To Freshman

To those we have lost

To those who are with us still

To those we have yet to meet

Contents

Dearest Ruby,

Thank you so very much for supporting me on this literary venture. It really does mean the world to me. I'm really looking forward to you having a

A Version of You

By

April Lee Fields

read of this. I hope that you enjoy my stories and are able to take something from them.

Stay the sparkling, fabulous goddess that you are and keep rocking the world with your infectious smile.

Much Love

Fields, April Lee

A Version of You

Edited by Rosana Rosli

Cover photo and tattoo artistry by Lolito Moko

Cover design by D Ladio

ISBN ISBN-13: 978-1542335683

1. Autobiography. 2. Non-fiction. 3. Travel – England, America, Australia. 4. Spirituality. 5. Poetry.

Contents (continued):

Part One

Leaving the Nest

Civil Slavery

3rd March 2014

Perpetual partying can really weigh heavily upon a dearly departing bag of bones.

Juggling the last few weeks of my time in England had somehow become a circus within itself. Circles of social prospects breathed fire upon the audience of my life. Affable bodies were charred with the black enigmas of Not Enough. Familiar pupils were widened by the amber glow of insatiability as the fire turned into gold, and their desires would always want more of me. Work commitments balanced on a tightrope above, wobbling and wavering under the weight of an evicted responsibility; they leaned with a casual carelessness that wore brightly-coloured socks, frizzy hair, and a clown's red nose of redemption.

The final organisational touches for travel were like hot potatoes in my hands. Connections; check... chuck. Travel insurance; check... chuck. Giving away everything that I had, except that in which I could take upon my back; check... chuck. My travel preparations were thrown out to the wind by the ruby of scorched fingertips that had habitually pressed down 5am alarms with an ambience of the greater good upon them. The necessity in continuity of motion had never been more apparent. That necessity sat in the quiet of the kitchen with me, though we did not speak. It was a necessity that wound its long, careful fingers around the sausage rolls of my packed clothing. Fabrics rolled their frayed edges back and forth between desire and need. As tenants of a retired, red Duke of Edinburgh pack, my clothes were evicted for reconsideration without sentiment, before being submerged once more into the darkness, alongside fewer garments than before. There sat with me a soft necessity that needed to consider the versatility of numerous eye shadows and underwear. There were mermaid lagoon eyes that fought for a place against the unweighted nudity that I knew would also find my skin. Silky undergarments that were hungry for browned buttocks looked nervously up at me from atop their piles; they knew that my derriere also desired the undressed freedom of swooshing around in the commando jungle of liberation.

Those same buttocks sat upon the cold tiles of my kitchen floor, a tiled floor that pushed cool air up into my skin and left me with cheap thrills. It was a tile floor that did not actually feel anything like a tile floor at all. It wore fake, plastic squares with diamonds inside of their impersonations. The oven broke the silence, attempting to heat away the fake that had joined me and the quiet necessity, for there was no real heating in my empty kitchen. Still, I began to defrost, and tried to entertain the idea that my destination could ever hold temperatures above the freezing English air. Winter held me captive, and the illusion of the sun mocked my subconsciously-packed woolly socks and jumpers. The Duke of Edinburgh laughed to himself with a fabricated tongue that hung down lazily beside a necklace tag; it read: 'Destination Asia.'

I looked around the soft walls of my little one-bedroom, bottom-story flat. My winter retreat. Our lovers den. Mould crept up the ivory walls like aged vines of untamed ivy. The Duke propped his fabrics up against the sofa bed like a drunk who had forgotten to pack his last legs and somberly, he looked upon the clothes that didn't quite make the cut. I admired the smallness of a kitchen that encircled me in the pit of its square belly and I rested my fingers upon its edges, as if to show quiet gratitude.

I knew that my dreams had been born from that kitchen's cold, plastic tiles. They had been summoned from the colourless kettle that lived a solitary life within its own kitchen corner, where it birthed for us hot tea and dreams of warm summer skin. Together, we had eaten toast with Marmite in the early hours of darkness before work, and then toasted late into the night, when we had all eventually gathered our tired bones and returned home. There stood three fragile glasses that constantly touched towards our future adventures. They clinked with our unified desire to be

4

reckless, to have fun, and to enter a life that was far from the schedules and governing clocks of this one. In that kitchen, we cooked our Sunday roasts at 3am on a Tuesday evening and imagined our Great Escape.

With one foot in this world, while the other dangled in another world of unknowns, my imagination began to sketch itself into the first pencil outlines of a reality. Winter ghosts chased away the cold draught of my transitions. The circus act of my fleeting life was a jester's best work.

One moment slid into the next, and the maintenance of an all-engulfing, full-time occupation was suddenly no more. My ass had been successfully busted by fifty-hour work weeks that served the rich and famous. Two years of departmental meetings, gold stars, and sharks, out for the blood of the weak and the financially needy, had finally fallen behind me. I slid out of the weight of responsibility as if it were a silken nightgown that gathered around the calluses of my worked feet. The metallic clank of £6-an-hour-minimum-wage shackles released themselves and sent shrills into my being. They jolted me, reminding me not to forget to pick up my soul on the way out of the door; it had been tucked away in the cash register for safekeeping.

I waved farewell to a responsibility that had been bubble-wrapped in slavery and did not stop to look back upon the polished shoes of airs and graces that masked a dark visage of gluttony and misguidance. The faces of grimacing wallets smiled their green, dollar-bill, toothy smiles at me, for they knew that falsified interactions of pleasantries were simply all in the name of Excellent Customer Service. We were buying one another over white, linen table cloths... but it was a civil kind of slavery.

I had tried it on and, after gaining success in the business world, I knew that I had worn it well. I had wanted to ensure that when I left it all behind me, it would not be because I was unable to function in the world of consumers. I would not be leaving because of the hungry mouth and my inability to feed it. I would not leave because the commercial world reminded me of dark things under large beds, but rather, I would leave down to my own personal choice. I would leave a productive member of those suit-and-tie lands. I would abandon my proposition for promotion back in the stuffiness of our monthly meeting-room, along with the memory of suits that had loomed over my underpaid contributions. I had aspired to depart a conqueror of the machine, though in reality, I was not a conqueror at all; I was simply a girl who had been wounded by the inhumanity of such a systematic structure. My colleagues and I had been carefully crafted into creatures of cattle; we voluntarily wore skins that never belonged to us. But I could not stand to be just another number for even one day longer. I was tired.

Being in England for the last two years had been long enough to let the grass grow between my toes for the first time in many moons. No sooner had I prepared to depart, did then my wavering heart show me all of the entwined connections that the past few years had offered up.

Christmas Day had been spent amongst my family of a reestablished connection, where together we had opened presents and had eaten ourselves into slumber. We had celebrated beneath the roof a familiar farmhouse that would always protect the quiet of our shared comforts; for too long had my familial chambers been vacant. The cold care of a Russian's voice had begun extending her family unto me; we drank wine and shared gifts of our precious time, whilst our worlds had connected very unexpectedly.

Sleepovers of forever-friends also continued to formulate, where the fountain of youth was forever flowing with stories of our connections between the pillows. Through the linen, there has always been those same, deep green eyes, searching out my frequencies. They are the emerald inquisitions that wear themselves upon the familiarity of my best friend. She looked at me through the white of her sheets and she wondered why I was leaving her, yet again.

Piss-ups often poured our pack of wolves into the park on a Saturday night, where we would be lost in a round-a-bout that was destined for Never-Neverland. Even though twenty-six years had found me, it was never the plan to grow up. A network of continuity had been formed and, as I prepared myself for an undetermined amount of time away, fevered farewells took precedence over solitude. Years swam around in my possibilities and, from the mouths that had become accustomed to my presence, there formed upon their curves the cool whispers of my abandon. The sense of simultaneous desperation and excitement sat in the diversity of their eyes. Each step that I took further from my friends seemed to suggest a diminishment in my love for them, but those were just the demons talking.

'Keep walking,' my loved ones encouraged to my dreams. 'Keep walking.'

Sleep was no longer as readily available as the winter had previously offered, for we were busy bees with bittersweet farewells and leaving parties to attend to. One final burst of playing in the park until three o'clock in the morning found me with socks in my hair for lack of a hairband. Bands were started in our Bathroom of Heavenly Acoustics. Carefully-orchestrated dinners asked me slyly if I could get used to them. Kitchen wars of Spatula Spartans had left my loved one's skin arisen with the swollen, red memory of me. Forget-me-nots of debauchery were pressed into the tenderness of our memories. 'Let no one be like me,' I say, 'for nobody is like you.' Captain Morgan stood proudly in honouring of the Wolf Pack, and the pieces of my life began to dissolve into black, leaving all the room that it needed to grow anew.

Dawn finally broke to find me still awake and void of any serotonin left in an over-driven neocortex. We spilled out of a souped-up van, wondering what could possibly be next. Tattooed hands waved us goodbye, full of smiles and disappearing acts. As the kitchen kissed my cheeks and began to retreat into the background of 'what it took to get me here,' the train station appeared from dawn's thickly-clouded uncertainties. The three of us stood there, with backpacks and hazy eyes that rested lazily upon the possibilities of our new way of life.

I stood beside Ben, my psychedelic lover; born of abandoned dreams and an angelic soul. We were two years in the making; together we swirled around one another with the curiosity of those who lock souls as they lock eyes and know their journey together to be grand.

Jon led the way on stumbled feet. He was our housecat compadre, born of all things chilled and groovy and dear to the heart of our friendship. We would lay on the sofa bed, sprawled side-by-side, our late-night conversations often drifting into the soft care of a roseate sunrise. My friendship with Jon was made of the morning's same gentle colours.

And then there was me. Self-appointed mother of the lost boys.

Ben, Jon and I dragged our tired, but smiling, bones upon that train together. Ties fell loose around our worked ankles as a sort of weightlessness carried us onto the carriage and we became lost in further alcohol-infused delirium.

Our adventure, my greatest adventure thus far, had finally begun.

Thick as Thieves

5th March 2014

I emerged from the grey halls of international transit sixteen hours after Gatwick Airport had initially swallowed me up. The weight of my eyelids hung dangerously close to my feet and threatened to trip me up as I stumbled out into the mad mouth of Bangkok city. My own mouth held yawns inside of its empty cavern as if they were prisoners of war looking for a way out of their gummy entrapment. But the weight of my lids soon called themselves to attention at the realisation that there was, at last, a new environment for them to rest upon.

Skyscrapers hung in the air like chipped, tinted teeth. Black taxis lined themselves on the pavement like cabby-stained lip liner whose only destination was a pronunciation of street curves. Delirium mixed with microwaved airplane food and swirled around inside the bloat of my stomach uncertainly. The smell of England still scented the cling of winter clothes that stuck to my skin and bones in transparent separation anxieties. My woolly socks laughed out in salted bubbles of perspiration as the heat swam out to greet me in a romantic gesture of taking one's very breath away.

Oxygen had put weight on in this place. With thick hands and heavy feet, he poured his formless body unapologetically into my chest as I took breath. The dull sound of romantic airline movies fell away from my ears and replaced itself with the pounding of car horns and offers of cheap transportation. Affirmations of "fit-for-royalty" accommodation threw themselves out of the taxi drivers' open windows and onto our sweaty curiosities.

Life felt like a chaotic transition between two very different worlds. The quietude of Cornwall became less and less real. Polite demeanours of hand-held doors and overly-apologetic hallway collisions became a fable of the British past. As I stood on the grey airport tarmac, my home simply faded back into the green rolling hills from whence it came.

I fell into the gaze of Benjamin and Jon as we stood encircled with arched eyebrows that invoked a potential recalibration of destination. The curl of clove cigarettes crawled quietly around our adjustments, as if to serenade the sweetness of our collectivity. The eccentricities that Bangkok offered us felt like an unwanted and drunken lover. We were sixteen hours past caring, but she greeted us with a loud, lip-lined mouth that would not stay together. Bangkok had bad manners and wore unfamiliar aromas upon the unrest of her skin. It was decided that we would not linger under the polluted covers with her any longer and, under Jon's advice, we decided to head further adrift to the island of Koh Samet.

With the freedom of no plans upon paper, our papered wings began to feel the breeze of impulsiveness blow between their fragile feathers. Three heads nodded in the certainty and necessity of change, for we understood that Bangkok could be revisited at the end of our circular traversing of Asia. This place required much more strength than any of us could offer at that point, and the quiet call of relaxing islands spoke tenderly to the exhaustion in us all.

Ben, Jon and I became just another group of tourists on a bus that bumped along the dirt roads of death. The sand threatened to swallow the tyres from beneath us on every turn. We melted into another boat that breezed through the possibility of too many passengers on board. Three bodies swayed, side-by-side, unaffected by mortality. Instead, we carried hope in the form of another bizarre destination that sat at the forefront of our wildest desires.

During the journey down south, I drifted in and out of consciousness. I rested my torso on what was left of my companions' stability and we all drank in the scenery with the eyes of curious children. Full of wonder and mystery, I sleepily gazed out upon my new Asian home from behind the bus window. Stray dogs roamed, buildings loomed, and scooters held whole families like precious pearls in an oyster shell of heaven and hell. Both places harmoniously entwined there, somehow.

Every now and then, I would catch a glimpse of my fellow travellers' eyes. They were wide with the fruits of labour that began to materialise before them, for we had each participated with unwavering commitment in the civility of our own slavery. Those working days were behind us, and Asia replaced our reality with unfamiliarity. Each mile that passed us by encouraged that the bond between us thicken, because each face was now a stranger's face, save for our own. Each place was now a mystery, save for the space that we kept in the unified memories of our home. Our backs stood against one another as three faces gazed out into the ever-changing backdrop of the world. Each of us quietly wondered what internal changes could befall our transformations. Our shoulders drew up treaties of unspoken protection and we signed on the dotted lines with blades that would have one another's backs until the end.

We were the three amigos. Thick as thieves. Behind our faces rested some sort of secret that the three of us could only ever keep. We had arrived in Asia. Hot, sticky, and damp with possibility.

We held secrets in our eyes because each one of us knew that, amidst the dust and deteriorated shacks that passed us by, there would be no going back from here.

Sweet Pennies

6th March 2014

The boat swayed backwards and forwards against the uncertainty of an ocean that sprawled out before me. Beneath the attentions of an afternoon sun, the monstrosity of a statuesque mermaid began to reveal herself upon the shores of my awe. The mermaid's dark silhouette hovered above me and cast shadows across my curiosity. Her stone skin shimmered in dreamy, emerald glimmers and, with grotesque features, she looked down upon me from a face cast with thunder.

I departed the boat with an outward inquisition that landed with unsteady feet on the dock of Koh Samet. My vision turned itself inward towards a Lonely Planet travel page that invited me on a journal's-journey of exploration. Explanations of the titanic mermaid's existence stained the pages with the professional language of Times New Roman. Local legend spoke in italic whispers of the whims of the mermaid's mammoth heart. Bold font declared to me of how she had boldly given her heart to that of a mortal man. I thumbed through pages that drew pictures out of language. They created imagery of a man whom she had saved from the ocean's deadly grasp. A man with whom she had fallen in love with. A man who, in return, saved his own love to bestow, not upon her, but upon that of a mortal woman.

The shadow that the mermaid cast upon my face sprawled itself out across the pages like pornography. The truth of her lover's betrayal cooled her burning heart until she had transformed into the stone that stood before me. She hovered in emerald green and extended a pointed finger that traced back to snarled and unforgiving lips. This stone mermaid is left guarding the sapphire shores of Koh Samet with a face that looks as though it will never forget. I looked upon her story and was reminded of the power that just one heart can hold.

I emerged from the pages of the mermaid's fate and gratefully found quiet distraction in the vision of a middle-aged Korean man who stood beside me. He wore a full smile and a dress shirt that extended the request for a lighter from its short sleeve. His enthusiastic face was generously pasted with the kind of sun cream that mixed solitude and adventure together with perspiration. He called himself Kim. Jon casually handed him a lighter as we began gathering our packs and, for no particular reason, this stranger began to make an immediate impact onto my familiarity.

As I walked down the crooked spine of the dock, placing my feet precariously upon fractured planks, I looked behind me and saw Kim still standing beneath the mermaid's shadow, looking rather lost. The plastic wheels on his suitcase crossed their arms uncertainly, as the sand silently mocked their curved roll with grains that grew hostile. The sun threatened to transform Kim's dress shirt into salted liquid and I could not help but to smile at his purity. Kim waved sweetly at our departure, and I found myself returning his wave with a gestured request for him to join us. His suitcase rolled on futile wheels beside legs that could not have carried him fast enough to our sides and, within an instant, Kim was a part of our pack... because travelling does seem to roll on like that.

There are often moments with strangers that one could consider potentially mundane, until they are no longer strangers and it becomes hard to imagine a life without them. We allow these people inside of our walls, and are able to connect somehow, even amidst our dress shirt differences. Whether wearing a sack of backpack dreams, or rolling upon suitcase wheels that cough out sand from their immobility, often these unique persons join us on the road for an undetermined amount of time. And each time, these connections inevitably turn our path into that which it would never have been without them. There lies a sort of conjoined sorcery within these connections; we throw into our magical cauldron: joined paths, first glances, presence, and an expansion of varied chances, because the more eyes that are truly upon you, the greater the potential of your personal growth.

The main street of Koh Samet was a ripened breast, protruding with strange sensations that sat deeply within its beach-kissed cleavage. Street foods sizzled in the soft of the day. Pieces of octopus wiggled themselves upon platters in a final dance, and Mad Hatter fruit queens walked effortlessly across the beach with elegance and grace. I passed by suspicious massage parlours that hung like loose teeth around the mouth of the village. Cheap and dusty accommodation dressed the island's bones, whilst dimly-lit rooms spoke to the tired that lived in the transit of my own.

Amongst the three amigos, plus our new addition of Kim, it was decided that beachfront accommodation would be the only thing to suffice for our first night on the island. Creaky wooden floorboards and a door that barely closed soon opened themselves up to me. Daylight shone through the dusty cracks of my simple, no-frills shack, just to remind me of the wild time difference that I had walked through to get me there. We had been travelling for three days and sleep felt like a distant relative that had finally made peace with the family; for how sweet it was when that bed opened its stiff, welcoming arms to me. A stray island dog slept peacefully between mine and Benjamin's adoptive bodies and, as I crossed the borders of dreaming and awake, I felt attuned with the proximity of the sea. But with the sea, lest we forget, comes the amplification of the night's beach parties.

As the sun dropped from the sky, so too dropped the bass lines of trance and techno. Their electro-swing melodies pushed themselves through the cracks and nestled into our bamboo shack from sunset until sunrise. I tossed and turned until all I could do was simply surrender and roll with the times. The adopted pup licked my hand thankfully, and I finally fell asleep in gratitude,

14

reminded that this was the life I did perpetually seek.

However, I had barely swept past the surface layer of dreams, when I was awoken by a knocking on my door. I moved the pup off the soft of my body, untucked myself from the once-cream mosquito net and dressed, despite the oven that I slept in. As my door creaked open, I was greeted by Jon. A Jon who, in attempts to save the sweets of his pennies, had decided not to book himself any accommodation for the night. A Jon that had once held ideas of drinking and dancing the night away. Though it was clear, as he stood meekly at my door, that the party version of himself had dissolved with the departure of his energy. However, the hour was late, and Jon's organisational skills were perpetually debatable, so I made room for one more upon the firm of our bed. Despite the intrusiveness of that bass-bumpin' music, I fell easily back into dreams.

The next morning found me feeling fresh and rested, though there laid beside me an empty space in the bed that Jon had never occupied. Ben yawned himself awake, the pup made its great escape and, as I opened a door that never really closed, I exposed myself to a slumped-over Jon. Jon sat outside on the wooden deck, folded over on himself, with coy eyes that greeted me in an assumption of pleasantries. Last night's intoxicated method of thought had encouraged Jon that it was best to not further distress mine and Benjamin's jet lag, or our new island puppy. Jon had decided to sleep outside on the porch, wearing only the clothes on his back. As I gently smiled to myself at the tone set for our travels, Jon reached up to my laughing mouth that humored his slouch and offered his hands up to me.

Jon's hands and back had become a Christmas feast for ants who were unaware that Christmas wasn't for another nine months. They had eaten alive a drunken and porch-slumped Jon-boy, with no regard for table manners. I saw a familiar mask of regret cast itself upon the curdle of his face. Jon's red and swollen hand-balloons looked at me blankly with no smiles to attach themselves to. The bites were enlarged, red bombing ranges that pushed their way out of his itchy skin until they doubled in size. His hands quickly became a topic of concern within a utopia that had encouraged us to leave all of our problems at the door; however, it was clear that the secret was to remember one's head when walking through those heavenly doors... otherwise we mightn't make it back without them.

I tried my best with the medical kit that I had, to nurse Jon up. I attempted to sooth his pains with Sudocrem, and to honor my role as a sort of mother to the lost boys. But it wasn't long before the familiar tough-tongue of my love showed face. I couldn't help but to state the fact that the silly fucker really should have sorted a room out.

For this lesson can't help but to teach that the sweetness of your pennies are empty in value if they are tucked away in pockets that fat and inflamed fingers will never reach.

Island Hopping

8th March 2014

Morning light shone upon the four of us as we darted through Koh Samet's markets like land-locked pirates, hungry for booty. Together, Jon, Ben, Kim, and I measured our adaptability against unfamiliarity with the effectiveness of our bartering skills. After indulging in the street markets, we washed happily up upon the beach to feast over our spoils of war; one-dollar fresh fish greased the sides of mouths that shared stories of theatrical, yet inexpensive, conquests. I looked across at Jon and witnessed the fat of his swollen fingers swallow the neck of a beer bottle, with no trace of inhibition. Jon itched and perspired, though we still cheered over our bounty without distraction.

Benjamin and Kim conversed over the meaning of 'kamikaze,' and I swore I felt 'the wind of God' blowing upon me. I looked down at my Thai red curry and somehow, I saw holiness. Street foods of traditional Thai sweet pancakes, chicken skewers marinated in tangy sauces, and sausages impregnated with rice noodles all offered themselves up like picnic virgins at our feet. But alas, the Thai red curry was my queen. She swirled with a perfect combination of creamed coconut and was kissed with a fiery spice that moved through her soup-like body passionately. My queen was light in a country where weight does you no justice. However, the heaviness of such a feasted breakfast travelled straight up to my eyelids and pressed them down with humid slumber, until I retreated back to my shack in the fashion of holiday freedom.

A few hours later, Kim politely called to me from outside of my bedroom door and advised me of an hour's preparation time before our island-hopping boat journey.

"I'm ready now, Kim. I'll be right out." I responded with the cracked voice of a mid-day nap and half a head of beach-blonde hair stuck to my face.

"Umm... You have one hour. The women... they take one hour," he replied, with confused, yet concise, facts from his own world. Kim and I had been keeping valuable company with one another during our island friendship and, through the maze of his unique ways, I was learning of South Korea. I was learning of their women and the multitude of differences between us; for travel allowed not just a traversing of the land that my feet physically touched, but it also offered an exploration of nations within the company that I kept.

"Why do they always need an hour?" I lazily fluffed out half a head of untamed hair as I yawned my way towards the polite mannerisms of a talking door. Although I could not see Kim, I could feel that his face had begun to lose composure.

"I... I... don't... know!"

Our worlds collided as I met Kim, just in time to catch the open of his jaw from a one-way collision with the shack floor. The two of us stood there, momentarily crossing cultures and changing. The mid-day sun caressed Kim's confusions as he looked upon me with questions resting in his eyebrows. I learned in that moment of how fundamentally opposite I was to a Korean woman. For the first time in my life, I felt like a big, gangly, foreign thing; full of strange independences and wild caverns. Kim smiled at me affectionately and accepted the forsaken necessity of 'one hour' without any further delay. I returned his pleasantries and, as we began to make our way to the main beach, Kim took my arm in his, just as a gentleman would. I watched him walk beside me with the kind of quiet calculation that gave away his occupation as a mathematician. He had observational eyes that sat trustingly inside of their sockets and, although he was looking for reinvented versions of himself to emerge, reservations still wore themselves upon the beige of Kim's skin, without intention to let go.

As we rejoined paths with Ben and Jon, the four of us fell into a boat that sleepily floated between the neighbouring islands, as if they were but alternate versions of this dream. The sun was shining and the pale of my winter skin also began to take a much-needed vacation, as I submerged within the warm, teal waters of an Asian ocean. A plastic snorkel pressed itself to my face without the respect of personal space, however, it made up for its close proximity by allowing me to see but a glimpse of the beauty that lived under the sea.

Schools of rainbow fish glimmered in colourful smudges past the blink of my eyes as sea urchins, with black spikes bent on world domination, tickled my feet. A bed of coral dropped off casually into the dark abyss, whilst warm air floated like gravity inside of my lungs and promised to keep me afloat in that underwater Eden. The damp of England, that had once clung to my clothes and sat in my lungs, finally began to wash away from my being.

I washed up on a private shore and walked with sensitive soles upon the boil of a powdered sand that mimicked cocaine. Chickens casually lounged around the free-range utopia that drew itself into my reality and, to my wonderment, I saw a baby rabbit perched in front of a shack-like bar. It nibbled on a discarded piece of watermelon and was as fluffy and still as any photographic moment could want for. I called over to Benjamin and together we crept closer to the bunny as if it were prey and our weapon was but a camera. However, as I drew nearer, I saw that in the nape of its neck there was a hole that carried itself down into the bunny's spine. Maggots had long taken up residence there. It soon became clear that the reason this small creature didn't move was not due to my photographic genius, but because of its pain and its weakness.

I looked over to the furrowed brow of Benjamin as he knelt down and cradled the rabbit with caring hands. Sadness creased itself tenderly into the corners of Ben's eyes as moral responsibility washed over his youthful face and made him appear older. We both knew what had to be done and Benjamin stepped boldly up to the role of administrator. Together, we began walking to a quiet place where we could aid the rabbit in a transformation of pain. But before we had taken even two steps, we were stopped in our tracks. The local barman ran towards us from the shadows of his island shack and waved his hands above his head as if they were touched by fire.

"Nooooooo!" He intercepted, with a rage that prickled up through his voice like a cactus.

I swiftly identified the potential that he could think us to be thieves and solemnly exposed the maggot-ridden hole that sat deep in the rabbit's neck bone, as proof of our innocence. However, despite our dissuasions, it swiftly became apparent that the man was well aware of the rabbit's plight. He quickly recovered his property from Benjamin's hands, placed it back upon the sand in front of his bar and threw it another piece of melon to keep it barely alive. The barman then watched with gleeful eyes as the next smiling tourist approached with their unseeing camera lens and stepped all the more closer to becoming his very own customer.

Disbelief crashed like waves inside of me. Fantasies of kidnapping turned on the crest of their breaking and I was sick to my stomach with the insensitivity of such a show. I felt fire blowing hot air around in my mouth as I began to make statements of my displeasure. Though, I quickly found that I had to talk myself out of such wildfire behaviour... because this was Asia; tied to the angry local that had recently intercepted our good intentions, there followed behind him a brethren of local eyes that cloaked us. Those eyes no longer exuded the same friendliness that they had once held and began to look upon me with the scrutiny of disturbing their fellow man's livelihood. A cold and uninviting feeling replaced the utopia that had previously courted me. Ben and I left the island with the draught of ineffectual coldness blowing against our bodies.

That night, I tried to warm myself back into the fires of meaning by feeling less; through the aid of cheap, sugary cocktails and suspicious cigarettes. I pushed helium balloons that had disguised themselves as didgeridoos deep into the frequency of my lungs. Afterwards, I laid back on the beach carelessly, just to let the ocean drink from my toes. My hair became the sand that held up the light of my body and together, we worked like gravity to keep me from floating away. I could not quite distinguish between heaven and hell in this place. The stars spoke in soft romances above my body and their twinkles seduced the light in my eyes so well that, at times, I thought they shone only for me.

Ben, Jon and I plastered one another's bodies in neon paint and danced away the faint odour of sickly tourism from under our noses. Drinks spilled carelessly around us, as Kim allowed that I also cover his body in the neon mess that we found ourselves in. I pushed colour into Kim's skin and drew over his reservations with the clichéd artistry of love hearts and sunshine-glow. He just sat there smiling, and absorbing parts of me in through his skin, touched by my neon print. The reserve of a mathematician fell from him and was replaced with a gangster hat that sat sideways atop his silken hair. A cigarette rested in-between Kim's lips and he pushed his hands up to the ceiling like he just did not care; we all worked on some kind of disassociation that night.

Benjamin and I made contorted, sweaty love for the rest of the night, because my faith in humanity needed to be restored and love, for me, is the only cure. As we climbed deeper into the tantric wells of one another, life was elevated just that fraction higher, and I felt the warm rush of actually giving a damn about something for the first time in so long. The robotic nature of my previous ways began to fade into the evening's shade and I breathlessly thanked bartering skills, broken rabbits, and neon paint.

Sweaty embraces of departure found us in farewell with Kim the next morning. A residue of faded paint transferred from one hugged body to the other, as if it were a gift of parting. Cambodia called us away but, as Ben and I dragged Jon's hungover torso onto the boat like a dead man, we all promised to stay connected. Kim stood alone and waved at three painted bodies that disappeared into the oceanic horizon. I watched as he returned to the same image of what he was before I knew him; a dress shirt that waved and smiled in the same exact way as when we had met, but how much of our parts had changed since then.

Upon the boat, Ben's well-defined chest became a place of rest for Jon's unsteady head. The bitter scent of alcohol-infused sweat glands permeated the air around us, but how sweet the two of them were. The purity of their friendship bobbed on waves before my eyes, and I was reminded of the gentleness in Benjamin. I thought back to how inspired I had been when first we had met; to simply sit amongst Ben and his male friends, in between moments of their debauchery, and listen to them speak of their hearts. It was a thing that I had not quite experienced until being amongst them; I had only ever seen how far removed some men could be from their gentility.

As the boat rocked, Jon slept and, as I lathered his swollen hands with ointment, I could not help but to look upon him tenderly. Benjamin and I had found Jon earlier that morning, resonating in a happiness that would forever change his dissolute ways. Although the endeavours that he had poured himself into during the previous night will go unsaid, there will forever be a black brassiere hanging from the Buddha statue of Jon's heart.

I looked with farewell eyes at the shadowed mermaid of lost love and watched her become smaller with each wave that carried us forth into our new adventure. Hangovers clung firmly to the motion in our boat-swaying bodies. Aged cocktails swirled around my insides uncertainly. Alcoholic sweat pushed itself out onto my skin's neon paint smudge.

And I couldn't help but to entertain the idea that perhaps we should all stop drinking so much.

You Want Happy?

9th March 2014

Maybe we should all stop drinking so much… but why stop short of something when in the midst of mastering it?

My backpack blurred into an endless array of borders. Navigations melted into half-noted observations, and the sweaty taunts of dehydration poured from pores that were still scented with last night's cocktails. The dualism of clarity and commotion was there just to remind me that hungover travel is undoubtedly an art form within itself.

A 7am South Thailand bus journey finally poured me out beneath the stern afternoon eyes of a Cambodian sun. The heat was like nothing that I had ever known. I collected my pack from the belly of the bus and stepped out onto a dusty new road with old leather boots that wrapped around my toes. I watched with the squint of half-moon eyes as the bus returned to the horizon from whence it came and was replaced with the mirage of snake-like rivers that pretended to run.

Dust and fear curdled in the air around me as the feeling of being abandoned in the middle of nowhere snuck up on my illusion of independence. Memories of my preceding travels rose up in me with the force of growing pains, because I had often intentionally placed myself in such unfamiliar places as this, in order to rid my heart of its sicknesses. The necessity of solo travel had long been fear-therapy for me and, as I stood there on that empty road, I felt that familiar cool draught that blew in-between the empty spaces of my skipped heartbeats. Travelling was not easy for the scared child that lived deep inside of me. However, as three shadows casually gathered behind me, I was softly reminded that, on *this* journey, I had the pleasure of my lost boys and our newly-adopted French-Italian friend, Piero, to keep me company.

I looked out over a long stretch of orange sand that rolled

itself out from beneath my leather-bound feet like a tangerine tongue. There were small shops on either side of the road, with keepers that sat inside of them and looked curiously out at me as I looked in on them. The whites of their eyes shone against dark dwellings that kept bottled water treasured inside of them. Cooked meat that resembled deep-fried cat guts hung like a carnivorous mistletoe above a bed of Asian sweets. My own guts swirled as foreign mouths desperately called over to me, heralding the urgent necessity of exchanging Baht into dollars with them. As I walked closer to investigate the rates of their livelihoods, I saw the reflection of my dollar-bill face in their piggy bank eyes and, breathing in the dry air around me, I caught a whiff of the distinct aroma of being fucked over.

Avoiding the stench of exploitation, with Baht still firmly in our pockets and a faint direction that moved upon our internal compasses, the four of us walked further down the tangerine-tongue path. The weight of life-condensed-to-a-pack pushed salted rivers out from the curve of my back and left wet patches on the thin of my clothes. The sun shone down on our movements fiercely without the intention of offering even a life raft, but it wasn't long before a building appeared ahead of us. The structure cast silent offers of shade beneath its body and appeared to be the border crossing that we sought; but as we made our way towards it, we were intercepted.

The motor of a local mouth appeared just above my waistline and did not stop running. It was fuelled with friendly advices on Cambodian adventures and promised to assist with our border crossing paperwork. As the man ushered us beneath the shade and encouraged that we lighten the weight upon our backs, I briefly noted a queue that had formed to my right, before my attentions were quickly drawn back to my first point of contact. I rested my torso on the cool, concrete table, filled out my paperwork, and enjoyed a brief moment of relief before it became apparent that the man did not even work for the border crossing agency. He held his hands out slyly as the motor in his mouth quickly demanded a small fee for his friendly service and travel advices. Dunce hats sat crookedly across all of our hairlines as shrapnel was extracted from pockets unexpectedly.

After joining the queue and getting in line, paying further for visa fees, photographs and transportation money, there was a sour taste of greed that sat upon my tongue. Men that took on the form of taxis argued with backpackers that took on the form of dollar-signs. The mid-day sun threatened to bring all of our brains to a boil until we each surrendered in our war of monetary ego and joined forces.

Sour tastes soon dissipated as we left that place on rubber tyres that began rolling their way towards Sihanoukville. As we bumped along the dirt roads, my heart fell into beat with the bounty of images that flashed past my window. I watched the scenery transition from tropical tree-top paradise into a dusty desert that was as orange as a Calippo sunset. The land was as rugged and as peaked as a courtesan woman's well-worn body and I felt my parts measured up against its mounds. Its harsh edges knew the cool angularities in me. Its softness reminded me that I too had the same fluidity.

The shacks that passed us by flashed me cheeky expressions from their square faces and gave the impression that they had been built that very day. They wore wooden window eyes that looked into me, unnerved as I met their gaze. Their rusted tin-tongues dared me to enter the mysterious lure of their doors, whilst stilts held them up like skinny legs that tried not to fall. The knobbles in their stilted knee caps told tales of a once-flooded terrain but, as I looked out across the land, I could not hear even one whisper that a single droplet of rain had ever fallen.

Families gathered beneath their stilted-house shade and bathed their brown bodies from within rusted tin buckets. A young girl sat happily in her tin tub wearing no clothes, although she did not know that she was naked. Freedom seemed to glisten upon the brown of her skin as water fell into the sand like a sacrificial offering to her family's thirsty home land.

Grey buffalo crossed the road before me in a herd of over twenty. Their prehistoric bones walked sturdily upon the warm mirage of the road as if it were a Cambodian catwalk. An ocean of thick skin draped over their bodies casually. Slowly, they crossed, and I watched each of their muscles carry the weight of their dense bodies. The buffalo were like true bad-ass models who cared not that we were watching, for life knew only how to halt in respect of their crossing.

The scenery passed me by like chopped-up scenes from a movie. My eyes were impregnated with their diversities and my lids became heavy with accomplishment and slumber. I leant my head to the right upon Jon's shoulder and held hands with Benjamin, who leaned drowsily on my left side. Piero sat quietly in the front seat and, just as a cat slips away into the night, the four of us slipped into a weightless and favourable dream.

It was 7pm by the time we arrived in Sihanoukville. Cheap and grotty accommodation was acquired with ease and, before long, I found myself bouncing between shack-like bars that gently touched fingers with the reach of the sea. Complimentary shots poured themselves down my throat, spilled over onto my clothes and left me scented with the wetness of what smelled like kerosene. Though I cared little of my aroma as the wild black cat that lives inside of me stirred from her slumber and arched her back in anticipation of good times.

The blasted bass of tragic pop-music transformed into melodious puppet strings that pulled at my bones theatrically. I moved as though I was possessed, with limbs that desperately climbed deep into their own marrow in order to evict deeply-rooted stagnation. It felt good to be out of my mind and present in the motion of my body. My calculations were on strike and with planes, borders and boats finally behind me, I began to allow myself to feel fully present within a moment that demanded nothing from the transition within me. The warmth of the evening whispered suggestions of freedom into my ears, assuring me that there was an age-old alliance between tropical air and liberation in there somewhere.

The morning found Benjamin and I huddled over a fragrant bowl of lemongrass soup. Our eyes simultaneously fell upon a chunk of fish that enthusiastically swam soupy depths as though it still had fins. The scent of lemongrass swum up my nose and nestled into my bones with a fusion of future culinary desires on the horizon. Ben and I giggled and blew bubbles of bemusement into our bowls as the shenanigans of the night before were conversed upon.

I looked at Ben's curious blue eyes as they hovered over the steamed yellow broth like patches of sky that were closing in on the sun. Ben wore a cheeky smirk that was drawn across his mouth in disappearing ink and hid itself well in the creases of his face, but I was well acquainted with his secret layers of seriousness and mischief. We spoke with tones of casual communication, yet the observations of entwined lovers dressed their common simplicity. The tales of the previous night were not, on that occasion, deep; however, in our usual fashion, Benjamin and I spoke over everything. He brushed my hand tenderly as it rested beside my abandoned knife and I drew myself closer to the drawings in his smile and breathed him in. Ben was scented with warm coconut oil and communicative familiarity. In the years of our courtship, Benjamin and I had somehow learned how to turn the abstract of language inside out, so that it could suit our own needs. We wore that romantic alphabet across our throats like a brooch of peacock feathers that pushed their wordy purples out in a mating dance just for us. He was my blue-eyed prince and he spoke to me in a genteel lingo of love.

Upon the outstretched arm of Serendipity Beach, a young flock of local girls gathered across my feet like ducklings and touched the blonde curl of my hair as if they had never seen such a thing. I watched the reflection of my springs bounce from the bottom of the irises in their awe-stricken eyes and jump back to the top, before their attentions were drawn to the shell of Benjamin. I have never been one to entertain company based upon looks, for it is true that a book cannot be read accurately by its cover, but somehow, the perfect male specimen had ended up on the bookshelf alongside of me.

Benjamin's thick, dark curls sprung out loosely from his head, as if they were corkscrew hipsters ungoverned by gravity. Years of Thai boxing had scribbled stories of triumph across the indentations of his stomach, arms and legs. The cream of his skin glistened with an abundance of coconut oil that temporarily blindsided women and men alike; they paid no attention to their toes and walked into things, fixated only upon him.

Those aqua eyes held a whole universe of oceans inside of them, with boundless waters that turned on tides of frantic and calm. I had often placed Ben's features at the tip of my fingers and traced his outlines in a pursuit to find at least one sign of fault in his perfect composition… though Ben's book cover body gave nothing away.

I watched as Ben and I slowly fell into the characters that Asia had mapped out in our destinies. I continuously attempted to capture the perfect moment in photograph and mental imagery, in order that I could one day pour its contents into the soup of my own unfolding story. I also took notes and tried to acknowledge every emotion that passed through me as though it was soul food, because my desire for documentation has always been insatiable. There are alternate lives that live inside of me and have crossed themselves across countless borders of diversity. The distances in between their grassy verges have left me with the need to merge worlds through words, as if, with them, I can connect the dots of my previous souls.

Benjamin inquisitively explored the Khmer language with a hunger that the people of Cambodia were more than pleased to satisfy. He took his own notes and connected the dots that merged the opposite worlds of his first full-time travels. Words of foreign flavour formulated themselves upon his tongue, and he practiced his new way of life as if it were a religion. Today was Day One of Devotion.

Upon one of our many street scientist explorations, Ben and I happened upon an establishment named 'Happy Herb Pizza.' Floating like magnets to that herbal pizzeria, we took seat upon its plastic yellow chairs as if they were pews, held hands of similar sizes and shared smiles that mirrored one another in the same flattery of those who have spent countless days together. I ordered the happy herb pizza with delight and watched the waiter disappear out of sight into the dark abyss of the kitchen. It wasn't long before the waiter casually returned to us, with rays of sunlight clinging to the outline of his body. He held a pen and pad in his hand and causally leaned over Ben and I with a broken whisper that quietly inquired,

"You want happy?"

It was a simple question. But, even after my gleeful affirmation of "*yes*... extra happy please," those few words decided to stay behind and linger on the empty yellow chair beside me. As the waiter returned to his duties, that query floated up from our table towards the sky and blocked out the light of the sun. 'You want happy?' replaced the sun's rays with its own light and I understood that particular inquisition to be the embodiment of my entire journey. Without question, I understood that without powerful questions, there could be no great answers and this felt as though it was *the* question that my heart was asking. The response that I gave the waiter was the same answer that I offered up to the sun because yes... we all want happy.

After the residue of the previous night's dancing 'til dusk had faded enough for them to endure the daily demand of the sun, Jon and Piero joined us at Happy Herb Pizza. In his usual fashion of an alcohol-and-smoke infused diet, Jon was of little appetite and declined any offering of food as though it was an unnecessary evil. He sat in a yellow chair with the oval of his face sucking from the neck of an Angkor beer bottle as though it were nectar from the gods. Jon looked happy without needing anything extra.

I moved my attentions over to Piero, who looked upon me tentatively with large, smiling teeth and an unwavering happiness that sat in the folds of his young, bright eyes. With great enthusiasm, I explained to the English virgin that laid nude and vulnerable across Piero's Italian ears, of the type of herb that resided within our pizza: ganja, weed, bud, happy herb, Mary Jane. All such adjectives were tossed back and forth between mine and Ben's verbal volleyball net until Piero's understanding dressed itself with the two-month-old cloth of foreign language. Nodding his head furiously in acceptance of the twisted pizza, Piero responded with little hesitation.

"Yes, yes, of course! Big... extra happy."

Later that afternoon, the five of us floated through the street markets like herb fairies. I was blazed and sampled Cambodia's fabrics and facades as if I were in a museum. An assortment of elephant trousers hung their fabricated trunks in the shop corners. Carved dragon pipes blew out ancient stories from their wooden mouths. A tequila bottle casually sat upon a shelf with a fermented snake wrapped inside of it and, as I followed the coil of the snake up to its head, I saw that it cradled a scorpion in its mouth like a tequila baby. The market museum was deadly.

As I drew my vision in from floated perusing, it appeared that we had lost our dear friend, Piero. After a fruitless hunt, Ben, Jon and I left the market in confidence that we would run into our estranged compadre later that evening. However, it was not until the next morning that Piero returned to us. We stood outside the departure gate of our room as he ventured to return to his. Dark circles slept under Piero's eyes and greedily hogged his dream time. His movements were glitchy and unformed as he recounted his tales of the previous night's disappearing act. Piero's account was as follows:

Piero found that he had floated further adrift from the market than expected, in search of a scooter that he could rent for our next day's adventure. However, during his estrangement, Piero began to feel exactly that... estrangement. Pangs of anxiety and intoxication had crashed upon the shore of his sensitivities and whispered to him that something was seriously wrong upon his beach. The potential of food poisoning, panic attacks, and malaria all rushed into the English virgin of his ears like an orgy. Intrusive thoughts clawed their way into Piero's paranoia with a frequency that was so high that nothing else could be heard, until Piero found that he had checked himself into the local hospital.

"You pay, you pay!" was Piero's first diagnosis, whilst needles poked and prodded with sharp eyes that were blind to his veins. He perspired and bled. "$150. You pay, you pay!"

Piero had spent the entire night in a foreign hospital for what was apparently just an accommodation fee, as the doctors could not find any signs of malaria or foul play in his cell bodies. He left the hospital that morning feeling confused and uncertain of the feeling that had come over him the night before and shared his story to us outside of our bedroom doors. Draughts blew around in his pockets. The tale that Piero told fell upon a press of laughing lips that were at least qualified enough to give him his final diagnosis.

I spoke in slow and clear, concise tones whilst Piero followed my words as if they were a treasure map.

"Haaappy Herrrb Piiiizzaaaaa connntainnnss maaaarrriijjuuaaannnaaaa!!!"

A light bulb finally flickered above Piero's Italian head and we each agreed that history had been made that night; the most expensive form of munchies to ever be acquired was awarded to Piero's enthusiasms. Language barriers broke and Piero breathed a sigh of relief that he would live to see another day.

And although happiness had momentarily left a member of our group, we laughed ourselves so hard into fits that, this time around, it could not help but to stay.

Koh Ta Kiev

14th March 2014

Benjamin's grasp on the Khmer language was coming on thick and strong. Every day, I watched him devotedly inquire about new phrases, whilst he held a notebook in his hands as though it were scripture. I witnessed each local's face resonate with the light of pride when they were able to teach something of themselves and their culture to a genuinely interested westerner. It was a culture of which the local Cambodians were fiercely proud, but far too often they were forced to accommodate and manipulate it in order that it fit our foreign needs.

I could not imagine a reversal of roles: Cambodian people flocking to America with talking dollar-bills placed in their pockets that expected the world to mould around them. I could not foresee Americans entertaining a change in their ways in order to profit from the Cambodian's coming. Guilty cuisine of buy-one-get-one-free Happy Meals would only ever frown distastefully at healthy rice dishes that swam in juicy Asian spices. The unformed drawl of American dialogue would not be adjusted in any way, other than to cement the reaffirmation that those in America should 'talk good English.'

Yet there I was, in a city that replicated so much of what it was not, in order that our western sensitivities were comforted. It made it hard to feel that I had truly travelled the country. It was as if Cambodia was just a quotation mark that highlighted an idea that I was yet to properly discover. But that is, I suppose, the fundamental difference between a tourist and a traveller; a tourist can stop in a place for a brief moment in time, carrying their own culture heavily upon their backs and barely skim the surface of their new surroundings. They leave with bucket-list boxes ticked and an album of selfies that overflows into forever; however, a traveller is more of a blank canvas, at least. A traveller can completely submerge his or herself within everything that is not made up of them, until eventually they somehow become a part of it. I often attempt to put into practice the art of being a blank canvas, and as I looked upon Benjamin's notebook devotionals, acknowledging the existence of that which was outside of him, I was proud to understand that he was just as blank as I. Benjamin grew and blew bubbles of Khmer phrases from his lips and I knew that I had never loved him more.

With each Asian day that passed Benjamin and I by, I fell further into the caverns of our love. So it seemed only fitting that our next destination would be an island that could further induce the flutter of our romanticism.

The bare of my feet stepped upon sand so white and fine that it crunched and fell away like powder beneath me. The ocean that surrounded the small island was so dashingly dispersed with blues and greens that it seemed to have drunk from the essence of a mermaid's deepest and most immortal of dreams. Tree trunks were so relaxed that they grew across the stretch of the horizon and dipped the drape of their green leaves into the water like rustled fingertips. The island of Koh Ta Kiev brought me peace like no other place on Earth.

Gifted with the sight of Koh Ta Kiev's untouched purity, it was as if my eyes had reprogrammed and replaced any of the ugly things that I had ever seen. The cells in my body did not verbally announce their changes, but I could feel the difference in me as they soundlessly regenerated. Jon, Ben and I walked the beach until we came upon three lazy trees that draped over into the shallow of the sea. We fashioned three hammocks across their triangular placement. The tide promised not to come up higher than our ankles, so that triangular tree patch was made into the perfect hamlet for our new home. Each one of our hammock strings was tied to the other's tree trunk and promised to keep us connected, even as we slept.

We tucked our packs away in the wombs of our suspended beds and left their fate up to the good nature of strangers whilst we explored. We proceeded to spend the afternoon sitting at a small bar that spread heaven out like promiscuity beneath our feet. Even heaven had a bamboo bar to bring all of the riff-raff together beneath. Glass mugs joined the heatwave and sweated through themselves without shame, whilst those who huddled over their perspirations shared stories and bridged the gaps of their strangeness.

The limp of my hand rested on the sand and came from a body that laid blissfully in a hammock beside the bar. I had found my placing in heaven and its day beds were complimentary. A fluffy puppy ran towards my hand and began to substitute my fingers for its chew toy, whilst Rachel emerged from the background with the kind of presence that could calm a lion. Curls the colour of mulled wine rolled out of Rachel's head, whilst freckles dotted her pale face like raindrops on a blank piece of paper. She walked towards me with a smile that parted itself across her mouth when it saw her fluffy fur baby beside me.

It wasn't long before Rachel and I began a dialogue of her life purpose; the impregnation of her dreams had recently birthed The Red Road Foundation. Its beginning stages stayed with Rachel in a light glow that rested upon her skin. She was passionate about the necessity of young children receiving an education and, as I swung on the hammock with a pup that licked my hand, she gently imparted her passion unto me. Too often had Rachel witnessed children sent out by their struggling families onto the hungry streets to work. I had become familiar with the sight of those young things that walked the beach with jewellery pressed upon their outstretched fingers like trophies, but repetition had left me with a numb resilience that began to tell me of its normality. Those children peddled goods upon tourists and had more street sense and credibility than most adults that I knew, but that did not make them grown. Kids could sell more than adults because they were just cute little eight-year-old boys or girls that looked with sorrow into our gullible eyes. Though the truth was that our misgivings would only keep them from an education; the cost of selling goods to tourists was seen as a better livelihood than schooling could afford. As Rachel spoke, the afternoon sunlight held her body as though she were an angelic creature that had forgotten that she was not born of this ether. Her 'Red Road

Foundation' would provide a place for that education to blossom, and she flowered alongside its gentle development. It was a beautiful thing for her to dedicate her young life to.

I looked into the sea and saw the faces of those street-smart children being kids for but a moment, as they played in tides much stronger than they could ever be. I went through the motions of feeling symphonies of pity and distress for their lives and I let the venom of monetary necessity rise and fall inside of me. I thought about that little white rabbit with maggots that festered inside of it until, finally, all my pity dissolved in the acceptance that I was a part of the reason that things like this happened. I was the westerner with big small-bucks and credit cards in my pocket. I held the unseeing camera lens and an ability to enrich the lives of others. So, I swung in a hammock silently and took responsibility for what it was that I despised. I offered a gentle honouring to the debt that Rachel had paid in order to make these things right.

That evening, our group of fifteen island inhabitants sat together and ate stew beside the bar. We shared stories and basked in the essence of a family that had formed itself in our small island community. I was far from home, but the necessity of family did not diminish because of it. It had almost been a year since the day that my nanny had passed away and that night was the first of her birthdays that I celebrated without her in my world. I sat amongst chatter and laughter and emotionally excused myself to visit the lanes of my memories where, that exact day, one year prior, I was in the hospital with my nan. I had painted her toenails, sang her birthday songs, and discovered secrets about her life that I had never known. But all the while, I never realised that my nan was slipping away. Beside the bar, upon a piece of heaven, I raised my glass to the first woman that had ever held me when I entered this life and I felt blessed that my hand had been the last that she had held when she made her peace with this world. My island family cheered with me towards the fleetingness of moments that so very quickly pass us by. It was a universal truth that brought the strangers within us together.

Later that night, Benjamin and I swam nude in the midnight ocean. Warm waters wrapped their waves effortlessly around my body as if they had somehow missed me. The sky held the promise of a nearby full moon upon it and, as I stood beneath its magic, I felt the undeniable kinship between that wise, white face and its pull upon my body. The water rolled off of Ben as if his skin were made of illuminated oil and, as I looked down upon the glow of my own skin, I saw that every inch of me was drenched in a heavenly light. The bright of the moon poured itself down upon me, watering me as if I were night jasmine; it pressed sweet scents out of my petals so that they could rise up past its lunar garden and be one with its light.

I looked up at the moon's feline face and finally gave thanks, because I knew that it had been too long since I had stood beneath her in honouring. Her metallic rays kissed me goodnight in a way that suggested that she had forgiven me my absence and she left lip prints upon my forehead that looked like the sun. As I climbed into my hammock, the moon pushed parting gifts of gentle waves at a roll beneath my watery bed and whispered aquatic lullabies beneath my cocooned body. I was like a child in the womb, connected to the umbilical of a waning moon that drenched me in silver dreams.

Over the next few days on Koh Ta Kiev, I arose each day before dawn and walked with the dusky rose colors that morning had cast across paradise. Circadian cycles began to taste my rhythms and align them with their own. I caught up on my writing and jogged the beach with Jon most days and we breathlessly laughed over the new ways in which we bonded.

One day, Rachel and I walked so far into the forest that we randomly stumbled upon an absinthe distillery. The jungle parted itself with treehouse secrets that gave the impression that it was just another shack in the woods, but as I climbed up the treacherous steps, I discovered a multitude of distilled bottles that glistened in the afternoon sun around me. Jars of mysterious colourings sat dustily upon shelves that looked as though they had never known a clean life. Couches sprawled out across the wooden floorboards like clouds in a dream and invited strangers in with an offer of creature comforts that hammocks could never compete with. The view of the island above the treetops stretched on for miles and, as I looked across its canopy, several strangers who were there before me placed a shot glass in my hand and we cheered to the random beauty of the moment. I allowed my body to be swallowed by the sofa as my head floated out above the canopy in pursuit of those rose colours that lived with the sun.

As I emerged from the jungle, I stumbled upon a young English girl laid out across a large black rock like a mermaid. She ran to greet me with the introduction of Africa upon her lips. Beach-blonde hair mimicked the oval of her face and bounced in its own curly ways as she took my hands and led me back to the fossil that she had devoted her body to. Africa encouraged that I take a seat and discover for myself that she had found the 'most absolutely perfect' rock for sunbathing. With hypnotised eyes, she watched as my buttocks slotted perfectly into the same indentations that her southern rounds had found. Alcoves for my palms carved themselves in the perfect place for my arms to take rest, and a mound of rocky headrest gathered itself beneath my neck. It was indeed the perfect sun bathing experience. Africa was scented with the wild gratitude of a star child that perpetually found peace in the most simple of things.

That evening, I washed away the taste of absinthe that still sat upon my tongue with a treetop dinner experience. A humble space opened up proudly atop its castle and, as I sat with Rachel and Africa on treetop cushions, I looked down to see Ben arriving with the remaining fifteen islanders in tow. The small restaurant barely contained us and just managed to sustain our group with ingredients that had been caught and gathered fresh that day. When we were full with the bounty of barracuda in our explorer bellies, we began the mission back across the island. The light of the moon ushered us away from the dark path that we had originally taken through a distilled jungle and lit up a silver pathway across the beach. We had wandered quite far off-track and continued to replicate our ways as we searched for our camp. I led the lost boys and girls of Koh Ta Kiev through the moonlit waters that hid rocks beneath their dark acquiescence and I recalled all the times I thought that I could never be a leader.

We materialised on the other side of the island with only a few war-story cuts that mostly belonged to she who tested the waters first. With blood that stained the scrape of my knee caps and ankles, I appreciated each moment that I had the chance to reinvent myself.

My last night on Koh Ta Kiev found me resting peacefully in a hammock, whilst the waves gently rolled in lullabies beneath me. My ankle stung with pieces of coral still stuck inside of its skin, but I chased away the pain with thoughts of the divinity that was held in this beautiful island. However, as I rocked myself against the waves, I could not escape the dark disturbance that had recently found me in the knowledge of the island's fate.

Tears had wet the empathy in a local woman's eyes as she told me of the Chinese businessmen that had bought the land beneath her feet and taken chainsaws to her trees. Her home. Her family's home; because the people of Ko Ta Kiev were not just visitors, but had long made the island their place of permanent inhabitance. They were the people who had cooked for us, hunted for us and invited us into their sandy living rooms, in order that we could seek refuge from our own worlds. Our love for their home inadvertently made it desirable, and therefore profitable.

"A casino," the woman said sadly, when I had asked what their intentions were for the destruction of Ko Ta Kiev.

"Me and my daughter hear them tear through trees with chainsaw… I bring her to me… we cry together." The reality of how her daughter's future had intended to grow alongside those decapitated palms could not be escaped and, as I swayed in my hammock that night, I revisited the inescapable truth of what our tourism can do. With thoughts perplexed by personal guilt and heavenly beauty, I allowed the ocean to soothe me and I gently drifted off....

Straight off.

Onto the ground beneath me.

Boom... crash... and other such comic book adjectives rang out around me as I realised that I had been a victim of Jon's imprecise attempt to adjust his own hammock.

Absent of any common sense of weight, Jon had fumbled with stoned fingers and proceeded to mistake my tie for his... until I hit the ground like an unsuspecting sack of shit.

Apparently, these things happen when we are so closely tied together.

Talk about a reality check.

Full Moon Rituals

16th March 2014

A secluded island, full of blissed-out stoners that slept and checked out of the world by 9pm each night, can only suffice for so long before the feet become a little itchy. That morning, Jon, Benjamin and I left island life behind us and headed back to the city in search of some unsavoury full moon party shenanigans.

From water to concrete, Jon and I splashed upon the maddened roads of Sihanoukville in pursuit of the legendary baking soda that Google had recently guided us to. We accelerated upon a rickety scooter, as trucks that sat on fat rubber wheels tipped towards us on the wrong side of the road. Five-year-olds sat astride black mopeds that wore themselves beneath their young bodies as if they were shiny school shoes. Jon clenched his fat, red fingers across my bony hips in anticipation of our unison with both parties. Although driving a moped in Asia was often an exhausting taste of life and death, I was well-versed with its company. After we located a pharmacy and returned to the beach, I lathered Jon's balloon hands in baking soda and watched their colourings fade from red back into their familiar British pink. Immediately, his swelling deflated back to normality, as if there had been air stuck in there somewhere. Baking soda pierced the once incessant itch and offered its first signs of relief. The happiness that moulded itself upon the round of Jon's face was well worth the deadly adrenaline rush that coursed through our veins.

Upon my return, I walked Sihanoukville's beach and stumbled upon a clothing shack that called itself The Hummingbird Boutique. Although I had no desire to buy anything, the shack encouraged that my feet come to a sandy halt before it and recognise the scent of synchronicities that flowered before me. The signature of the hummingbird has long etched itself into my spiritual journey. Wherever I go, this bird also seems to follow. As I looked upon the curvature of its dainty body, I smiled in the reaffirmation that I would forever be affiliated with its feathered symbolism. The boutique walls were dressed with a graffiti that spoke in spray-painted tones of the hummingbird's elegance and of its grace. Its joys etched themselves further into my joys and its effortless flight continued to form itself beneath the light of my feet. In this lifetime, I was but a creature of the land, though we were still one and the same, the hummingbird and I.

That afternoon, my amigos and I crowded the bars and danced away our unified English memories; we excavated the versions of ourselves that had stood together, clenched beneath a broken heater outside of our local pub back in Cornwall. Our hunched shoulders had attempted to form umbrellas over our bodies as we hid from a cold that crept up under our flesh and discouraged us from being present. We had piled layers of wool and cloth upon us to fight away the frost, but within those layers, our bodies had slowly become lost. Swallowed by gloves, our hands had forgotten the dexterity of their nimble fingers. Thick winter coats, hand-knitted jumpers, and world-dominating boots had solidified my immobility; the cold begged that we be still. Cardboard cut-out memories pierced through the Cambodian version of me.

Before I knew it, there was a tab of man-made love that dissolved selflessly upon the wet of my tongue. Bodies danced around me in appreciation of the shorts and t-shirts that laced them. A fable of skirts and sarongs hung loosely upon animated flesh and told stories of new-age summer rituals, whilst the sun cracked over us all like a yolky egg. There were no mirrors in the black holes of bar bathrooms to measure myself up against, but I could feel that my pupils were competing with the circumference of the setting sun. The sun and I worked together with the moon. We opened the flowers and navigated the motions of the tides. I became disheveled and wild in the awareness of the bag of flesh and bones that kept me. There were no reflections, but I could see that we were together.

Upon Sihanoukville's shoreline, I stepped out of the pale

light of winter memories and felt the warm breeze remind me of the curve in my thighs. I shook them to life against the radio station's top twenty cliché melodies. The mound upon my belly performed a speakeasy of one-too-many roast dinners that had been entangled within an endless story of winter. With three syllables running through my veins, I tenderly remembered that I had borrowed a body in this lifetime that was not made of wool nor cloth. My body and I met as old friends beneath the bounty of the setting sun and merged together upon the sand. I was reminded of my worth and gave birth to a reconnection of limbs, for I knew that I was but a child of the sun. The party shacks sprawled like a pleated skirt across the thigh of existence and I danced rituals of devotion that anticipated the moon's arrival.

The evening came and went like a one night stand whose betrothed morality had returned to her with the broken breath of dawn. I looked, wide-eyed, at the waking of the world and solemnly wondered how long the moon would continue to chase the warmth of the sun. So quickly she did run back to him, despite the connection that the night air had blanketed the two of us in. The moon and I were an unspoken lunar sin. Yet she and the sun were tied to one another by prehistoric fabrics that could never be broken. The sun would never know that I could love the moon's deep caverns just as well as him, that I could also sustain the moon's life force, for I too had golden hair.

Though, as the simple soundtrack of 'boots with the furs' faded behind me, I did not despair. I walked weightlessly down to the sunrise shore with the intention of cartwheels upon my mind. Benjamin appeared from the musical haze and watched the starfish of my body as I spun vertically across the horizon. A treasure, in the form of a wooden stick, washed up across my hand and asked me to stop my spinning just to admire it. So, with its point I drew upon the sand a globe, and sporadically placed us both within its continents. Somewhere on the shores of my imagination, as well as reality, Benjamin and I would always be together.

Hand in hand, Benjamin and I raced to the end of the pier and boat hopped from one sleeping sea creature to the other, until we found one that would suffice our pioneering. In the spirit of my sea captain character, I grabbed the wooden boat wheel with one hand and envisioned myself a pirate of the world. As the ocean opened its wet morning eyes to the sight of my cheeky face, I allowed my other hand to fall behind me and rest upon a seat. I greeted the beauty of the rising sun without jealousy. However, what I had thought to be a seat sleepily sighed under the weight of my oblivious fingers that rested upon its delicacies. Humour frantically climbed up inside of me and begged to be released as Ben took my trespassing hand and pulled me out of the boat, far away from the sleeping seat.

We clambered upon the dock, letting the chair alone with its dreams of phantom hands upon lower belly and laughed ourselves aboard a sunrise scooter. Ben was always an accomplice to my crimes. He and I took turns driving into the sun's morning rays with no destination in either of our minds; instead, we kept a unified thirst for perusing. I rested my head upon the broad assurance of Ben's shoulders and closed my eyes. Sweet smells of coconut comforted my need for control and, for perhaps the first time in the two years that we had swirled about one another, I found myself completely relaxing into Ben's ability to navigate our path. I exhaled with the sweet realisation of how far we had come with one another.

When I had first met Benjamin, his pursuits had been that of a casual nature. He had lived comfortably within his family home and had dreamed dreams that stayed up in the clouds with little sight of the ground. I was three years his senior and, in the realms of men and women, three years felt like a lifetime. I had left my own home at the tender age of fifteen and, at times, I had felt that Benjamin and I were lifetimes apart. Then, at other times, I found him teaching my hardened heart in the ways of his unconditional love. We were like the night and the day, connected by fabrics of forever and, on that day, Ben wore the full face of the radiant sun.

I tightened my grip around the solidarity of Ben's waist and touched my own fingers as well, because the morning wanted to remind me that loved ones can bring you closer to yourself.

43

I had met Benjamin on my twenty-fifth birthday and, even though I had always kept reservations about our differences, somewhere deep down I had always known him to be my gift from the universe.

The morning winds blew past my face and encouraged that I surrender my desire to be wide-eyed and navigational. I gladly handed over my reservations to the sun's warm pressings.

"Thank you," Ben whispered to the transition in our universe, with an understanding that needed no words beyond those.

When the time came for me to take the wheel, Ben showed me that, as always, he would trust me to the ends of the Earth. We swirled around in the surrender of equality and felt the warm fingers of protection press into the softness of one another's hearts. Upon the scooter, we cruised down bumpy dirt tracks and made our way deep into the heart of poverty. Rogue scabby dogs walked around aimlessly with tits that hung beside their feet, swollen with a free kind of abandonment. A calm and dusty state of awe blanketed our flesh as we watched young children carry babies across disheveled roads. The sleepless dirt tracks were laced on either side with every type of litter and waste, but somehow they still smiled at me through tin-trash braces.

As we passed all of this by, local eyes stared at the blur of our bodies through the dust, as if they had never seen two like us.

How far we had come.

The Comedown

19th March 2014

The late morning sun discovered Benjamin and I, illuminating four soft eyes that sat in the midst of an enchanted lake. Our bodies were drawn into the wild roots that grew above-ground like brown, curled hair. The lake's green waters ran through brittle bark like nervous fingertips that pressed down rough patches in anticipation of its new guests. I understood the kinship between that watery body of land and the aqueous body of me, so Ben and I made the lake our temporary home.

Benjamin and I stayed some time in that unsuspecting haven of a stumbled-upon lake. It was full of silent peace and interwoven grace that invited us to not only stay awhile, but to make the likes of it feel like home. My hammock poured down from the branches of wild things and collected our bodies inside of its waterproof pool as if we were but raindrops. I lightly touched my surroundings with no trace of greed in my prints. Trees caressed me in return, as green waters glimmered in the pools of my mirage eyes. I was reminded of my familiarity as the soft tissue of my lover brushed up against me. In our love, I felt that any place could be home and that everything around us could change just to suit that very feeling, if that was what we asked of it.

When the mid-day sun would not encourage our adventures any longer, Benjamin and I slowly made our way out of the jungle of thickened roots and love spells. We returned to the forest of broken buildings and busy-body civilisations; where scooters flew through the air on fire-touched tyres, fish sprawled out immodestly and rotted under the scrutiny of the sun, whilst unclothed children played carelessly amongst it all, in a way that only the adaptability of the young could. We began towards the quietude of Otres Beach for some much-needed rest after the full moon party had finally faded away. Long was the morning that had come to replace the blink of a night well spent and, with my head hung low, I quietly longed for the secrecy of the moon once again.

As I checked into a home-stay dome called 'Done Right,' my hands handed over passports and loosely searched for a tip jar in which to store my daydreams, for the beehive-like structure of my new abode was built upon such things. I had been in Asia for just over a week and, alongside the previous night's neon shenanigans, jet lag had finally crept deep into the marrow of my bones and came down hard upon me. By afternoon, I was cocooned in a space-age dome and was well on my way to checking out for almost two days. St Patrick's Day would be missed that year, for the mothership had landed... and she was bloody exhausted.

Over the next twenty-four hours, I trod softly in and out of consciousness. Each time that I lifted my lazy eye lids, I spied through the daylight haze that Benjamin was awake, carrying missions about his mind. He restlessly paced the floors until his legs carried him out of our bedroom door and ordered him to return our sunrise scooter on time. He stretched and meditated without any sign that he would find the kind of peace that offered sleep. The sensitivity of my slumberous skin felt him gently apply 'Benjamin's sodium bicarbonate and coconut-oil concoction' upon all of my scrapes and scratches. Ben tended to patches where mosquitos had left me raised and red in a reminder of how unforgiving Asia can be upon the delicacies of foreign flesh. Unaccounted-for batterings and deep bruises of momentary ignorance and delight all fought wars of colour between the purples and reds of my flesh. The jagged teeth of Asia secretly gnawed at me whilst I slept, but my heart keeper kept the wounds at bay, until I awoke the next day to see Benjamin involved in yet another task at hand.

I watched Ben's coco-concoction being generously smeared between the gaps in his toes, as frantic fingers lathered his little piggies with a pasty alkalization. His eyes wildly searched for confirmation, as if there were a secret language between his digits that only he could ever know. Ben's bent over body lurched above the inevitable and tried to assume the position of calm and collected, though heavily, laboriously, he breathed.

46

I sleepily inquired into the reasoning of his madness and became more and more alert with every moment of franticness that passed between us. Benjamin looked at me with the mouth of a pressed dam and broke into a complicated cocktail story that consisted of the previous night's scamperings. It was a mixed drink that created a monster, but I held my nose and drank down Benjamin's explanations. Ben crouched over his lower body and reminded me of his susceptibility to foot problems, such as dry or cracked skin. I recalled the beginning of our own relations, where a pair of frog feet shoes had followed me around my hometown, in an attempt to win my heart. I smiled fondly at our memories, until the reality of where those susceptible feet had recently stepped crept into our reality; lost shoes upon the shore of full moon rituals had floated out to sea and left Benjamin's feet vulnerable and tainted with foul things. The bathroom with no mirror was lined with grotesque and menacing floors. Barely-tiled tongues swallowed all of the purged parts of our beings without taste buds or a working flush. The cracks in Ben's feet were as hungry as his appetite for adventure. Our sunrise scooter antics had pushed dirt and dust into the cracks in his toes, whilst the mystical lake of roots and love had become an unapologetic swamp that feasted on the pleasures of the indisposed.

What sorcery was upon us, when we finally thought it safe to feel free and at home, that the green of the water not make its true intentions known? How it pushed deep tides into Benjamin's cracked and swamp-skinned toes and quietly replaced enchantment with the reflective hindsight of what we should have known. I parted Benjamin's toes for inspection and saw the green and yellow slime that was often found at the same party as his lover, Reflection; it was the trespassing egoic goo of Infection.

The soft, womanly curves of Reflection wet the waking of my eyes. The jagged penetration of Infection swam around in-between the crease of Benjamin's big toe and its neighbour. Infection and Reflection were neighbours themselves. They were two lovers that were usually seen together, however, it was always Infection that made the first introduction of the night. Infection was a self-absorbed character that needed to be seen first and foremost and often left his lover, Reflection, behind in the shadows. Infection is said to live in the warm climates of South-East Asia, but alas, it appeared that he had recently taken residence in the dark and dampened calamities between Benjamin's toes. I began compiling an eviction notice at once.

I quickly drove into town and acquired pharmaceutical supplies; miles of gauze bandages, cheap flip-flops, cleaning alcohol, and liquid iodine solution (God's own blood). Benjamin's coco-concoction didn't quite make the cut, for that slimy bastard, Infection, was well-settled and took no heed of the coco's alkalizing aggression. Having a health fanatic as a partner would prove to have its own setbacks, in that Ben's obsession with self-treatment often left my nerves calling out profanities at my own immobility. 'Man down!' they screamed. Man down. Together, Ben and I cleaned and separated his toes in order to let some air into his cramped-up minions and I left Ben with the condition that, if looks had not improved by the morning, then hospital would be the next appropriate step.

I left Ben with his walking stick and the good people of 'Done Right,' and attempted distraction by attending an open mic night upon the beach. Five people hung about the shack and spoke of complimentary drinks for performers, so I decided that drinking away the potential of our destiny would be the next appropriate step for me.

Jon and I pulled up a stool at the bar and got lost in comedy and song. When my time came to perform, I approached the microphone with not a poem, but a first-time song upon my lips. I sang in a capella about freedom, in front of an audience who were full of such pursuits, and amidst the feeling of despair that brewed in my guts…

…I felt my voice finally beginning to open up.

Infection's Reflection

20th March 2014

After indulging in a night of open mics, the next morning, Benjamin's feet looked up at me with a little less toxic sleep crusted in the curvature of their eyes. But he in himself looked slightly worse for wear. Salty sweat poured from Ben's sweet face like the stubbornness of a bathroom tap that would never surrender to the meaning of 'off'. His usually vibrant blue eyes cast across their encircled skies the look of an English winter's day. Grey and pasty pigments washed over Ben's skin with the imminent message that the light of day could soon go out from within.

Amidst the humid air that nestled within the cleavage of Cambodia's breasts, it was hard to tell if Ben's high temperature was due to his environmentally-bosomed suffocation, or if a fever had really settled upon his furrowed brow. Yellowed and ripe rivers oozed distrust from between Ben's toes and Infection looked as though he were pioneering a ship of his own. I intercepted a border crossing without further delay. The world expanded in the unfamiliarity of medical knowledge and my body shrank in its infinite vastness. But after I discarded tears of my own smallness, I sucked up the quiverings of my bottom lip and got on the phone to our estranged friend, Jon. The moment demanded that I put my childishness aside and ask for support.

"Jon, I need you to help me with our luggage. Its check-out time and we need to take Ben to the hospital before he checks out!"

As Jon arrived, the image of his concerns curved around the side of our spaceship dome like a satellite and became a warm relief to me in a place where everything felt unfamiliar. He looked upon Ben, then again up at me, and we needed not speak any further. Just like that, Jon had returned from the wanderings of his own journey and had put aside his frivolity, just in time to become a pillar of strength for me. I did not know it then, but that pillar would come to fortify our friendship in the years to come.

The three battered amigos poured out of a tuk-tuk and gathered outside of what was formally known as Sihanoukville's main hospital. We sat on three chairs in a waiting room that was a part of the street outside and stared out upon bustling roads that pretended to be walls before us. Fumes invaded our false walls and taunted the wounded souls that sat beside me, with a threat to seep into the accidents that were written across their skin. I looked at bandaged heads and scooter tyres touched with flesh all in the same glance and winced at their tragic love-making death dance. We each sat in plastic chairs and passed time with a language barrier that swirled around in the smoke of our empty mouths. Comfort did not live there, but it was at least a waiting room that was void of claustrophobia. It was a waiting room that bore no resemblance to any waiting room that I had ever known, but as I pulled on a silver-lined cigarette, I knew that I was privy to an open space that paved its own way in life.

Before long, Benjamin was carted off upon the gallant back of a metallic wheelchair and disappeared into the minor surgery unit with a doctor of foreign tongue. (Or was it I who was foreign-tongued?) The reality of Ben's departure into minor surgery caused anxiety to curl up like a scatty cat above my brow. The unfamiliar faces of Asia all blended into the brownness of one another and I could not escape the distinct idea that Ben's doctor had stepped right out of the streets and into a medical uniform with secretive ease.

"X-ray...x-ray!" was the only English that the doctor would repeat.

Broken things clanked about in my thought box and fractured the fragile fragment of hope that I held for things to turn out alright.

Half an hour crept by, with a slowness reminiscent of a teenager who painstakingly awaits adulthood. My feet tapped nervously upon the pavement to a silent song with no discernible rhythm. The images affront my vision were not in keeping with the things that I wanted to see on my Asian adventure. Time passed me by in a slow-moving freight train and I cautiously entered the carriage of 'worst case scenario.'

Phantom war stories of 'Asia's worst' echoed out from the memories of those battered souls whose paths I had crossed on my travels. Whispers of blood poisonings and amputations began to brush against the pounding drums of my ears, whilst my heart competed for its own heavy beat to be heard.

Infection was a thorough abductor; he had worked quickly, whilst Benjamin and I had played tag with our suspicions. Reflection wrapped herself secretly in 'too little, too late' packaging and pretended to be a peace offering. Jon allowed his shoulder to become a place of refuge for my tears and he sat there, in his soothing ways, calling me 'darling' and ensuring that I knew it would all turn out ok. Even though I did not trust Jon's assumptions, I at least trusted in the shoulder that I lent upon. I trusted in the three amigos.

Benjamin finally rolled himself out of the minor surgery unit, with a hardened smile drawn upon his face. His skin was still pale and perspired, but as he met us in the outside waiting room, a sense of relief seemed to encapsulate the grey of his eyes. They spoke in volumes that his fight for survival had been won.

In just three days, Infection had nestled so deeply into the caverns of Ben's flesh that he had handed over a billing address upon examination. Infection sat so deeply that no creams, nor ointments, could draw out the slimy beast. So rooted was Infection that the 'street' doctor decided it best to remove the majority of flesh from Ben's toe with a knife and a scalpel. The border between Infection and bone barely stood upright. If Infection were to reach the borders of bone, then blood poisoning would not be so easily treated. Therefore, the doctor's metallic weapons came closer to the soft of Ben's flesh and whispered amongst themselves that it was for his own good. Their tongues were like razors.

Benjamin had declined the anesthetic that was commonly administered during such an operation and instead requested that the doctor perform Infection's eviction under the clarity of day. I regarded Ben's dramatic actions as some sort of masochistic mantra that he offered up to the gods themselves: 'I didn't take care of myself properly and I shall know this pain. I shall know this pain as if it were my lover... I shall know this pain as if it were my enemy. I shall understand its secrets and never allow it within the same proximity as me again. I... shall know this pain.' I rolled my eyes at his unnecessary refusal for relief, but was quietly intrigued by such a choice.

For half an hour, the doctors had immersed themselves in the fate of Benjamin's toes. They had cut and pulled fleshy chunks of Infection out from his deeply-rooted residence. The scissors and scalpel tangoed all the way down into Ben's bone. The fluidity of blood and sweat were wiped away in a flash of towels. The instruments had chopped and tethered ties of poisoned tissue with rhythmic consistency.

Ben had laid stoically upon the surgery table and modelled an unhinged smile on his face that surpassed any earthly pains that the body could know. Floating on up from his tethered tango, Ben made an introduction to she whom had long awaited him. In the depths of surgery was where Benjamin became acquainted with the grandeur of Reflection; she stepped gracefully onto the scene with a mermaid lagoon ballroom dress. Images of 'immediate action' swirled across the satin of her elongated silhouette, as if projected. Her slender body pirouetted around gracefully on the melodies of hindsight. Reflection wore glass slippers that sat transparently across her feet to gently encourage footwear necessities. She had dark eyes that looked as though they could have done more.

Reflection was a beautiful tragedy and Infection would never deserve her quiet artistry.

Wild, Wild West

25th March 2014

After returning from the hospital, I splashed out on a room with air conditioning to help lure Ben's fever back down to the ground with us. Over the course of the next few days, I played nurse to his blur of codeine and happy-herb infused recovery. After bringing breakfast, lunch, and dinner to his immobility, I would also bathe his worries away and keep his company like the ever-present loose change within my pocket. Ben would often wake with a smile to find me still at his side, quietly caring for him in the way that lovers do. I hired a scooter and chauffeured him around every day that we returned to the hospital in order to get his wound freshly bandaged and cleaned. The nurses would cut out more green infection and scrape away war declarations, as I watched from behind horror movie eyes. I found that I was as completely submerged in the healing of that open wound as Ben was. It was as if his infection had spread into my mind too, but I tried to be strong for him, in all the ways that I knew how to be.

It was a time of quietude; a time of early nights that wrapped me up in the protective arms of my lover, and of early mornings that were awoken with desire to discover what the day may bring. I began rising before sunrise, just so that I could enjoy the cooler part of the day. I would sit alone upon our balcony up high, just to watch the world wake with me. By the blue light of dawn, the streets below me looked distorted, as if caught in a new light. A quietude that I had not yet seen seemed to have fallen over the madhouse of Sihanoukville. Local men and women's ambitious behaviour dematerialised with the knowledge that there were no westerners in which to unload their wares upon. They spoke nothing of "you buy... sunglasses... tuk-tuk... MDMA." The tuk-tuks instead took their bodies to work, with gentle faces and honourable natures that peered out from their open sides. School uniforms drove motorbikes to school with three little bodies that squashed up against one another's pleated skirts. The westerners slept and the ferocious necessity of business rested alongside of them. I began to see the Khmer people under the soft blue break of their true nature and, as I sat atop a balcony that was built upon their soil, I felt honoured to be there.

"I don't feel infected anymore," was Ben's jubilant reply, after my inquisition to his health a few days after the operation. The blues had finally penetrated through the grey skies of his eyes, but although sunshine looked promising, his ability to cope without prescriptions was yet to be determined. Walking, for him, was a mission that had to be supported by a bamboo stick. Pain pills had become a staple food in Benjamin's diet and they weighed him down with the lethargy of a desensitised threshold for life.

My sensitivities worked on overdrive for the both of us and brimmed over into a restlessness that I thought to be of a sexual nature. Benjamin was not so broken that he could not attempt to work out the kinks in me. Tongues of passion and hungry hands brought about a presence like no other, as the morning swiftly slid into the afternoon and lost me in its humble transition. As the day drew to a close, Jon knocked upon our door to discover the intentions for our usually unified sunset viewing. My excretions of love and sweat were quickly replaced by small beads of guilt and regret. For, within that knock, I knew that Ben and I had not been the travel companions that the three amigos had envisioned, once upon an English winter; back within damp, British kitchens where we had stayed up late into the night with only the half-light of Asian dreams to keep us warm.

However, our new reality lay in the unhealed hole of Benjamin's toe that wept for the flesh that it once knew. That truth kept us away from the island-hopping, mad-party travel that we had all envisioned. So, with a gentle reluctance, I pulled clothes across the hot of my body and followed Jon's offer to catch the slumberous sun. But as I walked out into the world, that same restlessness came out to greet me. I fumbled over my own desires to leave, or to stay, tripping over which things to take with me.

Strange thoughts apparently appear and then quickly dematerialise within your brain right before an unfortunate event slaps you in the face, but I believe that's what they call *intuition*.

I rode the pre-sunset golden waves of the afternoon sky, in the same way that a dragon would ride its own fires. Except that the vehicle of choice was simply a rickety old plastic scooter and the dragon was an uneasy and irritated version of me. Hospitals and flesh seemed to be getting up under my own skin, causing quiet meltdowns, so I encouraged tranquility within myself.

'Breathe in this beauty and exhale your pointless irritations of fire, so that you may ride in your own creation with joy. Feel your hair blowing in the wind and, with that same unbridled breeze, allow the ease of it to rush up the frilled thrills of your skirt,' I prompted myself, as the dragon scooter took Benjamin and I further towards the shore. My affirmations played an unknowingly naïve assistant to the events that were to unfold, but they granted me passage to a world without cares. Because, despite my mood, I knew that I was free.

Just as my consciousness shifted, so too did the body of my rickety dragon. It leaned with loud sound effects that mimicked the shifting of tectonic plates. My cares gathered themselves back around me like yelping puppies, in the realisation that something had come down hard upon Benjamin and I. The moment pressed a whispery wind upon me, rasping heavily of how anything was possible in Cambodia.

My thoughts fell upon the precious cargo that sat behind me in the passenger seat, with hands that dug into my waist and an outstretched infected toe that swallowed up first impact like a ravenous bumper. As I realigned the swerve of my scooter, I glanced a flash of black from my peripherals that maintained the same pace and alignment as I. I could not yet see any faces to ensure that they were ok, but it appeared that another bike had crashed into me. Amongst my own train of thought, I was unpleasantly brought back down to reality by a tugging sensation that originated from the strap of my shoulder purse.

Many great things can happen in the splitting of a second. Time is like one strand of hair split into numerous follicles, each representing a potential pathway into the unknown.

In the uncultivated time frame after the crash, possibility stretched out over the horizon, endlessly. I reached a strange state of enlightenment. I came to understand that the collision that had just 'happened upon me,' was in fact part of a well-orchestrated distraction to steal the shoulder purse that lay helplessly across my lap. My fake leather purse looked up at my driving hands with creased victim eyes and began moving from side to side, as if to taunt me with its will to leave. My hands clenched around the handles of the bike, tied to their own responsibility.

Playing tug-of-war with a thin, plastic purse strap at 50mph was like nothing I had ever tried before. One bandit drove the motorbike, whilst the other grabbed. As I tried to look upon the road, I could not help but to notice that it was, at least, teamwork at its finest. It was a cash-grabbin', high-speed, radical robbery idea that two strangers had formulated and carried into fruition right before my eyes. The only certainty in that strange scene was that a decision of continuity had to be made quite rapidly, if I wanted to emerge unscathed.

I saw two shirtless bodies flex their brown muscles at my stubbornness, as I retracted my belongings from their grasp. Two pairs of black leather trousers crouched over their getaway vehicle and leaned towards me with undeterred hands. Their dark eyes swirled in black-hole pools of determination and drew parts of myself into their hunger, but their eyes did not see me. Their only focus was the treasure that rested in between my legs.

One of my hands grasped a single handlebar feebly, whilst the other attempted to retract my treasures. The bandits and I ebbed and flowed for but a moment, before I realised that I was losing a war declared upon vehicular control. The dragon began to swerve without wings and I knew that one of us had to let go.

The proposition that time doesn't exist was in its fullest affirmation in that moment; innumerous questions flooded through my head in just those two seconds of uncertainty.

'Am I going to crash?

If so, should I just go for it and crash into them?

Will they soften the inevitable?

What would it feel like to have my skin removed by pavement?

I wonder how long it would take for the infection to heal?

Do they have guns?

Did Ben say that he had broken a bone before?

Why isn't Ben stopping them?

What would it be like to have four arms?

What happens next?'

As my questions bumped into one another unapologetically, it seemed that they could not find the fire exit of my mouth; t was closed, and its doors were bolted with awkward silence.

I let go.

Despite how independent I often pretend to be, in that moment of release, I found that I actually wanted the decision to be made for me. I did not want to have the wheel. I could not even fathom the responsibilities of the robbery's repercussions. I watched two small bodies drive away triumphantly and, left behind in their exhaust fumes, was a portrait of me that felt weak and helpless. One man's victory is another man's loss.

When the realisation dawned upon me that those biker bandits had acquired my debit card, $200 cash, phone, iPod and camera, all weakness and helplessness disappeared. Something primal came over me. I sped off spastically, in pursuit of my Cambodian cowboys, and accelerated with the memories of eight hundred pictures that were stored within my stolen camera. I revved the gas as if my scooter really were a dragon, pressed a weighted thumb deafly upon my horn, and suddenly remembered that I too had a voice.

"YOU MOTHER FUCKERS!" was the vocal choice that escaped me repetitively.

The chase was futile. The bandits rode a real motorbike that was well-acquainted with its road and, as they disappeared into its pathways, my rickety dragon just faded into their dusty background. The element of surprise stuck its sticky tongue out at me like a child with forbidden candy and Benjamin and I began to slow in defeat. Everything became hostile around me. I was in the Wild, Wild West and the disappearing act of two crouched silhouettes told me that it was not their first rodeo.

I stopped the bike eventually and became exaggerated with a fury of emotions. Benjamin stomped his walking stick into the ground as if to claim the pavement beneath him and I began to use profanity like it was my mother tongue. Onlookers cast curious faces across their expressions, showing that they were mortified by me and fearful to approach. Cambodia choked me with its falsity, for I knew that I was no longer an acceptable applicant for friendship, simply because no smile presently lived upon my face. Everyone stood by idly. There was no compassion, no hero, and no friend for an unfriendly face.

Although my smile portrayed differently, over the next few days I put myself into a state of emotional exile. I became unintentionally racist towards the Cambodian people, and like most who have had something taken from them, I became guarded and bitter. I no longer wanted to smile with Cambodia's people, hi-five the kids that chased my scooter, nor adopt the language of 'thieves.' After I had furiously protested the police officer's demands for payment of a police report, I realised that the magic of Cambodia had disappeared for me. It was as if one person fucked me over and everyone thereafter wanted to jump upon that train like a strap-on of misfortune. Gang-bang style. Close your eyes, bite your lip, and try to look sexy while it happens. Don't forget to smile, because they have your camera!

I felt completely weakened by my inaptitude to fight such an unsuspected circumstance and I was disgraced by my inability to remain in tune with my intuitions. I replayed my thought process, before that sunset adventure, over and over again in my head, until I understood what that unsettled feeling meant. My internal dialogue swam aimlessly around in the fish tank of my thoughts. I was weak; my weakness turned into anger and that anger reached out towards Benjamin, due to his equal lack of response. The crash had directly impacted his festering toe and caused him to be unaware of anything other than his pain. An abundance of pain pills and Mary Jane did not help our situation either, but I tried to keep my anger to myself because I knew Ben cradled his own demons. There was an unspoken unison in our defeat.

It was difficult to feel weak in a place where it was absolutely imperative to be strong within. I had not paid heed to the signs that had spoken to me from my guts. The dragon died and I tried to remind myself of how to not allow the robbery to ruin my journey. But my strength was challenged, and my foundations shook in their wild western boots.

Strange thoughts apparently appear and then quickly dematerialise within your brain right before an unfortunate event slaps you in the face. Yes... I believe that's what they call intuition.

Exit Stage Left

When a person's body becomes stationary in one body of water for too long, algae and scum can surround its outlines and mistake its skin for a part of their home.

Due to Benjamin's unforeseen foot infection, we were a week overdue for departure from Sihanoukville and, upon the night that my purse had been snatched from beneath me, I realised that we had all overstayed our welcome. It was decided that departure the following morning was imperative, in order to stop our waters from stagnating and our skin from turning a swamp green.

Although Jon's Asian stomach contents perpetually caused havoc with his English asshole, he nonetheless joined Ben and I for something other than a liquid lunch. We sat upon three yellow chairs that leaned on plastic feet beneath the yellow mid-day sun and, together, we reveled in one another's fleeting company. For it was the final days of the three amigos and we could not know when conditions would favour our reunion. Both of Jon's hands had finally healed. One of them habitually fused itself to a drink or a smoke in celebration of its deflation, whilst the other cradled his face in dreamy contemplation, as we conversed over the escapades of his bachelor life; of late night wanderings and questionable encounters. It soon became clear that Jon's previous liaison upon a statuesque Buddha, back in Koh Samet, was where his heart remained captive. Full French lips whispered Jon's name into the humid and fragrant wind, calling out to him with a seductive accent and encouraging that he return to her.

The three of us sat like well-acquainted knights upon our

plastic yellow steeds. I looked at Jon with nostalgic eyes and was reminded of how we had been but strangers just a year prior to that moment. Jon and I had met through mutual friends at a house party; I had scampered through the hallways, brimming with fiery rum and, as he stood against a wall, drinking and softly speaking with a friend, I had been struck by Jon's gentle presence. Jon wore a dark, dapper jacket and had strange, pointed shoes that made me entertain the idea that he could be an English gentleman. He was handsome, and had a warm voice that constantly pulled the word 'darlin' out from his full lips. Within that raucous hallway, the brown of John's eyes had softened me, and each mole upon his face became a secret that I would grow to love.

That last day in Sihanoukville found me in a lighter disposition, where waters began to flow beneath bridges and the fires of exploration ignited in my belly once more. Upon our stationary steeds, Jon courageously decided that he would return to his French love, whilst Ben and I planned to travel deeper into the heart of Cambodia. The three of us dined upon two-dollar monkfish and teased over the wild times that would be embarked upon when we were reunited. I revisited the importance of being able to make light of the heaviness that had passed us and attempted to release the generalisations and anger that were infecting me. We mulled over the unsuspected madness that had already crossed our paths, as fifty-cent draft beers cheered to our memories. Ben, Jon and I spoke fondly of the past and hopefully of the future, whilst the yellow chair and yellow sun slotted somewhere in-between our fun, unaware that presence was also a precious thing.

After a sunset power-nap, I awoke to a perfumed room, where the boys primped and prepared themselves for our last night together. I gently watched, with waking eyes, as Jon draped a blazer over his shoulder and set fire to a smile that burned across the galaxy of his face, his moles sparkling beneath the bathroom light. In a barber beauty-shop fusion, the boys cut, trimmed, and apologized to one another for overenthusiastic shavings. I sleepily played audience to their tentative relations. Together, Ben and Jon were an elongated comedy act that put most women's party preparations to shame.

When the mirror was freed of the boys' metrosexual affections, I walked into its reflections to primp myself, emerging to find Ben face-down in his own exhaustion. Pain pills held his free will for ransom, though I chose not to submit to their demands. Instead, I took Jon's hand and disappeared into the night.

As dance moves smeared themselves across my limbs, I embraced all of the tragic dance music that Sihanoukville had to offer. It was as if the town and I were old lovers and it was our very last night together. We put aside our differences. We forgot our petty disputes of who gave who what and who took what from whom and we thought only of the good times... if only for the night.

Upon encouragement, I discovered myself to be an exceptional wing-man for my gentleman Jon. I found myself dancing us into the smiles of many a beautiful woman, who bumped and ground against sound without a care in the world. Shots were the only thing that could contain the laughter in our mouths, as circles of silliness formed around our final night of togetherness. Jon and I became completely inebriated.

As the night pressed on, my wing-mania stretched further into the role than I could have expected. The night swirled around me in a vortex of gin and tonic, whilst the pursuit of beautiful women found me in a wild flirtation with some blonde-haired, soft-souled thing. She had long legs and a taste for adventure. My wing-man ability was compromised by my own ignited desire; perhaps it was the fountain of gin and tonic that moved like waves inside of me, perhaps it was the need to turn weakness into strength, or maybe it was simply my well-acquainted wild side that had come out to claim the bounty of what she rightfully acquired. Whatever embodiment reasoning took, it had me swapping saliva with Blondie as if our tongues were practicing Pilates with one another. As if we had never known a kiss. As if, for but a moment, we could be everything for one another. Blondie and I met upon the dancefloor with excited tongues that danced to the rhythms of an indifferent drum.

When the world came back into focus, I wiped the residue of Blondie's spit from my lips, just in time to see Benjamin amongst the crowd. He wore wide eyes that held hints of seriousness within their blues. I knew that my affection for women was not a surprise to Ben, so I did not think that his concerns were for me, as I stumbled towards his walking stick with thoughts of using it. Ben touched my shoulder lovingly and intercepted me with a string of words that sounded like 'Jon… timing,' and 'blood.' My head began to spin out of control at the realisation of my inability to digest whatever situation seemed to be unfurling beneath my unsteady feet.

Jon emerged from the shadows with a black circle puffed up around his eye like a smoke ring. A droplet of blood hung onto the corner of his mouth, as if it were afraid to make the descent down south, and Ben guarded over him like an attack dog.

Apparently, in my absence, Jon had encountered Blondie's boyfriend, who was not in the habit of sharing his possessions. In Jon's attempt to 'rectify' the hostility, he antagonized a pack of men who were fuelled with cheap booze and testosterone. They hunted him down like prey upon the beach. Fists were thrown at his gentle moles and kicks to the head extinguished the fiery smile that had once roared across Jon's face. Ben had roused from his slumber just in time to even out the numbers and diffuse any further violence.

As Ben and Jon relayed the story to me, my head swirled around in sickly waves of responsibility. I returned to my home-stay in pursuit of clarity and the remaining hours of darkness faded further into ebony dreams.

Waking at sunrise, I witnessed Benjamin tending to Jon's wounds in our bathroom. How different they looked from the two boys that had prepared themselves for a night out on the town. Jon's t-shirt revealed constellations of red blood against a white linen sky, and Ben's smile hid itself in the serious folds of his medical nurturing.

As Ben dashed off to the hospital for his final bandage change, I resumed the responsibility of bandaging Jon's wounds. Patching up our housecat had become a frequent occurrence, but this time around, I knew that I had been a bad mother to the lost boys. Our bus tickets peeked out of pockets and looked cautiously upon the approaching hour with paper frowns. Tick, tick… how the roles of the afflicted ping-ponged between the three of us. We had each taken a blow from disaster. Infection, robbery, and even physical violence had left us with little time to get the mess of ourselves ready for our 6am departure.

As I pressed a wet cloth across the swollen face of Jon, I tried to also make light of our new situation. I humoured him with a foretelling of his romantic excursion, where he would return to the girl of his dreams looking like an axe murderer. Jon's black eyes looked up at me with the same dark hues as the deep, blue ocean.

"It's not funny, darlin'," was Jon's final decision. He had sad love in his eyes and I apologised for what I could of my wild side. I was used to picking up her broken pieces by the light of dawn, but Jon's moles still turned their backs to me, unconvinced of my affections. Jon and I teetered between individual responsibility and personal connection until, undeterred, I resumed my motherly role. I packed our things just in time to kick Jon's blood-saturated body out onto the streets, watched him hail his bus, and smiled at the sight of him clambering aboard, right before the bus could rush off and leave him with the likes of me.

And then there were two.

Ben hobbled towards me with a silent humour in his step, as I sat upon our luggage beside the waking street. The three amigos had parted ways just in time for us to survive another strange day. I watched the morning sun rise over the city of Sihanoukville with a half-smile upon my face, partially concurring that our circumstance was not of a funny nature.

Ben and I boarded the bus and headed towards Phnom Penh, the emerald of Asia.

Genocide

The city of Phnom Penh was laced with silver-lined roads that wound into one another without the courtesy of dreams. I rode in a creaky tuk-tuk through the thick air and watched traffic dip in and out of view like quantum physics. Chaos crouched crookedly at every street corner. He had fat, unsteady thighs, man-made eyes and, greedily, Chaos turned over city life in his dirty hands as if he were its keeper.

Vehicles appeared at my attention forcefully, then disappeared back into the thick, grey smog of pollution without even a farewell. Breath was laborious. I watched as young men hoisted squealing pigs over their shoulders and carried them off into the dark murmurings of kitchens that I would never know. Their screams reached out of the prison of their snouts and grabbed at the geese that bumped beneath my prickled skin. It was hard for a country girl to see anything emerald about the grey chaos of Phnom Penh.

Upon arrival, Ben and I were led to a dark home-stay, where we planned to shack up for the next two days. It was a small, windowless room with no source of light, save for a dimly-lit bulb that flickered embarrassedly across the yellowed walls at its singularity. Tiles were cracked in defeat across the dirty floor and the fan gently wheezed of its short-comings. However, the price of the room saw that we placed our bags down upon its broken tiles without judgement and decided to make-do. Although our trip had just begun, Benjamin had run out of money a few weeks back. So, I attempted to be even more particular about our expenses, because innumerous hospital visits and air conditioned rooms had begun to leave my pockets noticeably dented.

That night, as Benjamin slept off the exhaustion of our transit, I walked the evening streets alone and tried to get a sense of the city that had offered itself up to me as a temporary new home. Tuk-tuk drivers lined the grey streets with an open availability that protruded from within their empty carriages. The faces of strangers nestled themselves into cheap bars that encouraged heavy drinking and conversation but, as they poured out onto the street beside me, I could feel no trace of our connectivity. Everybody seemed to be waiting for something, as if the city was just a place of the in-between that had impregnated us all with the unsettled airport-eyes of transition. Trees and beaches had long been vanquished from my surroundings, and the initial pangs of retreat tickled beneath the curved uncertainty of my feet. I stood alone on a dark and nameless road and began to feel captive in a place that would never pass for home.

The next morning, I left my windowless room like an escaped convict and spilt out onto the frantic streets in relief of daylight upon my skin. Ben and I mounted a tuk-tuk with the Genocide Museum upon our itinerary and, as we made our way through the city, my mood warmed to a boil with the prospect of seeing such a historical place. Everything danced around me under an adventurous and fresh light. It was a far cry from that single yellow bulb that hung itself in my room, having given up on life. Something close to wondrousness approached my face and turned up the folds of my mouth into the creases of contentment. Asian scents fused themselves together in matrimony and took a honeymoon beneath my nostrils, allowing me to relax and feel some kind of method to Phnom Penh's madness.

Ben and I arrived at Tuol Sleng, also known as the Genocide Museum. Guards with serious dispositions watched as Ben and I giddily approached. They were men with broad shoulders and stone faces that silently challenged us to match their demeanour. Benjamin had arrived in his usual fashion of topless attire and was instantly refused entry, until he respectfully clothed his body. We laughed amongst ourselves at the imposition of such petty rules and desperately tried to hold onto the lighter feeling that had only just made our acquaintance. With smiles as our armour, we purchased a shirt and returned to the gates of the museum, undeterred.

Limbless beggars lined the entrance to Tuol Sleng, as if

they were fencing posts that were missing parts of their dissuasions. Their full, black eyes looked up at me and dared me to assume that there was anything within them that I could relate to. I inadequately placed pocket change beside a man who wore tree stumps for hands and felt the cold draught of recent events brush against my skin. Two stumpy legs were wrapped with bandages that peered out from cut-off army trousers. Scars and amputations that were etched into this lifetime stared back at me and, I knew then, that I had walked into an un-aged war that was yet to collect dust upon the pages of its history.

As I entered the museum, my eyes fell upon a sign that depicted a yellow smiley face with a black 'X' crossed over its mouth. Those signs were placed all around the building, and without words or language barriers, they clearly instructed their guests not to smile or laugh. At first sight, I could not help but to grin nervously at such a serious demand, but as I walked further into the building, my humoured armour fell from me with flushed metal cheeks. My smile flat-lined. The story of the Genocide Museum began to emerge from a fabled fog of worlds that I was never taught about in school.

The ground upon which Benjamin and I stood had once been a center of learning for young children. Those children had attended school to learn of the world and their place within it, until slowly, their place in the world began to shift into the beast of an elitist vision. Phnom Penh had become westernised and, because of it, its people had begun to acquire work and schooling independently. An educated people emerged and distanced themselves from the rural community that Phnom Penh once was. Though, an educated people are a powerful people. The frightful potential of a civilian uprising had haunted the sociopath in power… a man known as Pol Pot.

In the five years of his reign, Pol Pot had perpetuated the execution of three million people, under the false pretense of traitor confessionals. Those three million people were his own. His soldiers, known as the Khmer Rouge, had taken the reins of

68

Cambodia with a Hitler-like mentality of communistic ethnic cleansing. The school in which Benjamin and I stood had been converted into one of many torturous genocide prisons that had begun sprouting up throughout the country just thirty years ago. With millions of deaths beneath the barbarianism of his belt, Pol Pot had given Hitler a run for his money. As I walked Tuol Sleng, I was baffled at the thought of how such mass murder could happen without my ever having learned of it.

Pol Pot had hypnotised local farm boys by dangling diamonds of superiority in front of their unknowing eyes. Those boys had lived lives that had been condemned to hard labour, where they had manually tended to their family's fields beneath an unforgiving sun. Their ignorance was made to feel shame, as Pol Pot had cunningly offered them the same riches that the city people held, in order to remedy not only the farmers' financial exclusions, but also to remedy Pol Pot's own illusion of depleted power. The farmers then knew that the developing world could suddenly be taken. Pol Pot whispered to them of how they had been done wrong. Under the promise of a better life, equality, and the cold knife of revenge, those young boys were swollen with responsibility and pride. A fairytale of fat wages sat firmly in their motivations. After recruitment and training, the farmers executed their leader's agenda of genocide and thus... the Khmer Rouge was born.

And so it happened, just as it has happened so many times before. Thousands of young men poured themselves into an idea of patriotism. Their allegiance was a dark jar with no top nor bottom, filled with empty men who simply wanted to believe in something. Dead bodies washed up wastefully upon their own blood-red shores, in the same seas that have countlessly pulled down other doors to equality. They were but men, who wanted to give themselves to the richness of a cause, but the truth was that they were just pawns in another man's war.

That center of learning was just one of the hundreds of schools, hospitals, and other places of creativity that had been converted into torture chambers. Windows that had once held childish daydreams are now barred and boarded up like nightmarish prisons. Barbed wire had replaced any thought of escape and the playgrounds had become grounds of play for the inhumane. Those transformations would forever shape the history of the Cambodian people.

Benjamin and I walked through the quiet halls, from classroom to classroom, and looked upon barbed wire beds that were decorated in shackles. As I crossed the cold corridors, I could feel the ghosts of children that ran carelessly through the halls with flowers still tucked into their hair. I turned a corner and thought that I heard the numerical whispers of hide-and-seek descending, as little bodies skipped with unattained dreams still tucked up under their wings. Pictures hung defiantly from the walls and drew portraits of the dead, without the filter of parental guidance upon them. Bodies were beaten, bludgeoned, scientifically experimented upon, and then bled to death. As I looked upon their memories, it was clear that the ghosts of smiling faces had long left.

I walked into the courtyard and was met by a man-made beam called the Gallows. His wooden poles made their way up towards the heavens, without repenting for his sins. His tall beams told cold stories of how they had hung prisoners upside-down, whilst they were whipped and electrocuted into unconsciousness. A rancid bucket of fouled water, to wake the prisoners, played as his accomplice. Rules had been written beside the Gallows, clearly stating of how any crying during torture would result in further whippings, electrocution, and violence. Amidst the sunshine and flowers that blossomed in the courtyard, the Gallows rested in a false sense of security but his cold, wooden weapons would never stand a chance of feeling the warm clasp of heaven's hands.

The Khmer Rouge kept an impeccable record of the thousands of people that had been slaughtered at that school. I walked upon blood-stained tiles through barbed wire hallways, and looked upon photos that were displayed in an endless row of tragedy. Black-and-white imagery captured each face of innocence, as they looked back at me with mug-shot eyes. I searched for signs of hope in the wrinkles of those who knew deep down that everything they loved would die. Young children wordlessly told me of their history, as if it could be a twisted bedtime story. The victims were of every embodiment.

I looked upon young women that were in the prime of their lives and caught my own reflection within their two-dimensional eyes. There was a sad beauty that rested against the reflective tones of their paper-glass skins, because those women had barely known the father of time. They would never experience the fear of crow wrinkles gathering beside the corners of their eyes. They would never feel the wisdom of growing old beside the warmth of the fire, and their grandchildren would never crowd about their feet just to ask them of the meaning to life.

There were children; hundreds of miniature faces that sat forever in their subject of circumstance. Innocence spoke through the worn-out pages and promised that they too would never age. We would never know if she would grow to have her father's nose, or if her blood would run the same red as the spirit in her mother's heart.

There were men and there were boys. There were men who could not protect their boys and they wore it like luggage under their eyes as they looked out at me. There were boys who looked upon their fathers' last defeat and knew it as their own.

The old lived there, too. There were intellectuals, teachers, fruit-sellers, shop-tellers; even the monks were not above being suspect to treason. There were snap-shots of freshly-shot bodies that breathed a sigh of relief upon the finality of their earthly departure. Human struggle and endurance framed their starved A4 bodies.

I came across the portrait of a woman who wore solemn eyes. As my vision descended like rainfall and rested upon the clasp of her hands, I saw that she cradled a newborn baby in her arms. My mouth became wet with the will to empty itself of all of the sustenance that was inside of me. Part of me wanted to join their emptiness and I grew nauseous with the knowledge of what we are capable of. A new thing that never stood a chance lay blanketed by an inescapable circumstance. I left Tuol Sleng with the need to throw up, or cry, or somehow attempt to remove the devil that had crawled inside of me.

The event that took place in Tuol Sleng was one terrible idea that stretched out in still-frames across history and wallpapered the world. Ben and I left with tears in our eyes.

My ears began to ring... but the dead said not a word.

The Killing Fields

28th March 2014

As Ben and I disembarked from our tuk-tuk in silence, the world around us seemed to move with an unconscious madness. Reality fragmented into particles of nonsense, as I tried to digest a mass genocide that had left blood-stained ghosts upon my boots. I looked down towards the rubber of shoes that moved with the fluidity of fear, and watched with a detached view as their tattered soles marched me on towards the Killing Fields.

Also known as Choeung Ek memorial, the Killing Fields had once been part of a peaceful orchard. Tree trunks had wound up from the ground and, once upon a time, had reached out across the sky with innocent stories to tell. Thirty years prior, their branches had only spoken of birdsong gossip and flowers that grew from little seedlings into dusty bluebells. The lake had once glistened with a virginal purity that had never known coupling. With the genocide, its own acquiescent clarity had been sullied in its mergence with the red water of thousands of dead bodies. Just thirty years ago, one million people had bled into the orchard's earth and waters, becoming a new topic of conversation amongst the concerned tree trunks. The trees' soil would grow to know the taste of tears, whilst it turned over inefficaciously with its inability to bury years of violence.

The orchard's tranquility had since been restored to its pre-war respect, but as I stepped across its manicured pathways, I knew that I walked upon a past that was paved with heartache.

I watched as flowers blossomed in bountiful bursts,

undeterred by the whispered folklore of their family curse. Two worlds of past and present put their backs up against each other. They drew a line between above and below, just so that we could stand upon their spines and be offered a glimmer of hope.

I stood upon that back-bone line of presence and history, with a head that felt weighted with misery and, once again, I looked down at my feet. Barely beneath the soil, I there lay thousands of hollowed bones that would never know what it was like to rest peacefully. Graves, dug by those destined to be their owners thereafter, became mass burial sites that were void of any ceremonial rights or privacy. Loose teeth and funny-bones dug their way further down towards the center of the universe, as if it would offer them a bed for the night. But, each time that the heavens had decided to open up, the rains would unearth the skeletal structures of millions of bodies that would never find rest upon a top layer of earth.

'Keep off the bones,' the signs beside my feet read. 'Keep off the grass,' is where my memories fled, back into their familiarity, in order to escape such confrontation and hide. To this day, millions of white-washed bones show up with each rainfall, just as a reminder that it will take more than three decades to bury genocide.

After Tuol Sleng's interrogation and torture had pressed prisoners into false criminalisation, they were then sent to the Killing Fields. After having nails pulled from fingertips, electrocution pulsing through flesh, and even being skinned alive, the prisoners admitted themselves as traitors to the government. They were also coerced into incriminating their families. As Tuol Sleng began to overflow with dead bodies, the fields would become the government's remedy.

My feet paced restlessly as I traced history back to the tales of trucks that would arrive from high school jails, filled with hundreds of fearful prisoners that had huddled together without words. Their eyes would be blindfolded and their hands and feet would be bound, whilst they were moved around like animals into smallholdings that were built from rusted steel. The Killing Fields would be the end to each prisoner's journey of insufferable captivity. They were gathered side-by-side in a dark room, unable to speak or look into the horror-story of one another's eyes. The Khmer Rouge had ensured that it would be a visionless and lonely walk out of the life of a 'traitor.'

Bullets had been too much of an expense for the millions awaiting death, therefore, more organic weapons had taken precedence. Handmade machetes and sharpened bamboo sticks were destined to be the fate that many prisoners were met with, as they hovered over ditches and anticipated the release of death.

I looked over to an old tool shed that stood shamefully in the corner. It had windowless eyes of repentance and rusted away in the hopes of its own demise. Its common tools told me of how they had also offered up a barbaric means to an end. But as I shuddered at its secrets, the tool shed did not ask for forgiveness. It just retreated back into the condemnation of years of silence that could not speak of the horrors of being an unintentional accomplice.

As the Cambodians' culture had apparently slipped away from them in waves of westernisation, the captives had walked a green mile that would always end at an open ditch. They would hover their beaten and weakened bodies over the holes that had been barely dug, by fingers that wore no nails... until execution finally let them go.

By any inventive tool that the Khmer Rouge could find, they would extract life as if it were a disease, and would dump body upon body into the insatiable appetite of the pits, in the pitiful hope of curing its hunger. Those that fell into the earthen bowls of hell, with breath still trapped in their lungs, were sprayed with complimentary DDT to rot their flesh into utter finality. As my brain drew up jagged imagery of being eaten alive by chemicals that feasted upon life, I could not help but to wonder, what gods play we?

What gods do we play, when we have cast the judgment to decide whose life can be taken and who deserves additional planetary time? As if there is a moral measurement not born of the human imposition to right and wrong. As if we are ethereal beings, casting our votes. So many times, we assume the role of divine control, when our earthly bodies are unknowingly saturated with infliction. Those who engaged in the brutality genocide were left blind to the higher resolve of love and contentment.

I walked with an empty mouth, and eyes that continuously fell down south upon my shoes. It was as if they were the only safe place that the vision in me knew. I walked through a tall, white building, where I was greeted by thousands of toothy skulls that were piled high in ascension towards a real God. They grinned at me with a thousand smiles; without skin, nor expression, I could never assume them to be frowns. Standing in a glass tomb of dedication to the millions that were lost, and looking upon their fractured cracks, they assured me that I would never know just how much their freedom cost. Memories etched disharmony into innumerous indentations and deformations. Fractured teeth told of their very own journey without the need for words.

I left the shrine of five thousand skulls behind, in search of some peace and relief to soothe my weighted heart. Benjamin hobbled beside me with the aid of his walking stick. Even the festering hole in his toe had turned into a mouth that felt sick. Sweat poured down Ben's face and a green bitterness swam across his skin. Walking beneath the aggressive Cambodian sun, I came upon a tree that stood alone in an unassuming field. The title 'Chankiri tree' was stencilled beside it. Thousands of handmade bracelets decorated the tree's brown bark in an array of colours. As I rounded its trunk, I soon realised that the Chankiri tree had been used as an instrument to take life; not only life, but little life. The lives of babies and young children, who had come to the fields upon the skirts of their unwilling mothers, had ended at that tree.

Pol Pot had not wanted the young that were taken from

their mothers to grow up and seek revenge upon him. He had instructed his men to swing them to sleep in a way that no child should ever be swung. Upside-down and gathered at the feet, like little chicklets, was how those children would come to meet their premature fate: by the bark of the Killing Tree.

That tree stood over a ditch which blanketed thousands of little bony bodies beneath its soil. As I looked upon its handmade bracelets blowing in the breeze, I felt that innocence had left me.

Benjamin and I left the Killing Fields with our tails tucked in-between our legs and rode the waves of our tuk-tuk back to our home-stay in silence. Ben's gentle features shook with shell-shocked stories written across them. My head rocked from side to side, without being conscious that it danced to silent, haunting harmonies. Dirty melodies swam around me, covering the outside of my body, and allowing me to become lost in dark thought. It was as if a choir sung to me with the splintered chords of lost souls. They wheezed their orchestra upon the roll of our tuk-tuk. We pressed forward.

As I looked into the black back of my eyelids, I recalled the faint whisper of English friends who had made mention that I 'do' the Killing Fields during my adventure. 'Do' joined me in my tuk-tuk waltz, as if he were a tall and mysterious accredit to my personality. As if he had stepped in like a prince, with a blue velvet blazer and eyes of forever that asked me to 'take this dance.' The Prince 'Do' wore dissociative eyes and held no notion in the depths of the questions that he asked me. As I danced with Do, my hands fell down his slender back and brushed against a buttock that was made up of empty boxes. Do pressed himself against me eagerly, as if to suggest that my ticking of his empty squares would get us both off. But I danced an empty dance, waltzing back into a reality that was far from Do could ever offer.

The Killing Fields had not been an accredit to my personality. They were not something to simply 'do' and, although I had not come from Cambodian culture, I knew that I was a part of a people that make up life's population. I pressed on, by the breath of lost souls, and watched as men and women went about their work day. I cast visionary spells upon tellers who guarded over their shops. I saw construction workers erect buildings amongst the busy streets and knew that, together, we were every person that could have been eradicated. We were the musicians and the painters. We were the educated and the foreign flavours that had brought in the fear of westernisation. We were everyone that had been dragged away and enslaved by stupidity. We were also the stupid who had done the dragging.

As the tuk-tuk weaved in-between the busy streets, those past events pulled questions out from the strings of my spine and softly asked me 'how many times?' How many nations, cultures and races... how many times would people be killed under the prospect of a better life? I wondered how much hatred would continuously fall under the false illusion of work done by a 'higher power.' I wondered how clean our souls really were after a 'cleansing' that had removed our mothers, our fathers, grandparents, brothers and sisters. How long will we kill off our intellectuals and creators, the lovers, and those of a good and pure nature? Until all that is left is a bunch of dumb cowboys who can only offer up the empty space in their heads, never knowing that they could have turned that empty space into a fertile and luscious garden instead.

Thirty years is not long enough for my comfort to rest easily beneath a top layer of soil, because that mass murder happened within *our* life time. There are girls my age who travel to those museums and thumb through paperwork in search of a father who had never come home from work; in pursuit of a grandmother who had never returned from her fruit market stall on the street, because she was named a 'traitor' to a government that had defeated everything that she had ever believed in.

Knowledge is more powerful than ignorance could ever pretend to be. The truth of genocide was not lost upon me, because I saw then that an educated people could be powerful enough to risc up against the reins of slavery. The fertile soil of our minds will forever be richer than any material riches that ignorance can offer us.

That night, Benjamin and I booked a 7am bus to take us far from the clouded emerald of Phnom Penh. I undressed for the night, down to my usual bedtime attire of unclothed freedom, and tried to find the words to communicate all that I had felt to Benjamin. It was the one year anniversary since my nanny had passed away and, as I lay sprawled upon the mattress on the floor beside Ben, I thought of her. Death felt all about me. Benjamin and I spoke into the early hours of morning. The fan wheezed quietly in the corner and attempted to reach out towards the nudity of my skin.

As the naked light bulb flickered with sepia dreams, every tribulation that Benjamin and I had endured suddenly felt trivial under the yellow light of reality. The robbery just past felt like a walk in the park, compared to the limbless beggars that had lined the polluted streets of Phnom Penh. I soberly understood the significance of their poverty and I was ashamed at myself for having ever felt such anger towards the Cambodian people.

In a moment of distraction, I checked my emails and opened a message from my old English teacher, Ms. Kessler. Enclosed was a photograph of myself and my friend, Freshman. For a brief moment, I saw something beautiful that I recognised as my own reality and I happily became lost in the years of our familiarity. I forgot the room around me; the wheezing fan, the windowless walls, the mattress on the floor. I forgot of the death that furiously clung to the life in me; instead, I just smiled in the safety of mine and Freshman's memories.

Letters gathered themselves beneath our single image and pressed their lines together, as if in prayer.

The message read: 'In memory of a dear friend that departed today.'

Yes… death was all around me.

Nudity

29th March 2014

The yellowed smoke of deceit curled itself around the dark length of my eyelashes and blurred my vision. Everything felt as though it were submerged under water, and even the tip of my nose became hard to distinguish.

It couldn't be true. Denial lay across my bare skin like an itchy blanket and caused my hairs to stand up on end. With cautious fingers, I clicked on Freshman's Facebook page and impatiently waited for the circular emblem to load and offer me the real truth.

I knew that Ms. Kessler could be a bit random at times and I leant against the memory of her quirkiness as if it were a refuge. She had been my favourite teacher, back in high school, but as adults we were of separate lives that bore only a connection to poetry. So I ushered Ms. Kessler back into the box of 'the first person who had believed in me and my words,' and I convinced myself that her correspondence was just a riddle between the two of us that had somehow emerged.

The connection on my crappy tablet gasped for breath and, as it wheezed, I stared into nothingness. *In memory of a dear friend that departed today. In memory of a dear friend that departed today.* The sentence swirled around in my head, absently. My eyes watched the blue circle on the middle of the page turn around and around. But with each second that passed, it gave no answers away to the question of Frenchman's death.

The idea of 'a bad joke' came in on a gallant, white horse and promised to rescue me. It waved a white flag of April Fool's Day humour across my imagination, in the hopes of peace. The two dates were close but, as I sat within that bleak, windowless room, I couldn't quite seem to figure out which day fell upon my time zone. Time and space crashed into one another without manners and I felt like I could be anywhere in the world. Not tied to anything. Not anywhere at all. My eyes frantically searched an oceanic room that emptily assured me of its lack of watery treasures.

Reality and Illusion were two strangers that made an acquaintance in the background of my mind and fell straight into the carnal passions of casual sex. They blurred into one another without shame of their hunger, and I could no longer tell them apart.

The corner fan wheezed in asthmatic rhythms. The prankster of Freshman's vampire-like teeth shone through my memories and smiled cheekily at my 'unnecessary worry.' As I turned in a prickly bed of frustration and fear, I told Freshman's memory that he was an asshole who kept bad and humourless jokes. The itchy blanket of denial that cloaked me began to turn into a grey weight of cement that held hostage my breath. I began to harden in anger and was uncertain of what structures I could build from there, but frustration felt a better temperament than death.

My tablet was like a mystic's ball that I hungrily peered down into for answers. But it was clouded. I was like an addict to the pipe, as I sat there rocking over my 21st century crystal ball in the hopes of regaining internet connection. My fingers began to swell above the keys as the buttons shrank in front of me. My thoughts fumbled with the sweaty lovers of Illusion and Reality, turning our situation into an orgy of terminology.

I was in the middle of nowhere, in the dead belly of Cambodia, far from any world that I had ever known. Claustrophobia began to settle into my room as if it hadn't noticed that we were fully occupied. Reality mounted Illusion without gravity. No windows. No phone. They pulled me in and I was part of them. I lay with a faded emblem in front of me that I desperately hoped to challenge the death of a dear friend.

Then, dressed in a timeless black, the Grim Reaper finally walked out across the dark catwalk of confirmation towards me. Reality pulled out of Illusion just before climax and I stepped back from the passionless truth of my screen.

Real people had said their real goodbyes upon an internet page that was a man-made thing. Phantom fangs retracted their parodies with haste and were ashamed that I could ever have mixed with Illusion and Reality, for death would always be a solitary thing.

There was nothing in the world that could have prepared me for that news. No robbery by scooter. No skulls cracked with genocide. Not even one thousand bodies piled on top of each other could have come close to the personal feeling of loss that I felt for my blood-brother.

I fell into the firm clutch of hysteria.

Each particle of darkness that swirled around my room slowly slipped under my skin and became me. Disconnection swallowed the breath in my lungs and I forgot to come up for air. Benjamin tried to comfort me but, despite his best efforts, I entered into a selfish state of loss, where Freshman existed only for me. He was my candy, and I was a child that had not yet learnt how to share properly. Despair weaved itself into the locks of my hair and bathed in the salty tears of my self-absorbed sobs. Panic attacks surrounded me with plastic guns and empty eyes that knew that I could not go on.

The Grim Reaper offered up his ebony palms to me and demanded that I give my cement blanket of denial up. He uncovered me without blushing and I lay naked as the day that I was born, upon a grubby mattress that sprawled out across broken tiles that pretended to be a floor.

Each time that Death has knocked upon my door and taken from my house someone that I have loved and cared for, I have been naked then too. The last time that the Grim Reaper had pushed his pointed nose into the crack of my ass and tried to know just who I was, I was just as bare on those occasions as the day that I was birthed. It was exactly a year to-the-day since my nan had passed away, making it hard to believe that Death's presence was once again due. Death's timing was impeccable.

I felt vulnerable. I had no cloth to mask the beating of my heart. I wore no linen to cover the quakes that escaped from my knee-caps. Each time that Death has sniffed me out, I have been transparent, fleshy, and so very alive.

And for my warm blooded-nudity, I began to feel the heavy hands of Guilt pound upon me.

I looked into Ben's eyes with a face that quietly asked him to make it better, but he drifted into a place that could not reach my terror. My tears slid down the curve of pointless questions and dotted their marks, without an offer of answer. *How* and *why* reverberated madly in my throat, as I choked on a sadness that expanded like a sponge to my tears. The ghost of my stolen phone ran in the room and pretended to be of use. But I knew that it was just me, a fan that struggled for breath, and my dimly-lit bulb.

Silence smothered me, until once again I could not breathe. Freshman was gone; at thirty years young. The sparkle in his eyes. The cheek in his smile. And just like that, everything that he had ever walked towards could be undone.

All of my preconceived ideas about death came at me like a stampede of wild animals. My hypothesis on 'the transfer of energy during the departure of this world' ran straight towards my head like water buffalo. They laughed at me with jagged, yellow teeth and ran their heavy hides over me, pressing my previous notions into the dirt. Their weight taught me a thing or two about the reality of loss.

I lay upon sheets that were becoming damp with tears, sweat, and snot. Loss was not attractive, but Ben held me close nonetheless. He gathered my unclothed body in the strong of his arms, Ben held me tenderly, as if any additional pressure upon my body would cause me to crumble. But I crumbled beneath him anyway. Ben rocked me in waves of lullabies, as I quietly drowned in a cold, black ocean. In the dark of the sea, I pleaded with the Grim Reaper to take me instead of Freshman. Ben swam out to find me and lifted my head up so that I could take in air. He wiped away the emotion from my cheek and lent me his sarong, because we were in a foreign world that didn't care for tissue paper. Ben tried to make it better, but I was like a squashed bug beneath his fingers.

Ben wanted to feel what I felt and, even though he did not know Freshman, he wept for my heart. But as I lay in the cradle of his arms, I felt anger boiling up towards Benjamin and I suddenly despised his presence. His arms were suffocating me. I loathed him, because he did not know anything about my friend, Freshman. Ben was from England and would never know my old life in America. To me, Ben suddenly became an outsider. I pushed him away coldly because, for my own reasons, I needed to drown alone in that sea.

Ben broke down. We argued, and he could no longer comfort me. I refused to comfort Ben, even though I knew that our journey had been hard on him too. I looked over to the crippled, beige bandage that wrapped itself across his toe and refused to acknowledge it as a greater sorrow than my own. Both of us were broken, but I needed Ben to be strong for me.

I wanted to stand up and break the room into a million pieces. I envisioned the sick, asthmatic fan being smashed up into tiny splinters that would finally put it out of its misery. I saw my nails bleed red, as a version of me scratched at the walls in order to make a window from where I could draw breath. I saw a heavy foot come crashing down upon the broken tiles of the floor. I saw fire and I saw brimstone. However, a cold reality showed that my strength had long left me, and all that I could manage to be was a weak body that hunched over a damp cigarette.

I had known Freshman for thirteen years. He had been a close friend of mine. He had been a close friend of many. Throughout our teenage years, we had shared countless strange memories and even lived as roommates together in a house that was filled with innumerable bodies. Those bodies had brimmed with teenage explorations and dream-chasing. They were bodies that had tried on who they had wanted to be in that moment, beneath garments of love and of folly. It was once upon a weird time in our history.

Those memories began to draw themselves up out of the dark of the sea and I wanted to meditate upon them. I wanted to keep them alive with me. But, as I sifted through the years that our journeys together had gifted us, my mind just drew a blank. Black waters surrounded me and I could not remember anything.

All I could recall were Freshman's vampire teeth and talking to him a year and a half prior, when last I had visited Florida; the Blue Lagoon bar; friends; slender beer bottles sweating generously beneath the thick of Freshman's dark, raggedy beard. As we had sat together upon two adjacent bar stools, Freshman had spoken of his sick father with sad love in his eyes. The rest of my memories were blank.

The wind howled against my empty memory bank. I tried to replace its emptiness with things that meant something to me, but each thought carried the residue of death upon it. I thought of my nan in the hospital bed; her heavy eyes and freshly-painted fingernails. I thought of my dog, Shaggy; the way that his eyes protruded from his head when he had left this world, and me, behind. I thought of many things that would only ever make sense and have meaning for me.

I looked down at my skin and was reminded of the nudity
that kept finding me in times of loss. For me, Nudity was an
accomplice to the bringer of death. Nudity walked hand-in-hand
with him, as if she were the Grim Reaper's favourite girlfriend.
She ensured that each time Death came to deliver his dark
telegraph to me, I would have just awoken from a dreamless
slumber, or casually stepped out of the shower. Together, Death
and Nudity were one body of flesh and bones that showed great
pride in the impeccability of their timing. Nudity was Death's
lover and it was her duty to ensure that I would always receive
him with the vulnerability of being uncovered.

Life and Death passed through the hole in my head like a
rabbit with a watch. And I was a girl called Alice, who lingered
around the rabbit hole and listened out for the tick of the tock. Life
counted itself down around me. I sobbed and I cried, deep into
what was left of the night.

By the time that 6am found us, I was going through the
motions of packing our belongings with the face of a zombie. I
looked as though I belonged to a B-grade horror movie. I felt
weighted down by material things that no longer mattered to me.
I squashed garments into secret compartments, whilst Ben limped
to the bathroom to change the bandage on his toe.

Just as a joke, fate had decided to make things worse for
us. Ben's bandage had fused its beige threads deep into the raw
flesh that tried with futile effort to grow over his toe. Iodine
(God's own blood) had served as the glue. Ben gently pulled at
the dirty fabrics that clung desperately to his fleshy hole, as he sat
in a bathroom stall that didn't cater for tissue. He screamed out in
sickly waves, from a place that was already bursting at the seams
with pain and death. The zombie on my face was unchanged as I
arranged our belongings. The fan wheezed. The lightbulb
flickered. As the walls closed in on us, it felt as though 6am would

last forever.

I carried our bags and helped Ben to hobble over to the bus, just in time to catch it before it sped off. We clambered aboard like refugees and I breathed a sigh of relief, as the bus began to remove us from the darkness of Phnom Penh. For ten hours straight, I sat in the back seat like a china doll and barely moved. I thought of no grand thoughts. I was as empty as a china doll would be. Fuelling myself on a diet of cigarettes and water, I left a trail of tears behind me, along the fractured spine of Cambodia.

As I stood outside of a bus stop and listened to a caged parrot mimic the sounds of oncoming traffic, I knew that I had to return to my old life in America. All around me, goofy foreigners high-fived their camera lenses, as beggars crawled from behind the bus and twitched their phantom limbs in disgust at the tourists' voyeuristic approach. The ghost of my old life twitched inside of me restlessly. Something was calling. I could hear it echo through the rush of traffic. I could hear it in the high-fives and the empty click of the camera. I could feel it in the pull of my cigarette. My past called out to me.

I surrendered my china doll head to gravity and watched through the bumpy bus window as the smudge of scenery passed me by. A momentary memory of youthful innocence began to finally stand still for me; I was with my sisters, Kasha and Trisha. We were smoking bongs out of a Mountain Dew can, crouched down beside wooden pallets, at the back of the pool hall. I was thirteen years old. The night was full of quiet mystery. The unfamiliar earthy smell of smoke curled up under my nose and rode itself down to the fuzziness of my toes. I looked up to my big sisters' glimmering eyes. The weed seeds popped and cracked in the aluminum can. Freshman was around front, chasing skirts with his partner in crime, Casey. They both grinned wide smiles that could barely contain their large, white teeth.

All of us had felt so condemned. Fourteen. Sixteen. Eighteen. I was the youngest amongst them, but we were all teenagers that were waiting for something greater to happen. We wanted to move out. We wanted to grow up. We wanted to be rock stars. Together, we dreamt of ways in which we could make those dreams come true, whilst we obliviously got high with the canned help of Mountain Dew.

I exhaled at the soft touch of a memory that had finally come to find me and, in that breath, I understood of how free we had been back then; freer than any of us could have ever known. In those memories, the strange and peculiar nights of our youth would never end. We were young and in love with all of the possibilities of life.

And, as I sat in the back of a bus that travelled across Cambodia, and allowed a broken china doll smile to crack across my face…

… I knew that I needed that feeling once again.

The City of Temples

31st March 2014

Benjamin and I were welcomed to Siem Reap by a glistening river that curved gently through the center of its small village, running with an exemplary fluidity that encouraged the stagnation in me to disperse; I could only try to mimic the river's calm movements. Thick trees grew proudly from the riverbank, without a memorial of cotton bracelets clinging to them; instead, I was relieved to see that there were only stories of life upon their brown bark. The village itself moved with a gentle longevity. It showed me that death had been left far behind me; back in a dark, broken room that I would always remember as Phnom Penh. As mine and Ben's tuk-tuk rolled to a halt outside of our hotel, I was relieved to find that I could finally breathe a little easier. Siem Reap began to offer Benjamin and I sanctuary during a very tumultuous chapter in our lives.

I awoke in my hotel bed from a deep sleep that felt akin to a coma, and stared blankly at the beige walls of my new chamber. The mid-day sun shone through our windowpane in appreciation of its opening and played gentle games upon Benjamin's skin. The sun's rays were hopeful fingertips that lightly pressed me into making the best of my time in Siem Reap, because life would have to go on… if only for some.

My original intention for travelling up the spine of Cambodia was to explore the infamous ruins of Angkor Watt. It sat atop of Ben's private list of things that he had always wanted to do, but I found that I was caught in a conflict that battled between living life to the fullest, whilst also mourning it. They were like two separate rivers that joined at my feet, right before they met the mouth of the sea, and I was caught in currents from each angle. I could not be certain of which way to swim. Many things had changed in the twenty-four hours since I had booked the bus tickets to Siem Reap. However, the city of temples stood patiently behind our bedroom window and waited for us,

90

undeterred.

The afternoon ushered me into the Cambodian Cultural Village. It replicated miniature floating houses and other things that half-interested me. I walked around like a real-life tourist, but the zombie in my body was uncertain of our exact location. I smiled in photographs to mask the darkness that festered inside of me, because white teeth just drew themselves across my face instinctively. Siem Reap's architecture was undeniably beautiful and it showered me with fleeting moments of merriment that were quickly followed by perspirations of guilt. The sun hovered above my shadow, as though it had just escaped straight out of hell and, somewhere inside of me, I believed it to be my punishment.

Walking towards a group of caged monkeys that swung wildly in their iron entrapments, I witnessed a baby primate cling desperately to its mother's back, giving me vivid flash-backs of the Killing Tree. In a cage of her own, there sat the long, black body of a gibbon. She looked out at me from behind iron bars, with eyes that were as red as mine, and together we mirrored the last decline of a summer's sun. The gibbon and I held one another's sunset gaze for a timeless moment, until she slowly turned her hairy back to me and pressed it against the bars. My tourist heart sank at our visual disconnection, but the zombie in me just stood there, staring at her back and the cold bars fixedly.

Ben walked towards the primate's prison and carefully placed his hand upon her coarse shoulders. I watched as Ben began to glide his hands up and down the gibbon's back in a motion that stroked her. Each time that he did so, she looked back at him in appreciation. Her droopy, bloodshot eyes told of a thousand lonely nights that had been spent in a cage with arms that couldn't quite reach those sweet spots. The zombie in me remembered that it had feet and walked forward to meet the two of them. Together, Benjamin and I scratched the broad of that monkey's back for half an hour and I gladly became lost in our offering. I touched the gibbon's fingers and her toes, as they wound around the bars and then parts of me. She gently entwined the soft of my fingers within her own and looked back at me with eyes that spoke of her permanence. My heart choked. I knew her isolation.

The next morning, I received word that Freshman's funeral would occur in six days' time. Despite my battle with guilt and death, I knew that I had come too far not to see the largest religious monument in the world: Angkor Watt, the city of temples. I felt rested, and parts of my heart were rejuvenated with sleep, so I devised a plan to take the day to investigate its ruins. I would explore the temples, book a flight to Florida, and then catch the 2am night bus back to Bangkok. From there, I would begin my journey back to America. Ben and I mounted a tuk-tuk, contented with a plan, and headed towards the city of temples.

Angkor Watt was a sight that took the breath from my lungs without any apology for its burglary, but I didn't mind at all. Colossal stone columns were etched with the faded faces of giants and stood proudly to welcome my passage. A glistening moat surrounded the entirety of the ruins like an aquatic guardian. As I walked across a grey, time-stained bridge, I looked upon tall towers that actually flowered in a peak of sandstone lotus buds. In its first glance, Angkor Watt showed me that it was a heavenly place on Earth. It was made up of gentle deities and I was drawn deep into the healing of its hallways.

A myriad of mazes laid themselves out before me and, as I entered their musty corridors, I became lost in time. I saw myself in a statuesque figure; it had the body of a slithered snake, with the head of a lion, and I felt a resonance in its dualities. Touching each ruined stone, I let my fingers follow the stories that had been intricately carved into their eternity. Some rocks showed me that a journey of winter solstice would always give way to an equinox of spring. Others allowed my fingertips to trace over chiselled battles that had been fought between heaven and hell. That same parody of beauty and barbarianism made up the holy temples that stood ruined before me. There was an ancient knowledge in those rocks. They were ravaged by war and desertion and were broken under the harsh eyes of father time. However, the wisdom within them still stood strong.

I inhaled every pocket of stale air that cornered itself in

the dark corridors of Angkor Watt, as if its wisdom could be absorbed into me; I inhaled in the hopes that its peace and purity would transfer from my tired lungs down into my pitiful heart. I climbed steep steps that ascended to the top of temples as if they were ladders into heaven. My flowery skirt lazily swayed in the breeze, unconcerned with the guest appearance of my underwear. Standing triumphantly at the top of a temple, I looked out upon my new world where, below me, hundreds of other tourists scampered around and enjoyed the very same moment, though our stories would always be different.

I caught sight of Benjamin and watched as he slowly walked the grounds below with a strained limp and his faithful old bamboo stick. He sweated into fever and hobbled with a clingy pain that decidedly took each step with him. But, even from a distance, I could see that he smiled. Ben moved with a broken, but ecstatic, step, because his intentions were saturated in accomplishment. Angkor Watt was a place that he had romanticised since he was but a boy, and it was a precious moment to look upon my lover's dreams as they became a reality. Because of my witness to his accomplishment, it was as if the moment also lent that smile to me and it rounded my watchful face. Fellow travellers sat up high, on the tops of other temples, waving at me with hands of personal pilgrimage and I began to remember the beauty of the world.

The grandeur of Angkor Watt shall always fall short of words, but as I climbed down from a ruined temple, I tried to remember every single thing about that moment. My mind began to wander without a leash, until parts of my own childhood inspirations came to life before me. I stomped around in my faithful leather boots and wore a rucksack that kept a medi-pack inside of it, to offer remedy to Benjamin's infected toe. In that moment, as I touched rocks that had been parted and cracked by the fingers of forceful trees, I left behind the grieving version of me. I remembered my own roots and gradually took on the form of my childhood hero. I was Lara Croft.

I casually searched for levers and secret doorways. I pushed my back against boulders that were larger than my entire body, and I shimmied across ledges that crumbled at the touch. Angkor Watt became my playground and it offered me a weapon. I shouldered a sandstone shotgun, aiming it at the sadness in me and coldly instructed that it take its final leave. I found refuge in the fantasy of dreams that had belonged to childhood and watched as they turned into a tomb-raiding reality.

Ben was lost in his own fantasy and he wore the face of Robinson Crusoe. Although we barely spoke, I saw parts of him become complete. I watched him breathe in the dusty air and become stronger with each breath. I could see his flesh thicken with each unsteady step that he took. The lion-headed snake bodies looked down at us expectantly, and I began to mimic their strengths.

For hours, Ben and I barely shared a word with one another as we stomped around the temples, lost in our own games of make-believe. At mid-day, the sun became murderous in his convictions and forced us to take shade beneath a forest of trees that had somehow become mixed up in the rubble. As I lay on a grassy knoll, I looked back at the trees that had pushed their way through the sandstone castles and I thought about their relationship.

After the war, the temples had been deserted and the whims of the jungle had crept in. It was as if the trees and the temples had long formed an alliance that was built upon the will to be close. It is said that trees are able to communicate with one another in order to ward off poisonous ants or leaf-devouring locusts. An alphabet of defense can crawl up their trunks and arm them with the ability to momentarily remove nutrients, or promote poisons that are deadly to leaf-eating creatures. So I lay on the grass and hypothesised; if trees were able to speak to one another, then surely they would have struck up a conversation with a bunch of ruined rocks that had crumbled beneath time, without the honour of an audience. Perhaps those trunks had stepped in at the perfect moment, just after the temples' break-up from civilisation, and simply asked to hold its rocks beneath the waning moon. Each day, the temples and the trees had grown closer and closer, and the ruins had gradually forgotten about the abandon of their previous relationship with the humans. The trees had lovingly wound their way into the rocks, as if their rubble were made of sunlight and, gradually, they had pushed their seeds into rocky cracks until they were one. Together, they formed an impressive companionship that was comprised of organic matter and man-made things. Silken trunks became lovers to what was once the backbone of Cambodia's spirituality and held the temples up with tender arms. Their union was a beauty that could not be forgotten.

Ben and I lay on a grassy bed beneath the temple-tree communion but, in contrast, our own isolation had never been more apparent. I had barely spoken a kind word to Ben since our escape from Phnom Penh. We had argued over matters of money and of strength, because I had thought it to be the ideal time that my unhappiness with him be heard. Ben's inability to be frugal was the perfect distraction from death, and I submerged into it eagerly and aggressively. My mannerisms were ugly and rigid and refused to take any comfort from a man that couldn't provide for himself. But Ben just looked at me with his unconditional eyes and he became like a tree that would never forget my beauty. So I surrendered into conversation.

Something about the magic of Angkor Watt began to break down my walls of miscommunication, and allowed relief to sit tentatively upon my lips. Ben and I pushed passed idle beginnings and began to speak of intimate things, exploring the perplexities that had befallen our pathways and comparatively reflecting upon the makings of each trail. I told him which flowers still grew beside my path and which rocks were tripping me up. We spoke of life and death as if they were our differences and similarities.

As my guard finally lowered itself, so that my body could take rest upon Benjamin's, a lone butterfly caught a ride upon the change of my heart and floated towards us. The butterfly had the colour of sunset captured upon its papery wings and, with its finality, I found the courage to put an end to my own bitterness.

A story of Freshman versed my lips in past tense. "He was…" was an unbelievably hard sentence to start, but I began it anyway, through a choked throat that tried to close. The butterfly took a seat upon my frilly skirt, as if to honour me with its audience and, silently, it began to drink from the flowers that were embroidered upon it.

Somewhere in the city of temples, upon a grassy matrimony of tree and sandstone, a flood of memories finally came to me. I had not been able to visit those memories since the news of Freshman's death, and I was glad to be included in their company once more. Ben looked at me with supportive eyes, the butterfly promised not to fly away, and both of them awaited a story in the form of my memories. Rock concerts, movie theatres, and kids that snuck out past bedtime all fell from my mouth for half an hour and that butterfly did not leave. It landed on the elongation of my fingers as I drew stories with them. It stared straight at my face and looked into my eyes with its own. The butterfly took rest on me and then on Ben and I was swollen in the simple elegance of its presence, because it reminded me of magical things.

I could have stayed in that moment forever, because it felt directly linked to Freshman and I was closer to him for it. However, Angkor Watt was a ruined city that was yet to be fully explored. Lara Croft waited patiently in my backpack and presented me with a map, showing me how to get out of my comfort zone. It was simply time to leave. Those three words rang around in my head and crashed into my inability. *Time to leave. Time to leave. Time to leave.* The wisdom of the temples finally offered a transferral of understanding to me and carved a message beside the equinox of spring.

It read: 'No matter what beauty surrounds you, at some time or another, we all have to leave. And death is no different, my dear.'

The butterfly fluttered on with sunset wings.

Transition

1st April 2014

Benjamin and I walked the streets of Siem Reap in search of a power source that had not been severed by Mother Nature's knife. A lightning storm gathered wildly above my head like a static crown. I did not feel like royalty, but nonetheless, I requested that the universe offer me a computer that would allow me to make further travel arrangements.

However, each establishment that I peered into had fallen victim to the power cuts. Each house had been abandoned to darkness, the windows to their souls looking back at me from an eerie blackness. Clouds swirled overhead like an endless ebony soup and the white light of electrical fingertips stirred them around like jagged spoons. The night air was heavy and oppressive. It sat so weighted in my lungs that even my heart could feel its pressure. Lightning bolts travelled down through the grey of the concrete streets and then continued their journey up through the bareness of our restless feet. The storm dispersed its currents throughout my entire body as if they were electrically-charged blood cells.

Mine and Ben's 2am departure drew ever closer, but I was yet to book my flight from Bangkok back home to Florida. My pursuit for a working computer had been fruitless and I could not help but to think that there was a force that stood spitefully against me. By the time that the power had returned to us, it was long past midnight, though I had time enough to scurry back to an internet connection and attempt to find a reasonable flight to Florida. Because of Ben's budgetary shortcomings, it was decided that he would not accompany me to America. I hovered over an outdated square box that offered up a connection to the outside world and grappled with the concept of venturing into that world alone. The path that I would have to tread would be a testing one, and the thought of the empty space that Benjamin's support would leave behind began to push an air of annoyance into my bones. The clouds in the stormy sky moved above me frantically, demanding that I make this journey alone.

Time pressed me into motion. I finalised my card details, grabbed my red rucksack, and embarked upon one final mad dash for deliverance. Together, Ben and I hitched a ride upon the back of a hotel security guard's bike and I felt the hot breath of Time breeze past my face. I could hear the tick of the clock as we rounded the final corner to the bus stop and 2am struck without any intention to retreat. Time and I moved together with such closeness that I could feel the bulge in his pants against my thigh. His clock hand urged me licentiously onto the bus with a premature pace and left a suggestive red imprint on my behind. I rejected Time's un-consensual advances and boarded the night bus as if it were a woman's refuge on wheels.

All night long, the bus rocked and leaned, as if its metallic body were too tall for its rubber feet. I struggled for comfort in my small, boxy seat and in the deep of the night, the bus attempted an improbable U-turn. Its small tyres were swallowed up by the hungry desert sand, and Time made my acquaintance once again. Time wore the circular face of slow-motion cinematography, paralysing everything around him with ease. I looked out of the bus window apprehensively, as it pressed its glass eyes ever closer to the ground. But in an instant, we stood erect, as if the breath that had been held in our lungs had escaped and pushed us upright once again. Exhalation had saved the day.

The bus creaked to a halt in strange, faceless checkpoints, for intervals that spread out across the forever of half an hour. The full volume of diabolical music tunelessly pushed itself out through a cage of loudspeakers and into the morning air. The windows taunted me like open legs. The monotonous tone of a voice that spoke in a Cambodian dialect blared out indistinguishable instructions into the tenderness of dawn. I could not determine what words were said, but it felt like a sick circus act that performed a masquerade of dark hypnosis.

Morning broke over our heads like a fevered teenage heart and bled into the dark of the sky. Ben and I gladly left the bus behind and began to cross the confusing border that separated

Cambodia from Thailand. I stood in one of many lines, clutching my passport to my breast as if it were my only ticket out of hell. It seemed a lifetime ago that Ben, Jon, and I had first walked upon Cambodia's soil with innocent promise in our eyes. As I stood at the back of the line reflecting on the days that had passed, I impatiently anticipated leaving all of Cambodia's beautiful tragedy far behind.

I watched as a stray dog ravenously tore apart the plump body of a street rat right before me, as if it were a delightful breakfast. The dog cast his accomplished eyes in my direction and strolled on by without embarrassment. The remnants of a bloody creature cradled the cave in his mouth as if it were a fleshy treasure, but I did not flinch. I had become numb to Cambodia. I fought for my place in line amongst a myriad of other bodies, who each had their own reasons to leave. I juggled with our luggage like a circus clown. Ben limped beside me as we hiked through the crowded streets like cattle into unknown destinations. The border brimmed with assumptions on how to escape the madness, though no direction was clear. I stabbed in the darkness, until I found myself squashed into an open-back van with fifteen other people that had also made the great escape. The heartbreak of the sunrise gradually blossomed into the yellows of a new day.

As the van drove away from the crowd of Cambodia, the wind tried to blow away everything bitter that was sticking to me. I looked back at Ben and saw his fingers clamped to the roof of the metal van. His body casually hung outside of the mobile cage and attempted to make its own escape from the sardines that we were. Ben caught my eyes and we both smiled with warm relief in the knowledge that we were finally leaving Cambodia.

After fourteen hours of travel, we arrived in Bangkok. I had tired and stiff bones, but within their marrow was the softness of hope. Long-haul travel was becoming second nature to me and my feet began to take me forward with very little effort and much more ease. I walked through the thriving capital of Thailand for the first time and I felt a part of its chaos. Bangkok's market stalls were built like pyramids. They piled their square bodies on top of each other and struggled for individual presence. Garments looked at me seductively with the eyes of silken love-spells woven into their enchantments. Merchants sang out in high opera voices of their incredibly low prices and tried to capture me, when I offered them second glances.

As I parted the crowds in pursuit of a specific restaurant, the sorcery of fabrics was soon dispelled. I stood at the dining entrance, looking disheveled, and the familiar face of Jon greeted me with round, caring cheeks. As Jon and I fell back into synchronicity, my heart calmed with the recognition of a familiar beat in an unknown world. Frenchie looked up at me from her menu with smitten eyes and, swiftly, she transformed into Hélène.

Hélène's features were gentle. She had a sweetness that had been delicately etched into the high of her cheek bones and the warmth of her smile told me that we were already friends. As I walked towards their table, my previous idea of Hélène took on a tangible identity. She had become a woman that had stories of her own; stories that were born from twenty-five years of personal growth. She had long, brown hair that gently poured past her small shoulders and a glow of soft skin that brightly showed off her light from within. Hélène looked vibrant and clean. She and Jon tenderly held hands upon the table top, as Ben and I took seat and fell like meteorites into their company. Together, we all fell easily into conversation, as if we were four that had always known one another. Jon and Hélène listened attentively to one another's frequencies, in the way that new lovers do, and I regarded their gentility as a foreign thing.

I looked upon the soft of Hélène's pale skin and then down at my dusty leather shoes. In comparison, I looked like nothing short of a car wreck. My hair was a mess and my clothes still had the dust of Cambodia clinging to their fabrics. I saw myself through the eyes of Jon when he had seen me last and I knew that I was different. Ben looked like a changed man, too. His eyes were worn and ragged. His bamboo walking stick took rest on the floor beside my dusty boots and pretended to be their friends. So much had changed in just those few days since the three amigos had separated and parted ways. Yet four smiles sat, undefeated, at an outside table beneath a humid grey sky and prepared to fill themselves with food.

I looked towards Jon, and he also seemed transformed. Perhaps his skin resonated with the love of a good woman and made him appear to be stronger. Perhaps he was just a stranger to death and easily lived his life in Bangkok to the fullest. But, as the street vendors sang out loudly with their monetary melodies, they made it difficult for me to determine the origin of Jon's happiness. The black around his eye had softened down to a barely-swollen blue, and a twinkle hid within its deflation. His brown eyes sparkled with the tale of a happy ending. Hélène looked like a picnic beneath a fig tree. Jon's moles no longer turned their backs to me and love floated in the stifled air of Asia.

As Jon and Frenchie ordered dinner, I absorbed their love as if it were my own and basked in their harmony. I ordered a double shot of rum for my meal because my hunger pains had been muted by loss and it seemed that they had stopped speaking to me. Fear tried to make its way in through the barricade of love and my wandering mind accidentally opened up the gate. My thoughts floated out towards my impending thirty-hour flight and fear triumphantly gained its entry without requiring a strip search. All around me, conversations of travel passed through my ears in appreciative tones, but the idea of Florida formed like a dark cloud above my head and I alone was subject to its storm.

A few years prior to that dinnerless dinner, I had promised never to return to America. I had lived in the States for ten years as a youth, with and without the support of my immediate family, but that family was far from me. As an adult, I had pined for them and had returned from the safety net of my home in England to make amends. But by then it was hard for my once-upon-a-family to hear my longing. Three years prior, the bitterness in me had made that promise of self-imposed exile. As I sipped from the warm rum that substituted my meal, I felt neither empty nor full. The promise of never returning to Florida suddenly broke with the clank of a single ice cube that pressed itself against my tooth. I swallowed it down and prepared for a journey back into a land that had become lost to me. I said farewell to my housecat, Jon and hugged him lovingly, unsure of when I would see him again. He just looked at me tenderly, with that same twinkle in his eyes and I left Jon in the safety of his happy ending.

I arrived at check-in with a tatty itinerary in my hand and the midnight moon upon my back. Immediately, the attendant made it clear to me that the flight that I sought out did not, in fact, exist.

'Preparations for departure unnecessary, please resume your normal lives,' she spoke over the loud speaker in my mind.

I wiggled my ticket in front of the receptionist's face as it were a real-life fairy, but she did not dare to believe in it. The receptionist's mouth was pressed with unhelpfulness. I left the queue to pursue an internet connection that would allow me to check my emails for confirmation, though it was to no avail. My inbox was empty of receipts. I left Benjamin on the airport floor with my tablet and pushed passed the queue so that I could plead with the receptionist. She greeted me with a face that told me I had become a problem and I confirmed her assumptions with big, wet eyes that pleaded for further instruction. The only change in her person was the shadow of Time, as he hovered over her pleated shoulder and spoke in a language of ticking clocks. It wasn't long before Time taunted me with a restriction of six minutes until the closure of my gate. I began crying and yelling frantically. The funeral loomed overhead and pressed itself into Time's restrictions, but it felt so far out of reach.

Time mocked me with his consistency, so I allowed my displeasure to escape my mouth with venomous tones. The wild woman in me was not particular and I threw my anger towards the receptionist and Time both. Fire took up residence in my eyes and I became hot with misunderstanding. It didn't make sense to me. The receptionist just looked at me blankly but barely, she spoke. 'No fly,' was her only answer. My rage became a universal language. Just as the sixth minute passed into the smug smile of Time, Ben came sliding through the barrier towards my place in line. His trousers were like rollerblades against the tile floors and, as he came to a halt, he offered up my tablet as if it were a gift to the gods. It would have been a heroic moment, if not for the fact that it was an incorrect confirmation that stared up at me from the screen. The unconfirmed booking put its finger on its nose and stuck its nasty tongue out at me. Time looked upon the scene self-righteously and I knew that I would not fly that night.

I awoke the next morning in a sour puddle of depression. I was stuck in a world of transit that I did not want to be in. Freshman's funeral grew closer and Time curdled like milk in my stomach. I lay there feeling sorry for myself and swore to stay in bed all day, as if I could punish the world with my absence from it. However, the world continued to turn and showed me that I was not needed. I tired of my self-loathing and pressed forward, so that I may figure out the booking mystery. After checking my bank balance, I was relieved to find that the $2,000 still sat fatly in my account and that Time had been the culprit yet again. The online booking had not had time to process, so I returned to the airport in pursuit of a ticket that I could purchase first-hand.

At the airport, I proceeded to do what so many of us do online. I walked hastily from airline to airline and inquired of their flight prices and availability. My feet were like the mouse that scrolled through an endless page, though there were no suggestions of help. I walked back and forth for some time until I was met with success. Washington was the closest that I could get to Florida but, with it being on the other side of the country, it was also the furthest. Attempting to organise a connecting flight from the maze of Asia proved to be futile, so I accepted Washington as my closest ally. Although I was an American citizen, I travelled

104

Asia under the guise of my British passport. Therefore, visa requirements would not allow me to fly that day. I took a deep breath and booked my ticket for the following night. Friday night. The funeral fell on Saturday and I was determined to see the eventuality of my departure from Asia. It had become a mission that I would not give up on.

The following day, the departure gate finally opened up its rigid jaw and welcomed me aboard. Ben and I kissed tenderly in our accomplishment and I tasted the saliva of a man that I had come to know with great intimacy. As I stood upon the jawline of Transition, I was ushered in by a red carpet that lay flat like a furry tongue. I waved farewell to Benjamin, uncertain of where in the world we would see one another again. I allowed myself to be swallowed up by the hallway of my past and South East Asia finally receded into the background. Time surrounded me like an army of urgency.

I slid down the metallic mouth of Transition in one grateful gulp.

Part Two

Migrating Home

Demons and Angels

4th April 2014

Bangkok to Dubai. Dubai to Washington. From there, I would have to make my way down to Florida on my own. As I boarded the plane, I wondered if I would make it in time for Freshman's funeral, though there was nothing that I could do to remedy my queries, so instead I just poured myself into a cramped-up plane seat. Time sat upon my lap despite my need for personal space and, as the engine whirred into life, I left my fate with the unaccountability of chance.

I watched as an air hostess walked the aisle beside my seat and cast her pleasantries upon me with a rehearsed kind of kindness. She wore a bright yellow suit that looked as though she had just taken a dip in a bowl of neon custard. Her plastic smile wrapped itself around the entirety of her face and caused her bubblegum pink lips to crack beneath its stretch. The air hostess asked me if I would like a drink for the journey and something within the pink, plastic manner of her mouth began to calm me. Familiarity spoke in southern tongues. As I employed the baby-blue headrest with relief, the distinct scent of western smells pushed out from its fabrics and swam around beneath my nostrils. I swallowed down my Washington anxiety from a plastic cup that was filled with foreign red wine, said a private prayer to help me get there safely, and closed my eyes.

The seat beside me exhaled sharply, as if it had been winded by a blow to the gut. I opened up my eyes as the large body of a fellow passenger fell like a falling star into the seat beside me. He looked over in my direction with glimmering eyes and skin that was as brown as mine. Mark and I mirrored one another with introductory smiles and together we departed the runway of idle conversation and made an immediate take-off into the arts of meaningful communication. Common talk on baby-blue seats and custard attire were surpassed as soon as the wheels went up and allowed our wings to take air. The tinder of two unknown worlds sparked a fire in our mouths and we began to be aflame with curiosity for one another. We had barely skimmed past the pavement of 'hello' before we were off the ground with the airy ideas of transcendence. Mark and I flew into that wide, open space that only two strangers ever go to. Our plump lips poured out ideas about God and karmic repercussions; we soared through ideas of life and death with complete abandon.

Mark gently told me of the faith that had put that twinkle in his eye and the strength in his step. I showed him the 'faith' tattoo upon my neck, but expressed that I leaned more towards an unclassified spirituality. Although our sacred stories were from different sources, thousands of feet up in the air, Mark and I met in the middle with absolute respect. The plane shook with the hands of a higher love upon it. I looked at the brown freckles on Mark's face and knew that he was one of the good guys in life. Mark had the kind of caring that sat atop of his glowing skin and would never wash off.

On a flight destined for Washington, Mark and I pulled similarities out of one another as if they were hairs on a dinner plate. We pulled sour faces over the comparisons of our military fathers and then smiled tenderly when we thought of their lighter sides. For hours, we sat upon that plane without the distraction of airline movies and engaged in a way that only two complete strangers could. Mark did not know a single person or thing about my life, besides that in which I chose to impart upon him and, because of his lack of assumption, I became completely unguarded. I began to speak easily of the last few weeks of my life in Asia and Mark listened attentively. His care pulled away the clammy hands that had been grasping at my throat, stopping me from communicating. We had nowhere to go and nowhere to be; it was just a version of him and a version of me.

Behind us, Time slept like a worn-out child upon a baby-blue seat that would never tell of our stories. Once words had begun falling out of my mouth, I was able to see my journey through the crystal light of clarity. I knew that Mark was a guardian angel that had been sent to me, and we both spoke ourselves into a peaceful sleep.

ॐ

I arrived at Washington airport to be greeted by a butch immigration officer that stood behind a glass cage like an animal. Her stern face told me that she thought herself to be the Gatekeeper of Humanity. Her thick arms were crossed firmly against the folds of her unwanted chest and as I approached her, she extended chunky fingers towards me that demanded my identity. I handed my British passport over to her with caution. The slick of her black hair ran to the back of her head and found refuge in a bun. Her greasy eyebrows followed their example and stretched themselves across her forehead in an attempt to make it to the same destination. The immigration officer looked down at me through her glass cage with eyes that said 'No'.

The Gatekeeper of Humanity made it undeniably clear to me that the U.S.A did not recognise dual-citizenship. Her thin, pressed lips spoke proudly of the country as if he were her father; as if the U.S.A were a person that I had never met. Her small, beady eyes looked disdainfully into me like I was merely America's mistress and the ten years that I had spent with him meant nothing to her. It appeared that the apple had not fallen far from the tree, because the Gatekeeper was consistent in her systematic approach. To her, I was not accepted into their family fold, therefore I did not exist:

"Where's your U.S passport?" She began.

"In England," I returned.

"Why is it in England?"

"Because I live in England."

"Why didn't you bring it?" She pressed.

"I was in Asia with no plans to return to America." I pressed her back.

"Where in Asia, and why?" Her nose grew bigger.

111

"Thailand and Cambodia, broadening my horizons." I smiled.

"Why are you here?" She asked, with the face of a bulldog.

"An unexpected event," I responded, vaguely.

"Well then…Where is your passport?"

Repeat to fade.

That strange representation of a welcome committee saw that I was held in immigration for forty minutes. The bulldog guarded over her country furiously and pressed me with the same questions over and over again in the hopes that I would reveal my true terrorism. The Gatekeeper wore the sickly perfume of rules and regulations upon the thick of her neck and the pursuit for power impregnated the grotesque swell of her round belly. She was undoubtedly the Gatekeeper of Humanity, and she had no intention of letting me into her paternal country.

So, I resorted to tears. I had spilled so many over the last week that my brave face felt wasted upon an immigration officer. I told her of my friend's impending funeral and fell into a dramatic sobbing fit that was full of snot and hysteria. The Gatekeeper of Humanity stepped away from me, quite disgusted at my public display of emotions; apparently, beastly ogres don't like that kind of quivering, gushy stuff, unless it is the warm kind that resides in-between your thighs. As I wiped my tears away, my American citizenship came running over the hill towards me, waving its unrecognised hands at me in familiarity. I left the ogre behind and walked through the gates with triumph tucked in-between my teeth.

I immediately booked a flight from Washington to

Florida with ease, though the flight departed from a separate airport somewhere in the city, demanding that I catch the bus across town within the hour. An airport attendant put me on the 5A bus to Ronald Regan airport and blew a large, pink bubble of 'bon voyage' out from her chewing gum. I confirmed my stop with the long, grey eyelashes of the bus driver and he fanned me with them in acknowledgement. After half an hour had passed me by, I yelled to the grey oracle once more. His wrinkled lips creased with thoughtfulness.

"Oh, you wanted the *airport*?" He emphasised the word 'airport' in a way that suggested I was going the wrong way.

"Let me off the *fucking* bus!"

I fell out of the mouth of the bus with a self-induced fever upon my brow. Time stood beside me amongst the busy streets and took great pleasure in my struggles against him. I desperately stuck my shy thumb out into roads that it didn't yet know, in the hope of a ride. As a car came to a slow, it showed two children that were pressed against a back seat window, looking back at me with curiosity. Their large eyes reflected the glimmer of my backpack as it shone like a red ruby in an endless silver city. It wasn't long before the car threw me back out onto the streets somewhere close to the train station. Two-thirty had struck and Time waited for three.

On foot once more, I began searching for the train station. I knew that I was close, though no maps nor phones could verify such things. I was but a simple traveller that had had such communicative luxuries stolen from me. As Time counted me down, I befriended a large, black lady that walked two steps ahead of me.

"I need your help, lady!" I blurted out from a mouth full of panic. The woman slowed her crawl down to a pause and looked at me with the same curiosity as back-seat window eyes had done, moments before. She stared at me from two wet bowls of brown broth and, for a moment, I became lost in their kindness. I threw my life scenario at her as if we were playing basketball, dribbling a jumbled mess of explanations across a court of desperation. I hopped from one foot to the next as if to suggest that I could take off at any second. My voice quivered and my eyes once again became wet. Upon a nameless road in Washington City, a stranger with broth eyes gently lifted a soft and caring hand up towards the sky... and then, bringing it down to eye level, she promptly slapped me in the face.

"You gotta wake up baby guuuurrrll," she slurred in her southern drawl, from a mouth that was full of tough love. It appeared as though Time had tied me up and enslaved me when I wasn't looking, and I became aware of the chaos that had taken over my mind. With a hand of gentle encouragement, that southern woman had released me from him. She began to walk ahead of me and mumbled gently to herself. The solar system of her thighs rounded each other as she heavily placed one foot in front of the other. I could feel something powerful happening, so I began to follow her. We covered a couple of blocks and, having seen the distress in me and allowing it to replace any thoughts of herself, that woman cooed me all the way to the train station. As I waited for the train, she stayed with me until it arrived, at which point I hugged and kissed her soft, pulpy skin madly. I felt as though I had just walked a block with my granny.

"Good luck baaaaaabbby!" She waved a caring hand that had tough love written in their fingerprints, until she disappeared into the blackness and became another gift from the heavens.

As I sat on an underground train with blinking yellow bulbs and junkies that were maxed-out into oblivion, the world didn't seem so scary. Having made it to the airport with five minutes to spare, I then sent a quick email to my family.

'I will arrive in Orlando at 5:30pm. See you in a few hours.... Someone please be there!'

There are demons in this world, and there are angels. One beast had obstructed me, but two angels had seen it in them to guard my passage that day, just by taking a moment out of their lives to show a complete stranger that they cared....

... even if one of them had initially slapped me in the face.

A Fairy Tale

5th April 2014

I was met at the airport by the big, blue eyes of my small, teary mother. Her long, blonde hair cascaded down her back like a silken waterfall and trailed off into a slither of rivers beside her thighs. My mother looked up at me with hopeful wells that poured from her pale blue eyes and wet her ruby face with wishes of my wellness. As I stood at the arrivals gate, I made a wish for our own uncertain future to realign and prosper, then poured myself into her arms as if I were a copper penny.

A year had passed since I had last saw those eyes. They are a mother's eyes; eyes that have distantly watched over the wayward course that has always been her daughter's life. They are the eyes of love and they are also the eyes of absence. For the latter, a year had passed since I had almost given up on them.

When last my mother and met, it had been under a similar circumstance of death. My Nanny, her own mother, had just passed away, unexpectedly. Thirteen years had passed my Mum by before she found reason enough to leave America and touch back down on the British soil of her homeland. It was a homeland that I had long left America for and returned to. Though, despite our common ground, it appeared that mine and my mother's paths continued to stray far from one another. During her visit, I was barely a character in her background and it mirrored every empty year that I had emptied my pockets for Florida in an attempt to be closer to her. In many ways, my Mum and I were strangers and it became clear to me that we had lost something precious long ago.

At the tender age of fifteen, without saying a word, I left high school in the middle of the day, climbed aboard a Greyhound bus and ran far, far away. I chose to leave behind the toxic trouble of a familial connection that had fragmented beneath the volcanic pressure of personal development. Its sharp shards had pressed themselves upon my wrists and had secretly drawn blood. The empty space that love left behind had caused me to no longer fit into my body and the suicide in me wanted to leave that ugly world. The Greyhound was my only chance for life.

Not only had I left my family, but I had also left behind the anchored weight of a house arrest bracelet. Amidst my familial troubles, I had somehow also fallen into the category of a juvenile delinquent and the system had a tight grasp upon she who had already struggled for freedom. At the back of a Greyhound bus, a Swiss army knife had been extracted from the pocket of a fifteen-year-old girl who wore the markings of a lost soul upon her leg. As she sat in the bathroom of the bus, the thick black jaw of her confinement was hacked away in vicious chunks, pulled like a bear trap from the delicacies of a young ankle. Freedom looked like soggy, pale flesh that had been exiled from the wisdom of the sun.

As the bus bumped along the highway to nowhere, a younger version of me looked disgustedly down at the black teeth of the perpetrator that had gnarled away at her for months. Her ebony jewellery was, without a doubt, deadly and had almost cost a sad little girl her life. In the confines of a bathroom stall, that little girl called high treason for forced abductions of impressionable flesh. She picked up her head and threw all evidence of her capture out of the bus window and watched it crunch beneath car tyres with unparalleled satisfaction. That fifteen-year-old girl returned to her seat wearing the triumphant smile of a prisoner of war that had finally escaped. Hundreds of busses have been caught since that very day.

I was fifteen years old when I left home because, although I wore a smile upon my face like an ivory back bone, I was full of broken things. I was built up on limitations. False faces had morphed onto my skin because of the roles that I had been forced to play and those falsities left me with no true identity. My hair was made of silver-tongued lies and my breath smelled like misguidance. My body wore an anchor of violence upon it, but I had stolen with me the first boy who had ever taken a chance on loving it. He had shaggy blonde hair and dorky glasses that looked into me caringly and I was fused to his gentleness because of it. I joined him on the bus seat bound to anywhere and together, we were gone for a year.

We drifted from Florida up to Texas, where we lost ourselves for months in underground raves that spat our contorted bodies back out at the break of innumerous dawns. I would travel home in unknown cars with the window down to my eye level and watch the skyscrapers split with the rise of the sun. As the wind whipped my hair like slavery and I watched the world pass me by carelessly, at fifteen years old I realised that I could be anyone. My freedom was inexhaustible and I pushed past the bounds of normalcy until I had no limitations left. I was certain that no one would control my life again and I went through great lengths to ensure that such a truth was upheld.

However, my availability of an identity allowed the world to offer me the cold tendency to become completely strung out on methamphetamines. I didn't eat. I hid away in a closet and smoked for days that timelessly slipped into weeks. I peaked and crashed and lost months beneath the ragged of my teenage eyes, but all the while… I had thought that I was free. After my 'identity' got out of control, I left for Illinois, Indiana, Ohio, and then back to Illinois without the gift of any real guidance. When we did eat, we lived on a diet of one-dollar burgers from McDonalds. When we found work in any way that we could, we never used our true identities. We were on the run from the law like Bonnie and Clyde. But more importantly, we were on the run from ourselves.

From drug nest to drug nest we had roamed, until I found myself living in the attic of a crack house in the middle of an Illinois winter. I treaded lightly upon a carpet of used needles and second-hand condoms in an attempt to turn that place into my home. My bedroom had windows that wouldn't quite close and allowed the snow in as if its openness were an invitation. The house itself had belonged to a man who replaced the purity of breath with a perpetual inhalation of crack cocaine. In the early hours of the morning, he would smash through the walls with an

118

axe, attempting to remodel his house in a frenzy of unnecessary construction. Then, his distraction would see that no job was finished and winter became a regular tenant in that house. His cracked-out company stole my possessions as I stood at the payphone at the end of the road, trying to reach out to loved ones. Snow fell regretfully upon my fingers as they clasped at an empty receiver and my soul began to feel a kind of cold that it had never known.

At sixteen, I was a broken thing that thought that she knew the arts of self-medication, though all I truly knew was that I was in need of great healing. Before long, my addiction saw that I progressed into dabbling in the mess of a brown toxin that most people don't come back from. I was sixteen years old with crack pipes for fingertips and cold shoulders that knew no true assistance. Although I had left home in order to save myself, I barely made it back alive.

That day on the Greyhound bus, I went away a girl and, although I did come back home, I never really came back to my mother. I was private in my nature and told her none of my dark experiences, but both of us knew that vast distances had grown between us. The recognitions of our souls decayed at an alarming rate, because we each resided in very different worlds. My mother began to regard my movements as independent of her own and in that independence, I became someone that no longer needed her protection. My mum saw me as a hard-headed woman with a maverick nature that was just like my father's, and for that I unconsciously repelled her. She would never know how much I had needed her back then… how much I have always needed her.

"You can't just stop being a fucking mother!" I recall screaming at her, as we walked towards my Nanny's grave in England all those years later. My eyes poured rivers from their pipes and I forced her to see the vulnerability that she had long confused with my coldness. My mother had looked up at me with those innocent doe eyes that were caught in the headlights of my rage. Despairingly, she recoiled and showed me of how she still thought a monster to live inside of me. However, those words needed to be said, because there were five of us children in total who had all lost everything that we once knew as paternal. Many years ago, my siblings and I had all strayed separate ways. We all bore heavy hearts for the theatrics that we had been made to witness. Five children had walked away from one another with belt welts upon the smalls of their backs and bruises inside and out. A curtain never closes on the dramatisation of what love can do to two people.

As children, my siblings and I were each haunted at night by the memory of a monster that had thrown our mother down the stairs and left her outside in the rain to beg for forgiveness. I would wipe the cool of the condensation from my bedroom window and watch as the rain pressed my mother's nightgown into transparency. Its white lace sat weighted against the soft of her breasts and revealed her pink goose-bumped flesh. Even back then, perverse natures were clear to me. My mother would knock ever so quietly, so that the neighbours would not hear, but the door remained locked until the monster said that the coast was clear. Five children would fearfully crawl back into their beds with shell-shocked eyes and hearts that locked out the world without the remedy of a key.

We each involuntarily participated in a Jekyll and Hyde show of Happy Family and we each had grown into estranged creatures because of it. We were actors upon a stage; we were innocent and we were guilty; we were both the punished and the happiest of children, but each of us carried that diversity like the devil upon our backs. I tried to remember that when I thought upon my family, especially when I looked into those blue eyes that have watched me grow into everything that I am. Those tragic eyes that could never save me; those pale blue eyes that gave life to me. But once they had left their monsters behind, they seemed to have forgotten me in their own final pursuit of happiness.

My mother and I spoke of many things beside Nanny's grave that day, a year prior. Our guards finally fell and we conversed over the importance of family and of cherishing life whilst it is here. I wanted us to be people that were more than just subject to their circumstance and I wanted her to join me in my desires. My mother and I cried beneath the cool spring air and held one another for a timeless moment. The damp grass held us up without reason. My mother said sorry. I said sorry too and, before she returned to America, our shores shifted just that little bit closer.

Amongst the commotion of the airport arrival lounge, I felt myself relieved to be in my mother's embrace once more. She wrapped her dainty arms around my disappearing waist as I rested my chin atop the flat of her head like a landing strip. The blondes of her hair told stories of western cleanliness and tickled out the happy endings from my nostrils. The nostalgic scent of a mother rose up into my lungs and filled me with a calm like no other.

Together, my mum and I drove to the unfamiliarity of her house. It was a place that the monster in me had banished us from a few years prior, when rage had boiled over in me and had burned her without care of the repercussions. Memories of my displeasure still hung about the shadows that were cast upon the kitchen table, but my mum walked past them without acknowledgement and began to draw a bath for me. Around the edges of the tub she placed thick, waxen candles and set them alight, as if her bathroom were a place of holy things. As I removed my soiled clothes, my mother took them in her caring arms, along with the contents of my filthy rucksack, and pushed them inside of a washing machine that had never known the taste of me.

I looked around the quiet of the bathroom with relief and was reminded of how my mum had always filled her houses with precious and holy things. I recalled tenderly of how she had put me and my siblings to sleep every night with her magical tales of fairies; it was as if they were woodland scripture and she were but a mystical devotee. I looked upon the porcelain of the toilet seat in delight at its slim resemblance to a grotty hole in the ground. Asia fell away from me as I stepped into the warm water and submerged myself in the curve of the bath. Closing my eyes, I finally felt that no harm could befall me. The wings of my mother once again opened up to me and I was like a baby bird beneath the feathers of her safety.

As I looked over the clean tiles of the bathroom floor, I understood that, although I barely knew my mother's home, I was well-acquainted with the things that lived there. Her collection of soaps sat proudly in the corner and conversed over the differences between circles and squares. Her candles stood fearlessly erect with the knowledge that they would always have a place at her table. Below the vanity mirror, her lotions gathered themselves and vainly whispered into each other's ears in an attempt to conceive the horror of my life without them. My mother's house was like a fairy's den that I had somehow found through a path that had been lined with death. It had brought me closer to a land that I had thought to be lost to me.

Tentatively, my mum brought me a glass of red wine and blushed the same rouge of embarrassment as I lay naked before her. As she turned to leave, with her own glass grasped in the small of her fingers, I intercepted her with my own tales of recent travels. My naked body was born from her own flesh and I had long learned that I need hide nothing from her. My mother casually took a seat at the edge of the bath and we swam in memories of our togetherness. I shaved my hairy legs and tenderly recalled of how I had watched her shave as a child. My wide eyes used to line the rim of the bath like a rising sun, looking upon the beauty of my mother as she bathed. My mum would sing and hum, undeterred by the presence of five curious children. My mum was the first glance into womanhood that I had ever seen. I remembered the thick of her calves and the way that the razor used to drink in her strength like a calf thirsty for milk. Whilst I shaved my legs and drank my wine in a bath framed with candles, I sat beside my mother for the first time as a woman. We started to return to the love that we had once known and for the first time in many moons, I began to feel like a daughter again.

As I sat in the evening, cloaked in darkness and blowing smoke out into the air, my sisters, Britney and Shannay came running through the screen door to greet me. Their large, white smiles competed with the light of the moon and soothed me in the same ways that the tides do. As they swarmed me with cuddles, their brown curls wrapped me inside of an eternal love spiral. The three of us fell, as always, into the little girls that we will always know one another to be. My sisters and I were goofy. We were intimate. We were unceremoniously jealous without the repercussion of ever losing one another. We wore similar styles upon the earthen tones of each of our skins that would never go out of fashion. Britney's fawn eyes held mine tenderly beneath the starlight, twinkling like an alternate reality of gentility. Shannay's long fingertips played with the tips of my blonde hair adoringly and proved that I would always be her favourite doll. Half of ourselves were strangers, yet half of ourselves were soul mates that would always be bound by blood and childhood adventures.

Britney was a mother to children of her own and they gathered beneath me like two raindrops that were about to burst. I dragged their squirming bodies into the swimming pool fully clothed, just to remind them of our connection to the innocence of youth. My niece and nephew's lips exploded with water-logged laughter and I solidified their unified idea of how their aunty was a movie star.

"You still makin' movies, Aunty April?" Terrance questioned from behind the purity of a damp lisp. It was a child's hypothesis on why a family member would stay away so long in lands that they had never heard of. As I held her in my arms, Kiara looked up at me with the same sparkling lights that twinkled endlessly in her mother's eyes. The tired of my bones began complaining of exhaustion, but I wanted to feel like a movie star, if only for one night. So, the black furrow of Terrance's brow back down to neutral, I avoided his question with a distraction tactic of adulthood silence.

I looked up from the commotion of the swimming pool and saw a small silhouette standing in the frame of the screen door.

Beneath a halo of light, our mother looked over us all tenderly like a winged guardian and, as the well of her wishes shone against the blue of the pool water, she watched us all with motherly eyes.

Celebration of Life

6th April 2014

I travelled down an open road and watched the sunlight dance and weave through the curvatures of tree spines like an enchanted ballerina. As my vision followed the lurch of their brown bones up towards the gathering of luscious leaves, it was as if I passed beneath an organic chapel that guarded my passageway into another world. Silver rays of light pirouetted across the windscreen with clothed feet and danced upon its glass as if no one were watching. As I squinted into the shards of angelic choreography, footless footprints prismed in the creases of my sleepy eyes, reminding me that morning had perhaps found me too soon.

From the driver's seat, my younger sister, Britney, momentarily withdrew her view from the road and cast her concentration upon me with the benevolent thievery of second glances. As we pressed on towards Freshman's funeral, I sat in the passenger seat, feeling as though I were a fragile antique that could break at any moment. I knew that if I were to show any signs of cracking beneath the pressure of loss, Britney would be there to put me back together. She took my hand and held it there upon the Middle Earth of two front seats that propelled us into a dangerous land of forgotten things. Britney's skin was made from the soft glue of sisterhood and her clothes were tailored by the rocky fabrics of 'lean on me.' She cast her eyes back upon the road, though her support stayed with me.

My own eyes blurred into an aquatic blindness, allowing me to become lost in the vision of a memory; it was Britney's twenty-first birthday and, as I had led her down the reckless pathway of legality, Freshman had made my sister feel welcome amongst a disheveled group of lost children. His kind eyes had kept Britney company throughout her intoxicated rites of passage and I recalled tenderly of how he had embraced her alcoholic excess with his unfailing affection. Freshman had been in my life for far too long not to extend our friendship into the realms of one another's families. As a prism gave me the gift of a rainbow's end upon the windscreen, I remembered that hug. Freshman had the kind of embrace that was akin to warm winter blankets and Eskimo kisses.

Knots tied and untied themselves in the pit of my stomach like pink, intestinal shoe laces. Nervous energy rose up inside of me and eagerly gathered in the salivation of my mouth as if it were a swimming pool. My stomach wanted to evict those shoe laces. I let in some fresh air and tried to dry out the impending sickness like a canine in a car window, though I did not feel the same pleasures. Britney squeezed a hand, reminding me that it was mine, and with her touch she brought me back to her. The air held a respectful silence around our passage, as if it knew that words of consolation would be lost upon us.

Alongside the grief of loss, there also lived a great fear inside of me. As the car curved through the quiet air, I realised that I was approaching a life that I had left behind many years ago. It was a life that I had pushed, with all of my might, to break free from, because I had every single reason under the sun to detest it. Four years prior, my feet had been bound and set to fire with the furies of my own replications of violence. So, in remedy, I had begun to run on the spot. I kept running on the spot until my ankles had broken free of their chains and my feet had caught up with the turning of the world. Before long, I found myself a million miles away from Florida, without even the kind gesture of a goodbye.

Freshman had also left his old life behind. It was as if his wild spirit had ran so fast on the spot, with such fevered emotion, that his body simply could not keep up and it had to be left behind him. Freshman had not been given the chance to say goodbye, nor had he the same option to return as I. So, although fear swam shoe string laps in my mouth, I counted each and every one of my blessings. The morning sun swirled around in elegant tragedy and I knew that my potential to make amends with my old life had been offered as a gift to me.

More often than not, a funeral is a deeply morbid chamber of loss. Rigid bodies are dressed in dark shadows, in an attempt to mirror their own personal sorrow; for black is associated with death, rather than an eternal mystery. Cold walls loom over a hollow room, accentuating a smallness of person that is already so very apparent. We mourners patiently listen to a robed stranger read aloud from a piece of scripture that may or may not have meaning to us. We try to draw comfort from its words because tradition feels like the last one standing in a battlefield of transcendence, but many of us just stand alone in our emotions and are lost in the war. Often, a funeral is an endurance which, when completed, sends us running back to the lighter parts of our worlds. We privately exhale with relief from all of the feelings that were caged in behind the bars of formality and not properly released.

In contrast, such an oppressive scene bore no resemblance to Freshman's final Celebration of Life.

As I stepped out of my sister's car, the green of the grass hungrily caught my feet as if their soles were nourishing dew drops. Grounding swallowed me up. I looked out towards an open field and saw vibrant colours belonging to a multitude of bodies that played merrily beneath the Floridian sun. Rainbows sought to end themselves in that field. Peacock-coloured garments and familiar smiles began to mix together in a whole new shade of love. People, young and old, threw Frisbees against the approach of the horizon and the day casually began, as if it were just another beautiful day in paradise.

As my feet took me towards the crowd and I began to recognise the faces that were attached to those colourful bodies, I understood the importance of a unified grief. The asthmatic ceiling fan and yellow flickering bulb of Asia fell far behind me because, in that field, I knew that I would neither cry alone nor struggle for memory. Loss could be a familiar thing that would unify the strangers in us all. We had each been granted permission to grieve beneath the warmth of the sun, where there was no pressure to feel formal or small. Together, the eclectic gathering of Freshman's family and friends could attempt to exorcise the demons of sadness out of our hearts with no reservations, until our aspirations could transcend our loss into the remembrance of cherished things.

Freshman's friends grouped together in various corners of the field and I anticipated being closer to them through his memory; for we were all known in different ways to a kaleidoscope of dissimilar people and we were brought together through one common cause. Each circle of friendship honoured a unique shade of the person that they had known Freshman to be. He had been a man of many faces, with an ability to merge into different shades of people's excluded groups with the neutrality of a chameleon. Though, despite our boundaries, Freshman had always maintained his true identity. From the grassy corners of our own self-imposed categories, we began to tie ropes around our unified memories and pull them into our dissimilar bodies until we became one.

We were an endless sea that was comprised of Friday-nighters, punks, preps, colleagues, and psychedelic trippers. We broke upon the shores of the loose-goose debauchees, the grab-a-coffee-on-a-Tuesday-morning crew, and the ones who had known Freshman through all of his personas. I sat beneath an old American elm tree with the old-timers, where we were like veterans to a war that we couldn't be sure was over. Our friendship was the kind that was akin to family and, for it, we drew comfort from one another's familiarity. However, shell-shocked stories could be read in the creases of our eyes. The elm tree alone knew of our sorrows.

There were many of us lounging upon the field that day who had once been subject to the bitter entwinement of rivalries. However, as the day pressed on with or without us, our disputes softened down into the tender care of compassion. It was apparent that time spent clinging onto bitterness, white-knuckled, was time

128

not well spent at all. The inescapable truth of life's fleetingness was all around us. It whispered through the tops of the trees and asked us to lay down our weapons at the feet of forgiveness. I heard its request loud and clear as Casey parted the crowds and walked towards me with the same confident stride that had once been the most familiar thing to me in the world.

Casey had been the love of my young life, my once upon an everything. He was also the reason that I had exiled myself from an entire country just four years prior to that field. His tall, slender body came to a stop and stood in front of my own, both of us knowing that we must let go of our failures. We began to close in on the years of our absence with the first attempt at a friendly embrace. Our bodies were like cardboard cut-outs of themselves. We touched one another with a disjointed affection, trying not to focus on the heartache that we had once caused one another. As the chalk of Casey's skin met my own, I attempted not to recoil in venom. Casey looked down at me with a face that said I knew nothing of his troubles and, for the first time in many years, my stubbornness allowed him to be right. My cardboard cut-out softened in the brutal knowledge that Casey had just lost his best friend.

The reacquainted gathered themselves beneath the shade of a gazebo and sat together upon plastic garden chairs to watch a slideshow of Freshman's life. Photographs of fancy-dress parties versed the screen with unparalleled hilarity. Days spent in the innocence of an afternoon park balanced out the wild nights that so many of us had spent with him at bars. An eclectic storm of fanciful friends all showed their love for Freshman in the projected and colourful memories of how we used to interact. Raspberries were blown upon swollen, round faces that were bursting at the seams with the sweet juices of laughter. Asses were casually smacked amongst male counterparts who held no fear of homophobia. Family took on many faces.

My own face was also in amongst the still frames of friendship, but I was startled to look upon our image; Freshman stood in the center of Stephanie and I, as we leaned against his shoulders like inebriated angels. Stephanie's red lipstick glossed over and pressed outwards with playful youthfulness. Our smiles were wild and silly. The round of Freshman's bearded face rested generously against mine like a thick winter blanket and I was surprised at how taken I was with our beauty. It was a beauty that bore no ego; rather, it was simply a picturesque loveliness that reminded me of how death held no pardon for neither the young nor the beautiful. When the old are ready to pass, we are at least able to see some kind of visual confirmation of their imminent departure. It is in the tired of their eyes as they kiss us goodnight; it rests in the loose skin that drapes from their elbows and shows that they will no longer need a body where they intend to go. But when death suddenly snatches the young from the prime of their lives and leaves us with only photographs of their beauty, we cannot help but to feel forsaken. No... death pardons neither the young nor the beautiful.

I cast my eyes across an ocean of plastic garden chairs and watched as teary eyes stared hungrily into the projector. As if I had spotted an island of land amongst the sea, I rested my vision upon the statuesque body of Freshman's mother. Lorna's small back stood unconsciously to attention, as if she were a soldier at war. Her eyes were glossed over with a wetness that said she was present with us in our world, yet there was also a distance in them that disputed that presence. Her dainty hands held themselves upon her lap, whilst the heavy hands of death lay cloaked on top of them, though she did not try to move them away.

Lorna looked calm, as if she could no longer struggle against the fate that had been dealt to her. Instead, she just sat there, like a spectator to the war that was her life. The day had pressed her features. She looked upon her son's pictures with a perfect face of composure, though I could not even begin to imagine the turmoil that fought inside of her being. My heart quietly broke for her. The warm draught of abandonment blew through the colours of her clothes and her image became a painting that I would never forget. Lorna was a modern day Mona Lisa who wore the enigmatic expression of a mother who had just buried her son. The lost children of our tribe unified and gathered around Lorna's statue like a halo. We reminded her that, despite the loss of her son, she would always continue to be a mother to us all.

Looking away from the Mona Lisa, I thought upon the memories of when Freshman and I had once lived together. We had shared a house that was perched just outside of our planetary rules and confined alignments; it was a house that had not belonged to normality nor time. It was the one place in which I would come to know Freshman the best. Freshman and I had lived closely with about twenty other bodies and, with the assistance of those bodies, I had taken the first imperative steps towards getting the shy girl out of me. Communal living had lovingly pushed away my self-restrictions with the hands of hard parties. We ate together, slept together, and had desperately fought over the last Hungry Man by chasing one another around the house with our laughter, together.

Amongst the lucidity of our explorations, Freshman and I had bathed together, brushed one another's teeth, shaved one another's legs and, in trusting that we would not cut one another, we had found absolute friendship in our wayward ways. When the day was done, we would all curl up like cats on beds, sofas, and floors and sleep peacefully like the lost children that we were. It was an interesting time in all of our young lives. During those hazy days of development, Freshman had taken many photographs to commemorate and capture our strange journey. Stephanie and I would often kidnap his camera and sneak into the bathroom to view his perspectives. We were two little girls with a promise to protect one another from the hardships of our worlds and we would harmlessly amuse ourselves at the expense of others. The bathroom tiles never grew tired of our laughter. Stephanie and I would look upon the photographs that Freshman had taken of himself and quietly giggle over what we had thought to be vanity.

Though, as I sat upon a plastic garden chair, I found myself endlessly appreciating every single self-portrait that

Freshman had taken for us. At the time, Stephanie and I had been far too busy laughing into bathroom mirrors that had only reflected our fun, to ever capture the light of Freshman's true character; only he knew how to do so. Looking upon the slideshow of his life, I found myself wishing that he had taken more. I imagined that perhaps Freshman could fill the world with so many photographs of himself that he could materialise from their pixels and become tangible to us once more.

As the afternoon sun slid into its evening attire, those of us that were left behind gathered in the center of the field for the final goodbye. Chinese lanterns were placed like an offering into our empty hands as the sky grew darker with a ceremonial silence. Casey's older brother, David, stood beside me with an air of protection. As we lit a single lantern together, we realigned in the long-lost fable of our own friendship. As David and I stood side-by-side, I sought out refuge in the deep brown spirit of his eyes, knowing that it would always be there.

The breeze tenderly tipped my chin upwards and held my face towards the sky. Together, David and I watched our lantern ascend up past the dark blue sky and float on towards the heavens. The lantern's soft, orange ember was surrounded by a myriad of other singular glowing lights. It was a sight of absolute peacefulness that sat atop of our heads like a star-kissed halo. As the lanterns travelled into the horizon with the grace of silence, I could not be angry at their departure. I had come to peace with the fact that all of us must leave: the friendship of Freshman, butterflies beneath sacred temples, and ceremonial lanterns, because they are no different.

Each and every thing rides upon the cosmic winds of change and its light is ultimately destined to travel alone into the dark mystery of the setting sky.

My legs felt weak and I soon became a puddle on the ground. There, I drowned myself in my own tears and pushed out as much of my fear as I could muster. I cried for our separation;

for our geographical and our spiritual differences. I wept for our great capability of love and of loss. For we were all there to celebrate a wild little fucker who, over time, had made us all laugh, care, cry, and choke in shock over the shit that had come out of his mouth. As if he had heard my thoughts, David placed a hand upon my shoulder, wordlessly telling me that he was there. It was strange for all of us to be there together, with Freshman nowhere to be found.

I expected to see Freshman around every corner. Any corner would have done. I wanted to watch him set alight a lantern, any lantern, and grin widely with his smiling teeth as the wind caught its paper body. I thought I had seen him earlier, sitting down beside his mother and taking the weighted hands of death out from her lap. As we left the field that was set at a rainbow's end, I was sure that I had also seen him through the darkness, shaking hands with the guests in appreciation of their coming. My mind tricked me into believing that every sideways smile belonged to him, every laugh originated from the pit of his own stomach, and every bearded man morphed into the winter blanket that was him because, after all, Freshman was the guest of honour.

Although no one quite caught sight of him, we felt his presence there all the while. Freshman was a family member to many and his friends gathered like a rainbow's end and celebrated the vibrant colours of his life. Freshman was everywhere and, together, we were the different shades of his love.

The sun set and joined us in our smudge of colours. Our lanterns became one with nothing and everything. The rainbow children each said their own goodbyes to cocky grins and bearded embraces.

We celebrated the joy of life, together.

Family Ties

16th April 2014

Time sure can fly when you are having fun. Time can also fly by just as easily when you are angry. For the sun will still rise and fall every single day, despite our internal temperaments. Weeks can easily turn into months. Months can drift like autumnal leaves into the seriousness of years and, before long, it becomes hard to understand how time snuck away so stealthily with our compassion in tow.

I found that I had returned to a life where street lamps lined the lane of my memories; their long bodies had 'missing' advertisement signs stapled across the thin of their wooden poles. Upon the weathered paper there lived black-and-white faces that stared out at me and wondered where I had been all of those years. Their tattered imagery represented every single loved one that I had missed. Broken bridges arranged themselves around their shoulders blades like winter scarves.

An impenetrable fortress of resentment had somehow formed inside of my own body, built from a begrudged brickwork that had stopped me from truly letting go. Water could not properly flow beneath its bridges and its tall walls were cemented with a thick callous of cowardly skin. Four years prior, I had retreated from my old life in America with my tail in-between my legs, but it seemed that the time was upon me to make peace with the fact that it was I who had been that coward.

'Go deal with your shit.' The gods spoke to me with gangster mouths.

My last visit to Florida had been a bit of a sorry affair. I had returned in the hopes of establishing familial connections, though I was offered the material possessions of phones and car keys instead. I had allowed myself to be pushed out of a house that the wild child in me had previously been banished from. The lights were turned off and they pretended that no one was home. Doors closed and ironically stuck out their 'welcome' sign tongues at me.

So, I just stood alone in my mother's driveway, weighted by superficial things that I did not care for and solemnly made a promise never to return. It was no longer necessary to get all worked up over the empty offering of a phone connection that attempted to substitute a tangible one… I knew that couldn't be forced. I was more than ready, but I had no reason to expect others to mirror such emotions, so I swallowed down the repetition of history with the sweet saliva of each-to-their-own-pace and focused on my life back in England.

However, during my unexpected visit back to Florida for Freshman, everything felt different. Perhaps it was the presence of an untimely death that finally shifted our emotions, or perhaps my family and I had simply synchronised at last in our unified desire for closeness. However the change came to be, it saw that during my twelve days back in Sebring I spent every single day with my family.

Together, my siblings and I sat in the comfort of Britney's family home, a home that had always been open to me despite the transgressions of our family. Our sisterly bodies were swallowed up in hungry sofas as we watched countless romantic dramas together. Sparkling rosé washed down the taste of our unity as our mother stroked my hair with caring fingertips, offering me more of her fairy tales whilst I listened with childish ears that drew pictures from her words. Britney unconsciously played with the silver of each ring that rested upon my own fingers and I told her tales of how each one was a constant reminder to me of our own familial eternity. The ring that she had given me as a teenager still sat on the skin of my index finger and Britney smiled in the knowledge that she would always encircle me.

At the request of a young girl who had missed her Aunty April, I slept in Kiara's small, boxy bed with her almost every night. We would each fight for covers and personal space, though we both secretly enjoyed being in such close proximity. Kiara's little angel legs would stretch with the morning sun and push her five-year-old feet into the soft of my gut, waking us both up. Her morning eyes would always be full of sweet surprise to see me still lying beside her and every morning she would smile with the pleasure of my company whilst I offered her the same in return. How beautiful it was to feel like an aunty again.

I attended a game of soccer that my nephew, Terrance, played beneath a warm summer sun, his gangly legs running wild with ferocity and me, standing in the crowd and meditating upon the serious look of competition that he held firmly in his young jaw. At seven years old, Terrance was just as talented in sports as I had known his mother to be and I smiled proudly at his accomplishments.

Shannay and I stood side-by-side and cheered on every little pair of running boots without specifics or particularity. In my absence, my sister's body had curved and drawn itself into the makings of a beautiful young woman, yet we still laughed like hyenas into one another's goofy teeth without the fear of being ugly. I looked upon the cheek in her laugh and knew that, despite her growing up, she would always be little Nay-Nay to me.

Amongst an impressive variety of big-screen computers, I spent an entire day locked away in a cave-like bedroom with my gamer brother, G. Together, we watched films with the curtains drawn and chased out the intrusiveness of the sun. We were in a timeless place of comfortability where G knew that he would always be my favourite brother. We spoke about his developments over the years and he answered my questions with a voice that was still humble. My brother's afro was huge and out of control, but I could only mirror him with my own wiry wildness. I smiled at the handsome man that he had grown into and was glad that G had kept his quiet artistry in him. He looked into me with kind eyes as we said our goodbyes with entwined fingers that did not want to let go. Out of all of my siblings, G's soul is the twin to my own. As we released our identical hands from one another's grasp, I dreamt of kidnappings.

During an afternoon at my eldest sister's house, I was offered the gift of a tattoo from her to me. Kasha's physicality had not changed; she had the same swollen eyes that drank everything in and brown freckles that still dotted her face like raisins. However, my sister's insides seemed to have been rearranged. I sat upon her tattoo chair and watched as she prepared to transfer a symbol of siblings from paper onto my chest. As she carefully mixed her ink with the ashes of my late grandmother, I understood Kasha's growth and knew that she was stepping further into her own creativity. Her children swam around our feet as if it were Christmas Day and we were their favourite presents. That evening, they were granted permission to be up past bed-time and my niece, Breyanna, held her pass up in the air with toothless pride, her eyes setting alight the sentimentality within me. I focused on the love that I felt for her, as my big sister pierced me with needles that showed me, in their own way, of how she also cared.

As my sister adorned my chest with a permanent symbol of love, my mother sat beside me and clasped my hand within her own bandaged one; Kasha had just tattooed a small hummingbird upon the space in between her finger and her thumb. My mum squeezed my hand as pain rolled out in waves across my chest and I knew that with that bird, she would always carry a piece of me with her.

Five hearts were entwined on the left side of my chest, representing five siblings who would always be connected. The balance of yin and yang were like a mother and father who kept our symbol centered and the ashes of my grandmother pulsed through us all.

Despite the knots that were in our family thread, life endeavoured to tie us closer than we had ever been.

Show and Tell

16th April 2014

A few weeks prior to my arrival in America, a dream of front porches found me; a wooden chair creaked beneath the weight of laughter, ice melted innocently into a glass of sweetened tea, and the mischievous face of my friend, Audrey, giggled itself into existence. It was a snippet of a dream that foretold of the times to come.

I found myself leaning against the arches of that very house just three weeks later, looking into the same starlight of Audrey's eyes as we reminisced upon the good old times. The porch did for us what it had done through countless years and silently guarded over our happiness. I had come to know the green shades of that porch well. Audrey and I had spent many a year looking out into the world from its wooden throne, with glassy teenage eyes that had always wanted to run away from home. Olde E' beer bottles would roll around at our feet, as we would pass blunts back and forth between fingertips that had the prints of perpetual hunger upon them. I spent so much time in the refuge of that porch that, one day, I just never left and its sanctuary became my permanent home.

Audrey's own mother, Mary, had seen it in her to adopt the orphan in me and, to this day, she is the only person that tracks me down on my birthday, wherever I am in the world, just so that she may send me a present; an inflatable travel vase, a mini needle and thread kit to fix my tattered garments and a variety of other useful gifts always seem to find their way to me. Encouraged by Mary's maternal nurturing, Audrey and I became akin to sisters. As I leaned upon Audrey's iridescent front porch that stood in the heart of Florida, thought of our relationship. I thought about everyone whose faces had been stuck upon my 'missing' advertisement signs.

To me, Audrey will always be a colourful stranger. Many secret people live inside of her soft flesh and take up residence in her personas. In our youth, I had found parts of my selves to match parts of her selves. We used to sit upon her front porch and dig through a treasure chest of our inverted characters so that we could release them in the world to play together. Audrey wore the red ruby shoes of beauty and insanity upon each foot, nervously bringing their sparkles together with a whisper that said *'there was no place like home.'* We found endless pleasure in our roaming and I would always feel sheltered wherever our adventures took us, for Audrey will always exude a strange comfortableness. She is like wearing my mum's favourite dress at seven years old; her frills follow me for miles as I go out onto the streets feeling grown. I look great. I look ridiculous, but I feel safe. That is what Audrey feels like to me.

Seeing Casey was one of the most difficult things for me during my visit to Florida. Just four years prior, we had been wrapped so closely together that there was no determining where one of us began and the other ended. He had been my friend for many years before we became lovers. During that time, we would lay beneath the night sky with our bodies pressed against each others, fingers gently touching, and together we would watch the stars die. Knowing that everything must come to an end, we were hopeful that when it did, that we would still be together, holding hands.

Casey and I were pioneers of the unfished seas and captains of camping in the great unknown. When we finally committed to a kind of normality and moved in together, we then became professionals at playing house. The kitchen and bedroom would fight over our attentions as carbonara dinner was repetitively burnt in our quest for ecstasy; for years the bedroom always won the war. We would emerge from our back garden with leaves in our hair after sleeping in a tent whose permanence saw that it became a secondary bedroom. The dirt upon our fingertips would carefully draw bubble baths with the cleansing water of a blue aching dawn. Spatula wars were often declared in the kitchen on a Tuesday evening as we chased one another around sofas and table tops until our lungs lunged out in excitement. Laughter was always our accomplice. Casey and I were once wildly in love with the best parts of each other.

However, Casey and I were kids and the young will never understand the repercussions of their actions. Somehow, in our ending, our love began to change objective. We had seen the best that the other could offer and we unconsciously adopted the cold curiosity of children that looked upon forbidden things. Like animals, we began baring our teeth at one another just to see what kind of demons we could summon because Casey and I thought that we should know every single version of the persons that lived beneath our skins if we were to love one another properly. After a few years, our silly spatula games transformed into the ugly face of violence. Our once-blue bath water, born of aching dawns, began to run dark with unnecessary suspicion. Those elegant hands that once fit so perfectly between my fingers also sought to understand how well they could fit around my throat. I retaliated with a razor blade tongue and a measure of personal violence until our worlds ended... and it was apparent that we were no longer holding hands. All I could remember were the stars. Two fucked up puzzle pieces had once fit perfectly together but as they lay side by side, the outlines of their identities were lacerated. So they pushed themselves deeper into one another's jagged edges and would always bear the wounds of their closeness.

I have spent many years since those days exorcising that darkness out of my heart and reintroducing some kind of tenderness. And as I walked upon the crumbling soil of my past life, I found that it was the perfect time to show Casey that truth.

'*Look how much I have grown.*' We each silently said to the other.

'*Show me how different you are, but tell me please that you are still the same person that I have loved all along.*'

For this was a show-and-tell of fractured tales.

One of the hardest things about a break-up is not only losing your 'one person' but also involuntarily breaking up with an entire family. During mine and Casey's time together, my blood family were distant from me, therefore, Casey's family became my family. His mum became my mum. His brothers became my big and little brothers too. Though, when we parted ways, his family and I never had the opportunity to sit down to dinner and have the long talk about why 'it just wasn't working out for us.' They just sat on the sidelines of neutrality and slowly disappeared into the past.

A warm afternoon offered me the chance to sit with Casey's mother again and whilst a chain of incessant smoke clouded around Kim and I, we got lost in catching up on gossip. The afternoon light wandered in through her living room blinds and became disoriented with my returned presence there. Nevertheless, for seven hours, Kim and I sat amongst one another's company and put the world to rights, sharing what the past four years had offered us. We each gladly gave our stories to one another like Christmas gifts in the nostalgia of her home where parcels of our progressions parted the smoke. A bundle of bad news fell apologetically at our feet, whilst Kim and I embraced one another in the totality of ourselves. I was finally able to show her the version of me that was undistorted by the third party of love. Kim showed me the whole of herself, ungoverned by the primal force of parental protection.

David and I sat together at his house on a nameless evening and conversed deep into the early hours of morning. Before he was Casey's older brother, David was once my friend. However, the constrictions of love had coiled themselves around my throat like a sultry snake and restricted our communication.

141

David and I sat around his dining room table and reintroduced ourselves to one another as the people that we were before all of that; two friends that had similar ventures and interests. You could find us lingering around poetry and art with a glass of red wine in our hands. You could also find us sneaking into an old retirement building and taking a dip in their outside pool. As I looked at David from across the dining room table, his dark hair pulled back casually from his dramatic eyes, I remembered him tenderly as the guy who had given me my first Joni Mitchell CD. David's pathway was lined with philosophy books whilst mine was lined with maps, though we would each be better off because of a friendship so abstract.

Lest we not forget Stephanie, my queen of crazy. Look into the empty night and you could find us disappearing into its eternal mysteries, holding hands, with adventure ripening the whites of our wild eyes. Stephanie and I could be found climbing to the top of the highest building, sidewinding and woozy... but not afraid to die. We would scamper naked on rooftops with an owl statue fumbling between our drunken hands, its feathers, as black as the night from whence we found it.

"Sacrifice him to the gods!" Stephanie screamed, as I spun around and around just to throw the owl overboard into the pool below us. You could find us running wildly through the orange groves at the break of dawn with our Mexican counterparts, Himee and Romeo. *Romeo oh Romeo, what beautiful green eyes. Himee, my amigo for more than just one sunrise.* We were reckless. We were dirty. You could find us caught up in barbed wire, screaming to the concern in the other with words that sounded like:

"No... I need some REAL help.... Stephanie!" Whisky on the pull of our collective breath as helping hands were pushed away. Together we pushed and we pulled and we pushed and we played. Because Stephanie and I were magnetised to each other with a force so strong, that nothing could truly exist outside of it... no matter how hard we tried.

You could find us in the trees guarding over things like two wise old owls for the day, even though Stephanie was just a young thing. You could find me saving her ass. You could find us running through the forest, being stalked by hippies with ticks that were in need of eviction. You could find her leading us to a safe place where we could laugh with full abandon at the hysteria of our circumstances. Stephanie's long hair, falling into her open mouth and fighting for space with her tongue; she was a perpetual picture of ravaged innocence.

You could find us chain smoking, eating cans of cold ravioli with red-stained lips that never stopped laughing. Stephanie and I were made up of green and purple peacock-coloured stars. We were private pirates who would take things from places that we were never invited into, but somehow always became ours. You could find us rolling on the dreamy green grassy knolls full of secret languages, imagining that bright blue water of Elsewhere. You could find us dreaming.

There were just two of us... and well, you could never really find us.

Until there was just one.

You could find her becoming wilder.

You could find her pushing further and further.

You could find her lost in the darkness.

Until even I could barely find her.

Stephanie and I met peacefully one afternoon with white flags above our heads and fortified friendship blowing in the breeze. I hugged each one of her grown freckles. I loved each one of our past stories and sat comfortably within their memories. Until we got too comfortable. Until Stephanie and I fell into our old reckless ways with too much ease, loosened up by too much cheap booze. The white flags were soon torn up and used as bandanas, because it was obvious that there was some kind of war going on between the two us. The white headlights of her car shone on my back as we left the bar and screamed at one another upon the roadside. Stephanie drove alongside my freshly-exited stroll with unwavering enthusiasm. Injustice was in the air and she wore a familiar freckled face. I had left Stephanie behind and she could never find her way back to me, no matter how long I did wait. Therefore, bitterness was also in the air and she had the same eyes as me. We did what need be and screamed it all out, purging all of those angry children that had been sitting cross-armed upon our laps, crushing our bladders for so long.

"You never gave a fuck about me!" Left-hooked me from out of nowhere. I looked into the glare of her headlights with stunned eyes.

"Well, you never even tried!" Escaped the wound of my mouth. Round after round, we fought until there was nothing left to say. Our emotions were high. The untimely death of a friend can apparently flare such things up; apparently too many cheap beers can do the same.

Stephanie and I would reconcile during the time that I was in Florida, for those things had to be said between us, but it felt like the end of something. Our truth was inescapable. Mine and Stephanie's impossibility couldn't have been more apparent; the single dream that had once unified us beneath peacock-coloured stars was the one thing that kept us separated between thousands of paradoxical miles.

We were also just two kids. I watched over Stephanie's wildness and she loved mine endlessly. Once upon a time, Stephanie was every ounce of my gravity. We only had one another and, for but a glimpse in time, that was enough.

Years later, time had tested us all. I leaned against the green of Audrey's front porch and daydreamed over our involuntary surprise review.

'Show and tell, ladies and gentlemen...please complete this examination without further delay. There are no multiple choice options, only long answers.' Instructed a faceless teacher of life.

We sat together, the students and I, with sweaty brows and restless feet. The question reads:

'Show me how much you have changed, but tell me please, of how you are still the same.'

Each person filled in the blank empty spaces of time passed, with the same familiar hands that I have loved...

... Since we were all just children.

Day of Double Birth

17th April 2014

When Audrey and I were both but stardust in the cosmos, we devised a brilliant plan: to be born upon the exact same day. Such a strategy saw that, down on Earth, the two of us may join forces and, together, celebrate the divine power of our birth.

Eleven years prior, we had chosen to have our party-for-two at Disney World. Two stoned teenage girls twirled around in a myriad of blissful magic, full of obsessions towards Dorothy and Pocahontas that they would never ever grow out of. Eleven years later, fate had brought Audrey and I back together once more. I wore a red beach dress that had travelled all the way from Asia just to be there and Audrey modelled a tie-dye top that captured the essence of her wild child nature. We awoke at my sister's house at the break of dawn and sang out tuneless birthday melodies to one another with tone-deaf excitement. It was my last day in Florida and I had turned twenty-seven years old. Stephanie met us at my sister's house that morning, with peace flags draped around her aura, because a part of her knew that no party would be complete without my queen of crazy. Audrey was a recent divorcee from a destructive love pattern that had left her craving fun and affection. Stephanie stepped off and on her own wagon, though, I could only watch her tragic dance from a distance. It was inevitable that much hair (frizzy, straight, and curly) was destined to be united in their kindred strands of wildness and let down upon such a day of double birth.

Audrey, Stephanie and I stood outside of my sister's house and squinted beneath the blindingly bright light of our perpetual poverty. Six pairs of pockets warmed like empty ovens that were heated by the morning sun, though we had neither money nor buns to fill them. What we did have, though, was an ammunition of brains and beauty and the invaluable ability to envision anything. So, with our girly brains and pleasant faces, we drew up a plan and began to set it to action. Stephanie, Audrey and I were armed and dangerous.

We piled into Audrey's soccer mom van and, although we were penniless, the van abundantly overflowed with Asian ruby dresses, tie-dye threads and white peace flags. Our sturdy tyres rolled to a halt at a tall white building that had the markings of a Red Cross foundation upon it. Six long legs stepped out of a beat-up old van and made their way inside. There, Audrey, Stephanie and I took it in turns to sweet talk the kindness of strangers, explaining to them of what the day meant to us. We were honest in our intention for festivities and asked if they could help us, for life was a thing to be celebrated. The ears of strangers listened as I drew stories of a dear soul that had recently departed and expressed to the Red Cross of our desire to bring everyone together on a day of double birth. Our truth was not challenged and their kindness sent us forth with reinforcements. We were gifted three large hams, three boxes of food, and a complimentary feel-good vibe to carry with us throughout the day. Three broke pikeys walked out of the building with slender legs and pillaged goods cradled in their arms. Some things are simply not destined to change.

The three of us arrived at the mouth of a lake that glistened like glossy teenage lips, full and inviting. Boats floated upon the lake water like dreams that had been cast out into heaven before practicality anchored them. A group of boys gathered on the sand beneath the beams of their makeshift shade and waved at our arrival. They were the boys of my past. Three male hands waved in unison at three arriving females, with the similarity of brothers. A Casey-shaped wave greeted me. A David-shaped wave beckoned me. A Camron-shaped wave tickled me. They were so different, yet so similar. A Malinda-shaped smile drank down my first jello shot with me. And then there was my run-away, house arrest compadre, Jake... my pen-pal when in prison, Jake. My strawberry, my Peetree. My we died together on psychedelics and came back together reborn, Jake. He waved a manly hand at me that I did not recognise, inviting me into the boat party that he had thrown for me and Audrey. I hadn't yet met the man that Jake had

147

become, though as the day pressed on, we would find that we were still very fond of one another.

Early into the afternoon, the sun drew dark clouds around its own warm body and impregnated its circular swell with a thunderous storm. Our bikini bodies could only shudder at its coming as the rains began pushing themselves back into their origins of ground with an alarming efficiency. Their droplets were swollen with a mission of reunion and no one dared to intrude upon their desires. The manmade shade that the boys had constructed as a labour of their love had become our only shelter. A single stick stuck out from the center of the ground and acted as a crooked pillar to a hat that was made of flimsy tarp. As the heavens opened up, my loved ones and I desperately clutched onto the tarps plastic corners in an attempt to stay dry. The winds sent geese marching in flocks across our skins and the sky lit up with electric adventure.

Despite our best efforts, all of those who attended the birthday celebration, became completely saturated in our susceptibility to the weather. I looked across at each drenched face that furiously held down a corner of the tarp whilst simultaneously holding a serious disposition that was pressed into their mouths. Casey's hair ran down in rivers across his pale blue eyes without the courtesy of a dam. Stephanie's jello shot ears struggled to hear anything over the storm, placing an energy of confusion around her movements whilst Camron adopted the eyes of a scientist that would surely figure it out and save the day for us. A cut upon Kim's leg ran a deep ruby red and followed the arch of her calf with a wordless confession that spoke of her maternal love. In that moment, we could not help but to recognise a power that was greater than ourselves and we fell into a shade of hilarity. A gathering of saturated friends each surrendered with a great big smile into greater and bigger things.

After the sun had made his point very clear, he returned to our appreciation like a long-lost king and rained over us all with his warmth. The rest of the day slid by in a soft haze of Sailor Jerry's and innumerous jello shots, both of them swirling around inside my swollen gut with the throws of an inside party. I stood beside my friends at the mouth of the lake and took note of how our bodies had changed. We were each much plumper with the process of the days, months, and years that had passed us by. Gangly teenagers were people that we could barely remember, the thin fabrics of our bikinis kept no secrets.

I stumbled out into the great lake that stood before me and attempted to conquer it with a disregard of responsibility. After all, we had a boat for the day that belonged to the grown up, not-so-grown-up, version of Jake and we intended to use it. As we sped off across the water, the wind gladly blew all of our wet parts dry. The boat had a tail of inflatable tubes trailing behind it where in which, you could often find a complimentary version of intoxicated Stephanie attached to it, drowning. You could find me saving her ass and laughing. You could also find that my ass needed saving on several occasions. It has been said that water and alcohol are not an advisable combination. However, I managed to stay afloat with the help of a Sailor Jerry's tongue and the arms of a boy from the past who was asked to prove his love to me.

The sun shone down upon our reckless fun, admiring our efforts at unity. Together, my reckless fun-having friends and I each put our issues aside and focused purely on the making of new and improved memories. Water rushed under bridges and inflatable tubes. Rap music blasted out through the speakers of the boat and nestled itself beneath our bathing suits. That afternoon, you could find us being high-time ballers upon a boat of reinvention, our bodies having been abducted by the liberation of dance.

Day eventually joyfully rolled into night. Stephanie rolled into the darkness without even the whisper of a goodbye. Audrey rolled around upon the soft, warm sand, bathing beneath the luminescent love of the moon, whilst I rolled another cigarette and stared dreamily into the orange embers of the bonfire. As I inhaled from my own fire, I began approaching my daydreams with caution.

In the calm of the night, I began to entertain an alternate version of myself that decided to stay there in Florida. I stared deep into the flames and wondered what that girl looked like. I searched her eyes for signs of contentment, explored her mouth for creases of joy, and looked upon her hair, measuring her happiness up against the size of its wildness, (for radiance is always displayed in the diverse ways of my hair.) Though her blazing tendrils gave nothing away.

I heard the phantom footprints of my nieces and nephews playing in the sand beside me.

'You could sleep in my bed every night, aunty April.' Kiara began, imaginatively. Her brown eyes, wide with hope.

'You could come to all of my soccer games.' Terrance spat, through teeth that were full of growing wonder. My self-imposed suggestions began to run into one another with an energy that was akin to the urgency of children.

'You can make movies here.' They both chirped in unison.

'You could protect me.' Breyanna waved a one-armed wave at me and the buck of her smiling tooth kicked me right in my softest spot. Guilt travelled up the base of my spine, swirled like a snake, and coiled itself around my heart.

'We could have lunches together regularly. You could be here for longer than a few weeks and we could maybe... begin to rely on one another.' A vision of my sisters fictitiously formed in the fire.

'I could protect you.' My brother's humble voice calmed my growing hysteria.

'Oooh... Oooohh... We could go shopping together!' My mother squealed playfully as her innocent eyes sent me an invitation, then merged with the familiar faces that I saw in the flames. And despite my distaste for shopping, I wondered if I could enjoy it... with her.

Then there was Casey.

'I could finally be everything that I was ever supposed to be for you, and more. I will love you the best, for I know every single part of you that others are yet to explore. I alone will love you the best. Just try to love me again, mi amor.'

The real-life version of Casey looked up at me from his seat beside the fire and said everything without saying anything at all. His elongated hands sat a seat over from mine and, as the fire caught the light of their creative beauty, my own fingers twitched in recognition of his. Our hands began a secret dialogue that explored the tale of how they had lost one another, somewhere beneath a midnight sky.

'There were stars, I remember... and then you were gone.' The hands that were once side-by-side, entwined in love, unconsciously gravitated towards one another in an attempt at a reunion. Muscle memory navigated our bodies and, before I knew it, Casey was looking down at me tenderly and I was curiously looking up at him, the evening air cloaking us in a blanket of mystery. Casey's definitive features were softer. His blue eyes were kinder and he had become gentle in all of the ways that I had prayed for him to return to during our final days together. Casey stood before me as that man, with lips that conjured up love spells.

A long-awaited kiss softly fell like a shooting star upon me; however, the kiss found that it landed upon a loving, but turned cheek. Casey and I stayed in that moment with neither urgency to move nor the need to speak. I held his slender body against mine as we said our final farewells. Closure looked like two soft puzzle pieces who had remembered how they could fit into anything.

As the firelight flickered with happy birthday wishes, a snake slithered away from my heart and I knew that my Floridian life could only ever be a fable that belonged in the past.

I chose to be the girl who was in the midst of her greatest adventure. For I would forever be the kind of Pocahontas who sang out breathlessly, perpetually questioning what was around the river bend. I hand-selected the version of myself who knew love to be absolute kindness and, with that version of me, I chose Benjamin.

4am struck with three hours left until my chariot would depart for the airport so I gathered my changed heart and disappeared into the dark of the night.

I couldn't keep that version of me waiting any longer.

Queen of the Dump

18th April 2014

For one hour, whilst drunken slumber gathered in the corner of my eyes and called itself sleep, I dreamed a dreamless dream. The alarm clock begrudgingly brought me back to the other side and I awoke to the realisation that, although I was due for immediate departure, I was also yet to pack. I stumbled towards the bathroom tap and, after splashing cool water on my face, crept around my sister's sleeping house in order to begin the tedious task of gathering my things.

My own personal collection of treasures were scattered around like seeds amongst Britney's living room furniture. A red bandana, which had been given to me years ago without a second thought, looked up from the floor with forever in its eyes. It was lifeless, yet somehow over the years it appeared to have gained an essence of life. The inanimate objects that orbited my existence knew that they would undoubtedly need no ticket when they travelled with me. They were excluded from the requirement of bus tickets and taxi fares because their threads paid the high price of a deeply appreciated life. They were well-worn around the world and had the pleasure of travelling for free, based purely upon their funk factor. I picked up my 'I can't live without you' sarong, screwed up my faded red hoodie into a ball and pushed them both into the Duke of Edinburgh's awaiting mouth.

As I heard my mum's car pull up in the driveway, I left a few garments behind so that they may try to forge a better life in the Americas. They opened their stitched mouths and gratefully thanked me for getting them there. I stuffed my toothbrush into my purse and reminded him that his wasn't a free ride; some things have got a higher price to pay.

I walked into the bedroom of my sleeping niece and nephew and softly kissed them goodbye. As damp foreheads met my lips, Terrance and Kiara opened their angel eyes up widely and, with a cloud of sleepy confusion blowing beneath their long eyelashes and tickling their tear ducts, they looked at me with a conjoined sadness. It was difficult for children so young to understand what the word 'soon' meant.

"But WHEN igzaktley will you be back?" Small droplets of sadness began gathering in the corners of their brown eyes. The concept of 'movie making' sat heavily in-between their teddy bears like a playmate, but offered them no real comfort. I looked at the empty space in Kiara's bed where I had lain and kissed both of her furrowed brows sweetly until they flat-lined back into dreams.

Britney and I stood before one another in a casual sincerity. Her smile was warm and full of pure adoration. I looked upon the shape of her tall, womanly body, but could only see her as the little girl that I once knew her to be; her socks pulled up over her calves and folded down twice, exactly. She had always had an incessant desire for perfect proportion. Britney herself was perfectly wholesome. Not one curly hair on her cover-girl head was out of place. She was the sister that used to make the bed whilst I still slept in it, just so that our room would always be clean. I would protest her obscene obsessions and try to push her out of her calculations by being an exemplary wild child. I had electrocuted hair and mismatched socks that inadvertently mocked everything that my sister stood for.

I would blindly lead Britney and my other siblings on strange adventures, down dark underground tunnels that may or may not have been sewers, where they had gotten spiders caught in their hair. I once made us resort to making a den in the forest in an attempt for us to live there forever. For fun, I had played in the cold, green swamp that was tucked away in an overgrown dumping area beside our house and I tried to teach her and my other sisters how to be queens of the dump like me.

I was the sister that broke their Barbie dolls, put worms in their hair, and chased them until they cried because, even though I didn't have two pennies to rub together, I knew that the outside world was mine. Britney would hang upon the skirt of our mother and voluntarily wash the dishes, wash the spiders and wash the worms from her hair. The inside world had always belonged to her.

"See you soon." Two sisters smiled, without false promise.

As my mum beeped the horn in recognition of my late departure, Britney and I embraced one another outside of her front door. She curved her thick eyebrows down towards her nose and wished me well on my next adventure. Her freckles told me to be safe and wear a seatbelt. Her sleepy angels gathered around her feet like fluffy slippers, clinging to her ankles affectionately. The image of Britney and her children became a 'wish you were here,' postcard that I would always remember. Yes; the inside world belonged to her.

Just as my mum had collected me, she saw that she also drove me the three hours that it took to get back to the airport. As the miles were put between Sebring and I, I deliriously tried to outrun sleep, though it began catching up with me. Leaning against the passenger window, I gently fell into dreams, mumbling in cryptic messages to my mother about the previous night's shenanigans. I whispered of marital bones that were evicted and a shooting star that had fallen upon my face. My mum stroked the place where the star of lost love had landed upon me and guarded like an owl over my ever approaching dreams.

Yet another departure gate swallowed me up, but this time felt different. I looked back into the sad eyes of my mother who looked like a teapot that was just about to boil over. Her long, blonde spout curved around her small body and made the world around her look disproportionately large. Blue waters poured over her eyes as I disappeared into the crowd with my red rucksack and a smile. I looked back and she still stood there watching me leave. She looked back and caught sight of me still watching her. We played visual tag until both my mother and I became tiny little smudges of transit and disappeared back into our own lives.

At twenty-seven years old, I cried all the way through the

shuttle bus. When I reached customs, I felt the uncontrollable urge to proclaim to the attendant that:

'I just said goodbye to my mum, to my old life. I got closure on love... and that I have chosen... that I have chosen to...'

"I just need your shoes... and for you to step forward ma'am!" The attendant interrupted my daydreams with her cool demands.

I handed her my shoes gratefully and kept my narrative to myself. As I stepped forward, I stepped forward in gratitude. I stepped forward in forgiveness and I stepped forward in many more ways than that check-in girl will ever really need to know. My twelve days in Florida had finally given me reconnection and closure on a precious chapter of my life. Such was Freshman's final gift to me.

I boarded yet another plane that was bound for the outside world, though this time, I was finally free to move forth into my self-appointed role as the one and only... *Queen of the Dump.*

Part Three

Flying South for the Winter

French Toast

19th April 2014

When I think of flying, I think of white clouds that are impregnated with an air of anthropomorphism, their lining lightly swelling into the shapes of celestial creatures as I glide by weightlessly.

When the thought of flight passes through my imagination, I then visit that special place in my dreams where anything is possible and a cool wind whips across my face affectionately; the rush of a tenacious breeze grasps the soft of my feathers and then pushes my plumes up towards the divinity of the sun without any fear of height. I see Peter Pan gliding through the sky with green tights, endless fun, and a white cloud moustache resting above his unaged upper lip… I see heaven and all of its ethereal inhabitants. I imagine myself close enough to brush past a myriad of wishing stars and feel their golden dust in between my hungry fingertips. I see ceremonial fairies bathing their wings in the pure blood of a rebirthed sunset and, to me, ultimately, flying conjures up thoughts of absolute and uninterrupted freedom.

But alas, airports are no place for such fairy tales. In the transitory world of immigration officers and endless queues, there are just long, grey passageways that involuntarily press my shuffling feet into monotony and routine. Flying with an airline is, in fact, the complete opposite of what one would associate freedom with. By the hand of a calculating mind, something as phenomenal as defying gravity whilst flying alongside of a waning moon has been transformed into a cramped and godless experience.

Flying will spit you out at your destination feeling as though you have lost your religion; with their steel teeth and metallic mouths, if overused, airports can suck the very essence of one's life force out. After leaving Florida behind me, I travelled for two days through countless continents and wore that very truth upon my tired face.

Gate A. Terminal 2. Flight 2874 with a connecting flight to Georgia. Terminal 5... straight through to belt 4, baggage claim. Trains, trams and tubes all merged into an endless snake of additional tubes, trams and trains that relentlessly slithered across a collection of worn out, shuffling shoes. *'Please keep your feet inside of the baggage cart at all times, place your pocket shrapnel in this bin, insert your laptop into another, whilst you prepare to board a connecting flight into absolute oblivion.'* As I made my way through an endless array of directions, my head swirled around like an empty fish tank that had been repetitively filled and emptied over and over again without any true purpose... leaving my body saturated with meaningless airport terminology.

In just a month and a half, I had unintentionally travelled over thirty thousand miles across the globe: from Cornwall to London; London to India; India to Thailand; Thailand to Cambodia and then back to Bangkok once more just for good humour. Then, Thailand to Dubai; Dubai to Washington; Washington to Orlando; Orlando to Georgia; Georgia to Washington; Washington to Dubai; Finally, Dubai airport pushed me out into the busy body of Bangkok immigration area with the impending knowledge of Australia as my final destination. I came to a halt from my continental merry-go-round right there in Bangkok where I planned to meet with Jon's girlfriend, Hélène, recharge and take a necessary break from travelling.

My passport (English, not American) had been stamped by innumerous clenched fists that each came down heavily upon its worn out pages and proceeded to unceremoniously award me with the inky medal of an Official Globetrotter. As I stood in line at customs, awaiting entry into Bangkok, I clenched my passport to my chest as if it were a shiny medal that had been looped around my neck, suspended by an invisible gold chain. But, although such a globetrotting title had been something that I had always aspired to obtain, whilst I stood in a hungry crowd that fell over itself for permission to enter a barricaded country, I did not feel as if I had

160

won anything. I smiled for the paparazzi pictures in order that they may verify my identity amongst existence but, as I became lost in a herd of long lines, I simply sighed at the realisation that I had accomplished very little.

Within the confines of the airport, there were no glorious hills for me to wander out upon and enthusiastically sing to the sound of music as it passed through outstretched, animated arms. There were neither snowcapped mountains to measure my breath up against, nor were there any rites of passage to get lost within. Instead, there were just endless gates of terminal repetition that had been constructed beneath a guise of relative safety. For, despite the perils of exhaustion, modern-day travellers have it made easy and will find little danger in such transitory explorations. After leaving my globetrotting title back in the baggage claim and seeing a familiar object curve its way towards me from the left side of the belt, I decidedly swapped my medal for something more practical; a red rucksack that would prove to be my only companion in a strange new world.

Walking into the humid smog of Bangkok city, I was unconsciously perplexed with the idea of an Australia that waited somewhere out there in the world for me. Australia was an unknown land, laced with decorative voices that would bid me G'day and call me mate. Full of secret windows and trap doors that had been kicked in by kangaroo feet, it was a foreign country that the adventurer in me was yet to explore. It was also a place in which my lover patiently waited for me and with every step that I took closer towards him, I felt his longing growing stronger.

Full of wonder for another country, I absent-mindedly jumped into the back of a taxi with Hélène's directions smudged across my humid palm and, as I looked down at the disappearing language of its ink, I was at last brought back to the present reality. The sweetly-perfumed and sourly-polluted aromas of Thailand began to consume me with a thick air and as I inhaled its diversity, I heard the land artfully ask if I could dare to not completely belong to her. Asia sensuously chased all thoughts of Australia away from my wondering thoughts and reveled in my returned presence, allowing me the secret knowledge that she was a

161

demanding and jealous mistress.

Looking out of the taxi window, I watched scooters dart fearlessly through thick traffic, undeterred by the mechanics of life and death. It wasn't long before my clothes became weighted with lethargy and sleepily stuck to the damp of my skin as if it were a four-poster bed. As my breath easily escaped the cavity of my lungs and I found that I could breathe easier than last I was last there, I realised that I had actually missed the ungoverned theatrics of Asia. Whilst Thai dialect blasted through the taxi speakers and the ghosts of southern drawls whispered to me that they would never belong in the corner of any Asian mouth, I welcomed the madness of Thailand with open arms.

Although Hélène and I were practically strangers, having only met once upon-a-dinner in Bangkok, as I approached her apartment complex, the light of her smile greeted me as if we were familiars. Hélène affectionately embraced me as though she were a friend who had always been well-versed in the knowledge of my happy endings as well as my original sins and unbiasedly, she welcomed me into her studio apartment. After leaving my rucksack in her flat as if her home were my own, I followed her petite curves out into the busyness of a Bangkok back street and watched her movements with gentle intrigue. Hélène had the immodest kind of confidence that lightly wrapped itself around the beauty of her movements without ego and effortlessly displayed her long-term residency in the city of Bangkok.

I followed the sweet scent of Hélène's perfume until I found myself on the back of a scooter that was parked just outside of her apartment and after mounting it, lent my body against the back of a local driver. As confident Thai instructions parted Hélène's French lips, she secured two seats that would help us to slay the large appetites that were growing inside of our stomachs. Once in motion, I watched as our frilly skirts blew in the thick city smog without modesty, as if they were sails that had been set upon a sea of completely new journeys.

As Hélène and I sat upon our sails for dinner that night, instead of awkward silences, we alternately began to offer one another a lifetime of stories to catch up on. The floor of a bohemian paradise presented two pillow thrones to two ready participants whom talked late into the night over rum-based beverages. I caught Hélène up-to-speed with all that had happened during my time in Florida, whilst she listened attentively as if a part of her had somehow known all about my friends and family that resided there. As she perched upon a velvet cushion with a cold rum drink melting in her hand, Hélène was like an oracle whose advice I was always destined to receive. With jalapeños for ears, the spiced dishes sat quietly below our wagging chins and listened to our fiery testimonies.

Hélène informed me of the progressions between her and my housecat, Jon. Despite their geographical differences, a whirlwind of deep connections appeared to have collected momentum with their unanimous surrender to love and had only grown stronger with each day that passed them by. Hélène's eyes looked out across the circular mouth of her glass and twinkled towards me with a hopefulness that was as pure as the night sky.

At the first mention of love, even our rum-based beverages took off their umbrella hats and bowed in honouring of such a concept. My own eyes inadvertently teared with the potential of their happiness because a part of me understood the magnitude of their connection. Life had recently offered me a love that could heal all things and I knew that kind of love to be a necessity for development and something to be truly cherished. Understanding that it is what we wake for each day, what we search for in the corners of dark rooms and what breathes life and light into the very fabric of our beings, I asked Hélène to join me in a toast:

"I wish the sweetness of your souls the very best that love can offer."

As Hélène smiled at my sentimentality, our rum glasses clanked together in matrimony of a French Toast and I watched Hélène drink down its sentiment with her sweet, French mouth.

Cliché's swam down my throat then dove into the depths of my gut so that they could have a pool party with spiced foods and rum, causing the umbrellas to roll their rummy eyes at our simplicity. Hélène's ice cubes bumped into one another uncertainly and aggressively pushed the umbrellas around until they screamed out that they never signed up to work in such cold and hostile conditions. However, despite the mayhem in our drinks, Hélène and I drank to love... because even through its war-painted roughness, both she and I knew it to be the most powerful thing on earth.

The next day, I rolled around in the decadence of Sleep's loving arms and, after showering myself in his peaceful offerings, I promised never to leave his side. However, when the inevitable moment came to move on and I finally broke that premature promise, I found myself aimlessly roaming the city of Bangkok, refreshed from Sleep's heavy affection. I played upon futuristic sky trains and squashed myself inside of tiny places that were like a Pandora's Box of secrets. Holding onto the bars above my head, I looked down at my pencil-drawn map and attempted to avoid making physical contact with the solemn faces of the sardines that were squashed in on the train beside me. Humanity and I were so close with one another that I began to involuntarily sniff his armpits and, because of our proximity, humanity also sniffed mine in return. Humanity smelled like silk fabrics, curry lunches, and clove cigarettes. Though when I asked Humanity what I smelt like, he simply avoided my gaze and pretended to know nothing about me.

During dinner, I found myself surrounded by fifteen of Hélène's French friends for a birthday bash in Bangkok. We each sat like knights at the round table, except that our dinner table was square and although we pretended to know everything about one another, we did not sniff one another's armpits to gain such knowledge. One of the members of the square-round table sporadically broke into a dialogue about a pants-less man that had once appeared in her room unexpectedly and as she spoke, I began to feel the large derriere of anxiety sit down heavily upon my chest. I realised that I did not know a single person at that table, in fact, I barely even knew Hélène. In truth, large groups of people are always a dark sea that I all too easily become lost within and as I listened to the chatter buzz around my head, I quietly struggled for breath. My new environment shone with bright colours that I had never seen before, yet as my breath bordered on panic, laughter began to chase out my fear as if it were a boy that had been caught in the girls' locker room.

I loosened. Laughter that had been born from a man wearing no pants relaxed the irrelevant worry of, 'what does my body posture say about me?' I unwound into the moment and began to remember what my journey was all about. Up until that point, I had constantly been surrounded by the refuge of familiar faces, but there at the round-square table, almost everyone was a stranger to me. I knew that Ben waited for me inside of a secret window somewhere in Australia, my Floridian family had been pushed into the background of 'what it took to get me here,' and I could only look upon the people that I shared space with: the 'strangers.'

At that crowded table somewhere in Bangkok, to say that I felt foreign, in more ways than one, would be an understatement. I was completely unfamiliar with the way that the guy to my right side held his chiseled chin softly in his hand as if it were his lover. I was not well-versed with the absent twirling of the girl to my left's hair as she stared at the dance of the candlelight on the tabletop, daydreaming. However, I was well-acquainted with the lumps that had gathered themselves in my throat and, as always, I began to call their eviction. I was reminded that I used to have a shyness that was as painful as razor blades and my private petals had only ever been known by the peeled paint that hung upon the wall, unremembered. But too many years had allowed those lumps in my throat to stop many a brave word from escaping the nervous pit of my belly and more than ever, I wanted to change that.

As I sat for dinner, I knew that I no longer wanted to be a wallflower. Instead, I wanted to grow wildly and blossom in the lands of Elsewhere. I desired to be a flower in the garden, a lily that floated upon the pond. Or better yet, I wanted to be a single daisy that had enough strength to push up through the thick tarmac of the city just to prove to the world that it could grow and harmoniously exist anywhere.

That night, 2am knocked quietly upon my door and requested that I gather my unpacked rucksack in order to prepare to face yet another airport. I kissed Hélène goodbye with the sweetness of a blossoming friendship and ventured into the dark gloss of Bangkok's evening streets without fear. With not a single whisper of familiarity in the strange new world that surrounded me, it was a moment that belonged only to my well-worn backpack and me.

Together, the Duke of Edinburgh and I walked with the rays of the moonlight upon our backs and flagged down the nearest taxi with an abandon of childish frailty.

"Bangkok airport, please," I said to the back of the driver's head who acknowledged my request without a sound.

To Benjamin.

Wilted Wayfarer

22nd April 2014

Often, the places that we travel can simply be a reflection of the person or persons that we travel them with. No matter how breathtaking the environment, a level of contentment can always be measured by the breath that is also drawn in by he or she who stands by our side. Those well-known wry smiles that laugh heartily at my terrible jokes can forever immortalise a moment of absolute simplicity and easily solidify the majority of my experience in a place. The same slender back that leans up against an ancient colosseum with my own, those kindred eyes that watch the same sun fall and then rise in unison with mine are what I often find myself writing about in my scattered letters to home.

My first experience of Australia would come to be a definitive one. Whilst I had been away in Florida, Ben, had quietly memorised every single persona that he thought I had ever wanted him to be and, whilst awaiting my arrival at Melbourne airport, had intended to try them all on before me. I unknowingly emerged from the arrival lounge with a tiredness that wouldn't quite wash off but as Benjamin walked towards me, it wasn't long before I recognised the familiar fever that was burning in his eyes. In my absence, Ben had been struck on the head with directions on how to love me, knocked down with a slab of instructions that I had written long ago, as if they were akin to the Ten Commandments; though their only similarity being that they were both aged and widely ignored. Benjamin embraced me at the arrival hall, locked and loaded with relentless tokens of his love for me and began to open fire upon my flesh without a moment to lose.

Bang, bang, my baby shot me down with his bombardment.

Ben took my rucksack with fingers that could cure ailments then, manically, he mechanically recalled my wish for him to take more pictures of me and pulled out a disposable camera from his pocket and aimed it towards me. Ben's movements were saturated in good intentions but they became drowned out by the loud orchestra of his mouth as he began to affectionately sing out in out-of-tune melodies about flowers he shoulda' bought and hands he shoulda' held. Ben's smile could have cured cancer.

It was as if Ben was a soldier on the battlefield who had come dangerously close to losing his love to her old way of life, therefore, he endeavoured to fill every single empty space that stood in between them with stories and songs of his own promise. Ben wore the skin of a doting boy band member. His one-sided conversation was like a car wreck that could have been avoided, had he only trusted that his own skin had always been good enough for me. Amidst the frantic serenading that crawled out from between his teeth, Ben pushed down a black camera button and, although he was far too busy to see it, he unconsciously immortalised my displeasure. Undeterred by my quietude, Ben opened my hand and pressed a bunch of fresh, fat rose heads that demanded my acknowledgment of their elegance and beauty into them. I looked down upon their already wilted corners and heard as they asked of this world, one final request:

'Love us.'

The roses seemed to have had a common goal with Benjamin and after sensuously sighing from curved, petal lips, the flowers proceeded to hang their thorny necks, buckling from the plump weight of their heads and then simply gave up on life. My head hung with the same weighted lethargy, my thorns were just as spikey and, my own petals, it seemed, had become wilted with the wonders of wayfaring.

As I held the bunch of beautiful and elegant roses in my hand, I cast my eyes back upon Benjamin. Inside of his own head, I could see that Ben had determined every single possible way in which to keep me happy and would stop at nothing until he saw to it that I was completely won over. However, despite Ben's devotion, I was simply exhausted and devoid of amusement. Still, Ben took another picture from behind a blabbering face that spun around and around with no intention to stop, continued to sing unapologetically into the audience whist shoving thorny roses up my own wilted nose with intentions that could have saved a nation. The measurement of breath that was drawn in beside me rose up to the red and read *'manic,'* on the Richter scale, trying to push its way into me. Such affection and desperation would be my first introduction to the land of Australia.

Looking at the songful persona of Benjamin, although I neither felt swooned by his romance nor overcome by the beautifully fat faces of expiring red roses, the corners of my mouth still began to tug at a smile because I knew that I had left my familiarity in the care of Benjamin. And despite his unaligned intentions, he wore that familiarity upon him like a natural scent that would never soften. Ben had kept our love safe within his abundant romance, as if his heart were a bar and amongst that bars unruly interior, would always be a quiet place where a candlelit dinner-for-two perpetually burned; a version of heart-throb hero pulled out a chair and, feeling at home with the sight of him, I allowed my hand to be taken... because our bar was a place that he and I would never have to pay rent and a space that would always keep my best interests at heart. With that, Ben began to lead me out into the mysterious dark window of Australia.

I arrived at our hotel room to be greeted by a white, wide bed that had been decorated with additionally scattered rose buds. Against the white sheets their ruby petals looked painted and could have passed for spattered blood. The room smelt like a western room, ventilated and dry and the petals sighed one more with their unfailing request for love; it was written upon the silk of their rosy faces. Ben threw birthday presents up in the air and smiled adoringly into me as if we were having a secret tea party but I just stood in the small of our hotel room and I knew that I had never felt so tired. Something truly had been taken out of me;

a surgery with no anesthetic, a sliver of flesh that I had wanted to keep.

I stood in the center of our room, knowing that I had encouraged Ben's animated behavior and, because of that, I could only take responsibility for the reason as to why Ben's mind was possessed with worry. Whilst I had been in Florida and Ben in Australia, I had emotionally taken him every step of the way with me, explaining to Ben the depths of my old love and admitting of how that love had beckoned me to swim within its currents once again. I spoke of the deep longing for a family that had very nearly kept me there, and I did those things in order that Ben could also know that side of my life and walk together with me in its developments. However, it was obvious, during that unscheduled tea party in our hotel room, that my truth had been unsettling and caused Benjamin to become erratic at my arrival because of such a close dialogue.

Ben had waited patiently on the sidelines with his unconditional love and wore understanding upon his feet like army boots, trudging through me. Songs were sung and roses had been thrown because Ben had thought it necessary to reel me in from a sea of lost love... as if I hadn't found my way back to him of my own accord. Ben only knew how to support my emotions and for that, I only knew how to enter into a state of absolute truth with him. It was neither good nor bad... it was just the way that Ben and I had been wired from the very beginning.

Stepping away from Ben's erratic behaviour, I left an empty shadow of silence in my wake. Because we were not friends, Erraticism and I. We spoke entirely different tongues. Erraticism wanted fireworks and passion during our first reunited night together. Yet I wanted bubble baths and secret languages to blow softly from our mouths. Erraticism demanded proclamations of an eternal and undying love. But... I just wanted greasy takeaway food.

My brain was too busy attempting to catch up on all that had transpired over the previous month to entertain fireworks. My eyes felt sore, parts of me were oversensitive and other parts of me were completely numb. At thirty thousand miles, a truly mysterious month had occurred. It had been a month of backpacking and bike robberies, of gooey toe infections and black-eyed bar fights. There had been a short-lived lesbian affair with long, blonde legs, swollen dysfunctional hands that had been ravaged by ants and smiles that had no smiles due of the rapture of genocide. I had experienced familial rectifications and fallen into a head-on collision with a love that had once been my everything. And finally, there was a friend that had departed from the world with no option to experience such tender human affairs again. Upon reflection, it is safe to say that my heart was a little tatty around the edges.

As Ben showered me in birthday presents and pressed for additional evidence of my love, I decided then and there that I required some goddamned simplicity in order to maintain any sense of sanity. I needed some time to just… be. So, I fell into a flowery bed full of dying rose's and, shutting the rest of the world out, decided that the petals and I would quietly wilt together.

It would take me a couple of days, locked away in that hotel room, until the request for simplicity fulfilled itself. It would take the majority of those three days to realign physically and emotionally with Benjamin. We barely left the room. I found that I was glad to look upon the whites of his eyes as they bathed me in affection. I had missed him. I began to once more draw comfort from the dark curls that fell beside the soft of his face, setting his blue eyes ablaze with their shadow. I was grateful to feel myself in the way that Ben felt me. Each time that he touched the arch of my back, I discovered that I actually had an arch in my back and I could also feel the caverns from whence that arch came. When I brushed my hands against the flat of Ben's stomach, I then knew what it felt like to have the flat of his stomach be brushed against by my own hands. I lived through parts of Benjamin that lived through parts of me.

When he was not pushing his feathers out like a peacock, Ben and I were sensitive in ways that were saved only for each other. I could tell Benjamin any thought that crossed the catwalk of my mind and he didn't mind because we often sat at the same show. We discussed the same doorways and conversed upon the same clothes. Ben and I had a private dialogue with one another that not another soul in the world could begin to enter; sometimes it just took Ben a little longer to press his feathers down and quietly meet me there.

Together, we spent three days and three nights locked away in that hotel room until Ben finally got there. Snuggled up in our large bed, we watched old black-and-white horror movies until the roses finally wilted around us and died. Benjamin and I ate greasy takeaway food that he had procured with the assistance of my pockets and we slept in each morning wrapped in one another's arms like Christmas presents. When the moment finally took us, we slowly began to bring the love back into our bones… and not a moment before.

With all the time changes that I had encountered, I often found myself awake at 3am, staring through a big, open window that took up an entire wall of our hotel and would smile to myself with the reaffirmation that Benjamin had been behind a secret window after all. As my eyes rested upon the city below, a fire of glimmering street lights began to warm my curiosity for the outside world and I wondered what kind of people lived amongst them. I would stare into the speckled orange darkness until the sun rose up over the city and broke in clean, bright waves that rolled into our hotel room and crashed over mine and Ben's faces. Between the slithering of residential city buildings, an assortment Australian birds lived somewhere out there in the bush and, through their song, I could have sworn that they were wearing laughing monkey suits.

The world was a fast-moving blur of chaos and rhythm and Benjamin was the only thing in it that I could really focus on.

I watched as the day broke upon his sleep kissed-features whilst he gently traveled through the dream world. And with the white light of dawn as my only witness, I ran my fingers across his caring face, kissed his coarse beard and effortlessly loved my sweet prince in a way that he would never know.

The Mystic

26th April 2014

As my bare feet stuck out from beneath the covers of my hotel bed, upon the surface layer of their soles, they began to feel a familiar itch. Toes the size of gum drops began to wriggle and roll around uncontrollably. After three days of rest, the walls of the hotel had gradually started to creep up under my skin and become the very cause for that itch. I found myself restlessly looking upon four blank walls, wilted flower petals and then down through the open window into the outstretched city with a hunger that was new to me. Melbourne sprawled out like a carpet of plastic Lego mysteries and I knew that the paved pathways beneath my chamber were the only thing that could scratch that itch deep enough to offer it relief.

After escaping the encroaching hotel walls, I followed Benjamin's puffed-out chest into the city of Melbourne and each time that we passed an establishment that he recognised, his eyes glimmered with conquest, his mouth salivated with the juices of a tour guide and his chest nearly doubled in size. Ben was bursting at the feathered seams, like a male bird that had built our love nest out of shiny things called buildings and I knew that he simply couldn't wait for me to see it. As we walked past a reflective shop window, I caught the glimmer of his honey smile shining sweetly beneath the autumnal sun and I realised that the romantic in him would never stop trying to win me over. Ben pulled a secret gift from his pocket and provided me with my very own green, plastic Myki bus pass; a bona fide reassurance of residence. He passed it to me as if it were a treasure map of the city and I received it in the same manner. A few moments later, Ben and I unceremoniously boarded our first ever tram together and set our sails for the city center.

I walked the streets and saw working men speaking into their box radios with cautious eyes that gave them away as conspiracy theorists. Towers loomed over their heads with green

174

tinted windows that had the potential to hide anything. The city itself was like a plump creature who wore many layers and busied herself with strange tasks. Her silver dress had potholes in inconspicuous places. Cars got lost in the folds of her curves. People met for coffee in the privacy of her navel and cyclists peddled across her thighs with a halfhearted intrigue. The city was alive and no one seemed to mind completing their daily tasks across the complexity of her body.

In the corners of trendy cafes, girls with bowtie bandanas and cherry-stained lipstick waited tables with faces that promised Audrey Hepburn to be a distant relative. As I peered in through their windows, bubblegum smiles gave me a second of their time for free. Upon oak tables, beneath bubblegum smiles, there were bountiful bursts of fresh fruits and food spilling out onto the ripples of wooden age lines. Upon the table tops, sprawled across those wooden age lines, the perfectly round face of a tomato posed for a still-life drawing, its flesh blushing and unclothed. Pumpkin soup pushed warm cream into the corners of winter's approach and softened her harsh edges, comforting her. Sweet potato fries dared to revolutionise French fries without consequence or fear. All the while, banana and mint finally set their differences aside and a made an organic peace treaty inside of a tall glass of milkshake.

Melbourne felt like a fresh and powerful city... a city where anything could happen.

When Ben and I had had our brief fill of the city, we returned to our hotel to meet an acquaintance of Ben's that he had met that very morning. Sitting at the hotel entrance upon my old faithful rucksack, I watched the tops of metallic cars glimmer beneath the sun as if they were alien creatures until I was brought back to reality by a yellow taxi that blasted out Red Hot Chili Peppers as it recklessly swerved around the corner and came to a sudden stop at my feet. A croaky invitation arose from the back of a black spread of hair that was positioned in the driver's seat and tried to make its invitation heard over Give it Away;

"Hop in." The woman croaked without question.

I found myself extending an elongated and half-interested leg into the back of that stranger's taxi. Ben hobbled around to the front seat and embraced the driver as if they were old pals. Their friendship had been conjured that morning after Ben had returned to our room after foraging for our breakfast; the gypsy of shadows had been awaiting a client and they had struck up a conversation that was ignited by the communion of their walking sticks. The shadow gypsy was an old lady with a bad back and Ben's toe had still not properly healed from Asia. The two of them had exchanged stick admiration as if their wooden assistants were slender children, or weird prizes at a carnival.

As I made myself comfortable in the back seat, a pair of spectacles turned around and looked down on themselves from the driver's side. They rested their vision upon me, though I wasn't quite sure that they helped the woman to see at all because she seemed only to be looking for her reflection within my eyes. The Red Hot Chili Peppers sang out into the air around us and permitted us a moment of quiet. The driver had dark, wispy black hair that feathered her aged features. Her long nose parted the length of her face and dragged itself down towards her mouth like a story with no ending. Above the rim of her spectacles, the woman's dark eyes rose up like two half-filled black suns. I offered her a smile, placing it in the fine layer above the loud music until she cackled at me in return. The woman stroked her long, thin hair with fragile ivory hands that were immodestly dressed in black fingerless gloves; rough humour and white dog hair poked out from their cotton stitching. As fingerless gloves courted her worn face affectionately, the black spectacles looked me square in the face as if to say 'here I am.' The woman pointed to herself with a casual pride and Ben took his cue,

"April, this is Magz."

Magz smiled a broken-toothed smile, showing me that she was pleased with her very own existence and then extended a black, fingerless glove towards me. As we shook hands, I involuntarily took a part of her dog with me and, from that moment on, Magz entered into a perpetual dialogue about her life that never seemed to cease. The three of us drove out of the city and, from the rearview mirror, I watched the character of Magz solidify into an endless identity. I listened to her stories, uninterrupted, and in return, the woman asked no questions of me. It was apparent that Magz was the star of her very own show and I was but a passenger in her corn-on-the-cob cab, however, I was glad to not have to speak. From the windscreen, I watched the trees and houses roll past me in indistinguishable scenes and slid around on her black leather seat all the way to the House of Magz, without any verbal expectation.

Fate would have it that Magz, the self-professed Speed Queen of the eighties, would be the first person to make it through the defenses of our hotel retreat. During her and Ben's conversational admiration of walking sticks, Magz had offered Ben and I a place to live, with her. Our hotel, at a hundred bucks a night, could only suffice for so long and the offer of tenancy seemed to be aligned with the next step of our journey. Having long left behind $3-a-night Asian homestays and, with pockets that shuddered with the approach of winter, Ben and I decided to throw our cards to the wind and began to explore residential living with the dark, mystical creature of Magz. My finances ran for warmer climates because it seemed that money had no loyalty; it slips from fingers without the fear of missing anything or anyone, adaptable to any environment and any new keeper. No… money has no loyalty at all.

Far past the bulge of the city, we cruised through a multitude of sleepy residential areas that make up the majority of Melbourne. The suburbs were quiet places, full of beautiful gardens that extended out to perfectly good hard rubbish piles that were prime for the picking; I made a mental note of a discarded wooden cabinet that our new room would perhaps appreciate. Our yellow cab pulled up to an old house that stood alone on a quiet corner somewhere in Reservoir. Its garden had not been well-manicured like the others. Its wooden panel walls allowed off-white paint to peel down its sides without a care. The sun shone over the crusty head of the house with a blinding suspicion, unsure of why we had arrived at such a location. Through the truth of the matter was that I was not sure either. Something in me still felt rather frayed and I had handed over the decisional reins to Benjamin days ago. It appeared that Ben simply followed some kind of gut intuition that made sense to neither mathematics nor to the half-interest of me but, without any need for calculators, Ben and I walked that path together.

As I stepped out of the car, ducks vibrated with the world outside world as if to show me that there was a pond somewhere nearby and that I should not give up hope. Australian birds wearing monkey suits seemed to mock my movements and laughed at everything that I did, but I pushed forth nonetheless. I began walking up a wooden slope that lead to the house and also served as a wheelchair access ramp. As I zigzagged towards the door, grass blades the size of skyscrapers leaned towards my feet with a sharp curiosity letting me know that visitors had not been seen around those parts for years. When I reached the barricaded and paint-peeled door, a dog yelped out in an aggressive and loving obsession for a mother that had returned to her. As the door was unbolted and creaked open, the white hairs upon Magz' fingerless black gloves stood to attention in anticipation of a reunion with their owner. Skylar, the Staffordshire terrier who could turn herself inside out, did so at our feet. The screen door acknowledged our request for entry and ensured that the locks fell away cooperatively. As we passed through, the door handle even suggested that Ben and I could have VIP access should we require it and tried to win me over with a slender bronze smile that could only belong to a gangster.

With our passage granted, Ben and I entered a dark and still house. A black wheelchair sat quietly beside the doorway and guarded over it like a bouncer to the Crippled Club. Mystic Magz looked back at my attention and disdainfully touched her spine in response to a question that was never asked, as if to speak for the wheelchair's petulant silence. She paused in the middle of her previous story and interrupted herself with another story, where the main character was a wheelchair and the villain was her back problem. Magz didn't seem to mind her own interruption. Benjamin assured her that he was the best massage therapist in town and he spoke with truth upon his tongue, for that was his

178

vocation. We walked through a small hallway where boxes stacked themselves upon themselves in a self-obsessed love scene, touching the worn edges of their identical neighbors. It was like cardboard orgy. The cool, unmoved air smelt like Nag Champa incense and a dog that never left the house. I joined the sun in his suspicions.

As Ben and I waded through the unlit hallway, past the incestuous cardboard boxes, past fire-breathing dragons and past Nunchucks that chuckled over how they would gladly spill our guts, we deserted our rucksacks in the potential of our new bedroom. The barren room and empty walls looked upon us regretfully, as if we had intruded upon years of devoted silence and solitude. However, our backpacks paid them no mind and piled their red and black fabrics on top of one another affectionately; mine and Ben's separation had been hard on them both.

After making my way through the hollow kitchen and looking upon its unused functions, (its empty cupboards and spider web oven,) I then stepped into the back garden with Benjamin in order to hold a quiet conference. We each pulled a plastic chair out into the middle of the skyscraper grass and began to discuss the potential of our new residence.

Benjamin, my Benjamin, he is a 'yes man.' Any suggestion that is made to him wearing the mysterious cloak of adventure is often adopted into his care with great haste. Ben will wear that cloak of risk so closely to his skin that its business and his begin to morph into the same thing. Ben thirstily drinks from the nectar of adventure and does not take the time to wipe its remnants from his lips; a part of him wants everyone to see it. Ben feeds off of challenges without feeling full. He puts the deep oils of danger in his thick, dark hair and coyly attempts to catch the attentions of the sun. Ben is pickled with impulsiveness and I was well-acquainted with his nature because, as of that moment, he had never said no to any of my wild ideas. For better or for worse, in that way he and I were similar.

Four eyes sat across from each other and searched their varied shades of browns and blues for deeper answers. Tall blades of grass gathered around two pairs of feet and pressed their slender bodies up towards us, leaning their green ears against our plastic chairs and pretending to stretch. I tilted my head towards the heavens and looked to them for additional answers but the bright blue sky had not a single cloud to look to for silver linings, it was just blue. With the simplicity of the unclouded sky, the suspicions of the sun began to come undone. Once again, I searched Ben's blues for a final decision.

"Yes." Ben's head moved back and forth, puppet-like, as if pulled by unseen insightful strings. I trusted the intuition of his guts and, although we stayed seated in the mystic's back yard, I followed my yes man out to the ends of the earth.

Growing Pains

1st May 2014

The next few days were spent cleaning and harmonizing my humble new abode in an attempt to rectify its dark corridors with a suggestion of light and gentility. I softly opened the tattered curtains that appeared to have been bolted closed for many years and put my favourite song on the radio in order to offer myself comfort. As purple melodies rained down from the speakers in an attempt to sooth me, my own nature appeared to be quite fragile. So as I cleaned, I also pushed a mantra of appreciation deep into the weathered fabrics of the furniture.

Each shelf that my duster selflessly brushed past offered me a greater understanding of the place that I had begun to call home; secrets, large and small, lived inside of their ebony drawers. I rearranged the dragons so that they were not bound to a life of being face down in the dirt and, slowly, I began to appreciate their china skin scales. As I cleaned the cramped quarters of our living room, I also decided that I respected the warrior spears that hung ferociously above our derelict fireplace. I ventured into my barren bedroom, occupied with one double bed and two courting rucksacks, where there was no mention of the people who had lived there before us and I told myself, *'it's an open space that can allow for great reinvention.'* I ran my fingers across its ashen walls and watched as the cool of my breath escaped me, resting upon its blankness. With a duster in my hand as ammunition, I decided that I could enjoy the foreign land of my new home, if I could only accept that it was a kingdom that had long been cloaked in darkness.

I entered the useless kitchen and stumbled upon Magz crouched over a broken barstool with a cloud of smoke gathered above her dark head. Her cigarette ash seemed to go on forever and it invited me to take a timeless break with her. Finally putting down my duster, my cloth and my good intentions, I surrendered and accepted that there would always be residential mouse

181

droppings in the drawers, no matter how furiously I cleaned. Magz greeted me with a toothless smile and, as master of my own destiny, I decided to feel tenderly towards it. With a slouched back, the mystic crowded around her silver ashtray like a beggar and I allowed myself to grow fond of even her crookedness. Magz blew rings of grey stories around my body and pulled me into her world. My new land lady had a cynical kind of humour that sat in the saliva of her pressed mouth and, although that cynicism quietly bullied me into joining it, she was more or less harmless. It was obvious from day one that it was Magz against the world and that she had always been a creature of solitude; no family, no friends. It was a difficult place for a flowery girl to attempt to fit in amongst but I tried to anyway because I could feel her solitude echo through the emptiness of her home. Magz had lived alone for many years and, as Ben and I gathered around her, it was as if her long-awaited admirers had finally offered her an audience. Magz was on top form.

Every evening, Magz would hobble into her yellow taxi cab and, with her black hair accentuating its brightness, she would fly off to work like a nocturnal bumblebee with a bad wing. Each evening that she left, Ben and I had the chance to stretch out our own wings so that they may take rest from travelling. Each of us catching up on things that only being stationary allows. However, in the dark of the autumn night, I cautiously began turning on the heater. I found myself in an upside-down hemisphere from what I was used to and winter was unapologetically approaching South Australia.

I often find that I arrive in a country with no preconceived notions as to what it is all about; no study, no facts and no thermometer. With so many lands that have already been travelled, I at least like to feel as though I am doing the exploring myself, rather than following the guidelines of Google. However, to know that winter awaited Australia would have been more than helpful. My skimpy clothes gasped at me in horror as the temperatures began to fall without concern for gravity.

As I sat in my bed one morning, watching my breath take form after it escaped the warm cavity in my chest, the mystic entered my room. With black fingerless gloves, she held a bottle of Bombay Sapphire over my head as if it were a fish bowl with no fish inside of it.

"Thank you." She croaked in a bolshie Australian accent, looking over the rim of her thin spectacles from behind dark, half-circular eyes.

"Now... how many of these will it take to buy your silence?" Her black eyebrows ignored my morning sensitivities with a rising enthusiasm and as Magz leaned down closer towards me, a dark kind of humour swam circuits within her saliva and pressed me into joining it.

"How many of these will it take to silence you about the things that your little cleaning fingers would have found in my house?" Magz cackled wildly to herself as if she were employed in a private joke, though I knew the reference of which she spoke. I recalled the dark secrets that were in hiding amongst her shelves.

Magz crouched before me, her spine bent in witchy humour and her features absolutely impressed with the bounty of paraphernalia and narcotics that she knew I had come to find. When cleaning the house days before, they had poked their plastic heads out from beneath my rearrangement and seductively asked for some love and attention as well. Little baggies with empty eyes inhabited innumerous drawers where they lived and died with no name, tucked away in the dark corners of substance abuse.

"Just the one." I replied, grasping the bottle and remembering the acceptance that I was aspiring for. As my thin blanket tried, with futile efforts to keep me warm, I fell into the justification that a nighttime taxi driver had to keep herself awake somehow.

That morning, Ben, Magz and I cracked open a bottle of Bombay and began to form an alliance of those that lived together and were well-acquainted with such sapphire secrets. Magz talked for Australia. Ben, for Britain. I quietly sat in between the two of them like a deer caught in between the headlights of two continents. Amongst their conversations, each of them made side-handed remarks about the other's inability to quieten and our once hollow bedroom echoed out with joviality. However, something still didn't feel right inside of me and I just sat there wondering how much room there was for me in the madness... how much energy I would need to push in between their constant dialogue in order to be heard. I quickly grew tired and then I became very tired of being so constantly tired.

The ability to listen tentatively is a communicative art form that is lost on some. Some people only hold their breath and count down the seconds until they can speak again, bursting with memories that have been ignited from what was previously said. Despite how little they will ever be able to know about anybody else, those exertions feel good to them. I knew that such an art form was something that the three of us would really need to work on, but luckily we had Bombay Sapphire until then.

A few days later, Snot ran down my face in a rush to the finish line. Snot's fat, slimy fingers had been caught in an obsessive love affair with my lips and would not listen to reason of their improbability. Snot only wanted them to be together and quickened in his descent to make it so. Air pathetically wheezed in and out of my lungs, completely uninterested in their one function in life. My skin was hot and clammy, sailors could have drowned in its thick waters. And a shadowy ambience seemed to sit above my... everything.

Although I was in denial of my condition, as time went on, my lips continued to run so far away from Snot that they even considered taking a restraining order out against him. Despite death before confession, it appeared as though I had to admit that my body had become very worn down. Snot rags fell like sodden meteorites upon the dirty kitchen floor. I was congested, agitated and felt inconsolably sorry for myself; apparently ill tempers make for the best kind of hosts. As I grew worse, I sat in the desolation of my kitchen and tried to come to terms with my position; the eclectic events that had occurred over the last few months had quietly weighed me down, the recycled oxygen from innumerous planes stuck out its germy, ventilated tongue and laughed in my fevered face, asking *'how boring are we now?'* I could feel the cold draught of Melbourne's outside creeping into the inside with me and our house seemed to have no defenses and wore no protective clothing. It only modeled cold, damp panties. Our home, it was decided, was a passionless place.

I could feel that, without a doubt, some internal demons were swirling around in my lower gut and trying to surface into existence. I could sense them in that tender spot in between my belly button and the beginning runway of my pubic hair, pushing down on my private parts. The darkness of the house began to smudge itself onto me and, somehow, I became unintentionally obsessed with Death. Although I had had some time away from him, Death had decided to come and pay me a visit in Australia; apparently grieving comes in many different stages.

Death slept with me in my bed and, when Benjamin was sleeping, tried it on with me. He watched me tamper with the gas heater ineffectively and smiled from behind a hood of black holes as my fear towards him grew deeper and deeper. Death pushed me into wondering what ties I had left undone in my life and I found myself in a dramatic correspondence with my father that didn't really lead anywhere. Although Death was a veiled creature, I felt the unmistakability of his presence and I was onto him. I was like a snotty spy in the night, hunting down the bad guy who had done this to me. As I dreamt, I would stop and ask strangers in the street if they had seen a dark, menacing figure. They always pointed their dream fingers back towards the passionless house.

The longer that I stayed in that strange place, the easier it was for me to understand the bounds of agoraphobia. The outside air became cold and hostile, pushing me inside with wintery fingers and, although I couldn't quite admit it, inside was the best of a worse situation. Despite the house's dark grimness, I could neither escape its confines nor leave its small comforts. I knew that my body needed rest and our makeshift haven would have to make do until Death and sickness took their exit.

I felt as though I were being blown around by the sharp winds of a strange new reinvention where an alternate version of me began to surface.

And I moved with the fevers of growing pains.

Silver Service

14th May 2014

Ben and I gathered ourselves around a boxy, cream computer that sat buried beneath the Dark Ages and tentatively pulled a chair up towards its wooden desk. I sat on Ben's lap, for love and lack of an additional seat, whilst we made ourselves comfortable amongst a forgotten living room that had been sparingly cast with a dungeon's light. The working world beckoned Ben and I and we were undeterred as to what dungeons and dragons we must first conquer and slay in order to get us there. I pushed past sporadic piles of yellowed paper, fire-breathing ornaments and, worn paraphernalia pipes in order that Benjamin and I could bring ourselves back to the modern time and begin updating our resumes.

As I looked into the computer, a little picture of myself smiled warmly in the right hand corner of the page. I noted that it was an attractive smile, an available grin, an alternate version of myself that knew, despite how shallow it was, that looking good could very well assist in employment's gain. My square face smiled out towards each corner of its box, unchanged by those that are bound to professionally judge, and it said, *'I can surely represent your beautiful business with my very own beautiful face.'* After all, 'selling yourself' is just another synonym for the word resume.

I browsed past the diversity of my qualifications, personal attributes and work history with a cheeky smile because even though every single one of them were true, the truer truth was that I simply had a knack for making things sound good. The reality is that I'm not really qualified in anything at all; since school, I have simply blagged my way through my whole professional existence through just making it up as I flow with it and, through a learned lack of fear, it has worked… so far. I have tried on so many different work uniforms that I unconsciously incorporate them all in my lack of fashion. I was but a high school dropout who made the effort to get a GED but left her diploma in hibernation at the bottom of a suitcase sea…somewhere, where no one ever cared to ask for it. A spell had been cast upon me as a youth that had me believing that every test score that I ever procured would forever define my potential for employment. As if Florida's Comprehensive Assessment Test would ultimately define my happiness. The gradually spell broke and I came to understand that it had never even been about me, back then, I was simply just a measurement of success between other school's methodologies.

Don't get me wrong, I believe in education, self-development, and being well-learned but that empty kind of formal education could neither quite capture nor stimulate me. If I am truthful, algebraic equations never meant shit to me. Math was my weakness, therefore to me, it was weak because not enough people ever took the time out to focus on my capabilities.

Looking upon the italic curve of my attributes and role/responsibilities that decorated my resume, I began to look forward to joining the ranks of the young, the passionate, and the employed. Australia was offering up a generous eighteen-dollars-an-hour minimum wage and my mind was stuck somewhere in between distaste for civil slavery and also getting paid. It was a fine line for someone who had just spent the last two years working her guts out, but it wasn't exactly a rock and a hard place. I didn't need proficiency in algebraic equations to understand what those mathematics could equate to in my life; even my resume dropped its jaw in disbelief. England shuffled around in the background, knowing that his selfishness had been found out, and hung his country bumpkin head in defeat.

Holding hands and plastic portfolio pockets, Benjamin and I spilled out onto Brunswick Street. We were two lovers, untainted by rejection, who were enjoying an excursion into the outside world where even the simplest of things could be an adventure. Ben and I sang as the birds sang. The city buildings looked at us invitingly and the sun shone down on us in thin, autumnal paper patterns. I had Fat Freddy's, 'Hope' playing in the background of my mind.

Ben and I darted into various pockets of buildings and dropped our resumes off as if they were each a Kinder Egg Surprise. The air felt light and full of possibility and, as we passed by a glass building, I looked at my reflection and admired mine and Ben's casual, yet smart attire. Looking around the busy streets, I was comforted to see that there were no signs of penguins plodding along beside me in black-and-white business suits. My own pursuit of employment was then automatically given permission to be as casual and vibrant as my mood. Sickness had released me from its coils just a few days prior and I was back in action with an unarguable zest and passion to explore my new world.

I cradled in my arm a bullet-pointed proficiency of my attributes to society; my managerial qualities, my training history, my volunteer work with troubled youth… my time done. As Ben and I conversed over the potential of finding sufficient employment, a woman passed us by and, overhearing our dialogue, placed herself directly in our pathway and proceeded to offer both Benjamin and I a job.

"I've got a restaurant about an hour from here and I'm looking for staff." The woman looked me up and down, silently dressing me in her staff uniform. Her mouth, twisting and chewing itself under its own uncertainties whilst my jaw could not help but to drop to the tarmac floor. It would turn out that the woman's restaurant would be too far past our commuting boundaries, but the magic of the moment was not lost upon me. England shed yet another tear of shame.

Back on course, I passed an Italian restaurant called Mamavitorias and peered in through its large, glass windows. The restaurant was in between service, giving the place a look of graceful desertion. As I pressed my face up to the glass, a wine glass shimmered in the sun and showed a smudged reflection of my body within its curve, helping me to envision what I would look like in its world. That reflection halted me. An open fireplace placed a kind warmth upon the room and bathed everything that it touched in a soft, amber liquid. The restaurant looked inviting, like an old friend. A small woman stood beside the maître d' station and returned my gaze with assertive eyes until I found myself standing in front of her assertions, asking her for a job; the woman told me to return that night. Potential fertile pockets sprawled themselves across the horizon and sunbathed without embarrassment towards their swollen parts. Although my distaste for hospitality had long become a part of my flesh and bones, I proceeded to gather them together, instructing them to walk towards a shop in which I could purchase clothes for my impending shift. As I emerged from the changing room in order to ask Benjamin how good my black jeans looked, he sent me a smile that could have led the cavalry to war.

Benjamin sat before me upon an eternal bench of support and, after confirming the goodness of my new black jeans, cast his eyes back down towards his own resume. With encouragement, Ben had decided to attempt to acquire a job in his specialised field of health and fitness. A few years prior to the boy who sat outside the changing room waiting for his girlfriend to model her new jeans, Ben had been a bright-eyed university student that had an insatiable desire to learn about everything, endeavouring to know every single mechanism of the human body and what their functions were, what it eats, how it responds to stimuli, grows and what alkalizes it back to health. In many ways, Ben was a mad scientist of the flesh and bones because, predominantly, he sought the knowledge on how to heal our fickle bodies. Ben aspired to combine the medicinal together with the spiritual and make at least a contribution to healing the people of the world; through massage and the power of touch, through health and ultimately, through love.

Yet when Benjamin had returned home from university, his desires and goals became caught somewhere in between the concrete and the clouds. Part of him had been weighted and

190

immobile whilst the other part of him couldn't stay down long enough to place his feet on the ground. Ben had been high up there when first I had met him, doing a few sporadic home treatments here and there but never completely adopting his desired profession. Benjamin's heart had been half and, although I undoubtedly believed in his contribution to the world of health and fitness, I also gradually grew tired of his indecision and pushed him into the working world of hospitality. Encouraging that, *'you've gotta get a real job Ben, you've got to do it if you wanna go travelling.'*

Ben glanced back up from his resume and we each locked eyes with smiles that said, 'this will be different.' I would not allow myself to become worn down by the weight of fine silver and Benjamin would not let his desire for healing be extinguished with the waters of indecision. As Ben limped towards me, full of promise, although it didn't say as much on his resume, I knew that Benjamin had also been awarded great deal of healing knowledge due to the longstanding infection of his toe. There was no doubt that Benjamin was ready to step (or at least limp) up to his new role.

That night at Mamavitorias, I enjoyed the mundane simplicity of my shift because restaurant work was a world that I was well-acquainted with and took little effort for me to employ. I polished an endless array of wine glasses until they sparkled with the same authenticity as the stars. I served authentically-prepared Italian food to the laps of salivating diners and collected their gratitude towards the meal as if I, myself, had cooked it. I befriended boys that tossed dough for a living and, despite being widely ignored, I made the guests feel welcome with my most pleasant and inviting voice.

As the night pressed on, I caught a glance of myself in the reflection of the window and saw a face that represented yet another thing that I could not recognise as my own. I looked upon the endless row of glasses that thought themselves to be stars and I began to restlessly tap my toes, knowing that no wishes could really be made upon them. Authenticity could not be polished on. From beneath bejeweled cutlery, the tablecloths began to smirk at the return of me and, by the end of the night, I could only stare into the open amber flames and envision what it would be like to set those cocky white linen table cloths on fire.

At home, I decided that I could not join the armed forces of forks and spoons, no matter if I had previously fought many a battle by their sides. The white linen waved a white flag of surrender, knowing that on my departure from England, I had been so certain of its dismissal. Mamavitorias had only confirmed the truth in that hospitality, to me, was a toxic love affair that I was struggling to leave and, as visions of burning the building down had found me, Mamavitorias gave me one final push out the door.

For all of those that have lain in the same bed as Silver Service, for those who have clung to her easygoing hardships as if they were the only source of light on the planet and for all those who have smelled her gluttonous scent upon their sodden pillow case as they try to dream at night, there comes a time when we have simply had enough. There is no other alternative than to leave her behind. Silver Service is kind, yet demanding, bitter, yet sweet, but sooner or later those that have known her intimately will inevitably throw their pretty white napkins to their feet and scream 'enough!' She may speak with split, silvered tongues to try and make you feel as if you're the only one that truly loves and understands her. Silver Service may even try to follow you to the ends of the earth, however Mamavitorias was a lover to whom I would never return.

Hospitality work was not the only thing that I was capable of. I had administrative history, pharmaceutical technicalities, manual labour and even teaching beneath my belt. As each year passed me, I found that I could learn how to do most jobs and fit into many roles. I could fill prescriptions wearing a white cloak of professionalism. I could pour pints wearing short-shorts and a friendly smile. I could even become a teacher and impart things upon students that I had learned along the way as well as things that I had learned that day. Professionally, I found that I could learn quickly, that I could manage things and that I could even be a boss. My only downfall was that I could never stay long enough in one job to ever fully master it. Boredom is a stalker that will find me wherever I go. I have worn many faces because of Boredom and been many people. Boredom twirls my hair and pushes me forward, showing me the cracks in the system and whispering of luminous green grass that grows just the other side of the fence. Despite a restraining order, Boredom is yet to take his attention from me.

I decided to stretch my resume wings and search online for absolutely anything that was not hospitality. I was not being picky, any rebound would do just fine for me. I knew that a contented version of myself lived upon a perfect professional planet somewhere, awaiting the day that I discovered the right face to fit me. But until then, I accepted a job interview for a promotional agency that had been very vague in its job description and decided to try on the mask of being a saleswoman nonetheless.

Benjamin was asked for an interview at a massage therapy clinic and both of our interviews aligned on the same Monday morning at 11am.

Synchronicity swam shapelessly through our passionless house.

Madwoman's Macarena

8th May 2014

A mechanical handshake stretched, with forced sincerity, over the dark pleats of my skirt and inserted itself into my anxious palm; we began moving up and down in a ceremony of acceptance.

"You're perfect for the job!" The handshake promised. And although I should have been happy, it was as if my interviewer's robotic invitation of perfection had been absently rehearing for a pantomime that didn't seem to be particular in its casting. The specifics of the job were yet to be determined, but behind the tinted windows of the tall building I sat within, everything felt a bit vague. Nonetheless, I gathered my resume, pushed my pleats down, and followed the handshake along the corridor in order to learn more about my newly-acquired position with Alinta.

I walked towards a silver elevator that sat in the swell of the wall and absently celebrated laziness, promising to push lethargy up into oblivion. Stepping into its silver-lined promise, it wasn't long before I was spat out at the other side feeling as though my feet could have done more. The empty hallways were like concrete noses that followed the curve of my derriere with an unfailing protrusion; they inhaled deeply, just trying to get a feel of what I was made of. The scent of occupational desperation sat in between my crack but despite how deeply I breathed in the ventilated air, the building decidedly kept its life a secret from me. I walked its intrusive passageways without the intrusion of words and attempted to figure out who its people were that had so easily accepted me as one of their own.

During my brief 'personality interview,' there had been a vague mention of sales and electrical companies but that was all I had been allowed to know. I followed the handshake across a green, grassless carpet and, despite the concrete noses that pushed themselves within the crevice of my buttocks, I began to feel content in the knowledge that I had finally returned to the working world. As my chin tipped up towards the water-stained ceiling, I felt a familiar feeling of respectability wiggling its way across my body. 'Today, I will be a woman working in the great, unknown world of Australia,' I thought. An unspoken alliance was made between soil, tarmac and woman and I began to feel a part of the city in a way that only working within a country traversed can allow.

Selfies at sunrise and cocktails on the beach fall behind me as I easily transition into the barman who serves the cocktails, the waitress who is asked to photograph the groups of good times and I merge into the hard worker that lives simultaneously within the gallivanting traveller in me. Whilst I do have a sincere distaste for the soul-sucking lips of occupational slavery, there can also be something very humbling and grounding about its demands. If one allows, working can connect you to the very fabric of a place and, upon the other side of the same coin, it can be a traveller's rite of passage. For when we worry over the same bills as our neighbours, when the sweat rolls down our necks, glistening beside the perspiring bodies of the country's men or women, when we catch the same busses and join in with the similar lump of commonness that is trying to distinguish itself in the world, only then, can we truly become a part of the country's soil.

To have the opportunity to connect to the land and to its people… that is often the ultimate goal of travel. So, I believe that until you have worked in a place, until you have sweat beneath the same sun as working men and toiled within the same strange streets as working women, then you have not properly acquainted yourself with your keeper.

After my interview, I entered a grey room and slipped in amongst a gathered crowd where no one took note of my arrival but, as always, I took note of those that I stood beside. The team that I would be working with at Alinta seemed to have all swept in from different walks of life, congregating in a rush of individual energies before me. They were bushy-tailed, wide-eyed and anticipated the pressing challenge of selling door-to-door energy without a hint of fear. Their personalities were made from various colours of the rainbow:

There was the blonde, American girl-next-door; who, as you look uncertainly from your peephole, will ensure that her cherub face dare to never lead you astray. The large lunar of her eyes turn on the same ancient axis as the moon, for she has learned how to move you eons ago. A blue blouse budding with breasts opens gently upon the garden of her chest and bids that you no longer concern yourself with her wholesome face. Her sparkling eyes show traces of lightning storms as she insinuates that you can pick her flowers as you please.

There was the rampant 'Jack the Lad' from London; the short porcupines of his black hair penetrate the afternoon air in the same fashion as his personality, intrusive and jagged. Jack perspires beneath his smile but could still sell snake skin boots to a snake without a problem and watch it slither away, without legs, feeling better off. Jack transparently wears wolf's woollen clothing over his fangs but for some reason, his soft fabrics soften your initial reaction to flee. You find a 'friend' standing at your door, you take down your red hood and invite the wolf in for tea.

There was also the unguarded hippy chick; swirls of purple skirts and golden cowgirl boots laced with fur sway majestically beneath her doorbell spells. Her frizzy hair speaks of her communion with the true God of Electricity. She lives it, she breaths it, and assures you that her ancestors were born from it. Electricity passes from her furry foot, out to the ends of her hair, then pulses through the entire earth and you find yourself infatuated, wanting somehow to be a part of her intimacy. You look upon her from the throne of your doorstep as she cracks open

196

a cold one just for your royal loyalty and you find that you sign upon the dotted line with an ethereal ease, just to feel the same fevers as she who pulses before you.

Within the confines of a small office space, a group of electrical psychologists role-played, attempting to figure out how to insert themselves into the crevices of doorways by placing one foot firmly into, not only the doorway, but also the barrier of people's trust. I was simultaneously intrigued and yet also halfway disgusted at the methodology that was being taught before me.

In front of me, a bright red, bald head hovered above two short legs like a blood moon, encircling two dead tree stumps and, as the stumps mounted a chair to acquire height and respect, the moon adopted the role of my new 'team leader.' The cliché of a little man with a big personality expanded into a reality and, as my team leader's squeaky voice pushed itself out of his small chest, his efforts filled up every available quiet space within the room. Whilst I thoroughly inspected his gleaming eyes for signs of intelligent life, my team leader began to bark.

"Woof, woof, woof, woof!" The team leader's eyes examined the room for shock value, hungrily demanding our acknowledgment of his wild canine behaviour.

"Woof, woof, woof, woof!" He continued with eyes that were void of any signs of intelligent life but, alternatively, encouraged everyone to join in on the madness with a sparkling reassurance. My co-workers and I searched one another's faces for signs of approval until slowly, we began to part lips with our abandon and words started to circulate around in our empty mouths like the first sign of smoke in a dry forest.

"What are we gonna do?!" The team leader bellowed with a voice that filled any spaces of silence that he may have previously missed. The blood moon in his cheeks, almost completely full.

"Sell!" Poured out from dispersed voices that rose up

through the crowd with tones of exemplary enthusiasm. I looked around the room with eyes of scrutiny and saw traces of other people's uncertainty. Though some of those that I looked upon, those in which the word sell had come crashing out from behind their teeth, they were the old-timers and were not new to the game of canine-oriented relations. I could tell from their smugness, from the war wounds that they wore upon their rehearsed enthusiasms and from the cool calm that pressed their shoulders upwards. And for some reason… the rest of us wanted to be like them.

"How're we gonna do it?!" Our voices rose past one another, clambering to the top of the room until the word "HARD!" came pushing down through the teeth of the old-timers.

"Woof. Woof. Woof!" We became like animals in the secrecy of those grey walls and I found my arms elevated to a press in the air where the roof was raised in synergy.

"Go team!" Came over me.

"Now get the fuck outta here!" The team leader smirked into the folds of his mouth whilst trying to obscure the cracks that had broken in his pubescent voice. Descending from his chair without embarrassment, I approached the team leader and he became two stumpy tree trunks once again.

"It's not a con." The team leader roughly answered me from the oracle of his shiny, red globe. "We are just getting the customers to switch electric companies because we are cheaper."

"Cheaper forever?" I cautioned.

"Cheaper for now." He shone.

"Do you have any vacancies in your human resources department?" A painful silence sat like fresh blood upon a blade that suggested no other alternative, cutting into the quiet of the room. And as I stood in a puddle of crimson truth, I allowed myself to digest my decision. A few spectators patiently waited for me to walk away but, despite my initial reservation of egoic and canine-oriented relations, I looked around the room and concluded that my abandoned sense of self could very well attempt to be a psychologist of electricity. I promptly decided in favour of the continuity in trial and error because I simply had nothing to lose and because nothing was really an error... simply a reaffirmation that there is another path. I accepted my position as a saleswoman with the carelessly convinced conclusion that I couldn't possibly go wrong.

My typical training day saw that I infiltrated the tinted windows of a ten-story building every morning at 10am in order to practice my sales pitch with my new co-workers. Each group was split into different teams and each team would gather beside an empty cubicle, huddled into impenetrability and would try their tactics on for size. It was a battle to be heard over the fever of one another's enthusiasms but, undeterred, I pushed my voice out of my unconsented chest, attempting to woof and I tried on the clothes of what it was like to be a door-to-door salesperson. Occupationally, I had never been a Big Bad Wolf. In one breath, my tail felt a little mischievous as it hung from my buttocks and brushed my bare legs, yet in another breath, my new furs felt almost glamorous. The music in the office blasted itself out at full volume and distorted my already wailing sales pitch. The melodies within the music were forceful against our collectively strained voices, encouraging heart attacks and step aerobics. Within that ten-story, tinted window building, there lived a fight for power that demanded you either grow some balls and be confident or go the hell home. I've always liked a challenge.

"Hi!" I would shriek over the deep musical rumblings. "I'm April and I'm here on behalf of Alinta in regards to your POWER. Now obviously," (pause for dramatic question of customer's intelligence,) "you have noticed an INCREASE in your recent rates!" (Insert dramatic hand gestures with 'power' and 'increase' so as to suggest the world at its end.')

"Now it's MY job to bring those back DOWN for you." A version of myself rides in on an impressive white horse. I smile reassuringly and order the customer to collect his or her electricity bill for me as if it were but a refreshment for the long and perilous journey that I made specifically for them. Then, in their absence, I am permitted to go and kill myself for my crimes against humanity.

After our role-play, the Jacks, the lads, the wealthy, the poor and I would all pile into the work van at lunch time with our sandwiches in hand. My sandwich did not hold any carcass between the browns of its slices as I had recently delved whole-heartedly into the lands of fully-fledged vegetarianism. (I was still waiting for my badge in the post, but until then, the evidence of a tomato and cheese sarnie would suffice.) After lunch, the team and I would arrive at a residential area and prepare ourselves for the hunt.

Before leaving the van, the team leader would blast us all with one final dose of manic music in order to 'awaken the salesperson within.' A modern-day mantra that melodically attuned us to abundance reflected on the red globe of his head, shining like a private disco just for us. Because, apparently, it was all about staying pumped-up when you are a salesperson. I looked out of the window into the houses that were destined for our visitation and, despite the intrusion upon my ears, I understood the truth behind the music; we actually needed it in order to perpetuate our tumultuous voices so that its reverberations could silence the still advice of practicality that attempted to infiltrate our minds. We required the music in order to chase out any thoughts that belonged to us and, instead, only focus on how to get sign-ups, stay pumped, don't be deterred, get even more sign ups. Hell… get sign-overs, go and get 'em!

The Macarena played through the crackle of the radio. It pushed and pumped its way out of the van's dirty, grey speakers until all of its inhabitants spilled out onto the streets like first-time circus clowns who were scheduled for their biggest performance. It was just past midday and local legend says that this is how those who have come before the door-to-door people, acquired that mindful zone. With the assistance of the Macarena, my expression went from daydreamer to game-face in two-point-five seconds. I got into it, exhilarated with the play and dance of abandon. With a gentle hand of encouragement, I then reached up and clambered onto the roof of the van. An old woman peered out from behind her lace curtains and, looking upon the sight of me performing the Macarena on the roof of the van, rubbed her tired eyes in disbelief. Spectators were startled, roofs were dented and curtains closed in on themselves like black holes as my coworkers joined me upon my metallic throne.

One Macarena; I crossed my arms and circled my hips as my feet stomped upon the metal of an indented roof.

Two Macarena; affectionately, I looked down at my feet and admired the places that they had brought me. They felt light and didn't seem to care what the outcome of such a dance would be because they had a mind of their own and broken lips that were fluent in the ancient language of metamorphosis.

Three Macarena; Door-to-door sales was something to do at least, something to get me out of the house. I could actually be good at the sales job and if not, then I was looking forward to getting fired and not actually giving a damn about the repercussions.

Four; I became possessed with the Macarena of a madwoman. Along with the spectators, I was as startled as they were at my involvement in such a circumstance.

After the perfect amount of pumping up, the team and I would then set off towards the outskirts of Melbourne's many residential areas and begin our hunt. The pack would stealthily spread out into little alleyways, marking its territory with strange electronic devices that I began to fear; I would have preferred using urine as a territorial marking. Each day, I followed my supervisor through the residential mazes of Melbourne where I would learn to gauge where we were and were not wanted. A yellow sticker that depicted two black hands crossed over a cartoon door was a demand from content electric-consuming kinfolk that we could not ignore. 'Thou shall not pass!' It commanded. When we were permitted to pass, whomever opened the door would determine who my supervisor would morph into. He would stretch out his winning smile, make common talk about sports, should he see a game on in the background and he would win the door-dwellers over with an uncanny ability to govern his most potential clients. It was psychological brainwashing and it was coming to a front door very near to you.

Each time that a door cautiously opened and a brainwashing commenced, I just lingered quietly in the background and took occupational notes. The garden gnomes would catch my dreamy attentions and question where I expected to gracefully fit in amongst such competitive economics. With their questioning, I began to envision myself during my first shift flying solo:

'Oh, you don't want to talk to me?' I saw the 'salesperson within' saying as a door was pushed towards a close. *'Right you are, that's perfect. We are all entitled to free will so exercise the shit out of that right my friend. I'll just continue to do real life stuff here in Australia and photograph all of the beautiful flowers and gnomes in your neighbourhood... Who would have known that parrots flew wild here in this country? Have a lovely day!'* Epic imaginative fail.

Nevertheless, I walked that training walk for a week and boy did I walk. Six unpaid hours of each day were devoted to the potential of my participation in the world of sales. I looked upon door after door and it wasn't long before I began to hear doorbells in my dreams. I would see apartment buzzers that would never allow me access into their complex begin to creep into the folds of my night terrors. My one pair of boots began to fall away in anguish and they took pieces of my feet with them. Little chunks of worn-out leather lined the streets of my dreams, but all the while, I reminded myself of the potential for substantial pay.

There were simple mathematics within my madness, in that if I were to sign an average of three people up to Alinta per day, then I would receive an average of $1400 per week. Back home, I barely made that in an entire month. Therefore, I began to envision warm garments that could soften the ever-approaching scorn of winter. I found myself dreaming of a suave scooter that fit perfectly beneath my buttocks in a matrimony of adventure. Comfortable campervans also rolled into my hazy horizons and drove my salivating dreams so far as to show me a campervan that could comfortably fit a scooter inside of its belly.

Every day, hundreds of hungry backpackers patrol residential areas under the same guise of quick cash as I. And although I had never been a money-oriented person prior to my salesperson aspirations, it appeared that whilst in the intoxicating aroma of dream chasing and wayfaring, that my nobility had temporarily declared bankruptcy.

That nobility was replaced by large, green dollar signs that rolled around in the empty alcoves of my eyes.

Door-to-Door Disaster

10th May 2014

My first day in which I would fly completely solo as a door-to-door salesperson fell upon a fickle Friday afternoon that could not decide if it wanted to be a part of the week or the end.

I sat in the back of a shifting van, collecting fragments of scenery through the tinted window and knew that the day would mirror my own occupational deliberation. The sullen sky hung loosely overhead, wearing a clouded cloak of misfortune and the air was damp with the torment of rain. As I was kicked out onto the residential streets in order to sell electricity, I rain-checked my own aspirations of floral photography, put my camera away in a ravenous back pocket, and stilled the soft murmur of my daydreams with a will to be present.

With the assistance of the Macarena, once more I fell into the cool resolute of my game face. I hit the streets with my very best intentions wrapped so tightly around me that their desirous aspirations inadvertently became my new work uniform. I looked smart. I looked approachable. I cleared my throat and checked that my actual voice was as inviting as I had rehearsed it to be. And I wore upon me a piece of each person's emotional outfit that I had learned from; Jack the Lad's bowtie tied itself firmly around my neck. The hippie's fur boots weightlessly carried me across the street to an unmarked residency and an all-American jersey kept my breasts displayed, yet warm. *Woof. Woof. Woof. I can do this. One Macarena, two Macarena, three Macarena, four.*

For hours, I knocked on door after door, but each time that my boney knuckles made contact with their unyielding security, the doors simply folded their arms stringently across their wooden chests and insisted that nobody was home. The high of the Macarena began to wash away from my pumped-up ego like the scent of Saturday night's sin during a Sunday morning sermon, becoming but a memory. As time went on, the knocks that extended from my wrist announced themselves in a barely audible query and, as silence surrounded me, practicality began to push its way into my knuckles, quietening my efforts with its unfailing presence. The flowers looked up at me suggestively as I passed them by and seduced my fingers into wrapping themselves around the camera in my back pocket. *'I'm ready for my close-up Mr. DeMille,'* they teased from petals that pulsed purple with distraction. My pace, at last, softened down to dawdling and left a snail trail of captured moments behind it.

Most of those in the working world were too busy being employed to enjoy the pleasures of their own abode and their empty spaces made fruitless work for my 'salesperson within.' In the process of my egoic deflation, I had only made contact with one pair of speculative eyes who had seen me coming a mile away and, narrowing with detest, bolted the door behind them. A 'no thanks' would have sufficed, though I was in no position to argue with neither bolted doors nor narrowed eyes.

I continued to walk the streets and, as a new world began to unfold and scatter at my feet, I took to taking in the spectacles of strangers' lives. I passed through creaky gates that enabled me access to a multitude of private chambers; a weathered armchair braved the outdoor elements with no remorse upon its tattered edges, the porch light that he turned off for her each morning when she returned home from work flickered against the grey sky. I wondered what kind of stories lived within such an eclectic array of sanctuaries. No one was home, yet there were signs of life everywhere. I felt as though I were in a David Attenborough documentary that specialised on the unique dwellings of human beings.

'Here we have the 'Stayeth at Home-oth Mumosaurus'. As we stand in the midst of her lair, we can see signs of her young ones all around our very feet. Try not to disturb anything for fear of her abandon. Notice the array of her cub's playthings discarded violently in the corner. And here... a scuffle of some sort between

her and her mate. Take note of the broken beer bottles that guard her den from intruders. The Mumosaurus is truly a force to be reckoned with!' Thanks, David.

Brimming with daydreams of David, I stomped through the streets and recalled a comment that my Aunty Debbie had made back home, in regards to my future Australian job aspirations:

'As long as you're not working the streets.' Debbie had warmly remarked in the comfortable humour that her and I had long perfected with one another. Her eyes, like a mother's. Her smile, like a friend's.

Casting my vision down upon my tattered boots as they aimlessly pushed and worked their way through cracked tarmac streets, I smiled to myself in private humour. *If only Debbie could see me now.*

Whilst navigating the residential premises that make up a major portion of Melbourne, one comes across an alarming number of apartment complexes. What is more alarming, for a salesperson, is the amount of buzzers that have to be pressed in order to gain access through the complex's gateways. Such a thing was what my nightmares were made of. I knew the words that I had been trained to say into the silver-boxed guardian of doors would bear no resemblance as to my true intentions of entry.

'If you say you're from a power company, there's no chance in hell that they will let you in. There's no smiles to hide behind. How else are you gonna get access to all of those glorious doors?' The large round head of my team leader had imparted his final lesson of the sales person within.

Standing in front of a metallic box, armed with my final lesson, I began my first attempt at ascending the numerically suggested stairway to heaven.

Apartment 12; no answer.

Apartments 11-8; no bites. I began forgetting what buttons had already been pressed.

Apartment 7; "Hello?" Above the murmurs of a busy background, a woman's surprised and shrill voice began to query my identity.

"Hi, it's April... can you let me in please?" I answered casually. Training had armed me with the simple tactic of 'a forgotten key bearer' and, as I stood beside the buzzer, I felt halfway pleased with myself for my accomplishment but also halfway embarrassed. However, there was no time to decide which feeling was more prominent. Without further question, the woman buzzed me in and I pushed through the silky gates of the complex with a conqueror's stride. Floating through the building with a displaced pride, I began to attempt its stairway, when a heavy-set and vocal canine that was akin to a Saint Bernard began to descend upon my intrusion. I was met at the foot of the stairs by the power of a creature that, unlike Alinta trainees, did not need to pretend to woof.

Holding my ground beside a glossy stairwell, I watched as a heavily pregnant woman, (light only in her curiosity,) began to waddle down the stairs to meet me. Looking past her, I observed the glorious doorways that hovered above the woman's head like a halo and, feeling inspired, I pushed the will to get sign-ups back into my bones. A young boy clung to the soft tissue of the woman's hips like a koala to a eucalyptus tree; his eyes, red and weathered with a child's unpacified exhaustion. The Saint Bernard barked over the young boy's restless cries and above the rising pitch of confusion, I attempted a sales pitch that I had relentlessly rehearsed, upon my first real-life audience.

"Hello, I'm April from Alinta. Now, I know that you have noticed an INCREASE in your...."

"I wish you would have said who you were." The woman looked at me with the soft eyes of a disappointed mother. Before gaining entry, I had understood little of the clatter and confusion that was living on the other side the buzzer. Slowly, the commotion began to focus into the beginnings of a picture, however, I continued my dissuasion of intruder and converted myself into a money-saving hero in disguise.

"Now, what I am here to do is LOWER...."

I barely made it three seconds into my well-rehearsed bathroom mirror speech, when the woman's irritations cut me off in cold blood. A frenzy of disapproval carved itself into deep running rivers that ran across her forehead and she began descending the stairs with a heavy haste. For an instant, a bull appeared to possess her gentle features, blowing steam out of her ears until the woman transformed into the 'Stayeth at Home-oth Mumosaurus.'

"You!" The woman's eyes pierced me with blame. I looked behind me, certain that so much anger could never be aimed towards a simple door-dweller such as myself. Though there was no one there. *This one's on me.* My eyes met the mother's will to unload, with the openness of a landfill. She began to fill me in.

"I just got Henry off to sleep." The Mumosaurus broke her words up so that the silent spaces in between them emphasised their importance. Henry guiltily looked down at me from behind the trunk of his mother's lady lumps. His red eyes, declaring war on rest.

"I have not slept in days because of THIS!" The Mumosaurus pointed with two stressed and stumpy hands towards her heavily pregnant belly as if I were the culprit... as if I were the one who had caused her to swell in such a manner and left her alone to fend for her and her cubs without assistance. The woman's stomach rotated around on a galactic belt of its own, her eyes shooting me down with dazzling meteorites. The Stayeth at

208

Home-oth Mumosaurus began to waddle closer to me.

I stood at the stairwell and, unable to move, was star struck. The Mumosaurus was a heavenly creature of uncharacterised passion; she had small children for angel wings and a ring of doorways that sat above her head like a halo. Her dirty-blonde hair fell, untamed, against red flushes that had begun to populate her once pale cheeks. Inside of a hormonal body-bag of flesh and bones, the Mumosaurus was a beautifully dangerous sight to look upon. Remembering my legs, I edged backwards to the doorway.

"You rang that bell and woke up Henry. All because you're *April from Alinta*." The mockery in the woman's voice reached a crescendo. Hot tears began to boil over the volcanic rocks of her dark eyelashes and, erupting into a molten lava of hormonal baggage, left a path of destruction in their wake. My lips parted in shock and, as the Saint Bernard barked above the mother's tears as if they were both singing the same Christmas carol, I followed my initial instinct to comfort such sorrow. But as I approached the crime scene, the Mumosaurus only drowned further in her despondency.

Below that glossy staircase, amidst real-time barks, the foundations of my very nature were questioned right then and there. *Who the hell are you, 'April from Alinta?'* Well, it was apparent... I was the bad guy.

After offering my sincere apologies to the inconsolable Mumosaurus, I swiftly departed the apartment complex of which I had trespassed. And before the gate had even closed behind me, I phoned the round, disco-ball head that was attached to my team leader's ear and informed him of my decision to quit. After mentioning the door-to-door disaster, I listened as my team leader offered up his invaluable advice:

"You've been real unlucky for your first day... uh... April. But on a 'human level' you haven't really tried hard enough. You don't wanna quit so soon, do ya? Think of the pay!"

Crouching amongst a bed of picturesque flowers and digesting my team leader's words, it was as if I could literally feel his clammy hands patting me on the back and pushing me forward into the next doorway. His reassurance was a feral kind that belonged to an unconscious animal and it was far from comforting me. Through the small holes in the phone, I could feel my team leader's chiseled smile trying to lead by example whilst it poured through the receiving end, aiming to attach itself to my face. My end of the phone felt so sticky with bullshit that I found myself removing the receiver from my ear so that I could wipe my face before offering him an explanation.

"I don't think that this is a case of luck... um... Guy... But I do know that it's definitely a sign for me to pay heed to. And on an even more 'human fucking level'... I cannot be the guy that makes pregnant ladies cry." A cathartic silence resonated out from the line, suggesting no further argument.

The dollar signs that had temporarily inhabited the alcoves of my eyes were once again replaced by the quiet truth of practicality. After departing the maze of residential doorways, I ticked door-to-door salesperson off from the list of things that I had never done, but will now never do again... and I kept on walking those city streets with tattered boots that sought after my true identity.

Melbourne's Melodies

18th June 2014

The afternoon light was pale with decline, the air around my lungs was crisp with the texture of winter, and for the very first time, my eyes fell upon a neighborhood that was known as Abbotsford.

Abbotsford sprawled itself out before my leather boots like a Lego cul-de-sac. The thick, silvered stalks of Australian gum trees rose up heroically from the cracked concrete streets with the force of an undeterred development that could not be easily reckoned with. Walking past their prison breaks, I admired such resourcefulness. Each house had been built, brick by brick, with individual character and rubbed residential shoulders with its neighbour in an acknowledgment of contiguous distinction. Some houses were plain and practical; their miniature white picket fences humbly extending onto the concrete boundary of pavement in an attempt to exist without equating size into their white-washed aspirations. Other buildings had been decorated with an array of prayer flags and homegrown gardens that peppered the boxy streets with an infinite display of good intentions.

As I followed the directions towards my final destination, I glanced through a swell of green ivy towards a doors entrance and saw a silver sign upon it that read, 'Abundance.' That single sign, sitting upon that perfectly aged and time-taken house, pressed positive affirmations out into existence and gave the entire neighbourhood a feeling of affluent serenity. As I exhaled a breath of cool air from my warm lungs and allowed frosty shapes to form themselves upon the curve of my lips, I felt that serenity to transfer into every part of me. I could not know it then, but I would not only come to spend much of my time in that particular neighbourhood, but I would also be drawn back to that very house.

With my door-to-door days behind me, the need to fill my time with other ventures had become a prominent one. During my perusing of the city, I had been advised of a volunteer-based restaurant that served as a meeting ground for travellers such as myself. The restaurant was said to be a place where those that had become dispersed from their tribe could come together as a family and unite beneath the light of a new sun. Those days, I was surely feeling displaced and alone so, by the whisper of the grapevine, Ben and I decided to make our way to a community that was known as 'Lentil as Anything.'

Formerly a convent, Lentil as Anything peeked its decadent head up through the gum trees of Abbotsford and beckoned me towards it. After passing the skeletal structure of a cherry tree whose blossoms had been assaulted by the blades of winter, I made my way through a multitude of buildings that had been assigned to numerous community-based projects. Many of the rooms within the convent were dedicated to art, yoga and healing. Some were centers of learning, whilst other parts of the building had been recast into small businesses such as cafés and restaurants. The structure itself had elegantly endured a modern-day transformation, allowing that which is modern to coexist peacefully amongst that which is ancient.

After our self-guided tour, Ben and I poured ourselves into an open dining hall that was filled with colourful characters who sat chatting amongst themselves. Lentil as Anything was not only a part of the convent but also a dining cauldron of mixed strangers that swirled amongst one another over healthy home cooking and jovial conversation. The ceiling above the diners had a cathedral's height and the low wooden tables were fit to satisfy the appetites of Vikings. A line of hopeful candidates formed beside an array of freshly-cooked vegetables that offered themselves up in a canteen style of self-service. At the end of the queue, a donation box sat honestly upon the horizon, stating that *'everybody deserves a place at the table'*.

The room was so packed with participators that it buzzed and hummed like a seasoned bee hive. I moved with the currents of the crowd until Benjamin and I burst out the back door like a river, spilling outside to water a large grassy verge. Out in the open air, flower beds and soft, swaying trees waved at me from

212

the boundaries of the garden. Upon the soft grass there lay a dreamy body of satisfied customers that all soaked up the autumnal sun as if it belonged to the summer. Pierced noses hugged the red roses of blushing cheeks whilst hair follicles that appeared to have been drenched in a rainbow's end swept across shoulder blades as if they were pots of gold. Jugglers teetered in the convent's garden, throwing their wares high in the air with concentrated and unashamed smiles. All around the convent, a sense of timelessness played in the cool autumn breeze.

As an acoustic guitar rose up over the grass blades, playing sweetly to everybody and nobody at once, I came to understand Lentils to be a place where everybody had at least an ear or a hand to lend. There, despite the wealth of anyone's pocket, we each had something of value to contribute to the continuation of the canteen. Behind the scenes, a myriad of volunteers ensured that the service ran smoothly and efficiently. Each volunteer wore the same hospitality-splattered black apron of a work person, but it was evident that each of them had come to the convent from a different walk of life. Indian head wraps were gathered above the heads of the chefs like Lentilian toques. Korean lips enthusiastically asked for my order in broken English, glad to have the opportunity to practice the language of their new country, whilst coffee machines patiently trained shaky virgin hands in the sought-after arts of a barista. Lentils was a place for the dispersed and allowed anyone who was willing, to learn the necessary skills for their working world.

As I submerged myself further into the land of Lentils, I began to feel a softened sense of home resonating out from the thicket of the convent. Although I did not know the strangers that gathered around the communal tables like a family on Thanksgiving Day, I was drawn to become a part of them. I had not yet met those who stood in line, awaiting perhaps their only meal of the day, nor had I before looked upon the tranquil faces of the casual grass-dwellers as they lay sleeping. However, something inside of me recognised that I would soon become a part of their community. The soulless Jacks and the lads fell away from my company with a sigh of relief, as helping hands unknowingly began to elevate me with the possibilities of new friendships and purpose. From that very first afternoon, Lentil as Anything offered me refuge and normality during a time when I needed it the most.

Amongst my new stomping grounds was where I first met Jimi. The afternoon sky had not long melted into the soft dusk of evening and Jimi crouched upon an outside table that offered up two spare seats. As Ben and I searched for a place to rest our limbs, Jimi's lucid, green eyes welcomed us with a flicker of recognition. His hair was as wild and untamed as mine and, as I approached his table with an acknowledgment of our hair brethren, Ben and I casually took a seat. Jimi's date for the evening was the gentle curvature of his electric guitar and it sat proudly in the seat beside him, just waiting to be touched. After Jimi, Ben and I had breezed past common formalities, Jimi and his date began to make wild and melodic love upon the table right before our eyes. He was undoubtedly talented, becoming lost in his date's silky slopes as the bellowing of Hendrix gathered like sweat around his lips and perspired over my attentions. As I ate my first meal at Lentils, I watched my new friend as if he were a wild animal and, in that single moment, Jimi showed me that he had no regard for who was watching, nor the length of our strangeness. Thus, the first of many a Lentilian alliance organically transpired.

After the love-making had subsided and dinner digested peacefully in mine and Ben's bellies, we fell into a deep well of humour with Jimi. Laughter was like water to us and, until it touched my lips, I had not realised the depths of my thirst. Jimi had a thick and hearty laugh that repetitively made a pilgrimage out from the depths of his belly towards the endless night sky just so that it may echo into a prayer of hilarity without restriction. He was pure like a child. I could see it in the way that his eyes glimmered wildly whilst we all conversed over the divine and the spiritual. Jimi, touching upon their concepts with the enthusiasms of a virgin. A soft layer of innocence illuminated the brown of his skin and shone with a light that was akin to stardust, though without the infinite knowledge of the cosmos.

Beneath the star-speckled sky, Benjamin and Jimi

formed an immediate bromance. My new hair brethren became lost to me in a way that being in a couple can inadvertently encourage, if only temporarily. They bounced back and forth with a thunderous dialogue that could not be penetrated and I allowed space for it, knowing that couples must balance the divisions of their spotlight. It was not long before quotes from 'The Mighty Boosh' began pouring from our mouths, tickling mine and Ben's unified sense of home and bringing us all back together. Those quirky quotes slowly fused Jimi to mine and Ben's day-to-day developments and would become the foundation for our friendship.

During a day when the house was creeping up under my skin, I ventured towards the city under an excited invitation from Jimi to join him on a busking mission. Whilst Jimi drove, he also perpetuated the dialogue of so many stories from inside of him that I thought his skin could self-combust at any second. At first, I found it hard to get a word in edgeways, but after the necessity of Jimi's listening skills had been established, he and I began to nurture a well-balanced friendship.

We arrived at the city in a stretched station wagon that also served Jimi as a psychedelic home. The inside of his vehicle was a cosmic jungle that grew wild with constellations of rocks, notebooks, candles, crafts, books, Buddha heads, celery sticks and, even a partial straw roof that hung over our heads imaginatively. It was hard to make heads or tails of the galaxy that Jimi lived in, however, his home was a precious kind of mess. I maneuvered past his lucent crystal collection that laid across his bed like a clear-cut pillow case and pulled out an assortment of amplifiers and wires from within the madness. I brushed aside pot plants and cartoon sketches so that I could locate the last of our musical equipment whilst Jimi began to construct his stage at the corner of a busy intersection.

As Jimi waxed and restrung his beloved instruments, I stood against the wall and held one of his guitars close to my chest as if my fingers actually knew how to love it. I wore the casual mask of a musician who was accustomed to singing for their supper, though that concept could not have been further from the truth. I had never busked on the streets before. My singing was, in fact, not something that I had ever really done in public. As I looked into the busy streets, my heart rate began to soar with the tattered wings of an injured bird.

The inner musician in me began discreetly taking notes as I thought over the small jam sessions that I had participated within over the years. They were not many, though it was a place to at least begin. Jimi tantalised funky melodies out of his voice box like a snake charmer and, as he did so, I began to follow his lead. *I can do that too*, I convinced myself over the intrusion of traffic.

Whilst Jimi wailed unapologetically into the busy crowd, I began to quietly sing to myself, my voice just above a whisper. A few heads turned and sent a couple of my heartbeats amiss, then their faces disappeared into a mess of movement that congealed upon the street. Some that passed Jimi and I by smiled appreciatively, others just looked vacantly at me before also disappearing into the crowd. But most people just kept in pace with their destination and didn't miss a beat.

Cars with heavy breath and bad gas passed by our corner-performance tumultuously. Motorbikes growled from within the bowels of the city, whilst turbulent trams shot electricity up into the tram track in the sky. The city itself appeared to be alive... and it was talking to me, encouraging that I find my own groove within its jargon. Black tires screeched to a halt against the soft of the pavement like a DJ scratching a record. The affirming green lights of a pedestrian crossing monotonously ticked like a light-hearted snare drum. And the city of Melbourne began not only to talk, but to sing to me.

"Sing louder!" From behind his electric guitar, Jimi had not been fooled by my calm façade and proceeded to speak in cool tones to me. As everything comes full circle, it appeared to be Jimi's turn to advise me on my own vocal contribution.

"Use that voice... nobody's even listening." He rejoined

Hendrix and left me to my whisperings.

I stood upon that street corner and, exercising the trust of strangers, I found that Jimi was right. No one cared what I did in the few seconds that it took for them to pass us by. People would continue upon their pathways no matter how confident or embarrassed I was, no matter how terrible or talented I was, and no matter if I was there to psychoanalyse my fear… or if I was not. So, I searched my head for fragmented lyrics and, with a trembling voice, sung slightly louder into the unmoved streets of Melbourne.

Music had quietly been brewing inside of my guts for years but only shower curtains and bathroom tiles did ever hear of such aspirations. I was content there in the privacy of steamy bubble baths as harmonies ran up and down my throat and spilled out into the generous acoustics of innumerous bathrooms, reverberating off of tiles that would never judge me. I used to sing as a little girl, in fact it was I who was my Daddy's number one Spice Girl, but I somehow lost my voice back when adolescence had robbed me of the choice to feel powerful. Though, since those childhood days, each time that I have secretly sung whilst shaving my legs and washing my pits, I have felt the music quietly changing me. I would emerge from the shower as if my genetic structure had been slightly improved, purely based on the knowledge that singing simply felt good.

So, as I leaned against a dirty city wall whilst Jimi incarnated Hendrix beside me, I imagined what it would be like to be back in the privacy of my bathroom… and I sang. I sang to everyone and I sang to no one. Turned heads turned into green bathroom tiles, pocket shrapnel shined like saturated soap bars, and the smiles of strangers stretched out over their faces like flimsy shower curtains. After a few coins had been cast into Jimi's guitar case and a few random pictures were posed for, I convinced myself that I was bored and allowed for Jimi to steal back his one-man show. But as I watched him, immersed in the ethereal world of music, I felt the warm glow of a creativity ignite deep within my stomach.

A few nights later, Benjamin and I accompanied the bellowing Jimi to meet a gentle friend of his called Bengal, like the tiger. Bengal was a soft, young thing who apparently went into tangents of clairvoyance whist in the midst of a conversation. Standing outside of her apartment, I anticipated meeting such a creature. As Bengal opened the door and welcomed me into her home, I could feel that she held the same sensitivities as my own. With the brashness of Ben and Jimi's competitive male frequencies and my home life being swallowed up in a battle for communication between Ben and the Mystic, I simply melted into the quietude of Bengal as she gently embraced me.

Bengal's dark hair moved like an antenna around our bodies, picking up on traces of things that others could perhaps not see. She was a feeling creature that had no regard for practicality and, as we made ourselves at home, Bengal eloquently danced about her apartment as if no one were watching her. Her small bones cut through the stiffness of the outside air that we had unconsciously carried inside with us and she broke it apart with her sultry swaying. Each of us silently watched Bengal from behind the busyness of our own bodies because she was simply a lovely sight to look upon.

Bengal's features were like a clay sculpture that changed depending on how you touched her. I didn't look at her from the corner of my eyes like the others but instead, I looked upon Bengal directly. For she ignited a nervousness in me that my self-proclaimed freedom was in need of coming face-to-face with. In comparison, my own body felt rigid and shy and I wondered how free I could really be in this world when I was still emitting such fearful frequencies.

Through Bengal's dancing, I could feel my own failures and, despite how confronting those shortcoming were, they were an important thing to feel at the time. As Bengal fell into the crowd that had gathered on her living room floor, she also produced a

218

warm voice that, like an endearing haunting, easily followed the sporadic pickings of Jimi's guitar. Benjamin placed a drum upon his lap and began erratically spanking it with the fever of a heart attack. Jimi's best friend, Tay, sat across from me with yet another instrument of mischief and assisted in birthing the musical child that was trying to make its way out of us. Everyone was participating in the random creation of song and symphony, smashing and tantalising eclectic beats with faces that were cast with the blush of liberation. Everyone contributed... everyone except for me.

I found that, as I sat upon that soft, beige carpet, I could only play the silent witness. My stiff body would only lend me the ability to be a crowd contributor, a person whose role as an audience member to an artist was vital, yet not forthright in my identity. I was faceless. I shifted around on the floor, smiling through an encouraged cage of teeth and I felt itchy all over my body, as if my well-worn role was a few sizes too small for me; as if it had outgrown the ability to simply sit still and listen. The fire in my belly was at a boil, glistening in the darkness of self-development.

As the drum line was continued by the boys, Bengal and I shared a few mundane words together over the location of our tobacco paraphernalia... and then, she was off...

"You're a warrior." Bengal met my gaze with a glossy look in her eye as if she were looking upon an autostereogram in a Magic Eye book.

"I see you, tall as a sword; some pillar-esque embodiment." As the music continued in the background, she searched the corners of her mind without any regard for time.

"With women... small women, deities... unfurling beneath you... honouring you?" Bengal looked at me with a question that wet the corners of her eyes, though a moment later, she appeared to have found the answer.

"You are their protector. You are the warrior spirit sister." Bengal looked into me with a warmth that could no longer allow her and I to be strangers.

Although I did not quite understand the meaning of Bengal's vision, I felt quietly enlivened. A sense of recognition pulsed through my skin and threw me into the fever of music. Before long, I was a part of that intangible compilation of unrehearsed vibrations. I twisted words and mixed up sounds as I felt them rocking their way through the marrow in my bones. *Bee-dee buh-deep bap-boo…* punched through my lips. My body, but an instrument.

Benjamin had long liberated himself from the confines of self-restraint and he tapped loudly upon the drum without shame. He had found a melody within all of our in-betweens and, upon gazing into those concentrated blue eyes, I saw that Ben was on a different level. He was smacking that ass and I was overcome with the desire to jump his bones in a rock-n-roll frenzy. Bengal and I gradually blended our scatty-tribe and blues-ska-opera-funk into some sort of angelic harmony. I was on top and she was on the bottom. Then, we switched it up for the sake of equality. Jimi strummed his guitar into ecstasy and Tay remained the continuity of our breathing thread. It was a musical orgy… and I could not help but to feel that it had always been a part of me.

Whether one believes in clairvoyance or not is of no particular relevance to this scenario. What mattered during the occurrence at the Bengal residence, I believe, was that that clairvoyant cat was able to see me in a moment when I needed to be seen. Although I had been quiet and inflicted with the barriers of self-doubt, Bengal had been able to see the warrior within me that I am sometimes able to see within myself.

To be able to see the higher version of a person's essence in the same way that they can sometimes envision themselves to be…well, there is great power in that frequency.

A few nights later, I retraced my steps full-circle and found myself being pulled back into the magnetic field of Lentils. As I walked the grounds beneath the moonlight, the dark features of a well-drawn young man appeared from the darkness and interrupted my wanderings. The figure looked at me affectionately from behind black-rimmed glasses and allowed his aquatic green eyes to rest upon my every feature.

"May I draw you?" The soft curve of the young man's lips were as sweet as the French accent that spilled like foreign honey from in between them. Standing beneath the pale moonlight, in front of two jungle-green eyes that seemed to prowl around my composition, I met the artist known as Luca as he thirstily looked upon me in that tentative kind of way that only artists do. I allowed Luca to drink from me.

"Wild hair and soft features." With an alluring passion, Luca had already begun drawing me in his mind. Just as I was being swallowed up by the moment, Benjamin bounced into mine and Luca's moonlit bubble and introduced himself with the excitement of a puppy.

"And you," Luca looked generously into Ben, "may I draw you also, with your poetic Jim Morrison features?" With an unwavering desire to still-frame beauty, Luca was not concerned with what sex it emanated from.

That evening, Benjamin, Jimi and I followed Luca the short distance from Lentils to his house so that he could immortalise our characteristics upon paper. As I rounded the corner of Lentils onto Clarke Street, I came upon the very same doorway that had exuded positive affirmations of 'Abundance' from its entrance. The house of affluent serenity would be our final destination.

As four bodies walked casually towards the door, a wealth of untamed ivy reached out through the ink-stained night and serenaded our passageway. The syrupy scent of jasmine leaked out from within its petals and perfumed the night air with an assumption of awaited pleasantries. Following the lantern of

221

Luca's soft, brown hair, he led us down the throat of an elongated hallway that belched us out into the belly of the house. After digesting my new surroundings, I felt as though I had stepped into a French resistance film movement. The resident ceiling appeared to be as high as the convent's and its creamy walls had the deep imprints of cracks pressed within them that shifted silently in the dark, giving the house a sense of animation. Pieces of artwork had been scattered across the myriad of wall fractures, decorating the house with smudged faces and theatrically contorted bodies. The external limbs of the house were each cast in slumberous shadows and, although my interest for discovery was unparalleled, I dared not to disturb their dreams.

Under the promise of heating and red wine, I curiously made my way into Luca's bedroom. As the chamber door creaked open, I was pleased to see that Luca lived in a small room, no larger than an office. Though its space had been utilised to the fullest. Halfway up the wall, thick, wooden beams had been constructed in order to produce an extraordinary home-made bunk bed that looked as though it would last throughout the ages. The bed itself sprawled out with the wing span of a king, whilst various colourful fabrics hung from the ceiling above the bunk bed in a languid offering of privacy. The floor space below Luca's sleeping quarters was as available as a Tinder date and I approached its vacancy like a first embrace.

I assumed my position upon an irregularly shaped beanbag, pressing down its lumps into normalcy and, as Luca drew his pencil from the gun sling of his pocket, I too armed myself with a writing instrument. We each pressed pen upon paper as if we were cowboys in a quick draw showdown and we fired several rounds into the room. Jimi busied himself with the wild strumming of his guitar, whilst Benjamin played a steady drum upon his thighs. As we each embodied our stylistic poses of natural life, Luca fulfilled his promise with an abundance of heating and red wine. I swam in the green seas of Luca's eyes as he feverishly bounced from paper to body, swallowing the three of us up in appreciation. I recited my writings over the mellifluous makings of the boys, whilst the wispy and frantic strokes of Luca's pencil added to our unified melodies. Luca's commemoration was also a powerful frequency

In the midst of our still-life moment, three more souls poured into the small quarters of Luca's bedroom: Atom, Aiichiro and Andy. Our group had barely even skimmed past introductions before the music intercepted us without care for common talk about the weather. Atom and Aiichiro spat sick Japanese raps out from their mouths like silver bullets of speed and style, joining our creative showdown. Their lyrics were short and pulsing, chopped up by a sword of good vibrations. Although I didn't understand a single word that either of them said, as I lay sprawled out across a lumpy beanbag, I surely felt the funk.

For, no matter the mother of your tongue or the frequency of your flesh, Music will drown you in her. She is the goddess of emotion that rules the deep caverns of expression. She will lure you in with melodic dewdrops upon her fingers, beckoning you until you feel wet all over your body. Music will demand that you feel what she feels inside of her and that you know the truth in which she speaks because Music... she is a language that no one need be taught.

With his memory bank brimming with words, Benjamin flew into the hurricane of sounds, joining Atom and Aiichiro in a colourful rap trio. They twirled around one another, gathering creative speed and fanning one another's flames until they each pulsed into a freaky lyrical crescendo that seemed to shake the entire room. The moment of flighty passion was soon brought back down to earth by the soulful and baritone voice of Andrew.

Andy's long limbs crouched upon the ground in front of me, cradling the wood of his instrument as if it were a precious stone. A pair of pale and endless alien fingers gently plucked the strings of his acoustic guitar as though they were silver-stringed cherries. Andrew's sound tasted like blood-red cherry juice and it pushed rubescent flavourings into my flushed cheeks. As we each quietened to a new frequency, Andrew looked into each pair of our eyes and encouraged that we timelessly contribute whatever we please to the moment.

It was apparent from that first wordless meeting with Andrew that, without being forceful, he knew how to move the things around him. He had effortlessly calmed the musical storm that had gathered force and threatened destruction. A part of Andrew knew the importance of expansion through spaciousness and he proceeded to offer each person around him a unique and peaceful place to exist inside of him so that we may all grow. As I listened to the sonorous tone of Andrews's frequency, I felt it resonate within my lower parts. His voice pulled parts of me towards him as if it were gravity and I knew that beneath Andrew's skin, he had the semblance of his very own solar system.

As Andrews's eyes met my own, I threw a few *coo's* out there into the ether and parted with some *oh's*. Then, just as those around me had done so with such ease, I began an attempt at improvisation. With pen and paper in my hand, there was no doubt that I could run on for days. Yet, without such instruments, I became painfully aware of the great void that was resting within my mouth. It was as if, in the absence of paper, I had no medium in which to truly express myself.

Yet, amongst discarded drawings, red wine glasses and the ability for spatial progression, a euphonious seedling had been unconsciously planted in that empty space in my mouth. Watered by timeless contributions and warmed by the fire of creativity that had been burning inside of my belly, that seed began to grow wildly from within a forgotten part of me.

The melodies of Melbourne, sparking a creative growth deep in the wispy tinders of my soul.

The Lion's Den

15th May 2014

The massage clinic in which Benjamin worked had only been open a week, however he had found firm footing in his newly-acquired position with a natural ease. Each morning, Ben would open the clinic in anticipation of new clientele and when there were none, he busied himself with administrative duties in preparation for their coming. Each evening, Benjamin would return home to me and draw stories of how, under a guise of new employees looking up to the wealth of his knowledge, he was encouraged to awaken the teacher within. Benjamin had found himself to be in a position where he no longer recommended elixirs of health to an impartial ear, but rather found that he thrived in a place where ears thirsted for such guidance. My prince was finally stepping into the teacher that I had always seen within those eager, blue eyes and I was proud of his developments. However, each morning that Ben set out on his occupational adventure, I realised just how alone I was in Melbourne.

Beautiful people were beginning to insert themselves into my life, but there was still a continuity of long-ago forged friendships that I found myself pining for. I missed those 'pop over uninvited, no need for a prearranged rendezvous' relationships that I was yet to acquire within the virginity of my arrival in the city. I knew that such relationships could be mine, should I allow such alliances to grow over time, but I was damp with the cloak of winter's lethargy upon me and I found that my efforts were few.

So instead, I sat alone in my hollow kitchen with a cup of tea at hand and I thought of my best friend, Kay. I thought upon the citrus of her kitchen cabinets, welcoming us to sit down and have a cuppa beneath their retro ears. There, we would hover over our steamy cups like hummingbirds to caffeinated flowers, whilst endlessly dissecting and digesting life from every single angle, just trying to make sense of it. I pondered over the maternal care that held itself in Kay's dainty fingers when they wrapped themselves around a china tea cup, a microphone, or a braid in my hair. The deep green caverns of her eyes would always clear a pathway through the steam and look into me with an unfailing ability to make my business her business and often, I was strengthened because of it. Kay's orange cabinets would promise to always keep our years of secrets locked away amongst their crockery.

I sat in my own inhospitable kitchen and romanticised over mine and Kay's regular updates and of the grounding that I received because of them. They were twenty-two years in the making, making our connection the longest that I have ever had outside of my blood family. Kay and I had sat down beside one another as children and with that meeting, she had immediately become a fourth sister to me. Since then, Kay and I have each fought against the odds of entirely separate continents in order to maintain a place by one another's sides. As adults, Kay's children became my children too and we were impenetrable in our tribe. Our lives were enriched due to our unwavering determination to keep one another close because, despite the vastness of our differences, we knew one another's stories as if they were our own. But I had, as I always do, fractured that. I had put miles between our love with my impermanence and my longing for our connection... well, that was my own consequence.

With four months having passed since the scent of home had tendered my heart, I could not help but to miss Kay. I could not help but to miss many. I found that, in my homesickness, I wanted, as always, things that were not particularly possible in that very moment. So I left my longings upon the kitchen counter with my empty cup of tea and took what was offered to me. Bypassing the wheelchair that guarded the front door, I grabbed my worn leather jacket and made my way towards a secretarial job interview.

The words 'Gotham City' sat in thick, neon-blue letters above a tall, black building that was destined to be the place in which I would be interviewed. The vibrant lettering, contrasting a bored and unimpressed winter sky. My eyes scaled the gothic structure that fell like a funeral dress beneath its phosphorescent offering and loomed over an assortment of glimmering cars that curled beneath, as in silent prayer. The multitude of Mercedes Benz' and Ferraris encouraged an essence of respect, making the establishment stand out like the rich amongst paupers in the slums. As I made my way towards the entrance of Gotham City, I pushed through a thick air of secrecy that wrapped itself firmly around my body, though I could not yet understand its source.

A strange hotel. I thought to myself, as I brushed down the pleats of my faithful black skirt. *The 'night time receptionist position' has never looked so glamourous.*

At the reception, I was greeted by the gruff voice of a small woman who proceeded to comment apologetically upon the state of herself. The woman and I were cloaked in darkness and all too quickly she turned and showed her back to me, so she received no reaffirmation on my behalf. Instead, I obediently followed the hobbles of her body down a maze of dark passageways until the apologetic woman pointed before a door and told me to wait inside.

As I entered the room, the darkness of my new surroundings began to fade away and was quickly replaced by the grey sparkle of disco-infused tiles. The tiles upon the wall shimmered like silver teeth that smiled broadly at my arrival. As I stood in the empty room, my vision fell onto the floor where my tattered boots soon realised that they were standing upon the remnants of a dead zebra skin mat. The mat's black-and-white fur was flat and well-worn but, as I stepped forward, its hair stood up on end as if I were the one who had committed a deadly sin. Apologetically, I tip-toed to the red mouth of a leather sofa and sat down, staring blankly into a canvas of immodesty that sprawled out on the wall before me. Whilst I gazed upon the photographic curve of a gold-framed, two-dimensional breast, I wondered what lion's den I had stumbled upon.

I prayed to the gods of Google, sacrificing the words 'Gotham City' to the search bar and I had time to read:

'Gotham City: House of Sin. Proud to provide Melbourne with a multimillion dollar establishment. Australia's only 6 star brothel.'

I also had time to curse myself for flying blindly far too often, before a door on the opposite end of the room opened.

"The boss will see you, now." A woman's voice stated. I arose ceremoniously, as though I had been called to the witness stand and, brushing down my pleated skirt in nervousness, I wondered which truth I would tell from here. Although I could have turned around right then and there, gone home and admitted that I had attended the wrong kind of interview, I instead proceeded to make my way towards the door with a fever of curiosity upon my brow.

Walking the unlit hallway with preconceived notions as my only company, I began to imagine what the boss of such an empire could be like. I automatically envisioned her as some sort of sultry, sapphire sister that was hell-bent on empowering women and their best assets. Business suits and breasts solidified themselves into my imagination, open legs pushed my mind further open with the force of Girl Power, whilst KY jelly stuck affectionately to the dry spots in my daydreams.

As a door slowly creaked open before me, I was surprised to be greeted by a stocky male figure that extended a coarse, hairy hand towards the butterflies in my stomach. With a rough and impassive voice, he introduced himself to me as Fabio. Looking upon Fabio from top to bottom as he stood beneath the dusky light that poured over us from his office, I immediately crowned him the perfect candidate to run such an establishment.

Fabio was the Fonz incarnate. The dark slick of his hair

228

swam down the thick of his neck with greasy ease and he reluctantly removed his hands from it, but momentarily, to encourage me to take a seat within his office. Chaotic papers partied upon the desk in between Fabio and I, unaware of our attempt at a serious conversation; the stapler mounted the marker aggressively. Fabio's bare chest was barely restrained by a worn-in black leather jacket, allowing thick chest hairs to push their way towards me in an attempt to draw my attentions away from the disarray of his desk. After Fabio had returned a hand to the resting place of his slicked-back hair, he then bid me to tell him of myself. However, as I opened my mouth up to speak, I felt words linger upon my tongue uncertainly, dubious of whether or not they wanted to leave the safety of my orifice.

What if there was no secretarial job? What if this was how they interviewed the 'worker' girls under the cover of legality or secrecy? Then, 'hey, get under those covers you filthy little piece of flesh... that ass belongs to Fabio now!'

A version of myself wiped away the ejaculation of a stranger from my thigh.

Despite my well-masked paranoia, I was able to discreetly affirm that the secretarial role did, in fact, exist. I then went on to swallow down my uncertainty and valiantly put forth my best qualities of secretarial work history to Fabio's tentative ears. It was the Frankenstein of a resume, come to life.

"You've gotta be tough in this business!" Fabio proclaimed in a cool voice that spoke in commandments. "It's a fast-paced whirlwind of sex, drugs and rock-n-roll, where ya gotta always have your eye on the eye of the storm!"

I took shorthand mental notes; eye, storm, sex, drugs, rock-n-roll... *got it.* I put the notes away in a box for later and, stepping firmly up to the orgy of the table before me, I disrupting the papered pleasures of the desk. I then audaciously assured Fabio that he should not be fooled by my blonde curls and friendly disposition. For, "behind the soft of my skin lies a lioness that understands many a thing about sex, drugs and rock-n-roll, for I was born from the eye of the storm!" The grandeur of the place appeared to have evoked the theatrics within me.

Fabio stroked the serious lines that sat at the side of his eyes with the bejeweled ring-finger of a pimp. After a moment's consideration of my case, he invited me back the following evening to see Gotham City in its full glory, to see how 'feline' I truly felt about the real nature of the beast.

The next night, I returned to Gotham City, having abandoned any prudish preconception I may have unintentionally held. Because, in my mind, the mysterious world of fleshy fetishes and worker girls had become a test of my endurance. Gotham City had become a veiled thing that I needed to uncover.

I arrived to be greeted by Danny the Doorman, who advised me that he would be my guide for the evening. Danny played a tour guide that was akin to David Attenborough, except the sensuous jungle that we traversed together would require an R rating. Danny and I entered a large room that was elegantly laced with long, smooth legs that extended from the fabrics of decadent sofas. Club music poured out from the speakers as other women danced against the wallpaper, as if they were just out for the night to let their hair down. In the center of the room stood a tall, oval bar where men casually gathered as if it were the only watering hole in the valley.

"You see that man sitting over there at the bar having a drink?" Danny pointed to a faceless business suit. I followed his fat finger and nodded in approval. "Each girl will casually approach him, one at a time, and offer him their range of services. He doesn't even have to move, and it's all over a respectable martini." The enthusiasm of Danny's voice extended to the corners of his mouth and painted a vivid picture of seduction.

Danny the Doorman and I stood in the corner of the room, to show that we were but mere bystanders of the game. I attentively watched as each pair of beautifully long legs approach a faceless man, imitating a to-the-point bar scene. Self-sales were happening over grossly overpriced cocktails, but it looked harmless and almost natural. With bubblegum lips, she whispers in his ear of fucking and sucking offerings, of foot fetishes and maybe even violent things. "I can call you Daddy," and all the mysterious in-betweens. As I stood on the sidelines of neutrality, it was clear to me that Gotham City was a land where the hunter became the hunted.

I was led to the top of a spiral staircase that conjoined with a secret entrance for those who cared to not be seen on the sex scene under speculative eyes: men with wives, or sensitivities, or a reputation to upkeep. My initial observation of absolute privacy had been confirmed, as the brothel of Gotham City showed itself to be a place where the maintenance of an unpublished life was not taken lightly.

Gotham City was covert and mysterious, with hallways that were small and dark. Upon passing their doorways, I crossed many naked and ruffle-haired women departing from the doors' dark, wooden secrets. Many of the women were beautiful, with fresh stories that were written upon their rouged flesh in the red ink of passion. I was eyed curiously, for perhaps the women expected me to be their next piece of competition. Walking the shadowy halls, I wondered if the girls detested one another, squabbling for the fruits of the males' pockets, at war with one another. Or perhaps, there was a sisterhood amongst them, one in which only one another's used-up flesh could understand the other's; a unified liberation. Maybe they were in this together. My thoughts rolled into one another in cryptic veils of those $300 half-an-hour 'whores' who had liberated themselves from the participation of social restraints and flowered in the opening of an orifice... or two.

Once I was out of the belly of the beast, I met a real-time receptionist who proceeded to inform me of my new secretarial duties. Those duties included, but were not limited to, ordering condoms, taking bookings, managing the girls' time slots and chasing up the girls who had made big bucks on the previous night and had become lost on some bender. I was required to watch the camera footage at all times and buzz the girls' rooms when the clock only allowed their client a few more minutes of carnal pleasure. The small office was populated with an army of secretaries that were all dressed in black and stood watching over pornographic footage whilst pressing buzzers to the beat of the clock. The receptionists were the Guardians; the Big Brothers of the House of Sin.

"You must be the eyes and the ears for the boss… you cannot trust anyone apart from the boss. You must never lie to the boss!" The receptionist drilled into me with mafia tones.

"And Fabio is the boss?" I inquired, innocently.

"Fabio is the boss." The receptionist took her eyes from the screens and looked upon me suspiciously. "But you must never use his name. If anyone comes to the desk and asks for Fabio, then you know not of who they speak. If anyone calls and asks for Fabio, then you have not an inkling as to their required person. You have never heard that name before. Fabio does not exist!" The receptionist spoke in slow, calculated rhythms, with a suspicion that would not remove itself from the label that she had placed upon my forehead. And I left the beast feeling rigid and uneasy.

I would never hear back from the infamous brothel of Gotham City. Fabio's real name would never again cross my lips. I would not become a member of the black skirts and black shirts or Big Brother guardians to the House of Sin. And I would never know the secrets of the women that worked its dark hallways and innumerable doors.

Perhaps it was because I didn't have what it took, or maybe my inquiring of the boss's name and the secret photography that I had gathered whilst sitting in the waiting room had led them to believe that I was a spy in their House of Love.

Which in some form... I suppose I was.

Happy Endings

22nd June 2014

Each day in Benjamin's absence, I found myself doing either one of two things; I would halfheartedly roam the streets searching for employment, handing over resumes that became just another discarded piece of paper amongst an entire city that was already bursting at the seams with forgotten paperwork. Or, I would sit at home beside the computer, surrounded by a stack of hopeful CVs and scroll through employment opportunities whilst casually obsessing over the impending need to work. *Work, work, work, work.* It was the only thing that filled my thoughts.

I had left England with seven thousand dollars in my bank account, but four months later, I found that I was down to my last eight hundred. More specifically, I was down to *our* last eight hundred. Benjamin's own funds had run dry at the beginning of our Asian adventure, however, I had acquiescently suggested a peace treaty of *what's mine is yours*. Though, how quickly had *mine* faded with *yours* in tow.

Perching beside a computer that gathered resumes around its base like a crumpled tutu, I thought over the previous two years of hard work that I had already put in just to get me to Australia; the 2am ending of a shift that swiftly demanded my attentions once more at six, the time slots, the missed fun and the ass-kissing that I had mechanically puckered up for for so long. Back then, there was a light at the end of the tunnel because I had been envisioning a brighter future.

At the mystic's house, I sat within that future and, enveloped by the lightless living room, I felt as though I had barely even had my day in the sun. Winter taunted my idealisms, odourless smoke scented my dwellings, and I folded my arms in disapproval of such a predicament to bear the title of My Greatest Adventure. A part of me refused to believe that it was already time to slop back into the soup of preoccupation so soon. But the other part of me knew that, despite my reservations, it was time to buck my ideas up and get on with it.

As I scrolled through the opportunities of my livelihood, I came across a job advertisement that read:

'Seeking female massage therapist. Experience beneficial, though not necessary.'

By the time that I finished reading the advertisement, I had already convinced myself that my natural intuition for massage would ensure that I secured the position. Furthermore, I had my very own masseur boyfriend who could surely teach me the ways of his world in order to advance my natural affinity for massage. Therefore, without further ado, I applied for the *'no experience necessary'* position and received an immediate response inviting me to not only one, but two separate interviews; one of which was located just beside Benjamin's clinic.

After weeks of fruitless searching that had seen me roaming around the city like a CV zombie, I started to feel as though things were beginning to financially look up for me. From within the tenebrous attire of our sombre living room, my white teeth broke through the darkness and shone enthusiastically at the thought of Ben and I working side-by-side. I romanticised over the two of us meeting up during our lunch breaks and discussing our problematic clientele over a hot drink. I envisioned the Ben and I returning home together in the evening after a long day's work, yet still finding the time to massage one another, in order that we could perfect our new techniques. Even though I was playing a game of concords with codependency, I could not dispute the fact that I had missed my partner in crime and couldn't understand why I hadn't thought of such a remedy sooner.

I arrived at the first massage parlour feeling nervous, though before I made my way inside, I glanced across the road upon Ben's work clinic in order to confirm the destined synchronicity of my interview. The sight of Benjamin causally talking to a stranger through the window calmed and encouraged me to go forward into yet another role that I had never tried. As I made my way up the steep stairs to the top level of the building, I was met by lackluster-looking man who introduced himself proudly as Graham.

"So, have you hearda' Lomi Lomi massage?" Graham's pores opened up like the Grand Canyon as he spoke.

I stood within his sterile office knowing that I had never heard of Lomi Lomi, but felt confident that I could master it with ease. Graham ushered me over to his desk and proceeded to show me a video of a woman who hovered over a client, massaging him in the fashion of Lomi Lomi. Within the small screen, there was calming music and an assortment of essential oils that I could not quite smell. A yellow flower perched upon the woman's dark head like a petal crown and, as I watched her gently rub oils into a man's thick shoulders, I understood Lomi Lomi to be a professional and achievable style.

"So, this is how I interview," Graham's continued, his voice exuding an exhaustion that implied I should have already known of his methodology. "I give you a massage, you see how I do it and then you give me one so that I can see what we are working with." Graham's tongue pressed against his teeth as if it were too big for his mouth and needed to escape.

Wobbling beside an empty massage table, I thought it strange to be removing my clothes for a job interview, however, I understood that I was in a field of therapy that dealt in matters of the flesh. I would not be required to use my persuasive voice or administrative qualities, Graham only wanted to know what healing I could create from the language of my hands. Therefore, I vanquished the fear of any unsavoury behaviour, removed my clothes and dressed my private places with a crisp white towel. Patiently, I waited for my teacher to join me in the small, candlelit room under the promise that it would be the 'best full body massage' that I would ever receive.

As Graham's thick, clammy hands lathered my limbs in a

balmy and saccharine oil, I began to note the contrast between his and Benjamin's techniques. Having a massage therapist as a partner meant that body manipulation was not a foreign world to me. Ben's devoted hands were like hound dogs that were on the hunt for irksome knots, whilst Graham's, on the other hand, proceeded to lightly brush over my body like a faint whisper. Graham employed a methodology of 'relaxation' and, although I secretly loathed such a thing because of its undesignated and whimsical characteristics, I put my desire for hard and rough aside and continued to take occupational notes without judgment.

Whilst I was receiving the best-detestable massage of my life, I thought over the tales that Benjamin had imparted upon me in regards to the power of touch. Each evening that Benjamin returned home from work, he would draw pictures for me of clientele who walked into the clinic feeling rigid and uncomfortable. Ben would then explain to me that once those customers were horizontal and had their expressions buried in the privacy of a face hole, of how they would often relax into an incessant dialogue and unload their troubles into the quiet of the room. Some, it is said, would even go so far as to weep, showing massage to be not only a physical, but also an emotional kind of therapy. In a world where our troubles are often over looked and labeled as the sole responsibility of our own, I saw how a simple acknowledgement of another person's ailments could evoke touching results. The need to be soothed and held is a deeply-seeded desire that, since children, each of us have been governed by.

As I dressed the whispery, oiled version of my body, I didn't quite feel healed from Graham's massage, however, I nonetheless aspired to offer him something in return that was potentially deeper than a murmur. Graham laid his swollen body out across the massage table like a beached whale and I saturated his body in oils as if they were fragrant, replenishing droplets from the sea. Pushing my thumbs into the blubber of his thighs, I watched them disappear in a meaty whirlpool without a life raft. Then, after ascending the lump upon the back of Graham's neck as if I were mounting a camel, I tended to his hairy hump with vigorous affection, despite the hump's outward aggression. As I made my way down the prominent curve in Graham's calf, I dusted off the black grime that stuck like warm tarmac to the soles of his feet and watched as his bloated toes twinged and floated like ten inflated life vests above a black and bottomless sea. In that small, darkened room, I consciously implemented every technique that I had learned from Graham as well as my own methods until he seemed pleased. As the whale slowly turned over on his back, the towel that was covering his lower parts became wedged beneath his buttocks, revealing a flaccid and lifeless penis. It lay atop of his thigh like a pale, wrinkled, washed-up body. I could only cock my head to the side in curiosity.

After going back to work on the ocean of Graham's thick skin, I assured myself that there was nothing to fear from the naked human body. As I kneaded the knots in Graham's legs, I weighed out the pros and cons of working in such a position. There was the obvious $30-an-hour that was an unarguable pro. Training and qualifications were provided upon employment, respectable clientele and good hours had all been promised to me. Plus, the massage parlour was close to Benjamin's place of work. All of which were definite pros. As I massaged my way up towards Graham's hip bones, the pleasure-saturated exhalations of his breath began to foul the small enclosure of the room that we occupied. Graham emitted an acrid aroma that smelt like last night's dinner mixed in amongst a discharge of a malodorously aged cologne.

As I held my breath, the cons instantaneously flickered in the flame of the tea light candle and, as if a single flame could cause such a thing to happen, my body began to feel hot all over. Looking down upon the whale specimen beneath me, I saw that my fingers were swimming dangerously close to two sagging and wrinkled ball sacks. The shriveled sacks gathered below Graham's member like two orphaned raisins that had been left out in the cold, clambering for their mother's attentions. My heart began to pound out of my chest as the imagery of the most unattractive feature in the male's body confronted me without even knowing my name. Graham's putrid breath caused me to experience breathing problems and as he exhaled with enjoyment, I gathered my belongings and took my leave from the strange circumstance that I had found myself within. As I left the building with barely a trace of explanation in my wake, Graham's shrill voice began to chase me down the stairs:

"If you do this topless, you will make great moneeeeeeeeeyy!" His proposition trailed away, fading into a world that would have to continue on without me.

"I feel as if I just massage-cheated on you," I humoured in response to Ben's inquisition over my interview. Ben and I stood in the sterile safety of his clinic whilst hairy backs, cracks and ball sacks floated in the air between us as we discussed the diversity of female and male massage therapists and their potential sexual expectations. I kissed Ben on the cheek as he chuckled over my experience, revealing two rows of large white teeth that could tear away any kind of danger and then I dashed off to my second interview of the day, where they promised that no sexual propositions were associated with their clinic.

I approached an unassuming building where an 'open' sign flashed in red neon lights and struggled against the piercing brightness of an afternoon sun. After knocking upon the locked door, a young Chinese woman opened the door and greeted me with, not a handshake, but a hoover. As the woman placed the long black pipe in between my fingertips, she swiftly instructed me to prepare the clinic before the start of business. The woman then disappeared into the back of the building, stating in broken English that, "Today you work."

Armed with a red hoover called Henry, I began to make my way through the small building in order to familiarise myself with my new place of work. Immediately, I knew I had stumbled upon a land that was far from the white-walled and white-towelled world of Ben's massage clinic. All of the walls that surrounded me looked as though they had been painted with Pepto Bismol and even encouraged the dismal look of a poorly child to draw itself upon my face. The décor of the place was trashy. Ragged towels perched upon the ends of massage beds in unmatched colours and threatened to jump to their death. But I was able to draw comfort from the signs that hung upon the walls and clearly displayed their disapproval of sexual misconduct. Bright yellow cocks accompanied by hanging ball sacks each had large crosses placed across them, leaving no room for argument.

"We offer no sex service," the young woman had assured me after emerging from the darkness and looking upon my affection for her signs. I returned her smile appreciably and continued with my cleaning duties.

I've always had a knack for interior decoration. My mother bestowed upon me such a gift when I was just a child; she had the talent of turning a cardboard box into a palace. I found myself mirroring my mother's ability and mentally rearranging the furniture within the clinic, repainting the walls and suggesting matching towels. In my mind, the pink cardboard walls transformed into a sterile palace. In the midst of my envisioning, the dainty woman returned and, standing in the doorway before me, made it look as though it were a doorway for giants. There was evidence of trouble upon her pressed lips.

"Some of the girl, they offa this... but only for very regular customer." Before I could answer her, the woman disappeared down the hallway and left me to my cleaning duties. Henry looked up at me remorsefully, as if he had seen some things. I pondered over the happenings that occurred within those pussy-pink walls and settled upon the fact that some women just do what they have got to d and that I would be no one to judge such liberated behaviours. Henry agreed with me, grateful of my continuation and together, we pressed on with our duties.

A moment later, the woman returned. Her silky black hair slid across her creamy face like an eclipse. "We have maaaany regular," she smiled politely, questioning my response with arched eyebrows.

"Um, not me, thank you." I spoke into Henry's black tube as it were a microphone and wondered if the strange ritual that I was employing with the woman at the clinic to be my actual interview. The woman scuttled back into the background with no further commentary.

Remaining on task and undeterred by the conversation that had just commenced, I excavated what dirt I could from a place that was becoming dirtier by the minute. Once more, the doorway became cast in shadow as the small woman appeared at the foot of Henry's ravenous mouth. A serious look seemed to possess the woman's features; her dark eyebrows folded in on themselves, her lips pursed with unhappiness and her thin arms folded across her chest like a useless bike chain.

"You no allowed to say no to customer... we never say no, right away. You must say 'I am too shy' or 'Sorry, I am too scaaaared right now... maybe later' and then you no have to do the sex." The woman smiled warmly at me, as if I were a child that was about to embark upon her first day at school. Then, the mother in her left me to digest her parting words.

The 'no sexual misconduct' signs stood against the Pepto Bismol walls and shrugged their yellow shoulders at me helplessly. Try as I might, I could not envision myself in front of a hardened man, masquerading as part-time massage therapist and part-time timid Asian woman. The combination congealed inside of my imagination and began to suffocate me. Looking down at Henry, I decided to tell him that I couldn't see him again. *It's not you, it's me,* I assured his sad, white eyes. Then I gathered him in my arms tenderly and followed the sound of the woman's heels as they clicked against the tile floor like the rapid gunfire of a mouse protecting its cheese.

As I lay Henry to rest in the broom cupboard, one final inquisition stuck itself to my turned back.

"Your name April, right?" I turned to meet the woman once more and nodded, cautiously. "It bit too hard to remember. When customer call, they ask where you from, and your name, then they choose you." She smiled at me as if I had won a carnival prize.

"You have many clients already today. They want new

girl from England, but you must choose better name." An assured smile full of teeth wrapped themselves around me like prison bars, trying to keep me with her and Henry.

A name can say many things about the person that wears it. It can be a combination of destiny and evolution, where a name can shape a person or that person can be shaped by their name. For that reason, I have even been discouraged from the idea of taking someone else's name through the union of marriage. I thought over these reservations as I closed the door upon Henry and knew that if I had not been prepared to adopt a new name through the beauty or destruction of marriage, then surely I could not change my name in order to perform in a circus of sexual favours.

Hi, my name is Bubbles, I imagined a hyper-sexualised version of myself saying as my feet subconsciously carried me back out the front door. It was a shapely name at least.

I did not judge any of the services that happened within those candy floss walls, but I knew that I could not bring myself to become a part of them. After fifteen minutes, my one day as a massage therapist, no experience necessary, was officially over. I knew that I didn't need an accredited job title in order to show that I was versed in the arts of making him feel good or blowing her mind, but at thirty bucks an hour, I was simply not prepared to sell my wares. I was too sensitive to touch for such things.

That night, I went back to the dungeon of my living room, jumped on the computer and disarmed all of my reservations that I had towards rejoining the wonderful world of hospitality. Immediately, I applied for as many waitressing jobs as I possibly could.

Waitressing. Yes, waitressing I could do. There, I would not be a villain who makes pregnant women cry. I wouldn't have to order condoms or look upon an endless array of pornographic footage until I became desensitised to it. And I would never be required to look upon the sloppy wrinkles of hairy ball sacks or be encouraged to rub my breasts against them. Waitressing was a safe world where in which aprons and notepads would never demand that I change my name to Bubbles.

Closing the computer down, I turned off the lights and went to bed with a sense of my identity still intact.

As my corrupted daydreams swam out to meet the happy ending of my unsullied night dreams, I pulled my blankets over my head and whispered to myself...

... This is April Lee Fields... over and out.

Clarke Street

1st July 2014

When the wild ways of the world have exhausted me, my home is a place in which I aspire to feel refuge and safety within. Even when I am far from my abode, I try to wear the safety of its walls around me as if it were a second layer of skin. Home, in the same way that it is for so many others, is a personal environment in which countless hours are spent wrapped in its comfort and protection so that when we chose to rejoin the world, we are able to carry that comfort inside of us wherever we may go.

The reality of my home in Melbourne felt as though it were a far truth from such an aspiration. I found that I was living in a home that had inadvertently turned itself into a manic-depressive and had forgotten Benjamin and I to be guests inside of it. The house began carelessly leaving strange pipes out in the open for me to find. It forgot to open its curtains in order to let in the light of day and when I tried to suggest otherwise, the house just ignored my advice and sulked in its own darkness.

Despite my constant strive for cleanliness, the house sat in its own filth. Mouse shit began to fill the cutlery drawers and the table tops. The kitchen wore a dirty and derelict blanket that did not warm but instead, made eating within it unappealing whilst the cold air bitterly clung to everything that it touched. Our house had the kind of winter blues that I could not permeate, so Benjamin and I unwillingly retracted our wings because we were no longer made to feel welcome, our manic-depressive quarters had been perfumed with the inhospitable scent of narcotics.

My time with Mystic Magz had come to a stagnated standoff. The habitual tendencies that kept her awake for days in a haze of paranoia had begun to drag me into their dark peripherals. The mystic had not long lost her job and without work, an influx of peculiar nocturnal activity began to replace her prior evening absence. There was a self-medicated sickness that lived inside of the mystic and that sickness began to creep around the house at night and taunt my inability to banish it. It threatened me as I slept, with the cold, steel blade of contamination that pressed memories of my old addictions up to the forefront of my mind. Despite mine and Benjamin's best intentions of alteration, the house that once showed potential for transformation decidedly stood in defense of its dark traditions and it would not budge. Winter fell into the full force of a cold brutality and what was once a sanctuary to us, had turned into a frozen prison. I began to feel infected.

I had acquired some casual waitressing work in the city at a Southern diner that fortunately kept me out of the house and instead, kept me close to my adoration of Southern-style cooking. Though unfortunately, my attempt at vegetarianism had gone out the window with my weakness for fried chicken because I have the kind of black in me that is an absolute stereotype of my culture and I just couldn't help it.

I returned from work one evening and, after finding myself in the safety of the Lentil grounds, I crossed paths with my French friend, Luca. Beneath the dark of the night, Luca and I became entangled in conversation. He revealed to me of his plan to move out of his house and relocate to a nearby squat, where obviously the rent was much cheaper. Luca and I conversed over the lives of squatters and I heard myself asking of the availability of his room. Before I knew what I was doing, Benjamin and I were being escorted away from Lentils in order to begin the short walk back to Clarke Street. Back through the pulsing ivy, back through the sweet spell of the jasmine and back through the enchanted jungle residence, was where we were introduced by Luca to the Lady of the Forest, Leaf.

Leaf opened her bedroom door wearing the auburn of a season just passed within her hair. Her fingertips had colourful tales splashed across them and, as they extended themselves in the swift reality of a handshake, they also told me they had just returned from an alternate world of art and illusion. Leaf's mouth stood firm, showing me that she was not a woman who was easily impressed… and that unforced pleasantry about her impressed me. Ben, Leaf. Luca and I all sat in a hallway that had been laced with pictures and pianos where we began to gauge one another. We felt out each other's frequencies just to see what would come out naturally. It didn't take long for humour and sincerity to join us in that hallway, allowing us to resonate into the idea of a future together.

The Lady of the Forest would come to offer Benjamin and I a room with her on Clarke Street, but a version of Mystic Magz sat with me in that hallway and she looked down at her feet like an abandoned child. Guilt took captive the loyalty of my heart and temporarily held hostage my commitment, but I assured Leaf that we would think over her offer of tenancy and return to her with an answer before long.

Back in the dungeon of derelict things, I found myself to-ing and fro-ing over the question of whether it was, or was not, worth the hassle of upsetting our mystic because of mine and Ben's will to leave. Our time left in Melbourne was yet to be determined. Benjamin and I were unsure if we would be in the city for much longer than a month, therefore a severance with Mystic Magz felt potentially unnecessary. Despite her nocturnal activities, Magz had taken Benjamin and I in off of Melbourne's streets. She had opened up her dejected home to us as if it were her loving arms and even asked Ben and I to call her 'Auntie' because she loved us both in her very own way. I felt the weights of responsibility pressing down on me because I had not been a stranger to the constant dialogue of Auntie Magz' stories. It was clear to me that her lack of family had been softened due to mine and Ben's unexpected presence in her home. The mystic was fifty-two years old and, with the exception of her troubles, she was alone in the world.

I also pondered over the perks of Clarke Street. It was a

home that was closer to the city. A residency that was closer to the social thunderstorm that I had grown to know as Lentils and it was exactly the same amount of money that Ben and I paid to occupy the dishcartened dungeon that I was pondering within. Clarke Street appeared to be a house that was filled with love and its shifting walls were painted with an ancient paint that could perhaps teach me a thing or two. I sat in the dark room of my dungeon and allowed Clarke Street to tempt me.

Once I had been honest with myself, I knew that I could not falsify my desire to leave, however, my loyalty to the mystic seemed to mix like thick concrete into my immobility. So I asked myself what the raw tale of truth really sounded like and looked into the mystic ball within my own being. The truth was cold and told me that Mystic Magz and I would never attend the yoga classes that we spoke of each morning when her spine gave her pain. The truth swirled in a clouded glass only to affirm, in its resemblance, that the mystic would never leave behind those odourless whispers that kept her alone in the darkness. The truth even went as far as to suggest that, in many ways, our mystic was the darkness itself.

Benjamin and I gave Magz a week's notice, which she initially took with a cool calm until the reality of our imminent absence actually set in. The mystic was then predictably insistent upon the notion of our financially fucking her over and Ben and I inadvertently joined the ranks of those who had done her wrong. Suddenly, I adopted the face of a bandit that attempted to pull a fast one over her all-seeing eyes and in an instant, Ben and I became her bogeyman. We had given Magz the ammunition that she required to despise us and the mystic relieved herself of all love towards us with ease. We were like a heavy load that had further stressed her spine and, as we approached it in departure, her wheelchair looked at Ben and I in disgust. I knew that it was easier for Magz to relinquish her love for us, so I just brushed past the judgements of her wheelchair and made my peace with being the bad guy.

Leaf picked us up on the afternoon of our abandonment. The sky swamped us all in a grey confusion that refused the remedy of clarity and, as we pulled away from the driveway, the manic-depressive of our old house just looked back at me ashamedly; it had closed curtains for eyes and they blinked in wonderment of whether our departure was due to something that it had done. My new roommate, Holly, sat in the front seat and smiled at me with a Cheshire cat smile that could light up the darkest of nights. The soft of her dark hair framed the house through the passenger window and Holly's thick locks slowly brushed the house's boxy-ness back into the past.

Intimate chatter began to rise from the front seat and, although it was soft like a melody, the air felt weighted around me. I clutched my belongings upon my lap as if they were floatation devices. I looked across at Benjamin and saw that he mirrored my caution with a villainous badge that had been written across his face in an ink that did not require consent. The four of us drove off into the sunset and dared not look back. Depression receded into the horizon and with each mile that passed us by, I began to feel lighter. Ben, Leaf, Holly and I slowly made our way back to Clarke Street.

Entering a familiar house that I had once visited as a guest, everything looked different the second time around. The warm café crème of the ceilings looked to have endured a growth spurt in my absence. The walls seemed taller and the paint, creamier. The cracks that wore themselves in the wall like a lifetime of wrinkled laughter, they seemed deeper as untold stories whispered out from inside of their shiftings. The dark rouge of the lamps exuded a comforting light. Velvet things found the tips of my fingers as if there was a love between them that had been long lost. The bunk-bed of my new abode spread out before me like the wings of an eagle. Wooden hands offered a ladder of passageway and pushed me up towards a nest of lilac lullabies and a fuzz of fusia scented dreams. Soft, white sheets hung from the ceiling and kept the enchantments of the nest privy only to those who dreamt beneath its wings.

The house looked different to me because, as I walked amongst it, I had aquired the title of a resident amongst its inanimate things. My shadow began to cast itself upon the house's knicks. My eyes honoured its knacks. We became part of one another, that house and I, and before long my toothbrush sat amongst the many that had come before me. Clarke Street was a mouth that had been tended to by many bristles. As my scarves left the decoration of my head, they found a final resting place in a bohemian paradise.

I had been in Clarke Street for but a few weeks before the one-hundred-and-twenty year old structure of my home began to fuse itself with the twenty-seven year old bone-structure of my emotional body. My mood became as light as the sun that shone brightly through the slender opening of my bedroom window. Art work hung upon the walls like swollen hoop earrings and offered creative remedy to the volume of my loneliness. Colours splashed out from a multitude of canvases and left their rainbow residue on the fingertips of Leaf, leaving me elevated by their courageous display of her rapture. How nice it was to finally look upon nice things. How it calmed me to hear the echo of contented feet busying themselves around the house. With my homely relocation, my cynicism had been vanquished and it gave way to the close quarters of a sisterhood.

Before long, I came to find myself within the chamber of Leaf upon a regular basis. Leaf's bedroom was a place that would offer her and I the opportunity to know one another well. Together, we would smoke cigarettes and drink wine beside the open of her fireplace and chase away the blues of winter together. Mine and Leaf's conversations were a sea of uncharted territory and while employed in it, the painted faces that hung upon her walls would watch us from within their golden frames and form silent opinions on our perspectives. Leaf wore blue, silken kimonos that draped around her pale body like the ocean. She had long, white cigarette holders for fingertips and skin that was made up of gentle moonbeams. Her lips wrapped themselves around a Viking's smile that had been born of unrehearsed pleasantries. Leaf, she had a laugh like a saxophone.

Leaf's best friend, Christina would often enter the room without the need for announcement and unceremoniously sit down beside the fire in the casual way that neighbours do. Christina, with her gentle ways and sincere eyes, would nestle into our conversations without any desire to change them, offering a wisdom that seemed to have been extracted from star dust. The dark cascades of Christina's hair fell like wild waterfalls across her face, telling tales of her contentment and affinity to the natural world. It was in Christina's nature to ask questions rather than to make self-oriented statements and, whilst getting to know me, Christina listened to my story as if she had walked the pathway with me all along. With a sideways hat that covered one eye, Christina accidentally styled herself with magical and trendy clothes. A dog named Pearl was perpetually curled up beside her feet like a child and brought out the mothering nature in her for all to see. Christina was a guardian angel that, from day one, I adopted as my own.

My roommate Holly would often arrive home from work with her skateboard still clasped in her small hands. She would enter Leaf's bedroom to be welcomed by a dead tree that had been turned into a jewellery holder, its oaken fingers bidding her to enter. The women and I would sit beside the fire together and each day, unconsciously become closer. Soon, the chocolate saucers of Holly's eyes began to seek me out in my own room for advice. Holly would crawl up the ladder to my bed on the thick heels of her Doc Martin boots just to lay beside me and tell me of her troubles as well as her joys. I began to impart to her of how she came from the same fears that I once had within me. In her innocence, I saw parts of me. The soft browns of our skins mixed together beside one another upon my bunk-bed, displaying a story of true kinship. Holly was a priestess who was yet to see herself as such, though I could see her with great clarity therefore she easily fell into the role of my little Clarke Street sister.

Four womanly bodies would sit beside the fire and look

250

at one another; Holly's black top… her quiet adventure; Leaf's silken kimono… her lone wolf; Christina's jazz hat… her delicacy. A Doc Martin boot. A boy trouble. A spilled glass of red wine that reminded us not to cry. A fury of four woman. A fear of being alone. An indisputable strength. A dead tree that had been turned into a jewellery holder.

Those three titans of companionship became the perfect wave of femininity that I had so needed in my life. And, whilst I walked towards my dreams, I heard whispers that those women walked the same path as I.

That path… it was a path that we each knew as Clarke Street.

Concrete Daisy

4th July 2014

Each evening, bound for work at the Crab Shack, I would squash my body into a congested train, hold onto the overhead handrails and make an attempt to refrain from smelling the armpits of strangers whilst we casually collided into one another. I would ride my bike, with no breaks and dim lights that looked as though they had given up on life, through the swollen belly of the city, whilst unconscious cars roared dangerously close to my exertions and threatened to tie our fates together.

The icy wind would run laps around my body, then huddle against my flushed cheeks in order to catch its breath, seeking refuge within their warmth. The aggressive sound of car horns became a beat in which my peddling feet could cycle against. The drivers' ill-patience would remind me of my own tardiness as the chain upon my bike began to break, failing the test of winter. My frozen fingers were often rendered into a state of uselessness.

As I crouched beside my broken bike chain for the fourth time in one night, I looked down upon the pavement and saw a single yellow flower growing up from within the city's fracture. Through the cement of improbability, that yellow flower grew and I knew, as my frosted fingers wrapped themselves back around the rusted steel of my handlebars, that I too could surely grow amongst the thicket of such an impenetrable city.

That night, I served succulent crab legs that were afloat in a boat of garlic and I thought, in great length, about that flower. I began to hunger for a pathway that could lead me deeper into the forest of frivolity. As I lined the restaurant tables with a newspaper that was bound for buttered saturation, I tried to envision how I could take the next appropriate step into a further happiness. I knew that everything I needed in life was just within my grasp and, amongst my mundane work tasks, I began to recall a conversation between me and my childhood friend, Teri.

"I've got a friend who lives in Melbourne." Teri had spoken from beneath lips that would be eternally glossed with the soft pinks of Baby Spice. "Her name's Kate and you would both love each other." I knew that Teri's friendship was the deeply-seeded kind that had never led me astray and I allowed her words to swirl around me until, one day, I found myself in the company of her friend, Kate.

Kate and I were two strangers that had arranged a time in which we chose to no longer be estranged to one another. Sitting beneath my bunk-bed one morning, with a Lentilian breakfast still digesting in our bellies, Kate and I broke apart every step that we had each taken in order to arrive at that very moment. Five hours later, the morning sun slipped into its skimpy afternoon attire unnoticed, whilst Kate and I became further lost in one another's life stories.

In a world of foreign flavours, Kate tasted like home. Her soft voice poured a warm British accent out from her perfectly proportioned lips and soothed my homesickness from within. Kate's soft, brown hair hung around her face like pine needles upon a Christmas tree and her curvaceous body resonated with a similar joy of festivities. At the end of our communion, it became clear to me that the meeting between Kate and I had been destined to take place. It was fated from the forever-friendship lips of a blonde-haired angel named Teri that had unconsciously guarded over me from afar. Serendipity saw Kate to be the manager of a school called the Academy of Hypnotic Science and, after our meeting, Kate had been inspired to offer me employment at the academy with her. My days of dissolution within Melbourne's seedy underbelly began to draw to a close and a pathway of further happiness began to open up before me.

Not long after that fated meeting, I found myself ascending the steps of the Academy towards my first day of work. Kate had asked for my assistance on a temporary basis and my diligent fingers began to studiously file an endless array of disheveled paperwork that had been piling up for years. I

253

categorised file after file with an enthusiastic fervor for organisation that could not be denied until, one day, the temporary chair of the part-time helper was replaced with the permanence of a secretarial administrator. After being offered a full-time contract, I slotted into the Academy like a quarter slots into a jukebox. Each day, I answered phone calls, replied to an assortment of emails and eagerly searched for solutions that the students required in regards to their hypnosis studies. Without further ado, I became the friendly first point of contact for science and hypnosis.

The Academy of Hypnotic Science was a place in which a form of consciousness was being taught. It was a school in which a form of consciousness was also being learned. Some mornings, the students would disrupt me from my secretarial duties and inquire as to whether they could practice their hypnosis techniques upon me. I would then happily divert the phone, sit upon the soft leather chair that was usually designated to clients, close my eyes and then absorb what the students had learned as they practiced their hypnotic delivery upon me. It was far from a hard life.

With the learned voice of a slow and steady teacher, the student who aspired to make hypnosis their vocation would attempt to calm me into a state of suggestibility. I would breathe deeply and allow my thoughts to be guided down a passageway of quiet and calm. During each session, I took mental notes of the progressions that we had encountered whilst I entered a state of mind that was akin to meditation. There, my thought patterns were open and ready to receive the advices of the teacher.

"Now you are beginning to feel well rested and happy." The student-cum-teacher would assure me. "All anxiety will fall away… in three… two… one." No matter if tiredness still clung to me, the room would always appear brighter once my eyes had opened.

There were two types of lecturers at the school of the subconscious. Each party was from an opposing tribe that met in the middle of the Academy and drew up a treaty of peace that allowed them all to work together. There were the doctors of science. They wore lab coats of sophistication and displayed endless certifications of accomplishment from the proud walls of their offices. Those lecturers believed in the absolute power of the subconscious mind through the calculations of science. *'I am therefore I am, I speak therefore I have spoken, I weep because I am broken and I become that which I have spoken about...'* all sat on the tongues of the teachers like modern-day commandments. Those doctors combined the warm winds of faith with the prodding needle of science and, if allowed to do so, they could begin to reconstruct your belief patterns through mathematical manipulation.

Then, there were also the lecturers who belonged to the realm of the fairies. They had the same certifications as the doctors, though they leaned more towards the light in a person's soul, as if it were sourced from the heart of the sun. Those lecturers basked within elvish energies, love and healing. In dark classrooms, they would gather around crystal singing bowls that had been made from starlight and begin to change the structure of a person by the aid of angelic frequencies.

Both tribes' methodology was different, yet their vision was the same. After attending one of the singing bowl sessions, I exhaled in amazement as the resonance of crystals echoed throughout the entirety of my being. In the dark womb of the candlelit room, things began to shift inside of me and I understood myself to be on a path of healing that would go on for many lives.

During my time at the Academy, I found myself challenging my own feelings of inferiority that lived inside of me by sourcing their roots. *Who are you, Nervousness and why do you cling to me so tightly, Imbalance?* As if they were characters in a play, I began to ask them what specific storm they were each born from and requested that they suckle upon my teat no more. With the aid of the Academy, I started to rewire myself in ways that I had never felt empowered to do so before. However, it became hard to write home and respond to questions like, 'What have you been up to... dude?'

Everything around us becomes us. The words that we speak all bear a hint of that which we have seen, felt and tasted. We are each a product of thousands of other people's stories and suggestions that consciously or unconsciously live inside of us. And I pondered over those personal truths whilst asking myself the question of whether or not I *believed* in hypnosis.

Each one of us, consciously or unconsciously engages in the world that is spread out before us and every single one of our characters can be reflected by that in which we see. Often, we are reflected in the television programmes that we watch, the advertisements that plague us and the interactions that happen all around us. We submerge into intricately-constructed film dramas that sooth our souls, but are then spat out into an advertisement of *'Steve's wacky, wobbly, inflatable machine,'* as if Steve were some sort of heroine. Since the times of old, we have been creatures who adore entertainment and easily lose ourselves in his pain, her ambition, even Steve's story as a whole, undisrupted by a personal connection. In many ways, cinema reflects the world around us and allows us to see through the empathetic eyes of God. Yet, in this modern day world, our craving for drama has become a sort of demise. Lies are lacing the streets all around us, pushing us into the consumerism of 'buy-one-get-one-free', and leaving us feeling un-contented.

Therefore, I came to the conclusion that we are each hypnotised every single day in an assortment of ways throughout the entirety of our lives. At the Academy of Hypnotic Science, the teachers were simply attempting to hypnotise helpful things back into our beings.

They weren't saying, 'buy L'Oréal, because you're worth it,' but something more along the lines of, *'don't feel ashamed, because nobody's perfect. Just close your eyes and enter a soft and comfortable space…*

'Breath. One, two, three.'

'Exhale. Feel your face, your body, your divinity, and your personal grace.'

'Notice the tensions that you hold in your body; the dip in your shoulder as you're getting older, the clench in your chest. Realise and release them.'

'From your hairy top down to the hairs on your feet, release all of the things that no longer serve you. Maintain concentration, disarm degradation and do not accept defeat.'

'Because I am you and you are me… And I just wanna see your stardust.'

By the light of the elves, a deeply-rooted darkness that had been inside of me for longer than I could remember was finally beginning to shift. I wiggled around in the darkness of my own secret development and, without letting on to anyone else, began to push up through the cracks in my soul.

In the reflection of my eyes, there were perfectly formed yellow petals.

Breath

30th July 2014

The need to reach out and stretch my limbs had never been so prevalent. I felt compelled to expose myself, piece by piece, from the comfort of my purple blanket. I needed to pierce through the cool evening air with an indulgence of elongated body parts. And as my fingers reached out with curiosity from beneath their maroon safety, the world suddenly shifted two spaces to the right.

BOOOOM!

My pupils were like wet mouths that began to drink in everything that rested before them. The firm of my jaw realised just how tightly it had been clenched and instead, released smiles from its cage as if they were a canine defense system. Their curves attacked my face and left marks of quiet happiness across me. Engulfed with the pressing sensation to dance around my small box room, braless as ever, light as a feather, I softened into the moment.

What were those feelings that were sneaking up across my back and curving over the hunch of my shoulders with relaxing intentions upon them? What emotion could this be that ran through the prison of my rib cage and made its great escape out into the freedom of my heart? Through the psychedelic fungus that swirled quietly around in my guts, I tasted pure ecstasy. The caps of fungal spirituality had become one with my blood stream and after encouraging harmonious frequencies within me, I began to spill full-steam-ahead into attunement.

I gasped in remembrance of breath, in acknowledgement of the life force that sat softly around my body, never asking for praise but always keeping me present. Larger and smaller I became with each expanded breath. I tasted every single word that tied itself into knots on top of my tongue, only to come undone again with nothing to really show for it. I inhaled. I exhaled. I physically bounced up and down whilst my thoughts swirled around and around, until a myriad of colours exploded from behind my eyes and showed a purple circle centered inside. I saw the third eye imagery of a spherical maroon moon where lilac curvatures represented the shapely colours of love. In the privacy of my bedroom, I witnessed a continuation everlasting.

Opening my eyes, I found Benjamin's vision resting steadily upon me with great clarity. His iris soaked into mine and despite the two years of us journeying side-by-side, I felt as though fate had only just allowed Ben to see me properly for the very first time.

I sprawled out upon our bedroom floor like a feline creature that was born of Egyptian dreams. I was impregnated with a ball of divinity and Ben finally saw the truth in me. He paid tribute to my hands and my elongated limbs and, brushing past the relaxation of my torso, he looked tenderly upon the restlessness of my feet. The usual restlessness of Benjamin's mouth had been silenced by a new observation in him and he hung on to my every whim without fear. My body became a place of worship and silence was his prayer.

Although I said little, I was heard with no interruptions and it was a foreign land upon which Ben and I walked. For, with every description that I shared, where purple twirled behind my eyes, and with every breath that Ben synchronised with mine, with every glance that I caught beside the dim of the candle light, Ben showed me that he no longer wanted me to hide my true self from him.

"Goddess," he whispered into the warmth of the heater, as Ben drank gently from my deep waters.

And 'Goddess' I heard. 'Goddess' I felt, because even though I knew that I could grow on my own, in many ways Ben had been the one who had made the goddess so. He bestowed love upon me with such unconditional tenderness that I had blossomed into the person that the little girl in me had always dreamt to be. In that moment, Ben could see this higher version of me, as if it were an avatar that I was yet to meet.

She is the secret, sacred self that lies quietly behind the breast of every woman that I have ever known. She is the divinity in me that has laid dormant during normal working hours. She is a deity that has been brought to the purity of first light by Ben's love, assuring me that he and I have danced this dance many times before. But just for good humour, Ben and I danced together once more.

Our drums were different. Ben's beat reverberated with the roar of a lion's heart. Whilst my drum was not a drum at all, but instead, played like the haunted strings of a gentle harp. Ben's beep-bop careless swing conjured up funky melodies that clumsily crashed into beautiful things with handsome style. My ballet was unrefined and fuelled with the tragic beauty of poetry and cheap red wine. We were unified in our individualism, Ben and I. And as always, we met somewhere in the middle, beneath a bunk-bed of bemused dreams, where we danced as if no one were watching.

The beige carpet whispered funny jokes to my feet, tickling them into laughter. Ben and I held one another to music that existed only for the two of us and, as we danced a wacky waltz across a galactic bedroom belt, I saw the promise inside of Benjamin's being. I saw a version of him and a version of me. I was a restless, effortless bird and he was a foolish, trickster coyote. But despite our improbability, he and I would hang out together until the ends of time. There was no rhyme nor reason, no mathematics to us, other than the fact that I adored his company and he promised to always adore mine in return.

My reservations against forever came crashing down around me because it purely felt as simple as hanging out. There was no contractual agreement, we were just two creatures free to come and go as we pleased that had magnets in our hearts that would always pull us together. I saw the promise in Ben's eyes that said that he would love me past any logical formulations of time. His quietude sang out in volumes of a forever type of love that has known me for many, many lives.

"There is no moment but now!" I responded to Benjamin's unasked question. "No appointment next Tuesday. No 21st birthday. Just you and me, right now." I dove into the barrier of those blue eyes without, asking him to meet me in our Nowhere and Everywhere.

A soft laugh escaped me as I turned over the chronological 'coincidences' that fate and life had given me. I took a moment to appreciate our bunk-bed cavern and the flow of magic that had given Clarke Street to me as a home. I felt protected by the winds of the women that I had come to live with there. Leaf, Holly and Christina blew in gales of support around me, without the need to be physically present. A job that was drenched in subconscious dreams had recently hypnotised me and offered up a contract of permanent employment at its academy. And my blue-eyed prince, who could finally look upon me with clarity, perhaps because I could finally see myself better, looked into me adoringly. Purity and love passed out through the jungle of his dark, black locks and blocked out the sun. It was perfect madness and I fell into Ben's chest, breathless at the wonderment of our world. We were one.

"I think that I dreamt you up once upon a time," I confided into my lover. My words became bolder with each indisputable truth that I was tapping into. And I refused my heart no longer. Too long had I sat in reservations with Benjamin. Too long had I been cold to his unconditional care and too long had he fallen short of my complete happiness because, after heartache, I realised that I had been too much of a coward to love again.

Laughter formed like bubbles in my mouth and popped the thin layer of seriousness that surrounded me.

Ben and I were kept by the company of our house cat, Persia. He had round saucers for eyes and although he spoke no words, he bore witness to mine and Benjamin's truest forms. We joined Persia in his Egyptian lands. The tea lights flickered into the early morning as our bodies spread carelessly upon our sofa bed. Each soul was in harmony with the others and somehow, eight hours had passed us by upon the blink of an eye.

I lay my body atop of Benjamin's just to feel his breath and we inhaled the secrecy of our intimacy as if it were a spring day. Together we exhaled with the breath of spirituality and beauty as if it could only be spread by the breath of lovers... and that that was our true duty.

The fungus faded into a needlessness for words and somewhere in between dreaming and awake, I finally gave myself up fully to my super star love treasure. Because I saw eternity in his eyes. The candle light flickered with the hint of sunrise that waited patiently just around the corner and Ben and I lay together swimming in its light. A boy and a girl breathed with a single unified breath that had the possibility to change the world, then exhaled as King and Queen that had been reborn from the death of their fear.

In that moment of forever, Ben was all I that I had ever dreamt love to be.

Creativity's Children

5th August 2014

The fast pace of the city pushed out greasy fumes of development upon my thirsty skin. With each day that passed, I drank in its oily nourishments and found myself delving further and further into the unclouded essence of my true nature. Around every idle corner was a developmental conversation that was just waiting for me to bump into its unscheduled placement and beneath each concrete canvas was a crater of reinvention.

In that city, in the breathing, pulsing creature of Melbourne, I was remembering my youth. I was recalling my dreams and remembering the divinity within me that had become so easily lost after years of brainwashing and logic. *'Be quiet!'* I heard them say. *'Sit up straight. Wear those shoes and this hat. Add X to Y and equate to a good house wife. Be perfect in every single way!'* It was the mantra of a common child, however, it was actually after childhood had skipped far away from me that I began to remember the joys of jump rope. When I again played in the park without the restrictions of a curfew and, whilst swinging on the roundabout with absolute abandon and the strength of adult legs, had finally found my true voice and began properly navigating its purpose. Such a time is when real happiness began to seek me out.

Happiness encouraged that I finally have the courage to wear an assortment of odd socks and skirt-boot combinations of atrocious attire. Contentment showed me my style and taught me that, after childhood, I could become master of the washing machine, in order that muddy dresses were no longer problematic.

Being barefoot and breathless was when the fleeting fragrance of true Perfection came to knock upon my door; I wiped away the beads that gathered above the dip of my smiling lip and invited Perfection in for a tea party. We took seat and began to discuss the latest developments in our unified campaign for divinity.

For life during that time in my life was as sweet as a cherry pie and the blossoming of city life had me glowing with the emerald magic of labradorite. Each day floated carelessly into the next with a perfection that teased the outer edges of my world and, without further ado, I became a country girl who had grown to love the city.

My time spent working at the Academy of Hypnotic Science was drenched with fascination and intrigue. I would sit behind my black secretarial throne and watch patients walk in with concrete blocks clinging to their feet like scared children. The clients would then disappear into a vortex of official rooms, wearing an apprehension that drooped in the same way that their smiles had drooped. And then the phone would ring, I would avert my eyes and continue to do my administrative thing, until I could once again witness the departure of their bodies. With fresh sessions of hypnosis upon their skins, the patients would not only leave the office, but he or she would float out of the building with the lightness of those who are not afflicted. Concrete blockage was but a ghost to them and the leather of my black throne would turn on its heels and squeak, as if to applaud their accomplishments. The once-strange faces of my co-workers became a sort of family that I was privy to exchange presence with on a day-to-day basis and, for the first time in many years, I was happy in my work.

Benjamin and I still floated in synchronicity with one another, even after the residue of our trip had softened down. Because we had finally connected in a way that, for many reasons, hadn't been possible during our previous time together. My heart had cracked open and allowed itself to be seen by Ben. And, without further ado, Ben had finally closed his mouth and opened his eyes up to me. I came to understand how long I had guarded my heart from him and from anyone who dared to breach my walls of independence with their dangerous affections. I understood of how I had been grasping at the darkness of my pains with white knuckles, as if they were really mine to keep.

I watched mine and Ben's journey as if it were a movie and discerned of how Ben had been so completely absorbed with his ideas of self for so long, that those ideas had inadvertently made it impossible for him to truly know me. For the first time in our walk together, his incessant chatter had become quiet long enough to allow him to hear me. So I attempted to put my weapons down beside the feet of this unfamiliar gentility, before the cool of my care could learn to get the best of me. My walls crumbled and spilled down into the relieved face of an ocean that crawled hungrily up towards me, in order to swallow any evidence of my shortcomings.

They say that scent is connected through memory. And as I stood in a jasmine garden on Clarke Street, I smelt a fragrant reminder of how love can heal all things. It smelt like ice and sweet wind that saturated my body. Healing had lavender heather for fingers that pressed me gently, as if to remind me that it also occurred from the heavenly blue skies that rounded themselves in the chalky blue of Ben's recently-opened eyes. My heart valve began to slowly creak open with a sincerity that could not be mocked. I felt its rusted doors opening in the night as I slept, moistening my dreams with slow, corroded tongues. They were tongues that pressed perfection upon the dull pulse of my surrender and encouraged it to quicken. My surrender accelerated with such force that I accidentally fell through the valve doors, slipping in between the deep, rusted opening of my own coronary machinery without a harness. As I fell into uncharted territory, my heart rate quickened into a pace of be-all-or-end-all… because what happened next, could not have been expected.

It was a Thursday evening. As normal as every other Thursday evening that had come before it and as plain as any

Thursday evening that will surpass. Benjamin and I primped ourselves beneath the dim light of our bathroom mirror, fuelled by a dinner invitation from his boss. Woolly hats fell upon our heads, wearing softly-stitched smiles. Fabrics gathered themselves across our bodies in anticipation of the brisk evening's festivities. I, as always, applied my eyeliner like feline war paint, tied my bandana tightly across my head and prepared to meet Benjamin's co-workers from the massage clinic.

Ben and I arrived at our destination to be welcomed by a maze of unpacked boxes that had been stacked and mummified upon a cold apartment floor. The apartment was a place that lived a contented life, undisturbed by the presence of Feng or Shui. Winter also decided to join us there for dinner, so we kept our jackets on whist our bellies were warmed with an easy Chinese takeaway. The rounds of new faces all sat around a square table and made acquaintance with me, all save for the face of Andy, whose well-defined features had already begun to formulate themselves into my familiarity.

Andrew was a part of the cracked walls of Clarke Street. His creamy skin mingled with the ancient beige paint that saturated the entirety of my home. His alliance was already known to the whimsical painter and the bad-ass skater that were my room-mates, Holly and Leaf. Andrew was a part of all that had existed in that life before me.

The takeaway dinner soon dissipated into an eve of homemade karaoke and the microphone found its way to my lips without any trouble on the road. Andrew played with guitar string fingers to our tuneless melodies, until the rest of the group reached a karaoke crescendo and laughed themselves into other games. We sat around a table of queens and jacks with our jackets still on. Winter pulled up a stool and waited for a hand. An ace of spades unconsciously dug into the plastic remnants of our greasy takeaway containers without knowing what it was doing because, although nobody else would, those inanimate things took note of our tales. The guitar still strummed beside the right of my shoulder. Its metallic strings, speaking to me in silver plated languages that were older than anything that the room could offer. Older than the twenty-seven years that played upon my skin. Older than my soul encryptions that were only just beginning to make sense to me... and I could not help but to be drawn into the guitar's melodious story.

My mouth continued a harmony. Faces in the background cheered one another on in the revelry of their card games. They appeared to be having a nice night without my conversational contributions, so I tilted my head tenderly to the right and saw the tall silhouette of Andrews's body waiting for me to join him.

Andy had sky-blue eyes that, as I looked deeper into them, held ancient civilisations inside of them. The full of his lips leaked a speak-easy jamboree from them that was being held in a smoky jazz bar inside of his beautiful being. An abundance of brown hair fell from Andrew's head, locking around itself passionately as if it were an asexual creature that needed nobody else. And as Andy's features sparked to a glow in front of me, I began to see him in a light that glimmered in whispers of gold. Andrew and I began to sing together, falling into the blues as if it were a woollen blanket that simply came over us both, until we were completely cloaked from the outside world. And as the background continued to be a background, the deep of Andy's soul reached out and touched me, leaving a smudge of blue fingerprints upon my heart. My eyes glossed over in silver sparks of soul recognition.

"I win! I win!" Benjamin interjected, with cards stuck to his pink fingertips and triumph settled in his teeth. But although he knew nothing of it, Ben was fading into a background that seemed to suggest the opposite to such a triumphant testimony whilst I began to feel strange and light as music ignited a creature in me that seemed to have been sleeping. A lifetime of dungeons were simultaneously being unlocked with a single blue-stained key.

"I win!" Ben howled once more, challenging the possibility of loss that had slowly begun to cross paths with the two of us. I sang and it felt like freedom, as Andrews's eyes held

267

themselves around the entirety of my being. He had a still, calm kind of seeing that had me cocking my head to the right in curiosity of its impact upon me. Andrew and I played in ways that acknowledged our musical duty as the background to cards and games. However, something pulsed strangely offbeat as the background in us somehow crawled up to the forefront of my reality, leaving everything else to its own winning nothingness until all that could ever exist was just the two of us.

'I win,' my lover's mouth had spoken, but in truth, Ben was losing in a game that he didn't even realise he was playing.

Bound for Clarke Street, Benjamin, Andrew and I drove through the silence of midnight in Andrew's white transit van. The shadows from the street lights poured in through the open windows, casting strange, dark riddles across our faces until Andrew stopped the car. With his curious impulse, Andy playfully ushered Ben and I out onto the streets until we each scrambled onto a small hill on the side of the rode. Through the foliage. Through the brisk winter's air. Through the discard of late hours and care, the three of us just stood there from the high of a mounded road and together, we looked down upon the orange glow of the city. Melbourne looked like a golden egg beneath me and my eyes drifted over the ambience of a city that was bursting with melodies and transformations. The moment was still and full of quiet nostalgia.

Through the dark of the night, I sought out a hand that rested loosely to the right of me and belonged to Benjamin. Full of appreciation, mine and Ben's fingers entwined lightly with a need to touch something precious, just so that they could verify the greatness of existence.

And with that appreciation pulsing through me, I also felt a familiar love for he who stood to the left of me, the attentive stranger that was Andy. He who had acknowledged and played with the creative child that had lived lonely inside of me for so long. So I also took the hand that rested to the left of me and entwined my piano hands within the soft alien of Andrew's string fingers.

The warmth of some kind of holy trinity began to pulse through three open bodies that stood still upon an empty road, looking down towards the city.

We were drunk on music and appreciation and, as I pulled both Andrew and Ben a fraction closer to me, I dared to rest my head not to the right, but to the left of me. And I felt that I was familiar with the stories that spilt out from Andrew's body. Benjamin squeezed my right hand, grounding me. Andrew clasped my left, accepting me. The breeze blew through the carelessness of my hair as six unknowing eyes stared over the tangerine metropolis, letting time pass them by without consequence.

Gently, the breeze spoke to me and, although I thought that I could hear a warning being carried across its balmy lips, I also wore the blissful ears of a creative child who was having trouble hearing two sounds at once.

Was it the whisper of a warning, or simply a rusted heart valve... creaking open?

Tea for Two

7th August 2014

It becomes increasingly hard to focus upon the trivial happenings of the past, in order of continuity in story, when a heart is burdened and troubled to its core.

My heart wore the dark cloth of confusion. It slept in the tantric troubles of 'other love.' For how can a heart be stretched so thin as to find itself consumed with two souls that rested on opposite ends of the spectrum? For thin my heart had been, as I wobbled and wavered back and forth in between the paradoxes of my life. And I wondered, whilst on the brink of self-combustion, why we were given two feet, two hands, and two eyes. Why were we were armoured with two ears and two lungs, two nipples and two lips, yet we were only given but one heart? Would it be greedy of me if I asked for two? One in which each one of my loves may live harmoniously and the war for space could be waived?

Alas, the dream world was yet to awaken into my desired reality and I was left in my own co-created existence with the unmoved possibility that perhaps I was in love with two souls. I began to wonder how such a conflict had crawled into existence when everything had been going so well between Benjamin and I. There were no fights that I needed escape from. There was no unhappiness that tore me from his arms, because Ben was a dream that had breathed itself into my waking. He was beautiful in all the ways in which beauty can be beheld. Ben's erraticisms had softened down into a calm honouring of my being and all initial kinks in our connection had straightened, allowing us to sail the seas of equality. However, as the duality of my heart was pulled apart with separate strings, all of mine and Ben's romantic efforts seemed to be master-minded by a cosmic joke. Just a few days prior, I had entertained the first fancy of forever with my blue-eyed prince… and then… then there was this!

It seemed as though, once I had acknowledged the possibility of forever, life saw it fit to rattle up my heart box and throw some infinite ideas into it. A version of me clumsily sang out 'One Love' to the loyal heart of a boy, whilst life taunted me with riddles that questioned my melody with a response of, 'Oh, really?' Life, as always, decided to challenge the principles that I had been leaning up against. It wanted to break apart my illusion of solidarity like a bully, because Life needed me to know that he was not fickle and he went as far as to challenge even perfection. I felt like an unpopular schoolgirl that sat in the playground alone, quietly believing in perfection, until Life teased it out of me, until I had watery eyes that didn't care to know if they would sink in the memory of what was, or somehow learn to float. Uncharted lands surrounded me and change was the only constant. It swirled in deep waters mysteriously. Yes… change was the only constant.

The time that proceeded mine, Benjamin and Andrew's harmless hand-held high, was one in which the nature of my entire world was tipped upside-down and exposed for the little toy box that it was. Colourful contents of internal parts spilled out upon the floor of my developments with a fascinating urgency, revealing the guts of plastic wars and princesses that stared back at me with empty, glossy eyes. I was blindsided and possessed by the illogical beauty that I had glimpsed within the stranger that I knew as Andy, and I could not keep my thoughts far from him. No matter the danger. I had become infested. Things that I knew not of crawled around on the outside of my skin. I was submerged in ice cold waters and inflicted with something that I did not particularly want. I drifted to Andrew in dreams of night and of day, and as he came to frequent our house at much more regular intervals, it became clear to me that there was no escape.

'Face this!' Demanded my uncertainty, as each evening I

came to anticipate the chance to have but a moment between just the two of us in which I could bathe in Andrew's unfrequented frequency. A version of me wanted only his eyes to look into me.

The days began to pass me by in a blur of cheap red wine, intended to keep the demons down and before I realised it, Saturday morning was upon me. The Academy of Hypnosis slept and as Benjamin crept away to his working world, he kissed me farewell on the forehead until I resumed the sleepless eyes of a bunk-bed daydreamer; eyes that were swollen with new secrets. Sunlight swam around the swell of my room and Andrew appeared beside the beige of its door as if he had come right out of my dreams. Lightly beckoned me from my slumber, Andy invited me for breakfast with him at Lentils, so I roused gladly and followed his smile outside to the ends of the earth, for the time of spring was finally upon us.

As I sat outside of Lentils beneath that warm, spring sun, the white of the morning light took hold of my inhibitions and shook them out onto the grass beside me. It was eviction day. In those inhibitions did seep like little fearful seedlings, never to be seen again. And I found myself asking if Andy wouldn't mind leaving all of the smiling faces of Lentilian jugglers and smugglers and "come take a walk with me?" A rusted heart pounded itself upon a silent drum. Duh-dun… duh-dun… duh-dun… dun.

Two pairs of long legs strolled side-by-side across the park and followed the wind of the river down through the Yarra Valley. Bridges crossed themselves upon Andrew and I. Friendship forged our footprints as we stepped upon a pebbled pathway that pointed towards a clearing down by the river bank. We made our way down to its grassy keepings until we found ourselves in a still hamlet where the wind could not whisper to us of its warnings.

Andrew and I lay upon the grass with casual disconcert

and began to discover the stories of one another's lives. One-on-one time formed postulations upon our life-long equations as Andy wore the angular spectacles of a mathematician, figuring shit out. He lay sprawled beside me with no desire to interject and, as I shared my own life stories, Andrew simply listened wholly. I could feel each part of me seeping into his care as we sat there, sharing. And when he spoke... full lips, low rumbles... Andy spoke with the grace of timelessness that bid the manic within me to slow down into 'this'. This moment. For 'this' was all that there was in a world where not one drop of rushed correspondence fell from the pairs of our lips and I bore witness to the intimate ways of his world.

Our connection unfurled itself upon a grassy embankment somewhere close to Clarke Street. The river ran quietly beside us; gleams of brown, earthy streams awaited a meeting with the crystal blue sea. I was awash in a strange land of clock-less existence and I minded not when Andrew casually took my hand into his. We twirled one another with fingers of borderline friendship. Prints pressed themselves into the past memories of our lives as we lay, long-limbed, across the breezeless grass. I minded not that our bodies seemed to inch closer and closer to one another's, as if there were some kind of story that could not be shared with merely a voice. Though, try as we might, as we laughed, as we played... Andy and I were simply closer without choice.

Above all other conflicting emotions, that moment down by the river felt as pure as the water that reflected the light of the sun. For how warm the sun was with its auburn intoxications as it finally came out to greet us upon that day. Whilst we lay upon a verge and discovered other worlds, it was the first day that winter had decided to crawl back into its cave and allow the creative children within us to play once more. It was the first true heat that I had felt from the sun in months and I worshiped its warmth on my hair, my face and in my heart. It devoured me with rays that pressed warm fingers upon the rushing of my lungs as Andrew and I peddled upon make-believe bikes through the cobble stone corners of 'what used to be.' Together, we rode upon a lane that never ended with memories. *'Look Andrew, there's my old cat,'* I would point into my recollections. *'Hey Apes, that's where I used to go to school.'* He would laugh.

As the sun sank closer to the hands of the horizon, so too did my heart sink in the knowledge that life would need to return to how it was before. The chill of the night threatened to chase Andrew and I back indoors and although our connection, as I have said, all felt so pure, I would be lying if I told you that I ever wanted to leave that embankment. The setting sun placed further riddles upon my face and I could feel my heart sink into the hands of the horizon with the imminence of Benjamin's return from work. Sharp shards of reality began to pull me back into the moment of all that existed outside of that grassy verge.

It was a tea party fit only for two. A riddle of boy and girl.

Tea for Three

10th August 2014

Honesty.

Honesty would be the recurring theme for me during the next few weeks of my life. Attempting to actually solidify the events that had occurred into a verbal truth was a concept that had me weak in the knees. Honesty. My truth asked me to delve out of my head and share unknown things. It demanded that I establish what was real within the sincerity of my own heart without being affected by the emotions and reactions of another. For there was a delicate consideration that came with the territory of keeping close company and my company was always kept close to me.

The secrecy of one's own feelings can be a conflicting, cold case. On one level, I had a best-of-friendship bond with Benjamin, in which I delighted in divulging the details of my days upon him. We each shared and cared, drawing strength from the fact that we were in this life together. My joys were his joys and my sorrows were also his. My stories become his too and, because of that, there was a bitter sweetness about the daily developments of our relationship. I began to realise just how difficult it was to distinguish the space in between where one person began and the other ended. Benjamin and I were two bodies, amalgamating into one mass of common interests and invested dreams. Even our facial expressions had begun to mimic our similarities. Yet despite my best intentions of independency, I was aware that Benjamin and I had become all blurred up within one another. And I began gasping for air.

Moments between Andrew and I were delicate and precious. Shared without words or reason. Just a look on a faceless Tuesday or a pale song lyric that I chose to interpret into the fanciful alphabet of my own heart. Purple rain showered me with a lyrical suggestion that encouraged of how Andy *could never steal me from another.*

Each day, I sat at the park outside of the Academy during my lunch-break and forgot to eat. I was dazed and confused. My phone became an ancient relic of long-forgotten histories. My notebooks and pens deteriorated in the sands of time and I was consumed. I just sat there in the grass, replaying stolen glances and trying to make sense of them. Despite how much I tried, my feelings would not subside. I tried to figure out what the fuck this all meant in the privacy of my lunchless lunch-break, though no clarity came to me.

So instead, I began to drink quite heavily. A version of 'party girl' me emerged and gathered our friends in the evenings for dinner parties and poetry congregations. She who does not cook began to spend hours in the kitchen, bestowing gifts of nourishment upon the bellies of all those that came within the bones of her house: a paint-splattered Leaf. A holy version of Holly. The Andrew that lived in the cracks of the walls of Clarke Street.

We had recently acquired two more mates with whom to room. Carlotta was made of Italian mafia blood that dared that you fuck with us. Passion sat hungrily upon the sheer of her garments. Carlotta was dark and dangerous, with a heart that kidnapped me without violence. Reeta was her friend of forever. Reeta, Reeta, oh how the angels did sing for her. Reeta was as brown as my sister would be, with parts of me that fit into her similarity perfectly. Together, Reeta and I were another version of conjoined sorcery. Reeta was soft, secret and sweet. She poured poetry from herself into me and I did the same for her in return. We all began to live together in the harmonious chaos of Clarke Street. Each with our own silent wars. Each just crossing paths as the stars saw fit. So, another glass for each of us, the party girl poured.

A week had passed since the Thursday night of card games that wore the twisted Jekyll-Hyde face of triumph and loss and I could feel words brewing within the sultry soup of my soul, trying to make their way out of me. That morning found the hang of an over-intoxicated body within a bunk that belonged to the party girl within me. Red wine residue slumped her over in defeat, for her attempt at softening the flutters of her feelings had backfired. Sometimes wine makes things worse. Eyeliner smeared down her face like burnt- out rubber. She wore a car wreck in her hair and was bound by her own attempts at casually keeping everybody near. Ben disappeared into work whilst Andrew slept in the bed below.

With a residual liberation of last night's wine, I abandoned my reservations and crawled down the wooden ladder of my bunk-bed. Then, stepping gently atop of the mattress that sprawled across my bedroom floor, I crawled into the slumbering arms of Andrew. As he wrapped me up in himself, I exhaled a breath that had long been kept within the confines of my chest. The morning sun bathed us in purity and as Andrew held me in a way that spoke to the tenderness in me, I realised that such an unspoken language could only come from the mouth of an angel.

"What is this?" Andy asked, from the soft of his casual caress. My hungry skin swallowed the tips of his fingers as if they were raindrops falling upon the Sahara desert, but my mouth kept no words in its empty well. Dry. Wet. We lay side-by-side in a confusion that was as pure as the morning dew that gathered outside of my room, but despite my bewilderment, I only knew that it did not feel wrong. Tucking away my unshared emotions, I attempted to claim ownership over forgotten parts of myself. I wanted to find the parts of me that were not merged with the sickly scent of coupled love. Words bubbled and brimmed beneath a golden layer of quiet sin.

It was the silence that was pure. I knew it as soon as the question had left Andrew's lips, but words had unavoidably boiled up into existence and left an indisputable truth that many more would follow in their footsteps. Words, they were the foot soldiers of emotions and they carried forth the unavoidable truth in the best way that they could. The alphabet marched through me. Drums rolled and the countdown to communication began. So, saluting its war cry, I decided to meet its communicative soldiers on the battle field that coming night. It was time to speak with Benjamin.

A strange happening occurs when one attempts to decipher intangible feelings and solidify them into words. It is akin to the first outline of a portrait; messy, unformed and embarrassing. Still, I tried to describe indescribability whilst Benjamin looked at me through the darkness of our bedroom. The half-whites of his eyes replicated the half plight of the outside moon. A pillow kept peace between us, just in case as I began to state my case and, in between the silence of my own convictions, I quickly became sick of hearing the words 'I don't know' falling out of my own mouth.

Know bumped into *Don't.*

Don't crashed into *I.*

I was held up at the railway station of Andrew's heart.

A train was that was splashed in colourful graffiti, boldly depicting 'a different kind of love,' was crossing and I was having trouble reaching Benjamin on the other side.

Still, I put into practice the vocalisation of a perpetuated honesty and attempted to explain to my lover of how a deep connection had awoken within me and was navigating its way towards our friend, Andy. Ben ushered words of acceptance from between the pillows that night, as if he already knew that I might say such a thing. As if that unexpected curve ball had not been unexpected at all, but was in fact predestined in its cosmic placement and Ben accepted my truth as if he perhaps knew something of the game's outcome. The half-whites of his eyes shone in acceptance of my truth and, without knowing it, Ben eagerly turned my guilty plea into a personal challenge. Our situation then became a private tea party for three.

Benjamin reached across the pillow and caressed the same arm that had been caressed that very morning by another kind of love. But Ben's touch felt different. His acceptance felt forward and his heroic words filled up our bunk-bed with the language of what he thought I wanted to hear.

"I love you even more now," he promised to a girl that asked nothing of him.

They kissed one another goodnight, both silently knowing that words were just empty things until they were put into practice.

House of Love

15th September 2014

I now know there to be such a thing as too much love. Pen did not find paper for some time and, without the details of day-to-day progressions, it was safe to say that the previous month had been long.

My days were amplified and exhausting, mirroring the wayward temperament of love that held me tightly with timeless hands. A month felt like a year. Fairy tales and disenchantment met for battle upon my forehead, leaving me red with the fever of daydreams. Everything seemed to be upside-down and inside-out and caught by the light of two opposite worlds. There was bitter and then there was sweet. There was soft and there was also raw. My heart expanded and simultaneously tore with each day that passed me by, until I was left swollen like a dead thing that had been filled with life.

I could do nothing but surrender to my growing pains; I let them push me to my limits in waves of joyful insanity, because it was not in my nature to have such a fickle heart and I needed to understand how so many rooms had become occupied inside of me. I had only ever before been loyal or contented with being alone, yet my heart found itself to be a full house that read *'No Vacancy.'* The weight of its occupants pressed down on me, showing me that there was such a thing as too much love.

The warehouse was full to the brim of Friday-nighters and I danced and twirled to reggae beats amongst them, daring to stay late into the night... because he was there. Holly and I got down with the funk, Leaf and I spoke with great animation above the frantic music about the times of our lives and I pretended not to have a care in the world. I had a circle of supportive sisters who accepted the intoxicated version of me, the girl who was drunk on loving things. And they loved me even more for my imperfections.

After one too many drinks had fallen into me, my mind predictably kicked into overdrive and I began to think of one too many things. As I stood before Andrew, the air of not caring fell from my skin, because the demands of an alcoholic life were undoubtedly getting the best of me. Despite my over intoxication, rum did lines across my spine and pressed any and all of my reservations out of me. I knew that I had unintentionally built something out of what could potentially be nothing but, because of that fine sliver of hope, my determined heart would never change its mind.

"I think that I... love you!" Escaped the captivity of my mouth, as if it were a wild animal that would never give up on the pursuit of real freedom. A tender version of Andy stood in front of me, his dancing slowed to a still. The music tried to drown out the imposition of my vulnerability but Andrew looked straight into me with a warmth that had settled within his eyes. It was as if my love were a fire and Andrew warmed himself beside it, without needing to give anything back. I was in full view, a flame that curled around him, a window that wouldn't quite close. Andrew stood calm, awash in my affections, and he allowed my declarations to wrap themselves around him without any interruption of his person, even though it had everything do with him. It was a moment that sang out to the warehouse that was full of Friday-nighters, screaming that my desperate proclamations were all in the name of love.

I had been brutally honest in sharing the mixing pot of my emotions with anyone who cared to know. The quiet wall-flower girl that once had rocks in her throat faded away and, for the first time in my life, I began to pioneer my emotions with elegance and grace.

My rum lips, however, begged to differ, as Andy just stood there looking back at me; I had become a fatal car accident that he was uncertain of how to respond to. We pulled away from the moment and fell into the warm rooms of silly dance and laughter as if they were the part of a house that would always be our saviour. Andrew was my favourite flavour of careless fun. He was the room in which I playfully washed the filth of the world from me. He was, in a way, the very foundation that I had built my affections upon.

Finally, we poured our sweaty bodies back into Andy's transit van and returned back to where we had begun. Standing beneath the orange lights of Clarke Street, I looked up at Andy's tall silhouette. The red bricks in the wall behind me promised to support the instability of my rum body. And In return, I promised that the bricks could rest their rugged ears against the back of my chest and tentatively listen to what came next. Andy looked into me with that same kind of curiosity that had made me so weak in the knees and, despite any logic or reason, I acknowledged him as someone that just did something to me.

The light from the street lamps cloaked our bodies in orange fire. Benjamin slept sleeplessly next to a cold draught that replaced my place in our bed. The red bricks stood between us all with their own curious motives of support whilst I was out, as always, way past midnight, just trying to find myself.

"One love," said Andy, from teeth that could stop a war, with a voice that could sooth loss and with eyes that spent time upon me, no matter the cost. The version of Andy that only I could see began to speak of love's singularity. My proclamations shivered with the cool before dawn as I slowly understood that our connection had nothing to do with me. There was not one specific love but just 'a' love. A love that was as general as that of the family dollar store, as common as people pretend to be and as plain as self-rising flour. No matter the tenderness that had folded into our moments like the petals of a flower that, whilst blossoming, had perfumed the air around me all night and day with the sweetest scent I had ever known. Instead, I was shown that Andrew and I share a love that was as simple as the kindness between strangers.

Andy made it clear that when he would ride away from Clarke Street in his home on wheels, I would not again cross his

282

mind, because he would forever be present with whomever, wherever he was. I shrank into the red brick of the walls, ensuring that they kept their promise to hold me upright. Confusion nestled into me as if it were a kitten and softened me in the same way. The street lights looked down at me with an orange sorrow in them that wouldn't allow me to hide, then proceeded to show the world what I was made of; heartbreak and dark rum.

My lesson in affection rained upon me with the finality of a judge's gavel. I had loved a man who would only show the reflections of my desires in his eyes, or so he had said, in that intoxicating way that he had. "I'm just a reflection of you!" Andrew claimed, like a beautiful goddamned sponge who just sat there, saturated, and absorbed all of my eccentricities up through the holes in his fabrics. A soft half-smile sat upon his lips, appreciation dipped into their curve as he casually observed my journey as though he were not a part of it.

I had climbed summits of my own independence outside of the co-dependency of my relationship. I had cast away all fear that accompanied my confusions. I had pushed bravery deep into my being and spoke of my truth to all that had kept a watchful eye on my developments, as well as my delusions: the concerned Leaf, the curious Holly, the ever-present ear of Christina. The winds of my attractions whirled on without warning of where they were going and threatened to destroy an entire block of houses. I swirled in tornados of growth and destruction, until my own house of affection began to crumble. And maybe I was better off for it, but the moment would keep that secret pressed close to it, until I was ready to truly hear such a thing.

There was no disputing the fact that I had the heart of another. Benjamin slept behind the inquisitive red bricks that were supporting me and tossed in a sleepless slumber. Although he would not say as much, Ben was secretly troubled by his desire of acceptance, though he refused to forsake our love, just for an affection that may be dismissed. 'I will stay,' Ben had said, in the weeks prior to my streetlamp confessionals, when I had suggested that we each take time out and explore our own hearts. 'I won't leave you.' He was resolute and determined.

To Benjamin, my heart was a riddle that he needed to figure out, though it didn't make it any easier when I stumbled into our room that morning with a puzzled heartache drawn across my face. I was scented with rum and fun and proclamations that had soured into embarrassment. It was only then, when I was sick of myself, that I saw Benjamin's true mourning. His love had long left him and it was empty without her by his side. A version of me remembered who she was. She used to stroke his hair and pull the better sides of him out into existence.

Each day that I had found a new way of entertaining myself without his company, Ben had slipped into a silent darkness. Each night that I was not in our bed, he had tossed and turned, exhausting his own harmony. Ben had been haunted by dreamless dreams whilst my indecisive reality became his worst nightmare. I saw his sadness almost too late as the sun threatened to rise without us. Benjamin's bags were packed. His eyes looked as ragged and trodden as my heart and he wore a false smile upon his face as he greeted me at our bedroom door.

Ben looked into the selfish eyes of the one whom he had held so very dear and searched my face for answers. The house on Clarke Street was the only safe place that we knew; Ben had nowhere else to go, but the full belly of his pack revealed that destination didn't matter. In his final act of acceptance, Ben showed that me that he couldn't be who he thought I wanted him to be. I attempted to respond, to assure him that I had no expectations towards him. However, I could only feel foggy and unclear at the picture of his imminent departure. In that moment, I knew only one certainty; when Ben and I had laid in the dark of our room a month prior, as I offered up my first rough draft of the truth, Benjamin's pillow talk of acceptance had been cloaked with white lies. His words were empty promises that, when filled with existence, had somehow changed in their meaning; mot intentional not lies, just not true-seeing. A part of me had known it all along. My speculations were confirmed in the blue light of dawn, when Ben finally dismissed the idea of who he thought he needed to be in order to keep me. Ben and I were in a war that had cost Ben precious parts of himself. He was once a loud and invasive man, but those parts of him had died quietly.

"So stay," I said to the ragged of Ben's eyes, to the war that had been declared upon his unconditional love. Looking at his bags, I wobbled on my own axis, uncertain of how much I truly cared. None of my feelings felt real any longer, but beneath that doorway, Ben and I were a sight that was made up of sad things; a coyote that had been pushed out of his nest... a hummingbird with damaged wings.

"Let's both just get some sleep," I suggested to a willing body that allowed me to lead it up the steep stairs into our bunk-bed retreat. Ben and I lay side-by-side as two bodies that were not quite defeated, but undoubtedly depleted in their emotional energies. Sleep and food and all other basic human necessities of functionality had eluded us both for weeks. We were weak, inflicted with the intoxications of too much wine and too much rum. We were covered from head to toe with too much ugly fun. Both of us had overdosed on the strange beauty of life but, because we walked had separately, we were unaware of the other's plight. We could not understand each other's perplexities. There was a to-ing and fro-ing tug-of-war that begged for us to love and not leave, because time was so very short.

It had come to a head. I left Ben asleep in our bed as Andy and I spoke upon the living room floor. We knew one another's secrets. We knew one another in ways that made no sense, because by the time that dawn had found us, our friendship had turned into a kind of torture. I had wires that came out of me and forced themselves into Andrew. Benjamin had wires fused into the one single love of me, and Andy... well, he was wired everywhere. To any love that could be shared. To me and to his brother, Ben, whom he loved in his own way. Even to my sister Reeta, where her and I had to overcome the reflection of similarities that had almost defeated us.

Andy was wired to everybody and to no one in particular. In some distant land, he kept a queen of his hearts but, beneath the roof of Clarke Street, we all merged together in too much 'one love'. The living room cushions listened to our indifferences with red velvet ears that would not judge. The deep cracks in the walls began to retreat as they crumbled, and Andrew spoke in dark tones to me. The winds had changed, causing an excavation of blues-rooted music and creativity to surface. Blue-smudged fingerprints fiddled with cords and attempted to rewire us both. It was as it had to be.

"Sorry, or thank you," Andrew spoke, with unfailing appreciation. "You choose."

My choice.

I had not deluded been in what the outcome could be. My romantic illusions didn't see Andy and I riding off into the sunset together, though they had assumed that Andrew could at least care for me. However, as our house broke down, it was apparent that our hearts were not as aligned as I had thought them to be and I wasn't surprised by his coldness. But when Andrew left, as Ben slept, and rouge pillows wept, I also could not help but to cry because, to me, Andy represented the vitality in life. He pulsed with vibrancy when I looked into the blue of his eyes and I had become addicted to that version of him; a version that could have been close or far from the truth of who he really was, though my eyes only saw him beneath 'one light.'

So it was written, that Andy was but a reflection of me... apparently. Even though I could see a shard of the truth in the words that he spoke, I also knew that I was not that moved by my own reflection. I had seen Andy in ways that had simply stopped my world, but we were bound by multiple reasons that encouraged a discontinuation of our growth. That rational had many fingers and many toes and I counted upon them the ways in which I felt that Andrew would never care to understand the depths of my soul.

So, I did all I could by letting that love go and, in its

absence, I received a ticket of understanding from the parking permits of reality. That ticket of enlightenment was spat out at me and it read: *'There are many different types of love in this world, baby girl. Not simply the safe love of one boy and one girl.'*

I sat alone in my living room like a deer that had headlights for eyes. Monogamy and polygamy were recipes with many ingredients that did not make sense to me. They were causing me to go blind in a kitchen that was full of razor sharp knives. The exclusion of all others seemed to be a joke that we all unconsciously played, because, whether or not we were aware, I knew that each one of us was falling in love with strangers every single day. Love was not simply a black-and-white picture that was printed on the paper of forever, but more so, it was a teacher of colour that would even go as far as to burn the paper it had been written upon, drinking thirstily from its ashes.

I crawled back into bed that morning, knowing that things had spun out of control. I had officially overdosed in the exploration of other loves and the fascination of twin souls. Proclamations and explorations ran deep in-between the walls of Clarke Street and, as I lay on the bunk-bed watching my prince finally find sleep, I knew that I needed to nurture him. I understood that my selfish whims needed to be completely reeled in because they had damn near broke him.

However, love filled up every single corner of every single room and became an entire house that tried to advise me otherwise. It tried to say that there was no such thing as too much love. The house even whispered to me of how love was our only true purpose in life, and went on to tell me that I needed to understand its diverse shades and swim naked within its seas. The House of Love assured me that it was up to me to decide.

Thank you... or... I'm sorry. You say.

My choice... I choose.

Ben's Birthday: Chapter 1

29th September 2014

At some point or another, when faced with a forked road or some blunder, we all learn to accept a deeper responsibility in our lives. So, with that time upon me, I began to swim deeper and deeper within those responsibilities with a learned release of control.

Deeper and deeper my loved ones and I walked into the mouth of the forest, with one foot in front of the other and, together we anticipated forked roads and emotional blunders. The diverse feet of my housemates firmly pressed against loose soil with an assortment of shoes that reflected their personalities; open toes, heavy-handed boots, and bare unashamed feet. Downward we descended through the rabbit hole, in an honouring of the family that it appeared we had grown to be. The day promised to bring joy, so we met it in the middle of its offering and began coating the bush with our laughter.

It was my lover's birthday. Twenty-six years old. Twenty-six years young. I had sent word to all of our companions, requesting that they join us in a woodland celebration. Each of us understood that life was a thing to be celebrated, thus the family gathered in an honouring of our co-creation. The sun stretched its fingers out hungrily through the tops of trees, as if it were in want of skin-to-skin contact, as if its firesome fingers wanted to fondle breathing, living things and chose us as its subjects. As we all nestled into the soft lean of the grass, an abundance of food and wine spilled out across our picnic blanket. The shoulders of the pine trees shaded our plentiful spoils, whilst together we laughed over nothing and everything, constructing camp within the meadows of an ancient light.

Then, when a moment of perfect peace had settled upon all of those who dwelt within that private forest, I arose and began to walk amongst each body that sat or lay casually upon the grass, just breathing. Stepping over roots and stones, I knelt down beside my adopted kin and gently, I took each person's hand within my own. One by one, the soft plains of ivory palms presented themselves under the cultivation of my curious unfolding. White-washed acceptance pushed itself open without neglecting the reason of how we had each chosen to celebrate Benjamin's day of birth. Upon each palm I consciously placed a mushroom capsule within its quiet yearnings. It was a wordless offering, enclosed within a silent blessing. Skin on skin. Hand in hand. We swallowed down that which Mother Earth had offered us with a temperament of absolute respect. Breathing deeply into the moment, I prepared myself for takeoff.

The morning had awoken me with lazy eyes after the previous night had barely shifted into day. Ben's coworker, Madeline, and I had danced the night away at a nameless establishment where in which Madeline had worn the robes of self-abandon and become a familiar friend to me. And Andy, well he happened to be there too. It was the first that I had seen of him in what felt like a lifetime, but the instructions of our inability to love one another lined the dancing walls without a timeline. Rules numbered one to one-hundred sat stickily against the bricks of the smoking area. Pink bubble-gum peeked out through the cracks as Andy and I lingered outside, trying not to stick to each other. We spoke easily with one another, pretending not to be governed by rules and their instructions. Vague dialogues dripped from our mouths as we crouched down outside the bar's red brick backdrop, equipped with a cigarette that wouldn't quite stay lit and the falsity of a true cool. Too forward had I formerly fumbled, so I promised to hold my reservations close to me. It was a promise that I intended to keep, born of a night that had taught me what it was like to feel the cold draught of an unrequited love.

So we were casual. I held a damp cigarette that wouldn't quite hold light, whilst Andy and I laughed over things that were humorous to us. We easily steered clear of any deeper seas because laughter and comedy equated to safety and was a place in which the two of us fell into with ease. When Madeline lay down beside Andy in slumber that evening, beneath the bunk of *my* bed, nestled into the safety of *my* nest, I begged that my heart finally be still. For we were all friends in this jungle and the green venom of jealousy had not been a stranger to me. Unspecific love had, in its own healing ways, poisoned me. I looked upon Benjamin, who slept beautifully beside me with a peace that was born from the return of his queen, no matter how half her heart was, no matter that his heart had been poisoned too. As dawn rounded the corner, I laid in my bed quietly and practiced pushing peace into my quaking stability until the room began to fill with the light of day and triumph placed a half-smile upon my lips. For the first time in almost two months, I had managed to stay away from my crazed obsession with Andrew and there had even been time enough to catch a few winks before rolling out of bed into Benjamin's birthday celebration.

As I sat in an enchanted meadow of dreams with a wash of warm air surrounding me, I remembered that triumph. Monkey birds laughed wildly into the tall, silken gum trees. A mushroom capsule was slowly dissolving inside of me and I was very aware of the fact that soon I was to become even more so aware of the totality of my wins and losses. I knew that, as well as my angels, my demons would also be brought towards the light. My unbalances told me that they would hide themselves from reality no longer and all darkness would be brought into the purity of day. So I encouraged that inevitability and humbly, I asked for clarity within that beautiful mess of my mind. Because, as always, I sought clarity within my life; I wanted to clean the glass of my soul in order to see properly the reflections of those who sat sprawled out upon the forest floor with me. *Show me the light!* I whispered into the warm breeze of spring that was bursting at the seams with the promise of a new beginning. *Show me the light.*

Before long, undistinguished feelings began crawling like a worker up the ladder of my spine. In that imminent feeling of departure, I became painfully aware of every single soul that was sitting with me in that field and I could not help but to tune in to their frequencies. My empathy was, as always, getting the best of me. I felt incredibly drawn to each person, as if a portal was running from my body into theirs. Magnets were in full force, pulling and drawing me to other people's energies. It was as if a wave were just about to break upon us all.

I saw Leaf: The orange sunset fell into the autumnal waves of her hair and it shone vibrantly as ever. Her dragon tattoo began to crawl from the freckled crème of her arm up into the sunset of her hair. Together the sun and ink swirled into one another in a dance of light and power. Drawing in the will to dance around her, Leaf's laugh seeped into my funny bones and rattled away my serious tones until every bone of mine contained humour.

My eyes caught sight of Benjamin: He lay his body loosely upon the ground with a cloud of rituals surrounding him. Benjamin pulsed in his own messages of truth, whilst the didgeridoo travelled all the way up into the sky, carrying his questions of how and why. Whilst green grass lay like a lover beside the thick curl of his dark hair, Ben practiced a calm that I had rarely seen him try on. From between those blades of green, I could feel his will for me. It pulled at me with portal hands that placed themselves upon my waist and attempted to gather me into his body. Ben's blue eyes were wild with desire for the totality of our experience, because it was his day of birth, and on that day he was the prince of meadowed things.

Andrew and Reeta sat on the grass opposite one another and threw private alliances up into the ether. Green envy and bruised care brewed around me simultaneously, as magnetic fingertips pressed themselves upon my shoulder blades and beckoned me to interfere with their intimacy. Deep down, I knew that my disharmony with their connection could only belong to weakness. That allowance of push-and-pull that I had subjected myself to whilst in our weird love-squared-triangle spell was not strength, and if I could be governed by that, then surely I could find guidance in greater things. So, I removed myself from all that was inadvertently pulling upon the strings of my heart and instead, attempted to tether ties that had left me feeling frayed inside, because I wanted to walk back to the start. Back to a version that resembled me before my heart had become totally saturated in the distraction of others. I wanted that person back... *I think.*

I began walking along dusty trails that barely showed themselves, with feet that were well-acquainted to the path less travelled. Those trails led to nowhere in particular, but they kept me away from the acknowledgement of anyone else's eyes, because I just needed a moment to go inside of myself. The river found me before I could even begin to seek out its movements. The curve of her brown spine, offering me a cubby hole beneath the vines of a eucalyptus tree. The smooth silks of silvered bark began to quieten me, as I took the river up on her offer and perched within my new residency. Earthen hands held me upright as my body began to feel nervous and faint, as though it may take flight at any moment. Despite my rising panic, the eucalyptus promised to keep me grounded and would never laugh at my self-induced sickness. Exhaling with peace, I knew that only the earth was watching me.

I saw Mother Earth unfold before me and although she needed nothing from the likes of me, she gave everything back in return. And that calmed the likes of me. I wondered where that peace had been all this time. Had it crawled out from beneath a mat of dead leaves so that it could come and soothe me during my time of need? I retreated in the knowledge that it had little to do with me, because Mother Earth was always there, even when I was not present with her.

When I am boxed off in my world of paperwork and entertainment and I do not know the time for lack of the sun, when my breathing is restricted to recycled ventilations, she is always there. So I decided to join Mother Earth because she needed me not. Because there were no invisible fingers upon my shoulders pressing down from her desires. Because her intentions were of the purest form and because Mother Nature could teach me all that I needed to know about strength and growth. I inhaled and then exhaled, until she became the mother in my womb, placing calming hands upon the quakes of my breath and allowing one moment to sweep easily into the next without anxiety or obligation. Time slowed down and I could feel roots growing beneath the cross of my legs. I heard my skin toughen into the brittle of bark that stood before me with whispers of cool waters rushing through us both. My branches, yawning themselves towards the sun, as if they had awoken from an ancient dream. Ancient things etched themselves into me. I was still. I breathed.

I have spent my whole life in manic hunger. After having sought out a lifetime full of wild and wondrous things, in consequence, I have jumped from one plot of land to the next and have never felt settled. I have barely taken rest and perpetually attempted to escape the outdated versions of myself by placing my shortcomings upon an island and leaving them there as if they were never a part of me. The quiet sadness. The inadequacy that lived in the hunch of my shoulders for too many year to count upon my fingers. I would often taste the dirt for but for a moment, place some stones in my pockets for proof of my existence, and then move on in my search to be bolder. As I perched beneath the silvered linings of a wise old tree, understanding how stillness had always eluded me, I saw that there were unfulfilled chasms in my dreams.

The little feet of a child that simply would not stop moving made phantom footprints beside me. *'Stop running April!'* called the memory of a mother's voice to the bleeding scrape of the child's knees. *'Skipping still counts as running!'*

I felt that familiar pull once more. Those portals that pushed through the serenity of my own personal space. That anxiety that bubbled up to the surface and tormented my quietude.

'What are you doing out here alone?' Fear pried with a forked tongue.

'There are those who would worry, those in need of your presence... there are those who do not understand...those who want....'

Quieting the unrest of my thought patterns, I began to sing to my Fear a lullaby. I felt my roots seeking further depth beneath me, like little fingers of exploration that fondled through the dirt. Through the worms. Through the ancient civilisations. Mingled mounds of miracles danced below me, as the breeze blew through the turn of fallen leaves. The river flowed, undeterred, and the afternoon light softened down as if it may, at any moment, disappear. All hard angles and straight lines began to fade into the hypocrisy of my own hatred. Something inside of me was being rearranged. The ants crawled upon my skin and I did not flinch under the tickle of their legs, nor the sting of their pincers, because I looked up at the majestic gumtree's trees and I wanted to be like them.

'Stillness is boring!' moaned the little girl with scraped knees who hopped around beside me. Though I no longer paid her any heed and, before long, she faded away into the past where she belonged.

The life of a tree began revealing itself unto me. He was the King of the natural throne and groaned as ancient winds rustled through the green of his hair. The sunlight played tic-tac-toe upon his bark whilst the tree neighbours gathered themselves in a flock of three across the river and, speaking in riddles to one another, laughed over a private joke that none of them would ever recall. But, as the tree's prepared themselves for the light of the moon, I knew that it was not quite time for me to leave. There was still something that I had to remember.

The ants crawled further upon my undeterred skin. Dragonflies perched like giants upon the brittle tree bark, full of

294

rainbow landings. Fragile paper wings opened up and with it, I began to understand their transparent stories.

Stillness did not bear the dull repetition that I had kept in my childish expectations. I could finally see that to be still, one had to be strong. I watched the still of the bark offer refuge to the tickle of ants and those buttered-up flies that had dragons for wings until I understood a little more of roots and the strength of grounding. Finally, I arose from the embankment, free with my small discovery.

The journey was in full force. I bounced and skipped across the velvet grass with emotional cords that had been cut. I was barefoot in the forest and my movements were carried forth by the sounds of my tribe. I heard them before I saw them. They guided me back to them with lupine tones. There was howling and yelling that ran through my eardrums and escaped into the ether. Into him. Into her. Into the feeling that something large was orbiting my existence and hanging out on the grassy knolls of our unique souls, telling us all that it was time to play.

After sloppily fishing the abyss of Andy's reggae bag, I grabbed his camera from its depths with unsteady fingers. Its string hung carelessly from me and mimicked the looseness of my limbs, and I crept like a photographic spy into the bubbles of personal harmony that encircled my tribe.

Luca was like a cat in the grass. He parted the blades with the feline of his eyes and fished his own memories for a recent dream to cast upon his paper. Luca worked in spells of pencils and blank canvases, endeavouring to fill them with the magic of imagination. A lead-pencilled samurai protruded from his paper in a yoga tree pose and, as I followed the instructions of its paper-motions, I became a samurai of life, with a sword-like camera that hovered above a French sketching face. Then, releasing all of my body weight, I flopped down upon Luca in laughter. Together, we rolled around in fits of laughter because of those extroverted things that we called our bodies. Our floppy, unattached limbs were careless bundles of fun but before long, Luca and I quietened and realigned with one another. As the soft sun shone over us like a golden blanket, Luca and I touched base upon all the happenings in our minds, because it helped to keep the psychedelic swallowings at bay.

I looked into the feline of Luca's eyes as he spoke in soft rhythms and quietly I honoured the role that Luca had played in my life. I thought of the home that I had found just because, whilst wandering beneath a once-upon-a-time moonlit pathway, he had made a "may I draw you?' introduction. Luca had been a stepping stone towards the future and a door that had opened up to my new home. Salty gratitude washed silently over me. With a fumbling camera in my hands, those waves pushed me back up onto my feet and pressed me to move on. Looking into the black box of the camera, the black of my irises began to forge an alliance with its circular lens, and heard something whisper to me, *the world through my eyes.*

Luca and Reeta conversed beside a swinging pendulum. Their dark figures, silhouetted in the sunshine whilst time left us all to our own devices. Obligations slipped away on the brown current of the river. And as the sunlight bid us bon voyage, the pendulum swung in circles upon a French finger, showing us that our cyclical lives were but a mirage. And Luca, he was a black cat of jazz.

I found Ben laying upon the grass, speaking in rhythms and waves to himself. And I wondered if his mouth really moved, or if I could hear him in his silence. *Silence. Silence. When was the last time words had escaped my mouth?* I had been watching, quiet in the observation of my life for a timeless procession of moments. For hours, I had been busy writing stories in my head. Ben glistened beneath the sun, as if the light were seeping out from inside of him. His skin and bones, glowing with a journey of their own making. It truly was a blessed day to be born.

One moment merged into the next, until Ben's body flexed, crouched and screamed out into the skies. Passion pulsed in the caverns of his eyes, whilst Benjamin dared the gods to wake from their slumber. He measured up his own fleshy mortality against all that existed outside of it. His veins, pulsing purple upon the thick of his neck, as all troubles left his mouth and pushed their way out into the skies around us. Ben screamed in his search of clarity, until we were all screaming upon a verge of soft grass. Eviction... sounded like murder.

Andrew spoke some secret language between the twins of his soul and Mother Earth. The Geminis lived a gibberish life of philosophy and speak-easy mysticisms inside of him and only he would ever understand their balance. Andrew was experiencing a completely unrehearsed release, holding nothing back from the audience of us. Father Sky listened on the back of the ground, but just as a father does, did not say a word. Andrew's long limbs reached towards the heavens, as if they were possessed, as if unknown things pulsed through him. And I watched him as though he were a documentary.

Reeta frolicked through the woods with a disregard of weighted things, singing out in acknowledgment of the guidance that she too had found. Warm appreciation slept in the dark of her eyes and she knew, without a doubt, that as she pranced and sang, that she was truly alive. Reeta's skirt drifted like a translucent purple snake with wings. She was afloat, gliding over old inhibitions whilst running through the fields with bare, brown feet. Reeta left a trail of soft, lilac dreams in her wake.

Leaf looked down towards her cigarette in disgust and affirmed that she would never again smoke. Her freckles told me that they came from stardust. Con was curious as to which perfume was Kate's favourite scent in all of the world. Scents formed memories in my thoughts. Kate had seemingly materialised from nowhere, though I was sure that I had led her there, into that world of tripping tribes where Nowhere was Everywhere and everything was full of laughter.

Christina encircled us all. We were children of the tripping tribe and she, a mother to us all. Back and forth she roamed, wearing a coat of woollen mysticisms. Quiet mantras fell from the pulp of her lips and planted the promise of growth. Christina was like a ship that sailed our silly harbours, blessing our adventures. With dainty fingers, she touched the trees with the same hands that had wiped away my broken-hearted tears. Her feet were bare with sacredness and, quietly she watched the avatar of our bodies play. As I approached her wanderings, Christina and I fell into some kind of galactic decoding, spaced-out tribal dance. The forest watched us in amusement. We did not speak but, inhaling her, I hugged the wool of her coat and felt her nimble body breathing beneath it. Christina smelt like forest, pure love and weed.

As the sun finally began to set in our timeless world, Christina, Leaf, Reeta, Ben and I accidentally met down by the river to congregate in ceremony.

"Three minutes and your intentions are strongest!" Leaf's proclamations made promises into the setting sun, whilst we chased the last remaining minutes down. The changa bowl was lit and passed from grateful hands unto receptive lips. After inhalation, Leaf and Benjamin sprawled out upon the ground in order to set their life intentions. We all became lost in the midst of our own creations. Leaf and Ben looked up towards the top of the trees and explored their worlds silently… until melodies found themselves in the mouths of three. Christina, Reeta and I began to layer the quiet breeze with a gentle song. I lay upon the notes of low, whilst Christina and Reeta soared upon the wings of high. I wobbled in a deepness and they sung like angels who would maintain the purity in all of us. Chants that we did not yet know began to find their way into our mouths with a delicate rawness.

After the singing had commenced, Lilac-skirted dreams began to chant:

"Our own sacred ceremony... Our own sacred ceremony!" We each joined the glimmer of Reeta's eyes and verbally unified.

"Our own sacred ceremony. Our own sacred ceremony!" We began sporadically, feverishly touching one another and chanting.

"Me, me, me, me!" Leaf's tummy; *me*. Christina's chest; *me*. Ben's eyes; *me*. Our own sacred ceremony. *Me, me, me, me.*

For all was me, and me was all, and all had simply connected, shifted a couple of perspectives to the right, ran up that flight of stairs onto the roof, cartwheeled around the chimney top and fearlessly taken flight from atop the roof with lilac-skirted wings... until it was free-falling down onto the ground. Landing exactly where it had begun.

Nothing had changed.... yet everything had happened.

Ben's Birthday: Chapter 2

27th September 2014

The setting sun merged finally merged into the shadows that it once cast and darkness began to swallow us. With our ceremonies complete, we were about fifteen bodies deep in the woods. Fifteen figures spiralled out across the grass in a sidewinding strangeness that was ungoverned by the confines of time. The chill of the night soon began to call out our names and sought to attach its whisper to the warmth of our skins.

The tribe and I were quite a hike from civilisation and I knew that we must begin to gather the troops and return home before the darkness surrounded us. So, an organised version of myself left behind the fanciful tripper in me and emerged to find a way out of our comfortability. It was time to leave the jungle of twins and sacred things and pack away the spoils of cheese and wine that we had yet to eat or drink.

Holly and I led the way with Doc Martin boots, each stomping up the hill like two warrior princesses that were in search of the light. Although shadows cast themselves upon us, I could feel the light of Holly's purity mixing in with the cool air around me and we supported one another with our companionship, until the forest finally fell behind us.

Upon the tarmac, I saw a figure strolling towards us. He had the gangly vines of a willow for arms, and he stumbled towards us as though he had just awoken from a distant slumber. Through the haze of twilight, I soon determined the figure to be Andy, but he felt like a stranger to me. When I approached to pass to Andrew his reggae camera possessions, I understood that perhaps Andy would always be a distant and undistinguished figurine. Perhaps I would never really know him or the shadows that cast themselves upon the two sides of his face, but that potential fit in well with all of the perfection that was emanating from me.

"Chapter two... Chapter two... Back to the house!" Leaf laughed her instructions into the ears of those who were emerging from the woods. We were all forest creatures with grass still stuck in our hair and we stumbled out upon a world that had kept on spinning without us in it, all understanding that we were but halfway through our journey. *Chapter two... Chapter two...* The page had been turned.

Back on Clarke Street, a fire burned within the confines of a tin barrel whilst rust spots poured lava out from their jagged holes. The ground never asked any payment for holding us up. Nature protected our tribe from the outside world with big, leafy shoulders that pressed up against one another, blocking out the neighbourhood. Dark green rustles shook without words. The sun had fallen down, but the music was lifting us up. Dance took its first creaky steps into life as, between the hallways, lovers played a game of cat-and-mouse. Stolen looks were never to be returned. Our pupils dilated further into the abyss, because blessed was the hour of laughter and of sweetly-scented fragile flowers. And we each endeavoured to go full-steam into the evening. Bushy hands of protection delicately held the pearls of night jasmine, scenting the cool night air with a taste of holy things. Glimmering stars were a-pocket with perfume whilst the jasmine's white petals flowered in the darkness and replicated the ivory of the moon.

Presence was graced with presence. Presents were shared with my lover on his day of birth. Ben swanned from group to group, pushing his feathers out towards the black sky. He and I spoke into the firelight and felt that there had been blessings placed upon us all. The constellations formed themselves above our heads like crowns and, as I stared into the rusted fire pit, my quietude finally began dissolving. I needed to sing. I wanted to burst out in beauty. I needed to know that my external frequency was in harmony with the way that I felt inside. Noises began bubbling up in my throat and as the fire was stoked, I quietly brewed.

I lay upon Reeta's bed. Back-to-front. Upside-down. Andy to the left of me. Reeta to the right. They; the right way up. Me; the front way back. My head rested at the foot of the bed as the three of us lounged in the same three-dimensional triangle of love that we had often found ourselves in. We were wordless and pure because there was no sin within the golden dust of silence. Andy and Reeta wore the same glasses of mad mathematicians. We passed the blunt back and forth between fingertips that each of us had adored to our detriment and although we were similar, each print was still unique. We pressed into one another's skin with shades of browns, lilacs and creams. The air was thick with smoke and each of us tried not to damn the vision of our private and separate dreams. Andrew, Reeta and I draped our reckless limbs across one another with a casual, barely touching, yet we felt everything.

I watched curiously as spectators and participators entered Reeta's room, just to get a better view of us. They walked in on their heads. I was a bird in a cageless cage. An upside-down tiger that had postulations for paws. The ceilings grew tall as I took rest on a bed that swallowed most of the floor. Only a small patch of green carpet had been spared. The visitors' eyes found the upside-down alcoves of my own and, as I looked into them, I wondered where all of those people had come from, where they had really come from and where they would go from there. I wondered silently if the rendition of their realities had been as changed as mine.

I was wordless, smoking blunts that were passed by adored fingertips and my hair lay like spaghetti sunshine upon the one patch of carpet that was spared. The shave of Reeta's head brushed the paint beneath the windowsill. It was a chalky sound and as I listened to it surround the quiet spaces in the room, that sound sent shivers through my body. Andrews's hair rested on the thick liquorice of his spectacles in fat, happy curls. Whilst Reeta's shaved hair felt like sex.

To my left, the eyelids of Andy began to grow weighted. There was no air in our cageless fish tank and sleep was closing in on the white curve of an eye that had kept two brown-skinned sisters in their vision. Andrew was tired. The prospect of work cloaked his practicality but, as he drifted in and out of dreams, Andy was disturbed by a house that was fevered with vitality and rebirth. The first pangs of responsibility for the following morning emerged. *Work; it was a terrible idea.* However, I left my upside-down ponderings behind me and led the vines of Andrew's arms into the quietude of my bedroom.

Up the wooden ladder we climbed and I laid the tired of Andy's eyes to rest with the nurturings of a mother. I watched his sleeping skin like a specimen from some enchanted tale. Andrew was the museum, I was the human and we would always be from different worlds.

Cam was yet another spectator of the night; he poked his head up through the ladder, with voyeuristic eyes that were full of wonder in what he might see. The rouge of my blanket scattered itself in an array of stories, though there was no evidence of foul play. Cam creaked up the steps to join Andy and I in our elongation and spoke stories of self in order to rock us to sleep.

Two more hungry eyes rose up past my ladder, falling onto the horizon of my bed like dual suns whose only duty was to encourage the light of a new day. Those eyes belonged to Madeline. Madeline pulsed with infatuation for the recently-entered Cam. An awoken spirituality swirled around on the milk of her skin, making her a three-dimensional creature that didn't quite belong to this ether. Madeline was full of excitement and nestled herself in beside Cam like the cat that had caught the mouse as well as the cream. Capsules pulsed through us all. Madeline felt love and she proceeded to pin-point it onto Cam. I felt love and had pin-pointed it onto Andy. Rusted heart valves were creaking, but both men had been unmoved by our 'once-in-a-lifetime opportunities.' Madeline reflected my once-forward affections and, as I rested my head against the chalk of the wall, I knew that she could not hear Cam's half-hearted dissolution. Madeline's ears were swollen with the deafness of longing and as I glimpsed myself inside of her large, green eyes, I saw what infatuation could do to us... *brain damage*.

Benjamin's head was the third one to submerge itself into our underwater bunkbed and he looked inquisitively as the four of us laid together like children in an orphanage. We had no parents. No guidance. And we formulated questionable sibling alliances. We were like fishes swimming in a shapeless bowl of protection. Our aquatic lips, chain-smoking and chatting over whatever was relevant in that moment. Benjamin joined us all with blue curiosity.

Lastly, with queries as to our placement etched upon her brown brow, Reeta floated up the wooden steps and trailed over us all with her lilac wings. Her feet, barely sinking into the mattress as she walked between our sardine-like bodies. Gravity had long left the room. Without requiring an invitation, Reeta dropped like dew into the pool of our beings and became the last member to join our orphanage party. One bunk-bed swelled with six deep bodies.

The hour was late, but fate decided to magnify and reveal the feelings that had been pressing up against my perceptions like an insistent tongue. A circus show of precariously-placed bodies all commemorated the days and weeks that had passed them by. Together, we were a freight train of love-triangles that had been lost in a fast-moving square carriage and we lay in fractions upon my bed. Our connection was a literary type of mathematics... that was captured in still-life art.

Andy laid sleepily to the right of me. Benjamin was wide-eyed to the left of me. Reeta had spread her lilac wings and laid flat-out on top of me. Cam and Madeline were nestled to the left of Benjamin, rolling around like children that were in search of sweet things.

For a moment in time, we were a tribe. We were all meshed up into one living, breathing organism upon the flat of a bunk-bed that *I* would lay upon at night and dream. We began to sing. The brewing began stewing into melodious escapisms. I was lucid in my love for one-and-all, because we laid on a bed where *my* dreams were made at night and I understood my tribe to be a complicated dream that had finally come out into the real world to play.

As I stared past Reeta's shaved head, I realised, embarrassedly, that I had seen each one of those bags of flesh and bones that I had grown to love, glimpsed as my enemy. I had seen Ben as a pirate, holding captive my love and my time whilst forcing codependency down the throat of she who would not swallow it. The pirate bound her hands. He wore an eye patch and had a silver sword to match. *'No one dare enter these harbours!'* Ben snarled, pointing his silver sword in between my ribcage as well as my legs. It was not like him at all… because that pirate-like ideology was all my own making. I had held myself prisoner. Benjamin would love me no matter what currents I swam within, no matter what oceans I dove into head-first. He would love me despite the complications and riddles that had become me. Ben was there with me, as I lay entangled between two other bodies and he just laughed and beatboxed alongside of us, letting me know that it was all ok. The pirate walked the plank.

Reeta lay atop of me. Breast to breast. Laugh box to laugh box because, she was my direct reflection and we mirrored one another's joy. Reeta and I had the same caramel complexions and a similar laugh that was born of wild abandon. Each of us were made up of poetry and song. Reeta had even dyed the shave of her hair blonde like mine, and at the time I almost died, because she had been an intruder in a place that I still didn't understand. At times, her presence had only made my complications worse because Reeta had frolicked with Andy in front of my face, more available and intimate than I could ever be. During one of our nights of Clarke Street Poetry, Reeta had read aloud a sad and beautiful poem about an aloof boy, after which, her and Andy then disappeared into the darkness together. The white transit van began to haunt me and, alone in the privacy of my heart, I had seethed. Though how hard I had tried not to, because I knew that I had not a right in the world to feel such greed.

Reeta was my sister. A sister who had eventually allowed me to see how much they all loved me, in return of my affection. I was just another version of Reeta. I became Ben, Ben became me, and Andy... well, he just lay there casually to the right of me, not quite asleep. And although a part of Andy was a stranger, he was also more connected to us than perhaps any of us would ever understand. He was the man who spray painted the city, the artist that my heart had always longed for. He drew me, he saw me and he loved me without particularity. Andrew wore many faces, but his true identity would always be kept a secret by the Geminis that lived inside of him. He was a dreamless dream, a cold-blooded lizard that warmed itself by our blood. A clear, white stream that carved its way through land and rock just to rejoin the source of the sea. Andy had been the catalyst just by simply being, and I revelled in the moment of loving those three souls all at once without anger or guilt. Together, we sang and we pulsed shamelessly.

I needed to abandon all of Jealousy's green vines that had wound themselves around my hands and bound me to distress. I wanted to undress my delusions until there was only nudity left behind. It was imperative that I burn down the house of my misconception because, even though I was having trouble finding anywhere else to live, my house of love had been condemned for weeks. It was making me weak. I wanted to leave it all behind. I sang, 'show me the light.'

Aiichiro appeared atop of our bodies, his cheerful head, bopping in with the slick of his sunrise skin. As he hovered above

Reeta's shoulder, looking into me with black camera lenses for eyes, Aiichiro became a strange photograph that was coloured in the inks of music. Aiichiro beat into the box. Offbeat music bubbled up inside of us all, until we let it escape in a stampede of peculiar vibrations. "Show me the light."

Other people sang other things. Our voices, squirming and wriggling in between the spaces of silence, until there were none left. Unapologetic limbs began and ended, undistinguished in their positions, but in that moment, it was ok not to have an identity.

I did not know whose hand I was holding. I could not distinguish between whose toe tickled mine and whose beat bumped into my box. It mattered not, because my tribe and I had broken through the madness together and instead, merged into some kind of harmonised cuddle-puddle of puzzled pieces that fit together with absolute perfection in order to finally made up the parts of our missing fractions. We were a literary kind of mathematics.

As dawn broke in unison with my misconceptions, I knew that there was no other place in the world that I would rather be… than within those mirrors that hummed and sang and held my hands offbeat, truly looking back into me.

Mirrors were to the left. Mirrors were to the right. Mirrors that were atop and back-to-front had me surrounded, singing, and playing basketball within their delicacies. Screaming at the fragmented reflections that *you are you and I am me. Me, me, me, me. Our own sacred ceremony. Show me the light. Dive six bodies deep into those fish-less tanks and shapelessly-caged seas. Show me the light. Be still like the tree. Me, me, me, me.*

You will know my story, world, for I will tell it shamelessly. And you will know just a fraction… of the beauty that I see.

A Capsule in Time

3rd November 2014

It had been a month since last my pen found paper with the intention of capturing a moment within its ink. But despite my literary absence, my days had not been dry of material.

I had witnessed the sun rise over the hillside, glistening with colours that I had never before seen. I had lost myself for days in an Australian doof, drunkenly dancing within its dust as if its particles were my partner, whilst a red bandana separated the outside from my lungs like a bodyguard. I had sung to strangers in unsuspecting places and found release in the variations of my voice. I had even discovered a delicate vocal harmony that, whilst living inside of me, easily met with the screams of a rawness that had been pouring out from my insides.

Tribal life had taken up room and board in my throat, purging itself towards therapy. Because, during that month, I found that I had a lot of things buried inside of me that wanted to scream their way out. It was a rugged release.

I had partied beneath a bridge with a boy named Samuel, who pushed heavy bass from his speakers beneath the curve of the crossing, just so that we could all enjoy our time in this world. Together, Sam and I had screamed out in celebration of life and, during our scream sessions, I had actually heard my voice split in two. Something inside of me had changed and it needed to break the old me in order to come through.

Real love had dared to nestle into my bones; it was the kind of love that I had always known to exist, even when there had been no proof of its existence. The little girl that lived inside of me had never had anything to compare it to, but, always feeling its presence, she had not settled until she found that love. At twenty-seven years old, I felt as though that love had finally found me. I discovered poetry in the pulse of my blood and had made blood brother pacts with sisters and soul family. I had gotten to know and become closer to people than my prior reservations had ever allowed for. I had seen the inner workings of another's soul.

With those visions, I began to feel something calling out to me. It was a soft whisper upon the wind of change, but I could not quite make out what it said. I could only determine it to be a single word. My ears pushed themselves towards its murmur in pursuit of clarity, but the bass that pulsed out from beneath the bridge had been too loud, so that calling remained undistinguished.

During a night out in Melbourne's city, I found myself participating at an open mic night event. My mind felt calm as I stood in front of a full audience for the first time as a poetic performer. Paper rested in my hand casually, but the trembles in my legs travelled all the way up the page and gave away my fear like a gift. My throat was dry. My notebook shook with the tremors of my uncertainty, because I didn't even know what the hell I was reading to everyone or why my quiet obsession for expression had led me there. However, the audience just stared at me with eyes that turned into lips and, as I opened my own mouth, they began to drink from me. All eyes were on me and I felt sick, but I persevered and read from my script, wondering what I tasted like.

Then it was over before it had begun and I somehow felt bigger. The wet eyes of the audience glossed over like satisfied mouths that licked their lips, savouring the moment. And I was swollen with their appreciation; it was as if they had filled *me* up when they had drank from me. I then took a seat within the audience and transformed into a pair of lips that began guzzling up other people's intimate testimonies. A whole community of story-tellers started to open up before me. A woman performed a literary autopsy before the microphone and I saw dusty ribbons unfurl from her wrists. They were pink with the suicidal care of a lover's razor-blade kiss and her words… rushed into me.

After the spoken word had commenced, Madeline and I sat in her car that evening, parked beside the park on Clarke Street. We each discussed love in all of its variant forms, because poetry encourages such things. Madeline and I explored our own obsessions in the privacy of two front seats that softened our troubles with their support. The windscreen played witness to our verbal adventures and we mimicked its transparency. Words ran out of our hearts like escaped convicts that had long been imprisoned.

"I feel like running," Madeline exhaled, passionately. A residue of screams, sitting freshly upon the pink of her lips. Madeline and I had just finished an impromptu session of scream therapy.

I peered through the glass window of the passenger side into the invitation of the night. It was like a dark envelope, sealed with the orange wax of soft street lights.

"Naked?" I asked, extending Madeline's invitation past the point of normality.

Car doors slammed as Madeline and I abandoned our purses and jackets and everything else that had kept us weighted. Giggles tickled the air around us as we laughed our way down the bend of the Yarra River, following it as though it were the fountain of youth. Our bare feet pitter-pattered across the bounce of a wooden bridge and we began to throw our clothes down as if they were breadcrumbs upon a trail. My t-shirt went easily to bed with the dirt, as if they had been waiting a lifetime to be reunited. Our giggles transformed into the playful screech of howls as Madeline and I transformed into women who ran with wolves... and I found myself at the end of a braless bridge.

I felt the air breathlessly asking for every part of me as we curved into a field and shed the remaining layers of our fabrics. Madeline and I... were all jacked-up on poetry.

We did cartwheels across the grass and laughed at our abandon of the things that we used to take seriously. I stood in the center of the park, looking out into the dark of the night, only to be met by the realisation of my absolute sobriety.

Sobriety and I, it appeared, had become strangers. Sobriety asked me where I had been all this time, but I stood in the dark of the park and arrogantly brushed her off, because I had plenty of answers to give. Sobriety had the concerned eyes of a mother and proceeded to pull out a picture of me from her apron, sitting in my bed at 7am looking like shit and drinking wine. In defense, I showed Sobriety the Polaroid evidence of me crying because Heartache had sat heavily upon my shoulder blades for some time, pressing me into intoxication. Sobriety quizzed me like a maternal cop and tried to push me into false incrimination. But I reminded her of how the Grim Reaper had taken my friend, Freshman. I signed the names 'Heartache' and 'Death' beside my confession… but none of it meant anything to her because Sobriety was pissed. And she said to me, but one word:

Creativity.

I laid upon the soft damp of the park bench, observing Madeline's milky skin. The full of the moonlight played connect-the-dots with her freckles. Whilst her flesh moved with her breath like a rosy, ravaged thing.

Creativity had seen the possibility of my sobriety as if it was an open window that clearly showed that I could get high on life without substances. Poetry and beauty blew in the breeze like floor-length curtains and that possibility became a window that would not close. A pathway that had been lined with breadcrumb clothes shone beneath the moonlight and I thought of its solitude. I saw, in its lonely trail, that my distraction with other people's lives had left me stained me with tobacco fingertips and red wine lips. It was apparent that my heart was a hopeless romantic that had been saturated with the beauty of strangers who I had turned into lovers. The path stood alone, showing me that I too would need to leave it all behind. Because I could not use Death as an excuse as to why I was having trouble living a full and clean life. Sobriety showed me, by the light of the moon, that it was bad manners to stay in bed with Heartache at 7am drinking left-over wine.

Breathing into the night air with bare skin and wolf's breath, I began to entertain the idea of clean living. Whilst images of rainforests and meditation joined me upon that picnic bench, I knew that Sobriety had only scolded me because she had barely recognised my face when she had seen me. As Madeline and I followed the breadcrumb trails of our clothes, I looked upon their *clean* fabrics and I wanted to be like them.

The next morning, I crawled into Reeta's bed, impregnated with a glorious idea. I had felt an overwhelming urge to pay tribute to the friendships that I had formed on Clarke Street because a part of me knew that they would not last much longer. As Reeta and I lay in-between her summer sheets, my desire for documentation spoke to Reeta's sleepy eyes and shared with her the remedy of a time capsule. Reeta smiled a smile that spoke of sisterhood and together, we crept from room to room and secretly gathered trinkets from inside of them. The rooms inhabitants were not home in order to ask their permission of eviction, but Reeta and I were thick with mischief. She and I were like identical twins who could never tell on one another because it would only incriminate ourselves.

Two brown hands removed a shell from the bedroom of Holly. Two more brown hands kidnapped a scarf from the chamber of Leaf. I searched through the single drawer in my den and discovered discarded love letters that had been signed by Benjamin. Mine and Reeta's treasure chest grew. A drawing that had been birthed from the artistic fingers of Andrew hung upon my wall and I tore it down without anybody to tell me otherwise. Reeta simply encouraged me with her black bandit eyes. A note from Christina also became a stowaway in our cargo. Together, Reeta and I gathered rings, photos and, as we ate breakfast, we even acquired the hair of a Lentilian grass-dweller named Guido. With a backpack full of Clarke Street treasures, Reeta and I left Lentils attempted to come to a unanimous decision of where we should bury such treasures.

Amidst our very important discussion of burial, Reeta and I had unintentionally drawn in the curiosity of a girl named Ola. Ola had angel eyes that were framed by long, ash-blonde hair and through the common ground of Lentils, she and I had come to know one another well. As Reeta and I gathered our treasures and marched towards the ceremonial spot where Benjamin's birthday had been held, (crowning that spot as the perfect place to bury us all together,) Ola casually had hitched a ride upon our adventure.

Together, Reeta and I spent hours beneath the scorching Australian sun documenting absolutely everything that had happened to us over the previous few months. Ola sat on the grass, giving our ceremonial dedication an attentive audience as four brown hands joined together and scribbled feverish notes of love and appreciation upon scraps of paper. Reeta and I spoke to one another in our mother tongue language of poetry, writing stories of what each person in and around Clarke Street had meant to us, together and individually. Reeta and I also drew caricatures of ourselves just for good measure. Ola sat quietly and respected our space as we burned Indian incense into the forest air and recited our letters aloud. Reeta and I were soft as well as serious. Our chins tilted towards the sky in reverence, as we offered up our unified gratitude to all the weird shit that had occurred over the past few months. The incense burned in waves of sweet power as Reeta and I mirrored one other without anger or greed. I was able to see myself through her with great clarity.

After digging a sufficient hole, I lay my shovel on the ground, beside the tree that I had once tried to be, and with four brown hands, Reeta and I began to bury an eclectic treasure of intimacy. Then, after drawing a mental map in my mind, we each poured piles of brown earth over our ceremony in a final act of closure. Knowing that a time of change was upon our entire made-up, make-shift family, I felt a warm relief rush through me. I took comfort from the fact that we had all found one another for a single moment in time that could never be replicated. And, from the vines of a journey that was almost hard to believe, we had each wound our personal stories into definitive memories that would always be with us.

Clarke Street had torn broken things out of my body and had helped to push something new and improved back into it. Creativity then took my dirty, open hands and began leading me out of the forest. As I left the meadow of an ancient light, watching the branches wave farewell to the sisters in us whilst the river ran on without sentiment, I knew that I would be hard-pressed to ever forget those lessons. Emerging from the forest, Reeta and I blessed each and every one of the lessons that we had learned together and individually.

'January 31st 2018' etched itself into my X-marks-the-spot memory.

Part Four

Flight of the Hummingbird

Dream Walking

20th November 2014

Sitting upon my faithful red rucksack, I looked down upon a slim-rolled cigarette that drooped in my right hand like a pregnant cheerleader, parting my fingertips with her skinny, white legs. Christina's hand sat daintily inside of my left palm like an ivory lily pad and, sitting upon the beach together, Christina and I touched one another as if our hands could substitute for our new home. Together, we stared into the ocean and it stared back at us with white-crested eyelashes that blinked over the heads of small children, though they didn't seem to mind. Christina's hand represented the white petal of organic life whilst the slim-rolled cigarette, despite its pregnancy, represented an essence of death. Sitting with a tall, bronze back, I weighed each one of their offerings up in my hands as if my body were a scale. The air around us grew damp in preparation for a coming storm. And the sky wore a dark hat that was made of brewing black magic.

Whilst puffing on the pregnant cheerleader that was living inside of my cigarette, I mused over how little effort it had taken for me to leave Melbourne behind in order to arrive at my current location, Brisbane. A simple 7am alarm had pulled me away from the pile of sleeping bodies that were curled up like cats upon my bedroom floor. Then, swimming through a sea of early morning farewells, without the need for goggles, I hovered over the bodies that had been dream-chasing within the depths of my dark room and said goodbye to my buoys. Then, jovially, I had sailed out of the door to Clarke Street and fallen into the passenger seat of Leaf's car. After a short drive, the airport had sucked me, but left just enough time for me to look back into a pair of deserted blue eyes… and never forget them.

After a two hour flight and a bus journey to the beach, I had arrived in Brisbane with Christina. A Christina whom had casually chosen to accompany me on my pilgrimage for clean living and higher love, even though I had no idea where I was

317

going. So, with a few ideas in mind, Christina led the way to a hippie gathering in Brisbane, and I gladly followed her until my own path were to reveal itself to me.

Looking off into the fierce eyes of the sea, I watched as its depths transformed into Benjamin's blue eyes. Ben had looked at me so trustingly as I left him at the airport that morning. Though, despite his certainty, I wasn't sure how much I trusted myself anymore, because I was basing all of my instincts around a single dream. The storm overhead grew dark.

As the first droplets of rain came crashing down upon us like liquid meteorites, Bruce arrived just in time to be our hippie gathering tour guide. Following his bare feet through the car park, I familiarised myself with the calm of his walk. Bruce's shoulders, standing proudly above my head, assured me that I could lean on them if ever I should need to. His shoulders then disappeared inside of a long, white bus that took up three parking spaces in the car park.

I once heard in a movie that one's method of transportation should be an extension of their personality; such a concept had always stuck with me. That notion had also adapted itself into my leopard-print seat covers that sat in my boxy car back in England and, as I stepped towards Bruce's bus, I was greeted by the extension of his very own personality. 'Free West Papua' was signed across the outside of Bruce's chariot with tribal ink. As I ascended the steps to the bus, its doorways promptly closed behind me, swallowing me up like a hungry mouth. As Bruce paved the way forward, a deep-purple, velvet ceiling licked the top of his bald head like a tongue. Peacock feathers hung from the roof like crimson tonsils that blew sapphire with the wind. Snail shell trinkets and wooden totems lay slumberous in shelves and boxes like fractured teeth, whilst a zebra-printed bed crouched at the back of the bus and smiled at me like an Arabian night. The bus evidently belonged to the mouth of a tripper but, as I placed my bag upon its floor, I found comfort that such a colourful chaos could be my home for the next leg of my journey.

As Bruce's bus roared into motion, I surrendered to the

idea of stepping closer towards the dream that I had been blindly following. As Christina, Bruce and I drove in the mouth of a magical bus, passing through a place called Murderous Creek as darkness fell all around us, I knew that the beginning a strange and magical adventure was upon me. Staring out from the wide front seat and out into the open night sky, I thought about my dream. Because that dream had been realer to me than any dream that I had ever had, and it was the reason as to why I sat in a nameless bus, travelling far away from my love. As rain ran down the windowpane and glimmered with the headlights of oncoming traffic, I meditated upon the stream from my dream…

… Within the dream, a murky, brown river had snaked out as far as the eye could see and I travelled its waters upon the distinct curve of a Viking boat. The women with whom I lived with on Clarke Street were all aboard that wooden ship of my dreams. Together, we came to a tall house with many storeys.

As Christina, Leaf, Holly and I entered a house that was akin to the bohemian style of Clarke Street, it became clear that each one of us was searching for something. Maroon pillows lounged lazily upon sofas, whilst a ruby lampshade cast a soft light across all of our pursuits. As I sifted through inanimate items, I understood that my search was aimed towards the 'ceiling.'

A silver elevator materialised to my right, metallic and displaced. The women and I rode the elevator to the top floor in pursuit of the highest level. Spilling out of the elevator, we were met by the stare of giant, masculine creatures. The giants had bald heads and purple veins that pulsed out from the thick of their necks. Their pale eyes, piercing right through me. The creatures were undoubtedly Godly.

Neither party seemed disturbed by the other's presence and, as we each stood on separate sides of the room, there was a definitive contrast between masculine and feminine. I looked upon three giant bodies that lounged casually upon a black leather sofa, though they did not look back at me. Fascinated, I became lost in their world, entranced by the purple in their pulse and, without realising it, my mission fell from me. I forgot why I was up there and daydreamed within a dream until a male specimen that was standing directly in front of me caught my gaze without pleasantries. Letting his jaw fall open, the god revealed a hole that was as black as the night. And through that gaping darkness, he asked one single question of me...

"ARE YOU READY?" he roared, with an unfailing authority, right into the very fabric of my being.

I shrank in fear at the confrontation of such an intense query, fidgeting nervously and averting my gaze. In an effort at distraction, my eyes fell upon a mirror that hung upon the wall beside me. The mirror was beautifully framed with thick, golden ivy and held my reflection inside as if it were a captive in a fairy tale.

Looking into the reflection before me, I saw that my features were mine, but I was not completely me. A set of full lips sat victoriously on my mouth, high cheekbones glided down my face and my nose still buttoned itself, though my neck wore the elongation of a phoenix rising. My eyes were swollen with the blacks of a new moon that were so dark that they almost pulled me into them. Nervousness found me again as I remembered the deity's question of readiness and impulsively, I laughed at my reflection. I laughed at his question. I tried to deflect what I knew to be seriousness with an armour of humour but, as I looked closer at my reflection, I noticed three golden rings that sat in three stacks atop of my head. Those golden rings separated the dark cascades of my hair and, by the sight of them, I knew that I was ready. Those golden rings were somehow my ammunition.

Casting my eyes back towards the bald giant creature that stood before me, I watched as he took a boomerang in his hand and threw it towards the ceiling. In that simple act of movement, I remembered my mission. I remembered the ceiling. I understood of how distracted I had become on the top floor full of gods, even though they hadn't been what I was truly looking for. Casting my eyes up to where the boomerang had landed, I discovered an entrance to the attic. As I climbed up inside of the attic, I was pulled through to the other side by the helping hands of the women that had been with me all along. As if she had not accompanied me through the dream, Leaf, with lips that did not part, proceeded to ask me where I had been.

'Remember... remember... remember...' Leaf drilled into my confusion.

So, within the dream, atop the attic, I began to retell the dream-tale of how I had arrived. Some of the women sat cross-legged beside a fire, travelling out of their bodies into different worlds. Whilst others stood over them in protection. Leaf and I discussed, amongst ourselves, all that had happened within the dream. Within the dream, we hypothesised over the heights of ceilings and how they represented the highest form of love. Leaf and I compared notes regarding the distraction of the male gods and how that kind of love was high, but not of the highest form.

In an attic full of women, somewhere in my dream land, it had all made sense to me. And with that, the dream-ceiling began to crumble. The women and I found ourselves back on our Viking boat and together, we floated back down the brown murk of an endless stream.

Staring at the space in-between the split of rain water as it forked across the window of the bus, I returned from my dream. I remembered how I had awoken that next morning forever changed. Because I knew with absolute certainty that there were higher heights for me to seek. It was as if the dream had slapped me across the face and everything that I had been obsessed with, thereafter suddenly became small. The rain streaked the bus window in acknowledgement, knowing that I was on my way to find those higher plains. Murderous Creek fell behind me, dirt tracks of possibility formed in front of me, and a strange, bald man

321

named Bruce sat beside me, driving Christina and I into anywhere. Although it was new a new concept to me, I respected that dream as its own form of personal prophecy.

The dark of the night gave away no secrets as to where that road would take me, but as Christina and I disappeared into the darkness, I simply surrendered to the unknown powers of the universe.

And, with one foot placed in front of the other, I travelled blindly through the world… like a Dream Walker.

Mumbari Magic

22nd November 2014

After the ascension of a lumpy hill had been met with thin success, our nameless bus finally creaked to a halt and its wheels wheezed out in rested relief. The dark cloak of night wrapped its arms around Christina, Bruce and I, as we found ourselves at a halt upon a body of land that was known as Mumbari. Stepping through the white accordion doors of the bus, I allowed my eyes to fall upon yet another house-on-wheels that had been parked directly in front of us.

The mobile home ahead had been draped with white linen sheets that blew in the balmy breeze like cirrus clouds. The clouds then parted to reveal two sleepy faces who immediately retracted with the shock of headlights upon their delicate eyes. In an attempt to distinguish where we were, I observed the final resting place that would be our encampment for the next few days, yet all I could determine was that we were somewhere in the middle of nowhere. A rustle of leaves enveloped me in a swaying lullaby, encouraging that I be ok with my displacement. The late evening gave nothing of my location away, but instead offered me a warm embrace that was born of a midsummer's dream.

As four headlight-stained eyes peered out once more from behind a white mask of linen clouds, squinting into the darkness, they took on the slender form of four crescent moons. Two of the eyeballs were aflame with green fires, whilst the other two were as brown as the earth that crumbled beneath my bare feet. Their diversities, filling the night sky with whispers of chalk and cheese. Both pairs of lunar eyes belonged to two undressed bodies that began to part the clouds, pouring out from beneath them like diaphanous raindrops. One body wore brown skin whilst the other wore cream. One belonged to a woman and the other, a man. Their two tones met instinctively just below waist level as they tenderly held one another's hands and walked towards us. Like an oyster shell with two separate coverings, their hands clasped over the couple's differences, transforming them into one single pearl.

Our small group stood together in the dark of the night and huddled over a home-made kitchen that looked to have been constructed some time ago. Oyster shell hands began pressing halloumi upon aged bread, presenting Bruce, Christina and I with an offering of food that served to welcome us to the Rainbow Gathering. As I scraped a lump of mould away from my piece of bread, the late hours slowly slipped between my appreciative fingertips.

That evening, Bruce, Christina and I lay our squashed bodies to sleep in the back of Bruce's bus like three little piggies in a zebra-print row. After gazing around at the colourful character of transportation that had swallowed me up whole and, despite Bruce's sleepy reservations, I decidedly crowned the bus with the name Broomhilda. Broomhilda's purple, velvet tongue shimmered against the candlelight, thankful to finally have an identity, and I stared at her ceiling as if it held the key to my dreams. Yet sleep managed to escape my capture, riding off on an animal that was half-zebra and half-sheep. I could not know when the beast of sleep would return to me, therefore I cast my eyes out of the side window and pondered over where my path had led me.

Millions of stars dotted the warm Australian sky, shinning like the inverted image of ginger freckles upon an endless and pale face. Some gathered in clusters, whilst others sat apart in definitive isolation, yet every one of those stars twinkled with a fresh wish that had been cast upon its soft edges. The stars furiously flickered, as if they were pressing light so deep inside of themselves that every single wish that was made upon them would be compelled to come true. Whilst the world slept and dreamt, the stars worked the graveyard shift with little thanks from their employers, but continued their selfless labour nonetheless. Some stars winked at me, as if together, we shared a private joke. But as I lay beneath zebra sheets, I felt as though I had somehow missed the punchline.

The reality of me following a dream that had purely been based upon a ceiling, sent a cool chill across my body, leaving me with a conscience that said I shouldn't trust it. My eyes blinked in replication of the light that twinkled above me and I wondered if I could even trust in the dutiful work of the stars. Laying there in Broomhilda, with all of my comforts stripped away from me, except that which lived in my red rucksack, I could not help but to feel bare. Pangs of fear hitched a ride upon my heartbeat but I tried to breathe and be brave amongst their traversing company. Christina and Bruce slept peacefully beside me in Broomhilda's psychedelic belly, with faces that looked like spent children and, as I closed my eyes in pursuit of my own dreams, I began to slowly follow them to the other side.

The next morning, I awoke to the sound of innumerous birds singing wildly into the heat of a new day. Removing the zebra blanket from the clamminess of my body, I followed the bird song outside, as if their urgent chirps were the directions to an underground rave. They seemed to suggest that there was not a moment to lose so I dismounted Broomhilda with legs that were not yet acquainted with the vertical demands of the day and allowed the soft focus of my morning eyes to explore the magnificence of Mumbari.

Should I have been at the very top of a ten-storey building, my jaw would have crashed through each concrete level and dropped all the way down to the ground floor. Thankfully, there were neither traces of buildings nor tarmac around me, only splendidly green hills that rolled out in an endless wave as far as the eye could see. Our campsite sat perfectly perched atop of a lone hill and, as I walked towards the edge of that hill, my vision fell like a waterfall down into the river below me. The sun flirtatiously glimmered across its brown, watery skin, offering the river an excess of warm kisses so that we could embark upon an early morning swim if we pleased. The river wound in a brown murkiness that was similar to the dream river that had led me to Mumbari and, realising their connection, I gasped at my own private confirmation of placement. My feet stood exactly at the point where the river split from right to left, showing me that I had been led to where I needed to be.

Like a wild bird, my eyes caught a ride upon the sultry winds of change and soared up towards to the heavens, coming to a stop upon a tribe of treetops that stood alongside of the river. The wild crowns of the trees bunched together like an army of broccoli, silhouetting a bright blue sky that had not a single cloud in sight. I began to feel a great clarity coming over me. The hills beneath and around the trees rolled into one another like the lumps of lovers who had voluntarily become entwined for all of eternity, slumping into one another's self-imposed boundaries without caution. The scene merged and crawled before me, stretching and sprawling itself over my eyes with an undisturbed beauty. *So, this is Australia,* I sighed.

Four-hundred acres of ancient, indigenous land had been breathtakingly etched into the magic of Mumbari's landscape, yet there was something slightly offbeat within the rustle of the trees. Hot air pushed up through their thick, broccoli leaves, blowing a feeling of unrest all around my body, though it was a feeling that I could not yet understand. Returning to camp, I watched as Christina floated out of the mouth of Broomhilda and fell into a position of prayer upon the viridescent grass. Christina's nimble knees tentatively met the earth like a first kiss, whilst the palms of her hands opened themselves up and pressed into the ground upon which I stood. Although I did not quite follow intellectually, my body impulsively followed Christina's example and mimicked her movements. Christina straightened the length of her backbone and showed me, with the intimate language of her own body, of the unequivocal importance in paying respect to the land.

Mumbari was an entity that awaited my introduction, therefore, I too kissed the ground with my kneecaps for the very first time. Pushing my own essence out from the palms of my hands as if to introduce myself, I wordlessly thanked Mumbari for having me as a guest. The curl of Christina's fingers arose from the earth and rested themselves on the outline of her heart. I also rested the fingertips of my right hand over my heart and cradled its faint pulse. With one hand touching the brown of the earth and the other resting upon the brown-skinned beat of my heart, I began to feel the movement of a full circuit within me.

Together, Christina and I walked a rite of passage and I effortlessly fell into it as if it were a familiar bedtime story that I had not heard since childhood. It felt like a story that I had always known, only I had somehow forgotten once I had become grown. Christina was my reminder and imitation was her flattery. Together, we gave thanks to Mumbari, and I realised in that moment, that I could very well trust in the work of the stars, for the land and the cosmos were in this together; a full circuit.

The distant echo of "food circle!" reverberated from the bed of the river below us and, beneath the blaze of Brisbane's sun, Christina and I arose and began our descent into the Rainbow Gathering.

As a teenager, I had found great escape in the gathering of the rainbow souls. At nineteen years old, Stephanie, Freshman and I had discovered a world of rainbow children that gathered by the hundreds in Ocala's national forest. The rainbow children that I met there wore no clothes upon their bodies and attempted to also undress their egos. It was there that peacock-coloured stars had pushed themselves into the fabric of my being, transforming me from a broken girl into the beginnings of a flower child. The rainbow children had blossomed in the protection of Ocala's wilderness and, as I joined them in their organic transformations, their prismatic petals had lined my pathway to self-discovery. The years had long passed since those days of naked woodland creatures who sought out vulnerability in order to find themselves, yet as I walked the path down to food circle, I began to see an alternate version of them appear before me.

A variety of undressed skins walked casually through the forest of Mumbari without any material bounds attached to them. White light poured down from the sky and fell upon an assortment of pale skins, giving the appearance that their bodies were one with the sun. Brown limbs crouched down beside the mouth of the river, replicating its thick shades of enriching mud. Thin freckles stood out amongst chubby moles in a break for independence, as an alliance of released inhibitions dressed everyone in absolute starkness. Wrinkles lounged shamelessly against a sea of additionally uncurbed age lines, whilst misshapen breasts and heavy-set testicles hung from their owners like animals without need for fabricated chains. Everyone looked so free, but as I stood beside the mouth of the river fully-clothed, I could not help but to associate Nudity with its wayward twin, Sexuality.

Immersing myself within that sea of comfortable bodies, I began to feel the stirrings of my own body asking for acknowledgement beneath its tattered robes. Although I was undoubtedly overdressed with brown skin made hard work of a visualised embarrassment, pangs of exposure began to rouge my cheeks. However, hand-in-hand with their adult, children ran across river rocks with fearless legs that were naked as the day that they were born. And their innocent abandon caused me to question my hesitation. I began to disrobe.

As I allowed my resentful clothes to fall from me, I thought over the common association of Nudity and her twin, Sexuality. Though they are known to be identical, Nudity and Sexuality are very dissimilar from one another. Nudity is the extroverted twin; full of fearlessness and abandon, she leads the way forward with nothing to hide. Sexuality is more introverted; she can often be found following Nudity to the ends of the earth, with a loyalty that will never be extinguished. Sexuality has her own passions, yet they must always be inspired and permitted to exist by her sister, Nudity. In the lands of association, it is said that one twin is not able to live without the other.

The colourful people that peppered my vision at the Rainbow Gathering were more than just products of carnal nature. I watched as a young girl held the hand of a naked man, and together, they were as pure as the morning sun. Once I had become disentangled from sexual connotations, standing as bare as the day that I was born, I began to feel that sun upon my entire body. My unmasked limbs silently spoke out to me, saying, *this is just who I am.* It did not take long before I realised clothes to be the true imposters of the land.

The food circle hovered around the mouth of the river like a promised kiss and, as I joined hands with its occupants, I anticipated the fruition of such an affectionate oath. Together, we each began chanting out with sounds of joy and appreciation, filling the air around us with gratitude of our replenishment. It was a glorious thing to hold hands in the morning, chant out in nudity and sing for my breakfast. Whilst eating my porridge out of a silver dog bowl, I listened to the children and adults laugh as one, and felt like the most content stray dog in the world.

After breakfast, the talking feather circle began and, as a bristled bird feather was passed around from hand to hand, I recalled my own introduction to a circle where feathers had unknowingly taught me to talk. In my days of adolescent anger and confusion, I had unwillingly spent much of my time in and out of juvenile detention centers. Years of shackles and chains had kept me in an inescapable hell, until a Native American-based detention center called 'Vision Quest' had focused its iris upon me. Vision Quest would come to be the resting place for my misplaced youthful imprisonment.

Amongst horse therapy, boot camp training and sweat lodges, Vision Quest had also introduced me to talking feather circles. I had been a seventeen-year-old girl who had a mouse stuck in her voice box, yet with a feather in hand, I began discovering the whispers that came from that mouse. One cannot fly without wings, wings cannot fly without feathers, and there are many kinds of feathers in the world from which to choose from. The talking feather, specifically, serves as a microphone; no one is allowed to interrupt, cut you off, or judge. Those without the feather are only required to listen and for that, Vision Quest saw that I blossomed. Ten years had passed since that chapter in my life, yet there I was in Mumbari, encircled with love, as a talking feather floated between a hurricane of caring hands. When my turn came around, despite the incessant dialogue in my head, I had but one thing to say…

"Thanks."

The original caretakers of the land that we know as Australia are an indigenous group of people known as Aborigines. The Aborigines are of dark skin and tribal nature, for they lived off of the land for thousands of years before colonisation took over. They not only lived off the land but the Aborigines also lived in communion with the land, nurturing it, protecting it, entwining their life with it, as if they were mothers to their environment. Hence the title 'Caretaker'. Yet, like so many native cultures, the Aborigines have been forced under the sharp blade of European 'development' and their ways of life have been mercilessly mutilated into unrecognisability. It was amongst the talking feather circle where the unrest of Mumbari was finally brought to light.

The caretaker of Mumbari had opened up her property and welcomed the rainbows so that we may enjoy her land before it was to be taken away from her. Governmental hands feverishly rubbed themselves together over our heads with dollar-sign tattoos etched upon their skins. Apparently, with just a few million dollars, generations of good intentions can be eradicated; replaced by Chinese factories that leave a haunted memory of what once was. As gentle tree-dweller sat beside me with a feather in his hand, he mourned over the imminent loss of the land. Some hippies tried to gather themselves enough to do something about such atrocities, whilst others just shrugged their shoulders in helplessness. The pipe for peace was passed.

Aunty Bev was the caretaker to the magical land of Mumbari. Bev, like many native elders before her, was given the endearment 'Aunty' as a sign of respect. It was also a way to connect and remind those that spoke her name of how we are all but one family upon this earth. That afternoon, I sat in the refuge of Aunty Bev's home, amongst a select few, and watched a scene of family unfold before me. It was because of those whose circle I travelled within, that I found myself in such close-knitted company, therefore I watched quietly, as a spectator should.

The kindness in Aunty Bev's eyes sat in two brown pools of earthy ambience. Firelight flickered from amongst their concern and travelled down into the caverns of her heart. Aunty was a part of an indigenous tribe that had nurtured the bounty of Mumbari for three generations, working with its delicacies and flowing alongside of its fearsome streams. As Aunty Bev perched on a chair that shadowed her dining room table, The Man sought to take all of that away from her.

A PhD sat proudly upon Bev's wall, watching over us all and Aunty Bev explained to us of how she was a self-educated woman with a knowledge for flora and fauna so expansive that she had been awarded an honorary PhD. Bev had gracefully stepped away from the stereotypical categorisation of savage simplicity and showed that, through her communion with the land, of how she knew more about her surroundings than any government could even pretend. Aunty Bev had lightning bolts for fingertips and sat like a forgotten queen upon her wooden throne. The rainbow children and I gathered around her feet like naked children, resting upon the cool of her kitchen tiles.

Before long, Aunty Bev began to speak of Dreamtime, relaying to us the stories of her people and her culture. Smoky visions woke upon her lips, breathing life into the forgotten art of storytelling. Through Aunty's words, I was completely captivated. Tribal magic swirled with the winds of fascination around me, truth resonated through her teeth and went out to join the birds in their song, whilst all those who were guests within Bev's house understood our privilege in her presence.

Casting my eyes around the room, I peered into each pair of eyes that stared hungrily upon our storyteller, drinking her in words appreciatively. Deep down, we all knew that the city lives that we each lived to be incongruent with how our souls truly needed to be housed. Looking at us collectively, I could see that we each harbored a desperate will for Aunty Bev to sow the seeds of our own displaced souls in order to help them to grow.

Upon that cool tile floor, it was as if a spell had come over us all. We were lost children who needed our good intentions to be identified and recognised by a Woman of the Tribe. Whether we knew it or not, each one of us was embarking upon some kind of pilgrimage for indigenous acceptance, or at least, what it represented. We were like a book of empty pages that needed colouring in.

Whilst Aunty Bev sat tall upon a chair of forgotten queenship, she continued to weave her magical stories of Mumbari across our open hearts. The strength of Bev's words fell from her brown lips like an ancient ink, pressing truth upon a stack of dry paper souls...

... that had never been so thirsty.

Responsibility Whispers

23rd November 2014

I laid my weary body upon a blanket of damp grass and allowed the solitude of the evening to swallow me up. Looking towards the heavens, a myriad of burned-out stars twinkled by the thousands, lighting up the entire sky like tiny tea candles that had been cast upon an endless tarmac path. As wet grass began to seep through the thin of my clothes, refreshingly, it tended to the warmth that pulsed out from beneath my skin.

The evening air, save for the crickets and the rush of the river, was completely silent. Yet, despite the beauty that enveloped me, I found that I could not escape the fool that still lived within my heart; he juggled upon my pulse, walking a tight rope of loss, and began to take on the distracting body of a Benjamin that had become lost to me. I tried to blink his image away and appreciate the beauty of the moment, but as I opened my eyes back up, I swore that I could still see his angelic face twinkling within the stars, watching over me. My pining required the exhalation of surrender, therefore I closed my eyes once more and began to meditate upon a memory that was born from my departure from Melbourne:

A week prior to Mumbari, Benjamin and I had been sitting within the privacy of our front garden back on Clarke Street and had circled one another with emotions that were akin to opposing planets. Mars declared war through the sword of my imminent departure to Brisbane and Venus was only ever concerned about love. Ben and I were involuntarily ruled by the heavens above us and could not help but to be products of their governing. Each of, desiring to be freed from the solar system of our eternal connection but we were both bound by a gravitational force that would not let either of us go; our love was fractal, everlasting.

In that front garden, the bitter reality of mine and Benjamin's impending split could no longer be ignored, because my plane ticket for Brisbane had just been booked. Our knuckles turned white as Ben and I attempted to grasp onto that last sliver of hope that would not dare to envision us each on our own. The sun watched over us like a helpless mother-in-law, crossing her thin arms, wishing that she too could do more. But Benjamin and I just sat there, with silence salivating our mouths and we stared blankly at one another as if we were walls. Fear lingered around our uncertainty like a swarm of bees, buzzing with the question of, *who could I possibly be without thee?* If my sense of identity were a petrol gauge, it would have read *'empty'*.

Throughout the afternoon, the members of our Clarke Street house intermittently passed Ben and I by in a train of mundane work commitments. The gate would gently creak open and Leaf or Holly would look back at us with a disheartened smile that was similar to the maternal suns. And just like the sun, they too would also make an attempt at saying nothing, because Ben and I were a story of love that they would not interrupt. Our housemates bore witness to mine and Ben's silent exorcisms of the heart and just like us, a part of them craved the improbability of a happy ending. Though similarly, they could say nothing, for too much truth had been spilt upon Clarke Street already.

The air around us was thick and oppressive. For hours, Ben and I sat amongst our secret garden like two parentless children who had become lost in the world. Isolation locked us away in a cage of a desolate desolation. Droplets of sweat gathered beneath my breast and began racing down towards my navel, though I knew it to be a race that no one would win. The thick scent of jasmine permeated the air around us, haunting the breezeless garden. Silence rang out louder than rebirthed words. Through jasmine-saturated lungs, after too much silence, I finally wheezed out in surrender. My self-imposed defenses began to crumble.

"Why don't you just come with me?" I leaked. Sweat and tears, rolling down my face in a clear and salty togetherness that painfully inspired the probability of 'us.' The grass beneath Ben and I bent a curious ear towards the change in my heart. I looked into the lucidity of those adoring blue eyes that, for the first time, began to envision a life without me. It was a version of me void of a version of he who had been bravely walking along beside me for three long years and, the picture painted without him, it just didn't feel right.

"Forget our plans, forget the past, let's just forget it all." I frantically searched my mind for a lover's treaty of peace. The thought of being without Benjamin seized my heart, aiming a weapon of incomparable loneliness towards my reality.

"We don't need money, we don't need 'other lovers.' Maybe all we need is each other... maybe that's all that we have ever needed?" I pleaded.

A flash of hope struck across Benjamin's eyes like lightning and he signed out a breath that sounded as though it had long been kept captive in his lungs.

"That was the last thing in the world that I expected you to say, April," Ben's voice was barely a whisper, "but this whole time... it is the only thing that I have wanted to hear."

From the pale blue beginning of Benjamin's eyes, crystals formed within their damp corners. After a moment, the crystal droplets slid down the long curvature of his thick eyelashes and teetered at their curled edges, as if they were daredevils atop of a bristly cliff. As time began to slow into unrecognisability, Ben's swollen tears glistened beneath the sunlight like a forbidden treasure and then made the final jump into the unknown with no regard for their worth. Skydivers in Timbuktu will write books about the courage of Ben's free-falling tears.

As Ben's tear ducts gave way like a dam that had been standing strong against all conventional odds, a stream of transparent rivers of relief made their way down towards the parched ground as if it were the sea. Ben and I were no longer at battle with Mars, nor Venus, nor even gravity. Our bodies and minds tendered together beneath the summer sun like prime cuts of meat.

That afternoon on Clarke Street, Ben pushed through the thickly-perfumed air and took me in the care of his tentative arms, showing me that no matter what, their embrace would always be my home. The world courteously stopped for but a moment, just so that Benjamin and I may always remember such a truth. Amidst the secretive, jasmine-scented garden, with our roommates casually passing us by on a boat that knew no words, Ben and I clung onto one another like children clinging to their mother's skirts. Loss glossed our fingertips and as we melted into a mirage of tears, sweat, fractal fear and hope, we both knew that our prints would never again be the same.

What the heart wants and what the mind knows are often galaxies apart. "I can't answer you now," Ben, at last, spoke.

Blinking my eyes back to Mumbari, I found that my backside had become saturated with dew and as my heart pounded off-beat out of my chest, I could tell that it was still fractured. As if the light of the stars were too pure for human eyes to look upon, the clouds had gathered in front of their twinkling, covering the stars like grey bedsheets. Taking my cue to leave, I put my memories behind me and wearily returned to a slumberous bus of dreams.

The next morning, food circle was called. I swam naked in the river, chanted in appreciation and re-joined a world that would always continue to go on, with or without my participation. After returning to the small mound of our encampment, I was met by the bright brown eyes of Aunty Bev. Having recognised us to be but blundering children who knew little of the offerings that Mother Nature provided for us, Bev had arrived with the intention of taking anyone who wished to join her upon a walk of the land. Because often, children know little of their mother's sacrificial gifts.

Grasping a note book in my hand as my weapon of choice, I slid in amongst those who hungered to know more of their surroundings and began to follow the voice of Auntie Bev. Bev's words echoed out into the day like a winged bird, perching upon my imagination with talons that were shaped with the curve of history. I listened as great societies fell at my feet; the Romans and the Greeks who had all lost their empires to the sharp blade of war. I saw forgotten ages dawn and set, yet we began to touch upon something that the history books had never taught me. Bev spoke of a culture that had lasted throughout each rise and fall of the ages. Her people; the Aboriginals.

"We had a wealth of knowledge in the land," Bev spoke with a mother's tongue, direct and stern, encouraging that we understand the importance of them. As Bev imparted her knowledge unto us, I leant against a tree that promised to be of medicinal value and began scribbling in my notebook, like a mad scientist that had washed up on an unknown land.

'Whale Bone tree:' I transcribed under Bev's guidance, 'used for whittling axes.'

'Black bean seeds: can be eaten, although pod is highly toxic (must undergo detoxification from Dillibag.)'

"What is a Dillibag?" A bearded young man named Tobias, questioned as one piece of information inspired further questions. Answers pushed themselves onto my notebook with a mind of their own. As the group and I made our way through a thicket of stories and trees, the birds chirped wildly around our excursion, encouraging Bev to reference a 'songline.' We came to a halt amidst an overgrown forest as the word 'songline' resonated out through my imagination.

"What is a songline?" I questioned.

"A songline is…" Aunty cast her eyes up to right side of her brain, searching for a way in which to explain the intangible. Her furrowed eyebrows, reaching out across to one another as if to bridge a gap of confusion where rippled waters flowed beneath them.

"A songline is a fiber-optic cable that exists… but cannot

be seen. A songline can also be sent upon that cable as a specific message that can only be received by you." As Bev walked away, leaving me to transcribe her words, fallen leaves rustled with her steps, as if to applaud her explanation.

Climbing the nearest tree, I hung upside-down from its branches, so that the meaning of Bev's words could fully sink into my entire body. Fellow tree-dwellers climbed in amongst me, swinging and musing, conversing over the language of the bush. Whilst I swung, my un-brushed hair attempted to touch the ground, though it came up very short, therefore I just hung upside down and meditated upon the concept of a songline. It appeared to be a form of telepathy. A fiber-optic line that could carry a message from you to me without the need to be close or even use words. Closing my eyes, I began to envision the messages that were being transmitted or received by me. Although I was a novice to such a concept, I felt as though I could feel many messages and lines stretching out and into my little teleporter body. I tried to tune into their song, but it was muffled, however something told me that before long, clarity would find me.

Later that afternoon, I found myself in the middle of a field that had been peppered in an endless array of wild dandelions. And I began to recall all the wishes that the little girl within me had once made upon their pale 'weed-like' faces. My little-girl fingers used to glide across their soft seed pockets as if I were moulding the clouds themselves. The dandelion's milky stalks, smudging against my thumb like a teat to the mouth. I would wind up my largest wishful thought and blow with all the vigor and saliva that my young body could muster, always asking for the exotic and sweet nectar of adventure to find me.

A six-year-old version of me had begun wishing and dreaming for something better than her current situation since before she could remember. Yet on that day in Mumbari, amongst a group of rainbow children who sought out an acquaintance with the land, I watched as thousands of wishes floated through the forest of Mumbari and I felt contented. My life looked like a fairy tale. The little girl within me could not help but to smile because in that moment, I knew that I had found the exact place where all of the wishes arrived, just so that they could come true.

I picked a single dandelion that swayed amongst the thousands and, as its milk began sliding down my thumb, I parted ways with a wish upon the breeze. Tobias stood beside me with wild, wispy hair that mimicked the wind and brown eyes that glistened widely with wet wishes. Together, Tobias and I held a single milky stalk and blew upon the soft starlight of the dandelion's face, making our wish together. Tobias' beard rustled with the same race of the leaves, but as I looked into the hazy pool of his eyes, I knew that there would be no catching up with his desires. Tobias' was finally free and my wish had become an accessory to its escape... because I simply asked that his wish come true.

Back at camp, an invitation to party in the hills at a place called Federal, interrupted my short stay in Mumbari. Christina and I felt out the decision to stay or to leave and as the day went on, we subconsciously began packing our things. The time was upon us to say farewell to the magic of Mumbari.

As the afternoon sun nestled in the head of the broccoli trees, I made my way towards Aunty Bev's house so that I could say my farewells. Bev sat around her square dining room table, encircled with faces of her inner council that, amongst others, also belonged to Christina and Bruce. A few rainbow children sprawled out upon the coolness of Bev's tiled floor, with squashed, sardine-like bodies; observing conversations as though the words were a fridge door that had been left open, whilst outside voices discussed dinner. I tip-toed over their scaly bodies and took a seat within the small council. Knowing our group's intentions to leave, Bev began to make peace with each departee that sat within her living room.

Aunty Bev stood against Bruce's chest as it loomed over her small body in the same way that a full moon hovers over a weeping willow. Bev affectionately extended her vines, bringing

Bruce's lunar body closer to her, and she embraced him as a brother. Despite the white moonlight that sparkled upon his skin, Bruce's blood ran dark with indigenous roots. As Bev and Bruce hugged one another in the affection of a limitless tribe, the room was filled with their love.

Bev then went on to lean into Christina's ear, whispering to her of how she has known her beyond the bounds of years and time. Christina wrapped her cosmic arms around Bev and they lingered like two planets in the skies. Though when their eyes met one another's, Bev appeared to recognise something else in the essence of Christina.

"You look tired, sister," Bev whispered into Christina's frail body as she nodded her head in acceptance, promising to take rest.

Bev began to look around the room at the other women who sat upon the tile floor, looking up to her. Her soft brown face began to trouble itself with sadness. To Bev, each one of the women looked tired and she encouraged that they all take rest when they could. The women soothed one another, hugging and humming away each other's pains. From over the shoulder of a young woman, Bev locked eyes with me. My heart skipped a beat, reminding me that it was still working dutifully within my chest.

"And you." Bev began walking across the room in order to address me, "You are here by default."

Looking out towards the inner circle of Bev's life, I recognised my placing in such an environment to be true. I had been but a bystander within her walls and had curiously watched her and her family's transgressions, drinking in their testimonies with barely a shared word upon my lips.

"But there isn't such a thing as default." Bev smiled knowingly as she stretched her loving vines out towards me; something about her made me want to weep. Approaching Bev, I allowed my thumping heart to be softened by her loving arms, knowing that it was my time to have her truth imparted upon me. She pulled me in closer towards her.

"You are the strong one." Aunty's words pushed themselves into my ear like a cool wind.

"You are the strong one... and a solid heart will carry others." Bev paused so that I may digest her words. But despite her announcement of such a strength, my legs began to tremble.

"You have a great responsibility, sister... you have a great responsibility." Bev and I separated our bodies like tectonic plates that had been destined to shift. As we took a moment to look into one another's eyes, without the distraction of touch, I felt as though my legs might give out from beneath me. My mind felt as though it had the strength of a thousand wild horses, yet my body felt as though it belonged to that of a jellyfish.

Frantically, I searched my thoughts for a way to repay Bev's kindness and hospitality, automatically assuming that my responsibility was in regards to helping her secure her land.

"I'm not talking about me, baby," Aunty Bev assured my proclamations. "If you ever become weary from the burdens of the world, you are always welcome back here at my home. But until that time... you have got a great responsibility girl." Aunty Bev stepped away from me with no further instruction upon her lips.

I departed Bev's house in the same manner that one exits the realm of dreams: light and lucid, barely able to recognise the world outside to be a reality. Cautiously, I looked back over my shoulder to ensure that Bev had been talking to me: the quiet girl in the corner, the one she had bestowed such a vague, yet heavy burden of responsibility upon. Aunty Bev caught my eye and, as if to confirm my queries, she winked at me.

From that moment on, responsibility began to seep into the restlessness of my bones like a tank of gasoline that had been spilt upon the floor of a garage. If a match were to ignite my understanding, I knew that the whole house could blow.

Clambering aboard Broomhilda, I smelt petrol all over my skin, though I could not quite determine its source. Songlines and dreamy wishes stuck to the clamminess of my limbs as, in every way that I knew how to, I began to buckle myself in.

Knowing that it would be a bumpy ride from then on out, I hit the road with the extra weight of a gilded prophecy upon my back and a sense of identity that no longer read *'empty.'*

Phoenix Sun Risin'

25th November 2014

After hours of driving through long, winding roads, the house party upon the hill finally emerged from a bed of shadows and beckoned Christina and I towards its enchanting light. Gladly, I succumbed to the house's magnetic spell and shook the tiredness off from my bones like a dog shakes its wet coat after a downpour. The deep exhalation of Broomhilda's decrepit brakes ceremoniously announced our arrival at the party, though no one appeared to be around to take notice. Stepping out of the bus's disheveled belly with my sanity still intact, I began making my way through an ocean of cars that glimmered in waves of metallic tides beneath the pale moonlight.

In the front-garden-turned-car-park, hundreds of vehicles had been abandoned like forgotten toys in an overgrown sand box. The playground itself had no evidence of girls nor boys upon it, leaving the automobiles with a haunted look of desertion upon their headlight eyes; glossy, almost crying. The cars' abandonment depicted the empty space that childhood leaves behind after the pursuit of adolescence has found them. A Nissan cowered in the corner, unloved. The nose of a Ford enthusiastically leaned in towards the house, as if he were on the hunt for a girl who had left him behind for the night, in order to find herself in womanhood.

Despite their determination, the toy cars would never receive an invite to the party that pulsed overhead and captured the attentions of their owners. With unconditional car seats and inanimate understanding, they were bound to the life of forgotten play things and could only ever wait patiently for their children to return to them. Learning from the patience of the cars, I ascended the hill and followed the sounds of celebrated life, hoping that I too could find myself amongst the fleshy pursuits of the party.

A single, broad house spread itself across the hilltop like the lathering of a creamy butter upon a freshly baked loaf of bread. It looked warm and wholesome. Sparkling decorations gathered from the house's swollen insides and spilled out onto the garden, giving the entrance permission for Christmas to exist prematurely. As I clambered up the hill, past the sea of forgotten headlights, and ascended the deserted toy box, hues of greens and blues began to wink at me invitingly.

Christina and I were greeted at the door by a checkered referee. His small body, accentuated beneath a maze of black and white squares that sat upon his clothes. The bald of his head sparkled in a blinding haze of silver glitter and addressed our arrival with a language that seemed to have fallen straight from the heavens.

"Welcome." The referee gestured with a flat hand that extended towards the house. As Christina and I cautiously entered the party, the referee's lips parted once more under the pretense of a promise. "Enjoy the party," he gently commanded, his glossy, white teeth smiling a thousand Cheshire cat smiles back at me.

Inside of the house, an assortment of costumed bodies gathered amongst the living room furniture and gyrated to funky melodies. A lonely lamp gladly transitioned into a capable dancing partner. A fat sofa moved away from its self-imposed reservations and served as a stage on which intoxicated bodies freely danced. Whilst an eclectic variety of tasty music roared out from a live band that were getting down and diggidy with their own funk. Colourful afros reached out towards the ceiling and heavy glitter contaminated everything that it touched, as if to spread the outside starlight into every corner of the house. I stood, bewildered, amongst its cosmic chaos.

I could sense Christina feeling out the environment beside me. Our transition from peaceful rainbow children into civilisation's deep debauchery stood trial beneath the doorway, yet our naked faces could hide no lies upon them. The leaves that were still tangled up in our hair and the dirt that was still embedded beneath our fingernails were all called to the witness stand, though they gave us away immediately.

Arm in dirty arm, Christina and I surfed through a sea of sweaty human bodies that were clambering their way towards social ecstasy and attempted to determine where we could fit in amongst the madness. As we scoped out the blueprints of the building, Christina and I came upon little cubby holes that had been chiseled into perfect chill-out spots throughout the house. A balcony stretched around the outside like tight, white lips, as the sweet faces of party-goers lounged upon it like loose teeth. Midnight had just passed us by and the party was in full-force, though we hadn't even the courtesy of a forgotten glass slipper to prepare us. With leaf-sodden hair and dirty fingernails, Christina and I looked at one another tentatively.

'We're not in the jungle anymore, Dorothy.' Through Christina's smile, we both agreed.

Amongst the lampshade dancers, the sofa stage singers and the loose teeth makers of fun, the awareness of our absolute sobriety was undeniably transparent.

"Where's our rum?" I asked, beckoning for the wild side of Christina to join me in a necessary transformation.

After a quick trip back to the bus, where Christina and I rescued a bottle of Captain Morgan from the clutches of Broomhilda, applied some make-up to our naked faces and puffed some snow up our Christmas tree noses, we returned to the party feeling better equipped. Smiles danced all around my body… but it was the music that ultimately drew me in to the party.

A young girl with dark hair and a boyish chest bashed away at the drums as if her exertions were nobody else's business. When her thin arms tired, she moved back into the mass of drunkards and was swiftly replaced by a moustache. A variety of guitar fingers sat upon curved, wooden bodies and sporadically changed hands, as if their fingers were instrumental strings. A bass guitar glowed in the same ruby red as a spanked bottom, whilst singers sung out into the crush of dancers with delightful rhythms upon their tongues. None stayed too long upon the stage, leaving space for anyone and everyone to contribute to the continuation of a musical paradise. Looking upon a microphone that stood alone upon the stage, I felt a great appetite growl from within my eyes.

"Go on, darling." Christina had seen the hunger that had kidnapped my facial features and proceeded to smash a tambourine upon the small cylinder of her thigh in resonant encouragement to my musical contribution. The microphone stared at me from above a jungle of dancing afros and honed in on my immobility as if I were its prey, causing my heart to flutter without wings. A brown-skinned brother named Lolito emerged from the sea of unfamiliar faces and casually made our acquaintance. Joining Christina in her affirmation of my development, Lolito also encouraged that I put my reservations aside and make way for the execution of my heart's desire. Lolito's kind eyes were serenaded by the ruffled carol of the tambourine and, before I knew what I was doing, I began to part the tireless crowd. Stepping upon the stage, I curled my fingers around the black cylinder of the microphone and tentatively opened my lips to it as if it were an object of sex. At that very moment, the Christmas tree powder began dissolving in my nose and took ahold of my inhibitions. The surge was unstoppable.

For hours, I blurred and merged in rhythms and howls, following and leading with high notes that soared around the room on a butterfly's wings, then transformed down to the bass-deep nectar of a vicious scream. I swam alongside of guitar fingertips, and together we searched the ocean bed for new sounds. The other musicians pulled me into them like an undertow. A drum pulsed alongside me as if it were the aftermath of midnight pleasures. Together, we were a circle of melodic infinity. Our bodies would emerge from the harmonised sea and fall back onto dry land amongst the other limbs that stood chatting and drinking, until the music pulled us back upon stage with an even greater vigor than before. I began to find my own funk without fear. Words took form within the insatiability of my mouth, as if the crowd that danced before me were paper and my voice were the pen. Whilst partying on the hills, that version of me became the entirety of everything that I aspired to be.

A boy with brown eyes and shaggy hair stood beside me, singing unapologetically into the microphone. The lyrics of a 'Sublime' song versed our lips in synchronicity, and together we forged an ambient testimony.

"There was a riot on the streets, tell me where were you? You were sittin' home watchin' your TV, while I was participating in some anarchy!" The brown-eyed boy and I roared, whilst casually exploring one another through music.

Taking my hands in his, the brown-eyed boy gently pulled me off stage and we became lost in the endless crowd. With a bottle of rum nestled into a satchel that sat upon my waist, I followed his lead down into the quietude of the back garden. There, we sat upon a mound of hill and fell into a frantic conversation in regards to our musical vibration. Although we were cloaked in a darkness that belonged to the early dawn, I could sense that his brown eyes were leaning closer and closer towards my face.

"I feel like you want to kiss me." I broke the magic with my incessant need to state the obvious.

"I do," proclaimed the brown-eyed boy eagerly, with a cheeky smile that lit up the night sky like a lantern.

"But you don't even know me." My words ran into one another in an attempt to escape my mouth before the boy attempted to close in on it. "I'm a stranger… and I'm not in a current position to be kissed by strangers purely based on superficial attachments."

The brown-eyed boy hastily began to express his understanding of me, only to be met with a thick wall of denial. Defenses bloated my body like a puffer fish and my poisonous reservations proved me to be a far cry from the catch that the brown-eyed boy had been seeking. The rising dawn melted into a deep, blue sea just in time for me to see his silhouette sailing back

347

into the sea of music. I sat alone, huddled on the grassy verge with a sign above my heart that flashed in neon letters and read: *'No Vacancy.'*

A wild hair sprouted wings within my ass, pushing me up the nearest lonely tree. As I climbed higher and higher, branches pressed against my lungs as they lunged out in exertion, scratches materialised in evidence of my desertion, and I furiously ascended the stalk as if there were hidden jewels atop of its bushy peak. When I had reached the highest point that I could muster, without the thin branches buckling beneath my weight, I looked out upon the bounty of blue, smudged land that had begun to faintly materialise before me. And I saw that it was the sapphire jewel that I had been seeking.

At the foot of the tree, grass-dwellers had gathered beneath me in order to watch the sunrise. Whilst I curiously looked down upon their sprawled-out bodies, I accidentally lost my footing. Clumsily, I slid down a large portion of the trunk, using my forearms as a braking system which inadvertently caused them both to become as raised and red as hell itself. Their uncomfortable pain compelled me to jump from the middle of the tree. And as I took flight and hit the ground, I somehow managed to end my mentally-challenged performance with a ninja roll.

"Whoa dude, that was awesome!" A single tripper looked up at me from a bed of grass, as if I had just fallen from heaven. With an impressed grin that swallowed up half of his face, the tripper acknowledged my efforts. I returned his fanged affection with a smile but as I brushed out the additional leaves that had joined the forest of my hair, I knew that my efforts had not been for him.

As I joined the puddle of life-gazers and spaced-out trippers, the sky took its cue to perform one of its greatest acts of transformation and, with all of our eyes upon it, it converted from deep blue into a theatrical pink. Three-hundred-and-sixty degrees of mountains began to disrobe from their shadowy pajamas, conservatively dressing for the demands of day. The sun finally bubbled up from behind the bottled hill tops like strawberry schnapps and poured its pinks over everything. My breath left my lungs without loyalty and floated out into the alcoholic sunrise. The morning sky was pure theatre.

An old man with bones for a body sat down beside my entertained eyes and engaged me in conversation. The strawberry schnapps sun leaked over our limbs and, as the man's eyes folded over on themselves, he attempted to see me through their wrinkled gathering. His creases gave him the appearance of an old hound dog but his sight appeared intact. Without further ado, the hound dog decided to impart his inner elder upon me.

"You have a voice." He smiled through missing teeth. "You... have a great responsibility!"

With that, my forearms began to burn with the same fever as the rising sun. Itching and bleeding, I began pleading into the crisp morning air. *What the hell is this 'responsibility?!* I couldn't quite catch my breath and began to scold my exhalations for being so quick to leave me for the intoxicating sunrise. Then, tilting my head back towards the sky, I allowed a cup of laughter to brew inside of my belly. After a moment, it grew up through my windpipe like Jack's beanstalk and burst out of my mouth in comedic whimpers.

"What do you mean by that, hound dog?" I casually asked, trying not to give away my nervousness towards his proclamations. The indisputable fact that two people had seen fit to express the impending urgency of a bestowed 'responsibility' upon me, all within the space of twenty-four hours, was not lost upon me. I tried to stay grounded by looking into his eyes and examining the excess skin that framed them like a timeless portrait, but my body felt light all over. The hound put his paw upon my shoulder as if he knew that I may float back up into the tree at any moment.

"You've got something inside of you girl... something that we *need* to hear." He patted my shoulder with his paws, as if to let his words make their way down into my chest.

As the sun rose higher into the blue belly of morning, I

349

sought to mimic its smooth ascension and, pulsing with impulse, I stood up in front of the hound. It was too early in the morning to receive such attention from a stranger; I hadn't even brushed my teeth yet... or gone to bed for that matter. My face felt as red as the sun. Nevertheless, another wild hair tickled my backside and inspired me to retrieve my private journal from my backpack, with the intention of sharing poetry.

I then began walking in-between the horizontal bodies of the sun-worshipers and the grass-dwellers, passionately pulling words out from inside the depths of me and, theatrically, I poured my stories into their gaping mouths. The extroverted assertions of the trippers' evening had all dried up with the song of the early bird and, as I drenched them in my personal tales, the grass-dwellers seemed happy to escape into my imagery. Within the soft appreciation of their strawberry schnapps eyes, courage had finally found me. The bloodhound's wrinkles framed a picture of contentment across his face, as if he had known all along that I had always had such nourishment inside of me.

After my reading, a spring of ginger curls arose from the grass-loungers and bounced towards me. The curls belonged to a girl who took me by the hand, and together we skipped all the way back to the microphone. "Do some of your poetry," the ginger pixie encouraged me, as she parted her legs and straddled a thick drum between two freckled thighs.

The house, the living room and the stage were almost deserted. Looking through the large French doors of the house, I saw worn-out dancers sleeping peacefully upon the grass. A few guests quietly stood in the corner, whispering amongst themselves. And the quietude of the morning promised to apply no pressure upon my nervousness.

And so it was written, that on that humble Sunday morning upon the house on the hill, as my forearms burned like hell, as the sun showed me the beauty of a true rising, as three men sat at a picnic table watching me, as beautiful bodies entered the pool in an attempt to wash the previous night's residue off from them and as a pair of freckled thighs straddled a drum beside me,

I began to bridge the gap of poetry and song.

I found myself reading in a voice that I had never before tried on, rising into song... then falling back down into spoken word. The drum beat beat on, the grand piano gently dented the morning air and, as I tackled with my ability to improvise, a man with guitar-shaped hands approached me. The three of us lounged upon a deserted stage, pushing our creativity out, and during that hazy morning, I found that I sang for all the blue eyes that I have ever loved. From their indigo ashes, a phoenix began to rise above her fear.

I would come to spend the next three days at the mansion that beheld perpetual partying inside of it. However, every day after the first party, I became an introverted stranger. I did not feel compelled to sing with the other artists, nor let poetry verse my lips again. Instead, responsibility loomed over me like a raincloud, dampening my spirit. Silently, I sat in cubby-hole corners and listened to other people's versatile stories, whilst listening to a blonde-haired angel sing out in the background. And I could not help but to remember the calling that I had felt when leaving Melbourne. *'Creativity'* is what the universe had spoken into the deep of the night and, looking around at the piano, the guitars, the trees and the innumerably talented artists, I understood creativity to be what the universe had also efficiently offered me.

Yet, despite my appreciation for creative offerings, I was silently consumed by the concept of responsibility. I found it difficult to get my head around the fact that two complete strangers had, within twenty-four hours, decided to both anoint me with the whispers of responsibility. Responsibility began to weaken me into wondering if I should be doing something grand with my life, rather than dossing out for days in a haze of self-indulgence. *Should I be saving children that are starving upon the streets? Should I be leading the cavalry to freedom? Should I be much, much more than I currently am?* Such questions began to paralyze me.

In an attempt at distraction, I began to focus my attentions upon Christina. My queen of the Cosmo's was bubbling over with her own complications of the heart, becoming a garden that needed tending to. Christina and I became lost in one another, blessing trinkets around the house whilst we lounged and strolled the grounds. Before long, we began speaking to one another in a secret language, dazedly envisioning ourselves to be two oriental woman who were paddling down a canoe through the forest. Our syllables were made up of 'ting's' and 'dong's', leaving me with the feeling that we may never again use English words with one another. However, when we were able to find recognisable words within our mouths, Christina and I each spoke with clear intentions.

I had seen the sadness that was sitting within the lotus flower of Christina's femininity. Her lover couldn't quite embody what it meant to be good to her and tend to her garden; in fact, he had repeatedly stomped upon her fragile flowers. As I listened to Christina place her unwavering faith in the workings of the universe, defeat drew lines upon her face. Christina's surrender encouraged that her heart situation would be balanced and work things out for her and I both. For we were both broken in that regard, but I could not help but to fold my arms and ensure that the future needed to be made up of two parts; trust, as well as action. It was a delicate balance, but action was an imperative part, therefore I encouraged Christina to take charge of her heart, grow a pair and be firm from then on out.

As we sat talking in the long grass beside Broomhilda, Christina's sensitivities began to escape her and she wept. Christina not only cried for man and his inability to tend to her garden, but she shed a thousand tears for the injustices of the world. Her nimble body would always belong to the bigger picture, and those injustices sat heavily upon her boney shoulders and became a burden that was hard to carry alone. Broomhilda and I watched in curious despair as each tear that fell into the grass below us highlighted a sadness of the world. The long curl of Christina's hair cradled the small of her breast like cloud wrapped around a half moon and, as she unashamedly wept before me, I was able to see a different kind of strength within Christina.

Wearing the epitome of femininity around her bare skin, Christina was a kaleidoscope of every woman that I have ever loved. She cried the tears of Mother Earth, because man can be so brutal and she was but a mother that felt each blow that he had given. Without words, I could feel that pain seep out from her being and, although the snow and the rum had long dissolved inside of me, I felt that if I touched Christina, her entire body would smudge blue.

I knew then that I would be Christina's balls. I knew that she would, as she has always done, encourage my path of spirituality and that in return, I would be her protector. The dark night began to cloak our bodies, as if to commemorate my silent oath. The frogs started to croak with voices that were as deep as the south, the birds commenced to repeat the same old jokes about monkeys, whilst an orchestra of crickets emerged from the forest, playing deafening symphonies upon their bodies. Their sounds rushed deep into my chest, and played a game of tennis upon the court in my lungs. The ball; signed with *responsibility*.

Face to face, my ethereal fairy and I looked into one another's damp eyes. The world around us buzzed and hummed and cried out with life. I placed Christina's hand upon my chest so that she may feel how the forest played with my pulse. It beat out of me like an adult that had been trapped inside of a play pen. Placing my hand on the small of Christina's chest, we inhaled the sunset, the song, the animals, and the ache in both of our hearts. Then exhaled with the life that was pulsing all around us.

Then, the shifting sky performed its second greatest transformation of the day and slipped from its strawberry schnapps summer dress back into a sensual, black velvet nightgown. Christina and I, we were but two minute specks that had been precariously placed beneath its transformation, upon a cosmic party hill, touching chests, mimicking change and connecting.

A few days prior, one phoenix had risen up from the

indigo ashes of every pair of blue eyes that she had ever loved and, feathered with poetry and song, had soared with the rising sun.

She looked into the blue eyes of Christina, as the phoenix in her began to rise up through the ashes of her spilt tears. Releasing herself from the burden of man, Christina removed her hand from my chest and, returning to the goddess within her, began to soar against the setting sun.

Together, Christina and I were night and day, light and dark. As different as bloody forearms and tear-stained cheeks.

But as we soared above our imperfections, Christina and I were united in our dreams.

Stillness

2nd December 2014

Whilst jovial birds serenaded an invasive afternoon sun, I found myself standing naked amidst a tropical forest once again. Warm, golden rays peeked through the cracks in a homemade bamboo door and fell upon my unclothed skin without any desire to turn it red. I stood in the woods, somewhere in Byron Bay, inside of an outside washroom and, although it was only a temporary stop, I enjoyed my first hot shower of the week.

A hairy spider sat in a corner of the enclosure, eating popcorn-flavoured flies, and watched me, with a front row seat, as I washed away the feral that had become me. As the warm rainwater poured all over my grateful body, I peered back through the wide cracks in the bamboo shower-shack and spied upon my new environment. A row of solar panels lounged upon a wooden balcony beside me, basking in the warmth of the sun without the need for sunscreen. Like a Venus flytrap, the rainwater tank opened its hungry mouth up to the clouds and patiently waited for the sea to get bored of being up in the sky. Various homemade shacks hid themselves in-between the thickets of trees, portraying a community of people who all aspired to live sustainably. Through the openings in that bamboo washroom, as I lathered my hair with chemical-free shampoo whilst a pilose spider stood, watching my bushy body, a whole new world of simplicity began opening up to me.

With each step that I took further into that new and organic world, the higher the improbability for me to be able to return to life as I once knew it became. I had been away from the city for barely a week, but already I felt wild and uncivilised, in a way that brought me back to the source of my true identity. Trash Day Tuesdays and chemically-concocted careers had all been rinsed from my commitment, spiralling down the leaf-sodden drain. Armed with an organic soap bar and fluoride-free toothpaste in my hands, I pledged to stay as far away from as many unnecessary chemicals and commitments as I could. Simplicity became my mantra.

After showering in the bamboo enclosure, Bruce dropped Christina and I off at her parents' house in the Gold Coast and then drove away into the psychedelic sunset with Broomhilda. Bruce's lean-on-me-shoulder extended itself in a tender farewell, as he waved us goodbye from his dust-crested window with cartoon-like theatrics. With Christina's parents only living a two minute stroll from the beach, Christina and I planned to ritualistically stroll back and forth from home to sand, stopping halfway to visit the local juice bar and, for a week, become ladies of leisure.

So, each morning, Christina and I rose beside her mother's rose garden and felt out what the new day intended to offer us. Ever concerned with my heart, Christina's sleepy eyes would gauge how I was feeling, and in return, I would do the same for her. In the refuge of her parents' home, we became emotional thermometers. We would stroll down the street with bikinis grasping at our slender bodies whilst bare feet that lead the way. Upon the stretch of beach, we would stretch our limbs, smoke, and bask beneath the sun. Fruit smoothies eternally glossed our smooth lips, whilst we spoke openly about our boy problems. Taking a dip in the tropical water, Christina and I could only aspire to cleanse ourselves of their stickiness.

Whilst none of our employments were restricted to the limitations of a schedule, it became clear to me that Christina was not a creature who belonged to time. Her movements were like that of a snails, sometimes taking hours to prepare herself for our two minute stroll down towards the beach. I would sit at the ready, watching the clock with my feet nervously tapping, and I would count down the moments until we would reach our destination. It wasn't long before I aquired the sharp realisation that I had always been a victim of time. Memories of militant upbringing dressed themselves upon the readiness of my feet; two minute showers, races to get ready for school, and the time clock for work had all praised me for my punctuality. Yet, there in the Gold Coast, during a time when I aspired to be a lady of leisure, time still mocked me. I was restless.

As I looked around at my new abode, a part of me felt as though I had been there before. The Gold Coast bore a remarkable resemblance to Florida. The flora and the fauna were identical, the temperature seemed to have blown in from all the way across the Pacific, nestling into that particular spot in Australia, which left me with the thought that perhaps they had been brothers in another life. The comparison between the two places inadvertently caused a restlessness to stir up under my feet and I began to embody a younger version of me that only knew the word *retreat*.

Amongst my clock-governed confessionals, I decided to attempt timelessness with my snail queen, Christina. We had nowhere to be and nothing in particular to do, therefore stillness was the next necessary step in my development. Because there was no such thing as nowhere, somewhere was everywhere, and I began to sit cross-legged amongst it, smoking, stretching, and pondering over which pathway I would take next on my own.

As I sat upon the beach one day, staring out to sea and attempting serenity, my memories began to haunt me. Those recollections seemed to perpetually seek out my location whenever I stayed too long in one place. As I locked down my eyelids and bolted them with my lashes, a memory from Melbourne came knocking upon my door.

'Anyone home?' It pried.

Peering out through the letterbox in order to see who had disturbed me from my daydreams at such an inappropriate hour, I was met with a waterlogged version of me, slumped over into last Friday night.

A party beneath the bridge had been thrown and that version of me had tirelessly tried to pour herself into every single outfit that she had in her wardrobe, just to commemorate the occasion. It would be the last time that she would see Andrew for a while, and Benjamin had requested that she 'talk' with him that evening. The girl knew that 'talking' equated to the confirmation that Ben would not join her on her trip to Brisbane, therefore the party would serve as a farewell to both of the men that she could not help but to love.

As the girl had stood in front of her bedroom mirror, trying on an assortment of clothes, she felt satisfied and contented, knowing that she would be going out into the world alone. Her plane ticket was booked and it was obvious that her sanity depended upon getting out of the everlasting loop of her unholy trinity.

She stood before the mirror and tried on the red lipstick of 'the reckless party animal,' though its colours were too crude and suggestive. Her contentment began to dissipate. She then pulled the long scarf of 'the enthusiastic lyricist' across her neck, but it was too loose to look good. The girl wore the yellow petals of 'the wallflower' upon her dress, though its quietude seemed too childish and its colours, too bright. Running out of options, she frantically dressed her fingers in the gloves of 'the star-crossed lover,' but her hands became clammy beneath them and shook with uncertainty. As a last resort, 'the casual stranger' sat amidst the creases in her worn, leather jacket, but as she draped it over her shoulders, the leather felt cold to the touch.

None of the outfits would do. Every emotional garment that the girl had attempted to model was either torn, bleached, over-worn or shrunken in the wash. Knowing that no face would suffice, the girl just sat in the dark of her room, drinking wine and chain-smoking. She allowed her absence at the party to speak the volumes that her red lips could not. The candle light gathered beside her cheekbones and tried to comfort her, but her sensitivities could have fuelled a nation.

Later that night, Benjamin returned to her sleepless body. He clambered up the stairway to their bunk-bed and, despite her expression of sensitivities, Ben began to frantically speak of his and the girl's destined connection. The substances in his blood swirled in cyclones of eternal love and were deaf to her need for peace. Ben burned with a fire red, whilst her blood ran a solemn blue. Undeterred, Ben hovered over her candlelit body, with dark locks that fell across his pale face and obstructed the fever in his eyes. Yet, through the hair particles and the flicker of candlelight, she caught them glistening with a deeply rooted madness. The motor in Benjamin's mouth never stopped to refuel, as his mechanical hands began to claw deeper into her being. He became a mining machine that was on the hunt for gold. Exhausted from his exertions, the girl wearily bid Benjamin to return to the party with the connections that he had formed; with the him's, with the her's... with the Ola's... back to all the women in the world that could undoubtedly love him better than she.

I watched through detached eyes as that version of me had tossed and turned, enduring yet another sleepless night. The next morning, she finally arose from her bunk-bed, leaving the returned Benjamin to his dreams, pulled the covers back over him and then crept off into the kitchen. It was 6am, therefore I was not surprised to witness her take a coffee mug from the shelf, but she did not fill it with tea or with coffee; instead, she filled it to the brim with leftover white wine. The cup was as wet as her eyes. Still in her pajamas, the girl began walking out of the house and, careful not to spill a drop, she made her way down to the Yarra River. The joggers and the dog walkers that passed her by would never knew the lies were concealed within her coffee cup.

As I looked further into the letterbox of my memories, I saw the girl's purple slippers carry her down the river to the resting spot that she and Andy had lounged amongst on that first day of spring. A part of her needed to feel close to him. Benjamin's birthday had not long passed and, although she had thought that the mushroom tribe had healed her desires, she understood the heart to be a frivolous thing. Knowing that Andy flew in an airplane overhead in a pilgrimage to return to his queen of hearts, she simply sunk into the grass because, as always, Andrew was just out of her grasp. As wine and tears played together upon her face, that version of the girl in me lay pondering over her desertions. The mourning sky was wrinkled and grey. Whilst she gave herself space to completely feel the things that she needed to feel, the broken child in her began to surface.

For hours, she lay there like a child and cried over her lost toys. Through that letterbox of memories, the girl who was having trouble breathing was a sad sight to see. Benjamin eventually found her that morning and, wiping away her salty tears, had assuming that they were shed for him. Yet she shattered Ben's glass house of absorption with the next sentence that she offered.

"I love him very much, Ben... I love him very much."

Ben stayed with that pitiful girl for hours as she pined for the love of another man. He pulled the damp curls away from her eyes, held her hand, and fearfully watched as she became the broken china doll that he rarely saw. This time around, he understood her fragility. He listened to her sobbing with an endurance that is not easily granted of a partner and, in that moment, Benjamin became a better man than she could ever thank him for.

'Knock, knock.' The door to my memories creaked. 'We know that you're home.' But I stepped away from their demands, closed the blinds and locked the door.

As I opened my eyes back up to the Gold Coast, I felt the sand sift between my toes like an egg timer. The ocean arched its eyebrows towards me and questioned my pledge to remain in the moment. So I realigned and began, once again, to practice patience and stillness.

And, although it wasn't going very well for me, I also endeavoured to practice being present.

Love Encompassed

6th December 2014

The grapevine was swollen with clandestine affections. I had heard whispers upon its juicy leaves of Benjamin being romantically involved with another; with the 'her', with the 'Ola' that Ben had felt such a divine connection with, back on that night where they had partied beneath a bridge. And, despite not having a right in the world, I began to turn the same shade of leafy green.

Back in Melbourne, I had developed a gentle friendship with Ola and, like a sister, I had invited her into the chambers of my war-torn heart. Together, we had lounged upon the grass at Lentils and formed an alliance through our easy-going conversations and connections. Ola's ears had been like two dry sponges and the stories that I had given her were as vast and salty as the ocean. She had absorbed and played witness to the holy trinity of Ben, Andy and I. Ola had even hitched a ride upon my time-encapsulated heart proclamations with the spirit of a curious scientist. Her angelic eyes had followed me down the troubled path that I had been walking and, in return of my honesty, Ola made it clear that she had felt touched in discovering the wars that had waged on inside of me. Yet, as I sat upon the beach in the Gold Coast a few weeks later, armed with secret intel, I found that Ola had begun to infiltrate the love that I had left behind. The grapevine smudged green with deep jealousy and the foliage of our friendship, of our sisterhood, began to part.

Since leaving Melbourne, the few sporadic phone calls that I had shared with Benjamin had all been barren of intimacy or substance. Attempting to extract the scent of a long-term lover from my skin was proving to be difficult, yet our phone conversations could not truly encapsulate what transformative perfumery either one of us was wearing. There was a need to be communicatively close, though Ben and I either fell into fun facts about the acts of debauchery that we had participated in, or simply allowed silence to fill the line.

361

Crouching in the sand with Christina's supportive hand clasped within my own, I fished for my phone amidst the aquatic mess of my backpack and dialled Benjamin. After a vague update of our happenings, I began to inquire about the whispers that had unfurled from Melbourne's grapevine.

"She only stayed over a few nights," Ben proclaimed from the witness stand within the receiver. "We just cuddled."

The thought of Ola sleeping in *our* bunk-bed with *my* Benjamin suddenly right-hooked my self-proclaimed detachment. In that moment, I knew that all of my encouragements towards Ben's romantic freedom had all simply been well-disguised delusions. I envisioned Ola's sweet eyes looking longingly into Ben's. His blue pools, full to the brim with desertion. I could see Ola nurturing him and bestowing upon him the love that I had not been able to offer. My stomach churned around like fouled butter, causing my mouth to salivate in sickness. The image of Ben with another woman began to haunt me. And I knew then, undoubtedly, what it felt like to be on the other side of the war of lost love; the enemy had surrendered to another kind of affection.

As a fire set to flame in the furnace of my throat, I began to choke over my own jealousy. There was not a truth in the world that could justify my hypocrisy; no ointment could sooth the unfairness that had settled upon my skin, and no reason would be good enough for me to allow my temper to come out and play. Yet, as I stared out to a restless sea, I allowed it to anyway.

Knowing that no part of me held even half of the patience that the man in Benjamin did, I resorted to the tantrum of a terrible two-year-old kid and began throwing my toys out of the pram. Steam spewed out from my eardrums, tremors boogied across my hands and lava spilt from my lips, scolding the undeserving recipient. To my surprise, Benjamin began to retaliate.

Ben excavated the knife of betrayal that had unintentionally been stuck in his turned back and returned the bloody blade to its owner without hesitation. It was the first time that Ben had ever raised his voice to me and, in his stressed pitch, the heartache that I had caused him became clear. He verbally searched for the soft spot below my belt and began to repeatedly, viciously stab. Andrew's name flew into our conversation like a bird that was flying south for the winter. And although it was summer in the Gold Coast, I felt that winter chill all around me. As mine and Ben's argument ascended into madness, I met it there with the same hot-blooded fever.

"Why don't both of you boys just take me out of the equation and go and fuck yourselves!" As the receiver began to pierce my ears in retaliation, I disconnected from a phone call that was no longer barren.

I know, without a sense of doubt that my ways can be born of a careless storm and because of that, it takes a certain kind of man to be able to love me. That man, whether he knows it or not, is required to challenge me when the time comes, otherwise, there is the chance that my path of destruction will inadvertently crush him. Therefore, despite the fire of hypocrisy that burned in my chest, a soft smile began to pull at my lips. For the first time in almost three years, Benjamin and I had just experienced our first real argument. And I found that I was pleased to see that he had finally found the nerve to challenge me. Benjamin had obviously come to his wit's end in following me down the dark hallways of my own self-discovery and, with a heart bled dry, he had finally thrown in the blood-saturated towel. My smile faded into a river of sadness, knowing that Ben and I had begun to walk down separate roads... roads that both strayed far from friendship.

Whilst walking back to Christina's parents' house, I attempted to distract myself from the thought of Ben, but it was a feeble attempt. Looking down at the cracks in the pavement, I could only think of one question;

How can one really escape love?

It seemed that I had been on an endless pursuit of detachment where in which I tried to fill my time with a deeper meaning that was outside of the confines of my heart. I had perfumed myself with rainbow children and Aboriginal dreaming. Vulnerability had unclothed me, flora and fauna had educated me, and even the whispers of responsibility had found me and given my spirit a sense of higher purpose. Yet there I was, walking that same old fractured pathway of love.

How can I escape it?

How can I not associate love with every single thing that comes into my view?

How can I be bold in the world and give myself to my dreams, without using my heart as the vehicle in which to get me there?

The answer to my queries never strayed far from the question mark. I simply could not. I could not escape love, nor uncouple myself from it, because the compass in my heart spiralled out in many different directions, yet love was the magnet that turned them. My aspirations pointed south. My connections pointed north. East and west were dominated by persons of the opposite sex, therefore, my heart could not help but to be drawn to love in all of its various forms.

For me, there is no distinction between my inner romantic that proclaims love to be key, and my extroverted principles that make me who I am. I cannot distinguish between the sweet scent of the pink hibiscus flowering, from the warm scent of coconut that rests on the soft of his pale skin. Even if I turned into a mad mathematician that dealt only in algebra and fractions, I am sure that I would still find romance in X, slowly dividing the silky thighs of Y. They are all one in the same; an encompassed love, by any other name.

Knowing that there would be no escape for me, I simply turned my off phone and packed my things, with Murwillumbah marked out on my mental map. I embraced my fairy of the light, my snail queen, my guardian angel, Christina, and set out on my own to further my discovery of self.

Like a tumbleweed tumbling around upon an internal compass of love, I continued to blow about in the hibiscus-scented breeze.

Sweat Release

11th December 2014

Retraining the programming of one's own mind is, to say the least, an enthusiastic task. The weeks, months and years of specific thought patterns that slowly solidify into the backbone of our beings can often emit an appearance of being the only thing that is holding us up. We grasp onto our perceptions as if they are our bones, our teeth and our hair, as if they equate to the entirety of our make-up. However, our ideas are often just a crutch to the bigger picture. It is comparable to an entire universe leaning upon a man-made walking stick of theory; like our ideas, the wooden stick is built from the natural world around it, but it is not the entire world. Moreover, a simple stick could never support the weight of the universe, despite how hard it tries.

Some idealisms are as simple as not liking crooked teeth in a partner, or the man on the train standing in too close a proximity for our liking. Others delve deeper into the specifications of a person's character: her midnight skin with voodoo seeping from its pores, his lost religion washing up on your devoted shore, or the dangerous lesbian that swirls in the saliva upon her hungry tongue, threatening to magically encourage the elastic upon your daughter's panties to come undone. We box them all up, label them with a politically or emotionally correct stamp and then ship them off to the appropriate category of our minds.

It's all too easy to become tied up in thought patterns that have either been passed down from generation to generation or adopted from one bad situation and then passed on to the next. Our wooden ideas wind around our minds like the vines of a family tree, consciously or unconsciously, and fuse themselves to our bones. In order to undo their knots and rewire our self-imposed notions, an injection of blood and sweat, along with a belief transfusion is often necessary. Reprogramming the mind is a tedious operation and not all believe their fingers to be steady enough to make the cut. My shaky hands were no exception.

I rode in a bumpy bus towards Murwillumbah, knowing that I needed to evict my own outdated judgements of love. My last conversation with Benjamin had left me feeling possessed; rather than an operation, I instead needed something more along the lines of a demonic exorcism. It was clear to me that my concept of romance had become distorted and tainted. However, the overpopulated public bus was no place for such extractable aspirations.

I arrived in the mountainous area of Murwillumbah to be greeted by my gracious new hosts, Tony and Therese. Tony was Leaf's uncle and, through her caring nature, Leaf had put me into contact with him and his wife, so that I could stay at their house for the next leg of my journey. As I made my way to their residence, Tony and Therese's picturesque property swelled out before me like a pregnant belly that was just about to give birth. Full of curvaceous hillsides and rushing rivers, I followed a happy trail of trees that lined their pathway and found myself in the navel of Tony and Therese's serene home. It was a belly button of beauty that stood alone amidst the forest and appeared to be at peace with its own company. Three thunderous mountains pirouetted in the background, as if to demand that my attentions not neglect them. Though they were unnecessarily paranoid, for their splendour was so grand that could not have been possible to ignore their tripled mounds.

The walls inside of Tony and Therese's house were painted with the kind of blood red that I required for my belief transfusion, immediately reassuring me that I had come to the right place. Upon the life force of those scarlet walls, photographs of intricately tattooed bodies were decoratively placed like blood-splattered art. A small but contented library sat amongst a window seat, swelling in the same expectant nature of the forest that guarded over it, whilst signs of rainwater showers promised to keep my new-found desire for sustainability intact. Looking over towards the coal-coloured leather sofa, I was met by the kind eyes of Tony.

As the afternoon sun permitted Tony and I the opportunity to get to know one another, it became clear to me that, although he was a man, Tony also firmly believed in the raw power of femininity. The leather sofas began to creak beneath my curiosity, as Tony went on to tell me of how he was in repulsion of what man has come to be. Together, we spoke of war and of violence, of miscommunication and misguidance and, through his brown-speckled irises, Tony named but one culprit that was responsible for our historical atrocities. And he had the genitalia of man.

I sailed over Tony's hair, as it settled upon his head like a brown, baby wave and I could not help but to be amazed in hearing a man say such a thing. Tony dreamily stared off past the expectant bookshelf, past the large, open windows and past the pillow-drenched day bed, finally allowing his radiantly melancholic brown eyes to fall, as if hypnotised by their womanly curves, upon the three mountains that stood against one another. As if to fill me in on his daydreams, Tony began to draw stories of when, once upon a time, women had been worshiped. I followed Tony back into a land where women had taken charge of spiritual exhibitions and listened as he expressed of how man's heart had been plentiful because of it.

I sat in Tony's living room, looking out towards the curvaceous mountains whilst the desire for my heart to also be plentiful through the genteel essence of femininity became prominent. I thought back to my dream, of the women that had sailed on the boat with me, pulling me up to the highest level that I could reach. In that moment, I knew that my quest for a higher love had somehow also become a quest to reconnect with the divine woman that was inside of me.

That night, Tony's queen, Therese, and I sat upon a wooden veranda that wrapped around the backside of their house like a faded tutu and, with the impenetrable sky as our only witness, we began a never-ending conversation of philosophy. Therese worked the nightshifts as a caregiver for the mentally sensitive, therefore she bestowed upon me her personal pilgrimage of exposing and altering embedded thought patterns. Our wine glasses tentatively clinked with the twinkle of stars, as the more wine that we poured into ourselves, the further we crept down the dark hallway of mental afflictions. As always, I took notes, in the hopes that I could exorcise the terrible habits that my heart had been harbouring. The frogs roared out from the darkness around us with a hint of mania in their croaky throat passages.

The next few days in Murwillumbah came to be a time of reflective solitude. Tony worked at the sugar mill during the day and slept at night, whilst Therese worked the night shifts and slept during the day. For most of the time, my company was all that was available out there in the woods and like the lone house that sat in the belly of the forest, I aspired to be at peace with myself. No communicative distraction could detain me from the need to rewire certain parts of myself and the more that I thought about things, the more I began to understand how imperative it was for me to actually get out of my head. I realised that I needed to focus on getting down and dirty with my physical body. It would be the only way for me to exorcise the bitterness out of me.

Therefore, I began listening to the sequestered voice of my body in an attempt to couple it with my mind. Each morning, I rose like freshly-baked bread and, despite the thick air that flopped around like dough inside of my throat, I employed the excretion of sweat as my remedy. I began to do as many push-ups as I could muster, and then twenty more just for good measure. I would cradle my knee caps to my chest, feel my forgotten abs flex with redefined existence and allow the sweat to roll down into my eyes until they stung me back to life. I took to jogging around the entire property with bird song as my only soundtrack. Although my raggedy boots were not made for such endeavours, they pushed on anyway, appreciating the feel of grass beneath their soles. I could feel the fresh air billowing up into, and catching, the soaring kites of my lungs, until I almost floated off into the sky, breathlessly. I played peekaboo with the bearded goats, the timid horses hid for cover at the sound of my approach, whilst the bulls just stood there, indifferent. I was never truly alone. The sun pressed down on us all through a snow globe of deep greens and blues, kite lungs blew in the breeze and little particles of happiness began to fall upon me.

Those pertinacious exertions quickly became the most enjoyable part of my day. As I exercised, I called in health, I invoked breath and I began sweating out my own sickness. My mind attempted to practice equality with my body and my body was humbled by its eventual consideration. I would sit upon a hill, looking down at the goats, with my notebook clenched in my clammy hands and endlessly purge words as sweat fell upon the page. I practiced all of those things like a private religion, until I could feel each psychological string of bad thought that had fused itself into my being… slowly begin to untangle. The exorcism was proving to be beneficial. And I scribbled spells upon my paper.

Release me. I wrote.

Release me. I exhaled

Release me. I sweated the heartache out from me.

After a week of exorcising my demons, I lay upon the wooden veranda with fresh sweat stinging my eyes and, as if for the first time, I looked upon the scenery of Murwillumbah. Everything looked lighter and brighter, like a dark veil had been lifted from my eyes; after all, it is said that love is blind. Three mountains gathered their arms around their kneecaps and, knowing that nothing else was happening for the day, they rocked themselves into an afternoon nap. Shrubbery fell around their ankles like a safety blanket, the sky pierced their nightmares with a blue blade of clarity and they finally exhaled themselves into dreams. Feeling the peaceful wind upon my face, I took my notebook in my hand once more, gladly accepted that I was 1,600 kilometers away from the trials of Melbourne, and slid into the presence of Murwillumbah's healing.

As I sat in the alcove of a wooden chair, with sweat swimming above my upper lip like a row boat and a damp hand scribbling out my incantations of release, I began to hear a thud of heavy footsteps pounding across the veranda towards me.

The sound of laborious breathing penetrated the slumberous mountains, disturbing them from their daydreams. Releasing my eyes from my saturated paper, I looked up to my left at a shadow that had gathered beside me.

"Hello, April." The shadow spoke.

It was Benjamin.

Hitchhiker's Heart

14th December 2014

Each step that Benjamin had taken towards my placement on the veranda had echoed out in remembrance of the last few words that I had said to him on the phone. *'Fuck'* thudded out from his left foot, whilst *'you'* creaked out from beneath his right. Ben's body, upon arrival, was riddled with a justified uncertainty. However, with my bitterness having finally left me, I stood up to face Benjamin without a trace of venom. Disturbed from their slumber, the mountains began to wipe the dreams away from their leaf-crusted eyes and clambered onto one another's jagged backs in order to get a better view of us. The soupy afternoon air was filled with great expectations.

As I walked towards Benjamin, tear drops leaned out from the pale windows of his eyes and looked down upon me hesitantly, as if they were unsure of their commitment to the jump. The sweaty row boat that rested upon my upper lip began to take in too much water and, as it sunk, pressed my jaw down towards the floor in weighted shock. Like black-out curtains, Ben's eyelashes drew themselves to a close, wobbling and twitching in the same manner as the body that held them. After a moment of exhalation, they regained composure and the impenetrable curtains of Ben's thick eyelashes re-opened in order to bathe me in their luminescent light.

Ben and I stood upon the faded veranda that afternoon embracing one another tenderly. Though after a moment, the electricity that had been pulsating out of his body began to zap me. Chest to chest, I felt the freight train of Ben's heart pounding off of its tracks and it was coming straight towards my tranquility.

'See me.' Ben's inner desires throbbed, as they rode the rollercoaster of his heartbeat to the point of throwing up. The aromatic scent of his skin sent me into a wave of intoxication

whilst the clean air attempted to permeate the smell of cigarettes and desperation that clung to him. Our perspiration merged into one another's like two rivers that met at the mouth of the sea and, as I breathed in deeply, I inhaled the wild fire of a forgotten love. The mountains fanned us with their breath in an attempt at bringing our temperatures down, yet as the flames between Ben and I grew uncontrollably wild, I decidedly withdrew back into the safety net of my own serenity.

Placing his heavy bags down upon the floor, Benjamin put a cigarette to his lips, as if to stop his mouth from prematurely spilling tales of his adventure from it. Exhaustion gathered beneath his eyes like two sacks of earth-saturated potatoes and I knew from the sight of him that Ben had just arrived from an almighty adventure; a pilgrimage of love. A fleeting feeling of expectation pushed itself through the barriers that I had, just then, placed around my heart. Because although any girl in her right mind would have gone weak in the knees at such a heroic voyage of romance, the instability in Benjamin began to feel dangerous to me. However, as I looked into those eager blue eyes, I saw that, as always, they expected nothing from me.

As the mountainous sisters held their breath and leaned in closer for a better view, fuelled with the desire to insert new gossip between their tips, Ben and I gradually fell back into orbit with one another. The afternoon air attempted to loosen up our voice boxes as I listened to Ben draw tales of a hitchhike that had spanned out all the way from Melbourne up to Murwillumbah. 1,600 kilometers of truck stops, defiant thumbs and dangerous highways had all been crossed in order to get Ben to where he was standing and he wore the scent of sleeplessness upon his nicotine-saturated skin as if it were an aphrodisiac. I knew that before our conversation furthered, Benjamin needed to catch up on some rest.

Retreating into the kitchen, I made Benjamin a peanut butter and jam sandwich and watched as he tried to eat it without falling asleep in the jam. I then pulled back the covers of a bed that had once been just for me, and laid his electrically-charged body to rest within it, promising to speak more the next day. As Ben deliriously mumbled about a truck driver that had been touched by his pilgrimage and helped him along the way, the mountains dismounted one another's backs in an unsatisfied retreat, finally joining Benjamin in a warm and lucid sleep.

The next morning found me with a serene pep in my step. I had had time to digest the implications of Ben's quest for love and could not help but to admire his determination. When Benjamin had finally awoke from his coma, I introduced him to our hosts, Tony and Therese. Though, knowing that our tranquility had been compromised, due to that which I had previously told them about Benjamin and I, our hosts each circled Ben like two eagles protecting their nest.

"He's welcome here... as long as that's what you want." Tony and Therese had both unanimously decided.

What I want. What I want. Those three words bounced around the kitchen walls and did cartwheels off of the spatulas. They barely skimmed past the cookie container before crashing into the wind chime. Then, after falling down into the depths of a prism that was hanging beneath the jar, the words projected a rainbow of unity as my final answer.

By the time that the late afternoon sun had tardily punched into the timeclock, Ben and I had found a quiet retreat beside a ravishing and radiant creek. The water glittered beneath the laborious sun like a bejewelled prom queen, blowing watery kisses towards us and beckoning us to undress. Benjamin and I discarded our clothes, leaving them beside our spoils of bread and red wine, and dove into the creek's satin-gloved arms. The world appeared to be only inhabited by the two of us.

As Ben and I splashed each other with acquiescent diamonds and turtles slowly swam across our feet in a race that they would always lose to the hare, (despite whether he was there or not,) I realised that exact moment to be the first conjoined taste of an organic Australia that Ben and I were yet to share together. It encapsulated the very dream that had been born from our solitary kettle back in England, and almost forgotten. It was the fabric that had sewn our footsteps upon fantasies of the great Down Under. Together, far from looming buildings, peddling pedestrians and kamikaze traffic, Ben and I began to sample Australia as though it were a smorgasbord of serenity. It was not only the distance from city life that had begun to encourage my contentment, but the undulating illumination that came from being far away from the entanglements of 'other love.' As I said before, it was just the two of us; the rest of the world was on lunch break.

"So, let's talk." I eventually encouraged, as Ben and I ascended a mound of rocks in order to bask in the heat of the day beside uncompetitive turtles.

Whilst the diligent sun, as if to make up for his tardiness, feverishly warmed the rocks that were supporting my bare buttocks, I listened to Benjamin's testimony of travel. Ben began to fill the afternoon air with tales of his love for me, speaking of how he simply could not be without me and, despite whether or not I was ready to receive him, Ben assured me that only one thing had been certain in his heart: that he must try to find me, wherever may have been. In hearing this, the lily pads looked across at the reeds shyly, wondering why no such grand declaration of love had ever been bestowed upon them. The reeds could only bow their heads in shame; Benjamin had that kind of effect upon other couples.

Benjamin then theatrically retold the events that had transpired during the beginning of his quest for me, where he had aquired my address from Leaf, who had thought Ben's pursuit of me to be of great comical value. Penniless but undeterred, Ben had packed a rucksack, walked to the nearest highway in Melbourne and stuck a hopeful thumb out to the road. The ripples in the creek pushed themselves against the riverbed suggestively, wet with the notion of his heroism. The riverbed, glad to finally receive some action. Benjamin then went on to tell me of how he had met a truck driver who had been so compelled with his quest for love, that he had given Ben money from his own pocket, a ride for most of the way, and his invaluable respect. Even the hare, although he was still nowhere to be seen, was soaking wet.

Ben had travelled for days, sleeping on the streets, meeting a myriad of strangers and infecting them all with his tireless heart proclamations. That kind of love would always serve to be an inspiration and Ben's heart had carried him with wings of protection, his gammy toe had hobbled behind him, (still raptured with infection,) and Ben, with a hitchhiker's heart, had finally found his way to me. His love knew no distance too far, no hurt too deep, because, for me, Ben would have reached into the darkest depths of hell in order to save me. It was clear that, for Ben, every single path somehow led to me. The late afternoon sun, forgetting his duties, sighed out in dreamy relief, cradled his slender rays against his face, and thought about the steamy night that he had just spent with the moon. True love would always excuse tardiness.

I was officially swooned. Even with my best effort at filling my being with interesting ventures, I could no longer pretend that there had not always been a Ben-shaped hole that was living inside of me. Despite my initial reservation, I was glad that he had found me, (in heaven, not in hell,) and was happy that we could finally enjoy paradise together. However, clause one in the Bill of Our Reunion clearly stated that hands were to be kept off of my goods. All I could offer Benjamin, at that time, was my friendship. I had no intention of further stressing my heart; I wanted peace and tranquility and Benjamin respectfully understood. Therefore, we were friends… for 2.5 whole seconds.

Friendship, it was discovered, was an impossible task to achieve for lovers who had known one another's bodies for years. Therefore, Ben and I slipped back into our familiarity with hot-blooded ease. The hour was late and my guard was down. I felt an adoring mouth searching me out in the night and found my tongue swirling around inside of it like an eel. It was a cave of secrets that I had always known, a blade of grass that could only grow, a sticky toffee pudding that would always cause me to moan out in delight.

Benjamin and I grasped at the straws of our continuity; we drank from them, we put them to our noses, we even put feathers on their ends and tickled one another's private parts. I became lost in a forest of Ben's never-ending love.

Mine and Benjamin's connection was so strong that night, that it felt almost new to me. It seemed that the more Benjamin and I let go of the idea of ownership towards one another, or what we thought a relationship should be, then the deeper the well of our passion seemed to flow. Ben crawled into the caverns of my being like an insatiable stranger, but he touched my skin as if he had always known me. Together, we began to sweat in a new kind of sweet release.

Though, something still felt slightly amiss; as Ben kissed me, a missing link began to whisper of its identity but I couldn't quite put my finger on it. Then Ben placed his fingers in places that swallowed them up and, heaving and ho-ing, I forgot what I was thinking of. A sexual revolution joined our party and the fruits of his loins were saturated in possibility.

After all that had happened to us, somehow Benjamin and I had still managed to keep one another.

For days, Ben and I held hands and watched waterfalls do their thing. In a haze of renewed love, we walked together amongst the forest, stared out into the same sparkling lakes, and tentatively looked upon the same dead trees that had been drowned within their stagnant waters…

…both of us silently hoping not to endure the same watery fate.

Letters to Home

16th December 2014

A pool of afternoon sunlight fell upon the empty roads by the bucketful, chucking moist heat over every particle that it touched and causing the drenched tarmac to glisten and sparkle. Then it slithered off like a silver river that was bound for the honey dew horizon. My thumb sprawled itself out towards the river-road like an opposable rowboat whose own destination exceeded past the horizon and aspired to make its way towards Never-Neverland. However, after checking the map, it appeared that the third star from the right wasn't quite the plan, though I had heard upon the grapevine that Byron Bay held a similar kind of magic, so we settled for that sand-stricken star instead.

My thumbs were itchy and twitching with a responsibility that, since departing Melbourne, I knew would be theirs alone. It was to be the first time that I had ever hitchhiked in my life, though, over the years, I had often romanticised about casting my hopeful thumbs into the grey sea of possibilities. There seemed to be nothing more adventurous to me than subjecting myself to geographic luck and the kindness of strangers; therefore, I took to hitching like a duck takes to water. Ben and I stood on the hard shoulder just outside of Murwillumbah with our thumbs to the wind, and made an attempt in attracting cars into our optimistically-charged gravitational pull. But despite the fever of my romanticism, the cars just blew by like shiny little planets that were on their own orbiting trajectory. City life, work commitments and heartache were all, hopefully, far behind Benjamin and I. Therefore, despite our initial hitching rejections, I could not help but to smile at the confirmation of such a cosmic adventure. It felt worthy of writing home about.

Before long, a car stopped, a passenger door opened and another world materialised before Benjamin and I. I curiously walked towards it as if I were the first man to walk upon the moon, throwing my rucksack into its silver craters and touching skin with a stranger in appreciation of her vehicular offering. As I climbed into the back seat, my feet were seized by an assortment of children's toys that, due to their presence, convinced me that I was in no immediate danger of abduction, the driver appeared to have enough on her hands. As the engine started with its new passengers on board, and the lady smiled her introductory smile at me through the rearview mirror, I employed the headrest and was proud to become a part of the hitchhiking world.

Hitchhiking itself is a spherical bubble of continuity that will pull you into its rounded edges just to see how well you can mould yourself to its shape. Before entry, the hitcher can never know what resides behind the closed doors of the halted vessel and can only place the greatest of faith in the universe that no dangers are lurking behind its child-locked doors. Babies may scream, wail and demand a nurturing from you that you never knew you had, soppy dogs may take up the space upon your lap as if it were always destined to be their kennel, whilst uncertain teenagers may simply stare out the window just to avoid eye contact with your unfamiliarity. There are organised cars that sparkle with the whistle of clean life, whilst other cars demand that you fight for space amongst its crowded inhabitants if you want to make it to your destination on time. Some hitches are bubbles of awkward silences, in which there is no escape; others are filled to the brim with thick catalogues of unending dialogue. Whatever vehicle you find yourself in, once the door is closed, behind headrests and personality tests, the hiker is trapped in an inescapable vacuum of another person's universe.

Benjamin sat in the front seat with our driver and danced around idle conversation as if it were a second language. *Who are you? Where have you been and where are you going?* seemed to be the local dialect, and Ben answered the driver's queries like a well-informed tourist of himself. As I sat in the back seat and employed observational silence, Ben and the woman driver gradually came to a common conversational ground of health and elixirs. Upon listening to the woman's nurturing stories, it became clear that we had stumbled upon one of the good ones. She organically drew stories of clean living that were deeply-rooted in her memories and even went on to encourage Ben and I to attend a conscious festival that was scheduled to begin a few days from then; I pencilled her guidance into my mental map, beside the fourth sandy star from the right.

Within the world of hitching, there is always a time limit that one must consider. When a bond is formed with he or she who aspires to assist you in the furthering of your journey, a conversational desperation can also sit quietly in-between the car seats. That inconspicuous passenger will watch as both parties dramatically attempt to draw from, and unload, the entirety of their lives upon one another, spitting out advices and guidance before the end of the line rapidly forms upon the horizon.

With a look of melancholy in her eyes, our driver unloaded us upon the tarmac belt like a sack of groceries. One small step closer to our destination, but one giant leap from the beginning, the world began to pull Ben and I forward without sentiment. Yet, with our eyes cast down, we were like a trio of new lovers who, after being destined and star-crossed, were just about to part from their first date. *'Well, this is me,'* the glimmer in mine and Ben's eyes said as we kissed our date upon the cheek. The craterous car drove off into the sunset, though unlike the lovers, the hitchhiker's heart knew the improbability of ever seeing one another again. Hitchhiking is a casual lover that the hitcher is never bound to; therefore, after a moment of appreciation, our thumbs were back out in the wind, wriggling and worming, inviting another recipient in without particularity.

After a few more hitches, Byron Bay began to roll towards the horizon in sparkling, saline waves. Although we were about a half-hour's walk from the beach, mounted by my red rucksack, I began making my way towards Byron with the intention of meeting an old friend. The afternoon sun shone furiously overhead of mine and Ben's endeavours and began to frisk us, as if to look for a place upon our bodies that had not yet been drenched in sweat. Each item that I owned began to press down upon me with an unforgiving weight and I could not escape the fact that I had unnecessarily packed too many things. My red turtle shell spewed out demonic colours from over my shoulders and I began finding it difficult to swim through the heat of the day. Once Ben and I had made it the town of Byron Bay, I began to throw the contents of my life out onto the pavement, in order to exorcise those demonic burdens.

'But that's my favourite dress.' I pleaded to the sweat upon my forehead, to the ache in my back, to anyone who was willing to listen to the pampered girl within me. *'I can't possibly live without it, or those innumerable jeans, or my assortment of favourite lip glosses.'* Yet, Practicality seemed to be the only one to pay her any attention and he was having none of it. *'It can be someone else's favourite dress too.'* He responded coldly and, like an unhappy parent, threw more of my clothes upon the sizzling street. The charity shop gulped in most of my belongings, even my dream journal was not spared under the scrutiny of Practicality's gaze. The sun had worked as an accomplice, tempting every single luxurious item out of me, until all that I had left was one pair of trousers, one pair of shorts, five t-shirts, toiletries, and my faithful green hammock. The transition from unnecessary to simplicity was a swift one. I placed my shell back upon my shoulders feeling, not only physically, but psychologically lighter and began to make my way down towards the beach.

The pure, white sand that showered Byron Bay's beach squeaked and crunched beneath my booted feet, like an incessant rodent that had decided to make its home in paradise. As I made my way across the powdered sand, I was hypnotised by the teal-blushed water that twisted and turned beneath the sun like an aquatic ballerina, doing its best to appease its audience. Palm trees rose up in-between sunbathing bodies, brushed their leaves together and applauded the dance of the sea. Children played freely, unaware of any theatre other than their own, whilst the warm scent of coconut sunscreen and dry salt combined to produce a nostalgic result. Floating up through my nose, that familiar scent allowed my body to adjust and relax into the picturesque scene of Byron Bay.

As my eyes attempted to register all of the beauty that was unfolding before them, I looked out towards the horizon and saw a familiar face walking towards me, lending the scene an even greater beauty. The young woman's blonde hair gathered itself above her head in replication of the sun and browned the body that lay beneath it into the same shades as my own. Her translucent skirt blew in the breeze like paper wings and, as she walked towards me, the confidence in her step showed that she was home amongst the world of Byron.

It was my blood sister, Reeta, and I had never been happier to see her. Reeta and I began to run into each other's arms as though our extended fingertips had fairy tales imprinted upon them and the ending for our tales could not be determined until they touched. The seagulls eagerly squawked at our reunion as Reeta and I collided into one another's similarities like two tectonic plates that had always been destined to merge.

As a request for water fell from my parched lips, Reeta laughed at me as though we were back in our living room in Melbourne, rolling around on the floor and gut-laughing at our stupidity. Whilst Reeta and Benjamin embraced, I mused over the fate that had led us all back together. There had never been any plans upon paper for our reunion, yet there we stood, miles from Melbourne, and we stood together; it appeared to be the hand that fate had dealt us.

Before long, Reeta and I were like mermaids swimming in the blue lagoons of life. I allowed the waves to wash over my body, as if they could serve as a baptism to the disconnection that I had endured from Reeta. I watched as her dark body glistened in the water, like an iris that had been set amongst an endlessly blue eye. Salty beads ran down her skin, separating like water to oil, and she splashed me with the enthusiasms of a long-lost friend. It did not take long for Reeta and I to fall back in sync with one another and, as we made our way towards dry land, I knew that we had been reunited amongst a new backdrop in which we could reinvent our relationship upon.

Back on the sand, I began to do my daily sit-ups, Benjamin stretched, and Reeta played, in great animation, with her dog, Tarantino. In the midst of our casual reunion, a petite woman with beach-blonde hair approached us all, with a camera in hand, and asked if she could capture our persons in photographic form. Complimented by her request, Benjamin, Reeta and I unanimously voted. "Yes."

"Just keep doing what you were doing," Ness instructed to our open eyes. The lens of her camera closed in on us like prey, attempting to bring the best parts of us out into existence. Under the scrutiny of the lens, we all fell into great theatrics. Reeta and I ran towards one another and did running kicks in the air, laughing all the while with salt-saturated hair that whipped our enthusiastic eyes. Benjamin did backflips in the background and flexed his muscles for anyone who cared to look upon them. Cartwheels began to liberate themselves from our limbs and we each star-fished our way across the sands of time. Ness appreciatively captured every moment.

After our impromptu photoshoot was completed, and we had adequately fallen into conversation with Ness, she then invited the three of us, plus an absent Carlotta, to stay in her home with her for a few days. We were the lost children of Byron Bay who had nowhere to stay, so we gladly accepted her offer. The kindness of strangers became a random reality upon the beach of Byron Bay.

In the safety of Ness' house, her children encircled us as though we were clowns in a carnival. We each fell into family life with a natural affinity, dining together, playing games with the children, and conversing over life. Ben, Reeta, Carlotta and I, (plus Reeta's pup,) all slept on a single mattress that was sprawled out across the living room floor and couldn't have been more grateful for a roof over our heads. In an attempt to repay Ness for her gracious hospitality, brimming with wine and fun, we decided to embark upon some drunken modelling.

Being a photographer, Ness had conveniently acquired an assortment of ball gowns and costumes that hung in her closet, just awaiting our attentions. Transforming into a fairytale princess, I adopted a satin ball gown dress and let it hang seductively from my oiled skin. Carlotta dressed herself in the dark dangers of an Italian Mafia priestess. With a plastic gun in her hand and smouldering eyes, Carlotta slipped into a character that was second nature to her. Reeta adopted the look of an African queen and pushed fire into the camera lens' insatiable appetite. Ben dressed, or rather, undressed, as a tragically handsome slave boy who was bound to only his underwear. His thick hair was slicked back in a ponytail and his hands were tied behind his back as Carlotta, Reeta, and I walked amongst the cornfields, torturing him with our beauty. The camera was pleased with our efforts.

That night, upon a crowded mattress, I wrote a letter to my mother.

"Dear Mummy,

I met someone on the beach today who wanted to take photos of me and my friends. They invited me back to their house to stay the night. My friends and I oiled one another's skin up real good so that we looked tasty and put on very skimpy outfits for the shoot. I drank a lot of wine and posed seductively.

Speak again soon!

Love, April."

Though the letter, for obvious reasons, was never sent.

Divinity's Disconnection

18th December 2015

I sat on a park bench, with a paper tree at my back. Its bark curved around my body like unwritten histories, blowing curled, paper fingers across my shoulders and I looked out towards the streets of Byron Bay.

Conversations fizzled, evaporating in the heat of the day that held me. The full rouge of laughing lips touched the sea air without pressed reservations. Relaxation wore the face of youth, for there were young, swaying, salted hips rolling around and around the borders of such a happening beach scene. Bikinis held on for dear life to aqueous bodies. And everyone seemed to be having a good time beneath the sun, the sand and the sea. Musicians lined the streets and sat on the park grass beside me, gathering shade beneath the same tree as I. Our papered histories subconsciously entwined. Harmonicas hung upon the lips of creamy beach boys as drums awaited the attentions of well-versed brown hands. I could hear the saxophone symphonies of 'the Pink Panther' making its way towards me. The place was busy and young with little trendy things that materialised like children before me; they had no curfew for their curly hair, or anywhere else that they needed to be. Handmade jewellery lavishly sprawled itself out across the sand, shimmering beneath the sun, just to bait their young attentions. That picture of innocence showed me just a glimpse, in that handcrafted shimmer, of what Australia really is.

Another flash of perspective found me in the form of a woman. Whilst I sat upon the park bench, with my back against a paper tree, I made notes of my own personal history. The pen upon my paper consolidated a version of you with a version of me. As

I turned my vision out towards the sea... she approached me. She was about seventy years old with muddy skin tones that reminded me of my grandmother, wearing tatty clothes that rested lifelessly on her skin, reminding me of my own. The woman held a glass bottle of dark mysticisms in her hand, which stretched its deep shades out onto her skin, then further onto the shadow of the land and she introduced herself to me with slurred speech. Alcoholic undertones sat heavily beneath the light of her breath and pressed me with an introduction that bore the title of an Aboriginal elder. The woman went on to ensure that I knew that the fat of my ass sat where her past, her own history, where her land now kept me...

And yes, it was true that I did understand. I had heard the whispers of how her culture has been treated. To me, they were stories that had been diluted in disassociation, though she wore those pains like a choker upon her neck, because her reality would not be stepped away from so lightly. So I avoided a reaction of confrontation or desertion and humbly I gave her my thanks for sharing her land with me... but this moment of exchange in what two persons of respect should say... it felt empty.

The woman seemed unhinged, as though a ghost lived inside of her, because her memories of what once were the best days of her mob's existence had now been replaced by this young thing of Byron Bay. She slumped down next to me in acceptance of my peace and became lost in the wanderings of her mind. I made re-acquaintance with my thoughts and, without further words, our unified vision was lured into the horizon, where the sea shone for both of us... without question.

I had been in Byron Bay long enough to see that such meetings of similarity had been hunting me out. The brown of my skin was like a magnet to unspoken tribal alliances that looked respectfully upon my shades and, because of it, I was taken in with great haste. The disconnection of the past racism in my predominantly-white childhood was now replaced with, "Hello sister… come have a beer with us!" And hey, I like drinking, so I chugged it up. So too did my sister, Reeta. We cheered together on the park bench, for together we were made to feel welcome amongst our kin of the darker shades of skin. But as I sat with a black back against a paper tree, looking out to the unified glimmer of the ocean, whilst a slumped woman's beer bottle fell into the echo of the concrete, I could not help but begin to feel the rough fingers of disappointment upon me.

A younger version of me hung her pigtails in sadness, as the wish of being taken in by those in spiritual communion with body and land was slowly vanquished. The yearning for learning magic and its entwinements with life began to fall from the grasp of my small, childish hands. That little girl within me walked away with her head hung low, for what she had repeatedly been shown was that the magic of this place had gone. Been robbed. Been given up upon. It had become clear that a people who once believed in Dreamtime and divinity had now been reduced to stolen shopping carts and moonshine.

They sat on the streets with white people, too, brown and yellow. We were all unbiasedly defeated as we sat cross-legged upon a concrete pathway that wept for us. But still, there was a version of me that clung white-knuckled to the idea that people could still see a God in the scalding heat of the sun. That a Goddess could still take form within the craterous wane of the moon. That the Spirit could direct the people of which internal paths to tread because, I too had felt that same spirit inside of me and I thought that maybe these people, in communion with the land, that they could know me… and I could know them… and we could be true brothers and sisters who put down our substances and spoke of Dreamtime again.

For my soul hungered for it. And I had heard the whispers of other souls wanting the same thing, with similar hunger pains as I. I wanted to see those who could walk hand in hand with the four elements. I wanted to feel the fire upon the open of my palm but instead, I leaned against a palm, upon a park bench, with a dark bottle that rolled around on the ground beneath my feet, with the ghost of my lips upon it, too. I sat beside a woman who was slumped over into a far cry from who she could be. She searched the glimmer of the sea, though she could not quite see that she had forgotten, somewhere along the pathway, her own divinity. However, I just walked away quietly... for who was I to say such things?

The music played on in the background. The half side of a coin rolled itself into the Godless sun, while Reeta and I tried to have fun amidst the ugly things that stared us right in the browns of our faces. We slept homeless on the beaches, nestled away in hammocks that only knew how to sway. Tarps laid themselves upon the shore, offering a break from the cool hands of the night. But when we tried to dream, we were internally bullied, though we did not speak of it.

There is a dominant thing that has no face and steps in the shoes of a giant upon the browns of our backs and we become fearful of a faceless robber. We become small. We become drunk and we become unconscious, just as everyone else who is trying to get through this, whatever 'this' is at the time. Our unconsciousness becomes like a disease; it spreads itself into all the versions of our beings until we are angry in our small boxes, sleeping out on the streets with hands that push and shove at the cardboard edges... because we all need to at least feel free.

But, there are self-imposed emotional prisons that we need to escape first. There is a responsibility that begs us to tend to it, but until we step up, the anger turns into hate and the hate just breeds with itself until we are all inflicted... until we are all slumped over in our own worthlessness... until we cannot escape this unhappiness. And I see this in all kinds of eyes. Blues. Browns. Greens. Upon many different shades of skin. Blacks. Whites. Browns and yellows. Watered-down intoxicants sit in the beige of wet eyes, rolling like glossed-over empty wells, looking for new beginnings, though there is a sort of fear that swirls within us. So we just keep to our ways and we say nothing, however, half of our spirit... it becomes missing.

I love the idea of sacred soil, for all soil is sacred. I am blown away with the power that the People can place within the red of the earth, within the breath that we can breathe into life itself. Seedlings growing wild with desire and birth but numb... numb... numb. People are becoming numb. People are slumped over in defeat at disconnection with their true divinity.

So, who has the right? I found myself asking as I sat on ·the park bench, with a woman slumped over beside me, alcohol keeping company her breath. A paper tree with unwritten histories is the only one standing strong enough to support my queries. So, I ask it: *Who has the right to tell another being, a being of human experience, another human just simply being... who has the right to suggest a better knowledge of their true path? And how could we even govern such things?*

We have been told what is right. What is wrong. Which gods to pray to. Which colours are of acceptable respect. Whom to love and whom to hate. Pillaged, raped, and pushed from the land by transparent puppeteering hands and in turn, we clench our own hands, bound with the ghosts of a forgotten past, because we are implored not to make a sound. So, the People have become quiet and lost. There are no rites of passage. No communion with the land. Who still plants trees anyway? Apparently that is an age old thing that has passed us by and for it, we have begun to disconnect from organic life. I can see it all around me every single day. I can see it also in an empty and intoxicated version of me, for I am not above those slouchings. I try to remain happy and to play but these things quietly sadden me. They keep me up in the night whilst I lay in a hammock that sways in the cool beach breeze as these things... they quietly haunt me.

So, I did the only thing that I knew how to and I joined the musicians that lined the streets. I sung soulfully, attempting to pulse out joy in a way that could help us to understand the frequencies of love and fear and to choose consciously which path to tread upon. Love is much more of an alive thing than the sleeping dogs of the past, so I tried to lure those that passed me by, even if momentarily, into that frequency. I harmonised and tried on owning nothing and expecting even less. For I know only my truth; I have heard the angels singing to me in the deep of the night when my liberation of ownership has carried me upon harmonious winds. I have smelt lavender within the blossoming truth of my own life and have connected to every fibre, to every fabric, unweighted by the peculiarities of a division. Black, white, strong, weak, innocent, darkness and light all rest under the skin of my own existence, amicably. There are paper-bark histories imprinted with versions of you and versions of me, where we are owning nothing but our contribution to this existence.

I listened as the harmonica licked the wind's white-whipped teeth. I felt the pink panther crawling stealthily upon me and I reverberated with the dark drumbeat of my own heart. It pulsed in light, and too, in dark rhythms, where I had only my own contribution to keep.

But I can see, on one side of a faceless coin, shimmering with sides of duality... only the bark listens to the queries of which I speak...

I can see now, that my little contribution... well that is everything.

Holiday for the Homeless

25th December 2014

I lazily swung in my cramped hammock-turned-home, topping-and-tailing with Benjamin in the same squashed manner that we had slept in for the last month, and I listened to the oceanic lullaby of the sea. It serenaded Ben and I with salted carols that sprayed and hissed from its festively foamed mouth. Yet, despite the sea's intentions, Christmas Day turned out to be just another Tuesday afternoon that my nose appreciatively spent parting the pages of a wonderful book.

The holiday was, to say the least, an unceremonious event. Homelessness gave us no luxury of privacy, therefore Ben and I had simply found a quiet place upon the beach, where we consciously chose to not celebrate the holiday and also, unfortunately, to not feast. A homeless man named Dave lay upon a sandy tarp beside me and slept; breathing, twitching and dreaming with the force of a sleepwalking hurricane. I looked over every inch of his beached body in detail; his whiskers, his dandruff and his reddened wrinkles, only to stop myself from looking at a phone that couldn't muster up enough courage to ring. Holidays always placed such an unnecessary responsibility towards communication and gifting, but I was attempting to rise above that tradition, so that my heart would not be let down. My phone made not a sound and I looked back down towards Dave again in an effort of distraction.

Dave's relentless snoring pushed itself out through the wires in his ginger beard like a refugee that was in search for dry land. The residue of a kebab sat encrusted within his facial hair, as if to offer the refugee exhalations a vessel of hope. As the sea turned on its heels and retreated back into its own body, I recalled my own dinner; it had been a kebab that homeless Dave had gifted me. It was a tender act of kindness from the homeless and, although it was not quite a feast that was worthy of inviting Grandmamma to, it was definitely the most unusual Christmas meal that I had ever eaten.

As I feebly attempted to capture book pages that blew away with the balmy afternoon breeze, my imagination slowly wandered back to a place that it had begun to enjoy visiting. It was Dave's hometown, a place called Nimbin that I had often found him speaking of. Although I had never even been there before and all I really knew about the place was its affection for 'greenery,' Nimbin seemed to be calling out to me. The ideology of clean living that I had formulated back in Melbourne, back when I had more of a sense of purpose, appeared to have tired of my romantic distraction. Therefore, it had decided to pinpoint Nimbin as the place where higher love and clean living could come into fruition. Nimbin was only a stone's throw away from Byron Bay and, the more that I thought about it, whilst swinging in my hammock and half-reading pages from my book, the more I realised that I had, like so many others before me, become stuck upon Byron's shore.

I had spent an entire month bumming out on the picturesque beach with my Melbourne crew. Even Andrew had eventually left the city behind and arrived in New South Wales to enjoy some time at the beach with us. Byron Bay inadvertently became a place where we each attempted to create new alliances with one another, yet the similarities between our old connections were easy to see. No matter how estranged, the way that we all knew one another back in the city would always serve as a foundation for our friendship.

It was clear that, despite how far I had tried to run from those foundations, some things simply appeared to be magnetically pulled towards my journey. As the pages of my book blew and turned with the breeze, I knew that it was finally time for me to embark upon a new chapter of my life and leave Byron Bay behind. There was much more that I aspired to find within myself and I knew that I had become distracted with familiarity. All those months later, my dream still spoke to me. So, I closed the straying pages of my book, put Christmas day behind me, prepared my voice box to amplify over Dave's rambunctious snoring and turned my attentions towards Benjamin.

"I know that you planned to stay here so that you could begin a business in massage therapy, but, Ben, I'm gonna' go to Nimbin today and I wondered if you would like to come with me."

Ben's professional aspirations had long drawn up a plan in his fertile imagination that portrayed him running donation-based massage therapy upon the beach. He envisioned sunbathers soaking up the chance to have a massage therapist that would come to them and tend to their sun-kissed limbs, whilst they lounged around beside the sea. Since arriving in Byron, Ben had often spoken of such a plan and, although he had made little attempt in putting his plan into action, he seemed intent on the idea. Yet, as Benjamin put his own book down and chewed over my words for a moment or two, he began to nod his head up and down, graciously accepting my challenge. Benjamin's consideration towards me was, as always, unfailing.

With our thumbs extended back out towards the wind, Benjamin and I slowly walked the hard shoulder of Byron and began to embark upon the hottest hitchhike in our young hitching history. My red rucksack, no matter how vacant it was of belongings, left a sweaty river running down my back that poured out from my legs and merged with the mirage-stained tarmac. My eyes squinted into the horizon at the approach of cars, yet I could only distinguish a blurred brightness. The road beneath us sizzled and began frying the little piggies of my toes like swollen balls of bacon but, just as a waiter began adding 'April's Toes' to the special's board in a café somewhere in Byron, a swanky BMW pulled over in front us of and stopped. Benjamin and I looked one another up and down, aware of our tattered Beach Bum looks and were uncertain that such a car had halted for us. Though, before my toes melted into the tarmac and ended up on a specials board, I stepped up towards the passenger window in order to investigate its inhabitants.

"Oh for heaven's sake, do come in and get out of that heat!" An elderly woman exclaimed from the crack in her passenger window, furiously fanning herself with creamy hands that thought themselves to be paper. The driver, her husband, looked across the black leather seat and winked at me, as if to excuse his wife's exasperation.

Not needing to be told twice, Ben and I threw our backpacks in the boot of the car, slid across the cool leather seats and quickly closed the back doors to the thick soup that we had been swimming in. Air conditioning had never felt so good. The unsuspecting couple that had picked us up were in their seventies and determinedly stared into the passing scenery through their front windows with an obvious uncertainty as to what to say next. After engaging the couple in mild conversation, it appeared to be the first time that they had ever picked up hitchhikers. The maternal affection of the older woman had not been able to stand the sight of the two children in Benjamin and I subjected to such high temperatures and, despite her fear, she had been compelled to offer us assistance. She also appeared to have put her back out of place in doing so and sat in the front seat, looking stiff and unapproachable. After a few more attempts at relaxing our drivers, Ben and I began to chat idly amongst ourselves for a moment. We then joined our hosts in their preferred silence, both of us appreciating the cool air that stuck to the sweat on our bodies and revelled in the unexpected dapper attire of our vehicular environment.

After the couple took us as far as they could, and were adequately convinced of the joys in picking up hitchhikers, their BMW threw us out upon a busy freeway and drove off into the smog-saturated sun with a new perspective. With air conditioning long behind us, the air in front of us was so thick and permeated with exhaust fumes that even the idea of breathing became a task that required conscious effort. It didn't take long for Ben and I to determine the freeway to be a terrible place in which to hitch from. Most vehicles were going entirely too fast to even consider stopping and, along with the initial impracticality of picking up two young strangers from the road, the drivers also had to consider the ability to exit and reenter the freeway safely. I scribbled down mental notes in my hitchhiking guidebook, advising us to never hitch from the freeway again.

Yet, it was apparent that the only way that we could depart from so many lanes of furious traffic would be by car, so Benjamin and I attempted to persevere. After fifteen minutes of fruitless endurance, I took refuge under a shadow that had been cast from an overhead bridge and appreciably watched as Ben tried his luck against the chaotic traffic.

After buckets of sweat had fallen from our tendered bodies, finally a rickety old grey car, trailing a black slug of fumes from its exhaust, came to a sudden halt in the road. Ben and I gathered our things and ran towards the vehicle as if it were Noah's ark. One by one, we clambered aboard.

"Lucky we picked you two's up. The freeway is the worst place to be on a day like today." The thick, brown lips of the driver parted for breath and then spoke once more. "Where are you's goin'?"

As Benjamin made himself comfortable in the empty front seat and I squashed in the back with three other dark bodies, pressing my sweatiness against theirs, we began to drive away with Nimbin as our destination. The Aboriginal family that had swallowed us up was a far cry from the silent luxury of the BMW that had initially collected us. But, as our new hosts began to lavish us with water and ice, drawing dreamy stories from their plump lips, I knew that Ben and I prospered in a better kind of way. We were rich in an abundance of magic.

I sat beside the stormy, blue-grey eyes of an Aboriginal woman who began mumbling stories into my hungry ears. Though, with all the windows open, her words got caught in the whip of the wind and were carried off into a faraway land. I could tell that her words were of importance, so I strained the worn leather across my curious eardrums tighter, so that I could hear her better.

"When you go up north, don't look the black-skinned, blue-eyed man directly in the eye." She cast an intense look at me from her stormy, grey pools, as if to reiterate the power of eye contact.

"And don't leave the hair from your hairbrush anywhere." Voodoo spells began to fill any space that was left in our cramped-up car, swirling and twirling around my ear drum as if conjuring it to make sound. "Burn it! Otherwise, it will be used against you." The warm air flew through the open window and slapped me in the face with the force of a schoolteacher, ensuring that I paid attention to class and take heed of the woman's words.

"Watch over him." The woman looked towards Benjamin, who was caught in the midst of a hearty laugh at something the driver had said. "They will not want to see you with him, sister." The woman's affection begged for me to trust her, her voice quivered with the roar of the wind and her brown hands clasped around mine like a velvet glove. "You must protect him."

I looked once more at Benjamin, whose face was still held captive by joviality, and I wondered how I had ended up on the wrong side of the voodoo stick. The front seat and the back seat were worlds apart and the thunderous wind ensured that they would stay that way. No matter how I felt about such mystical things, I agreed to the woman's advice and when the time came to part, I gave my car seat partner an appreciative kiss upon the cheek. Our hair did not touch and our eyes did not again meet, yet we still aspired to see one another.

As I stood on the single street of Nimbin, ready to explore, I decided to associate my voodoo warnings with the air of good intentions. I washed the conjured-up fear away from my essence with the salted beads of sweat that my body had excessively excreted, and began to acquaint myself with the town. An assortment of colourful shops, hemp bars and cafés laced either side of the street, billowing out clouds of smoke from their open doorways. Rasta flags attempted to blow in the breezeless air, then settled for the meditative practice of stillness. The entire place pulsed with greenery, and an even more specific cannabis leaf green symbol had been decoratively placed outside of most café windows without shame.

As Ben and I walked down the street like two sweaty birds of a feather that could not keep from getting stuck together, we came across a three-legged dog that served as a doormat to a hemp bar. The heat of the day had paralysed the hairy dog into slumber and, as I stepped over its panting body, I could feel the realness in its woolly-haired struggle; my own hair was like a furnace. Time seemed to slow down in Nimbin, though a busload of tourists pulled up at the side of the road rapidly, as if unable to slow down from the force of their origin. Feverishly, they snapped some pictures of the dog, drank a coffee, smoked a joint and then disappeared into the horizon as quickly as they had arrived.

Nimbin wore a badge of peace upon it that, even at first glance, was evident to have been birthed from the seventies. Knowing that that peace was still in full effect, I took a seat upon a park bench, next to an assortment of colourful characters, and endeavoured to learn more about the history of Nimbin.

Once upon a student dream, an assortment of young and open-minded people had flocked to Nimbin by the hundreds, in an attempt to replicate the American Woodstock festival. Those free-thinking hippies of the seventies had aspired to create a festival where in which they could celebrate art and sustainability and where they could call in harmony and freedom, whilst having a lusciously green environment to do such things within. Their dreams were eventually achieved and thus, the Aquarius festival had been born.

With forty years having passed since the creation of the Aquarius festival, those hippies were still around. They had chosen to stay and reside upon the abundant soil of Nimbin, guarding its wealth and keeping the grass green. Scattered amongst the rainforests and the mountains, they lived in communities that practiced sustainability and exercised a sense of universal family. They bathed one another's children, ate, worked and slept together; the thought of such a natural lifestyle ignited something warm in the pit of my womb. The rainbow children had become a backbone to Nimbin's peace, standing firm in an ageless truth that war was not the only answer.

"Dem hippies..." A local man's dark lips moved beside

my thirsty ears, continuing to water my queries. "When I was young, dem hippies be the ones walking around butt naked!" His thick eyebrows arched like a cathedral and I paid homage to their storied scripture. "And we, the true local people... the Aboriginals... we was the ones wearing clothes!" As the man laughed heartedly at his adventure down memory lane, his face began to wrinkle and fold in on itself until he looked like a new man. From one stranger to the next, I cloaked myself in their silken testimonies and nestled amongst their words, knowing that they had not frayed by the hands of time.

The hippies that had stayed behind after the festival, deciding to make Nimbin their home, had also begun to formulate a harmonious relationship with the Aboriginal culture that lived there before them. It was a harmony that was previously unversed between the whites and the blacks, yet as I sat on a colourful park bench with the finest of Nimbin's homeless community, I could see the promise in that alliance. Each stretch of skin bore a different colour, each pair of eyes glimmered in a separate shade and, with Ben and I amongst their mixing pot, we all brought something separate and new to the picnic table of truth.

An Aboriginal aunty waltzed over to the bench and, as her wide eyes fell upon me with affection, she immediately adopted the orphan in my eyes. The blonde weave that gathered like a golden crown atop of her head suggested that the resemblance between her and I could make us mother and daughter. Immediately swooned by our similitude, Aunty's large, dark lips began to cover my entire face like a thick mud mask of kisses and she swallowed me up in purifying salutations.

"Come on, babies." She encouraged. Knowing that we were one of them, Aunty took it upon herself to take Benjamin and I on a homeless tour of Nimbin. We followed her winding, slender body down into the park, watching her flick her weave across her shoulder as if it were a fashion-veil until we came to a halt beside the library. Aunty showed us an external power source and opened up the unlocked box, assuring us that we could charge our phones there if we needed to.

"Neva mind that bag of mushrooms," Aunty announced, as she swatted a festering bag of sparkling, blue, magic fungus out of the way. "That's just Rogers, he will be back for dem later." Without further explanation, Aunty closed the lid and wobbled her way towards an outside stage.

The stage itself was a small area that had wooden floorboards and a thin, tin roof that arched above it like a pyramid, though its insides bore no resemblance to the internal intricacies of a pyramid; it was just a floor and a roof. A single mattress sprawled out across its wooden base, revealing the sleeping owner of the mushrooms. At the sound of Aunty's approach, Roger pulled the covers over his dark face, then resumed his melodic snoring.

"Welcome home, babies." Aunty extended her hands as wide as her teeth and invited us to live amongst her and the rest of Nimbin's homeless crew for either the night, or as long as Benjamin and I would like. Her fingers wriggled with happiness, pointing to every simple thing around them, and I decided then and there that it was a wonderful offer.

As I sat upon the park bench that afternoon, Aunty walked amongst an ocean of tourists and rustled up some loose change from their pockets under the guise of a kind smile. After her mission was successful, she approached the table, triumphantly threw a few coins down upon it as if she had just gotten checkmate, and instructed Benjamin and I to go and buy ourselves a few slices of pizza for dinner. In this simple act of kindness, I was warmed into the spirit of Christmas. A woman without a home nor income had just offered money to two strangers, in order that they may eat dinner for the night and, all at once, I didn't mind that my phone hadn't rung on Christmas day.

With that, ginger-bearded Dave appeared from the crowd and joined our table, reminding me that Nimbin, (a place where the wayward looked out for one another,) had long been his home. As I sat amongst the homeless, drinking beer and merrily singing along to the Bee Gees, I felt as though Christmas day had merely happened a little late for me.

That night, Ben and I attached my hammock to the beams of the stage and continued our ways of top-and-tailing. We hung over a sea of dreaming bodies like a half-moon that had been cast upon an ebony sky. As usual, Ben's feet pushed their way through my thin sarong and wormed their way towards my face, finding a final resting place upon my shoulders. The sodden scent of them had become all too familiar to me, so I just closed my eyes and attempted to feel as peaceful as how I assumed the moon would feel hanging in the sky, thousands of lightyears away from us. Though as I opened my eyes up to reality, it was possible for me to get much closer to other people's bodies, their personal scents... or their wriggling feet.

Twenty other bodies lay within breathing range of me. I could feel their exhalations swaying my hammock with their self-generated breeze. The mattresses shifted against the wooden floor like chalk upon a chalkboard. Big, swollen lips gurgled, blubbered and blew out snores like a whale blows out a fury of ocean from its blowhole. And as the deep of the night fell upon us, so too did the unmistakable aroma of sour body odour begin to float up towards my nostrils. It had been a hot day and it was plain to see how each person's salt-crusted pores had dealt with such humidity. Along with the snoring, the chalkboard mattresses shifting, the dream murmurs from beneath me and the weight of Ben's feet pressing down dangerously close to my face, the once quiet air decidedly became saturated in the creaking release of flatulence.

Amidst the musical night, I thought back to the second car journey that had taken me to Nimbin and I pondered over the words of warnings that the woman had offered me upon departure. I thought of stormy eyes and voodoo dolls wearing locks of my hair, yet I did not fret. Through the fog of the night, I knew that voodoo cast a pale shadow upon the evil stench that I had been subjected to.

It would not be the blue eyes in a black man that I should avoid for fear of demise, but staring into those soggy, semi-infected feet... that would surely be the death of me.

Oasis

26th December 2014

After spending a restless night swaying above a churning sea of flatulence, the next morning, Ben and I removed ourselves from Nimbin's homeless stage and embarked upon a mission through the town in order to procure a more private chamber. Just a stone's throw away from the town's single street, Ben and I stumbled upon a winding river that curved into a dense and luminous forest. An abundance of trees stood guard over the water's purity and, as we followed its sparkling, slithering body deep into the forest, Ben and I discovered a place that we came to call 'Nature's Honeymoon Suite.'

Entirely surrounded by vibrant green trees, crystal-clear waters and soft, worn pebbles that washed up upon the shore to our new front door, Ben and I fastened my hammock between two thick trunks that sleepily leaned down towards the embankment and finally, our bed-turned-home hung over the winding river like the half-moon that it had always been destined to be. Amongst the soothing sounds of the trickling water, rustling leaves and cheerful birds, an air of gentle quietude also hung around our new encampment like a crystal chandelier. There was not another person in sight and with such a glorious concept of space and privacy, my mood felt much lighter. I began to remove my cumbersome clothing in great haste. Ben followed and, in a ceremony of the accomplished, we began to wash and baptise ourselves in Nimbin's holy water.

The water itself, so clean that one could drink from it, so cool that the heat of the day did not affect it, and so persistent in its path that the odour of unwashed body parts ran away with it in the hopes for a better life, provided a great relief to Ben and I. We spent the afternoon indulging in our outdoor honeymoon suite, basking in the sunshine, loving one another and, when the thick heat of the day became impenetrable, we simply sliced it open with the cool knife of the river, bleeding it. The honeymoon suite

401

became a private oasis just for the two of us.

As the evening came to call upon Ben and I, it also brought with it the orchestral song of crickets and bugs that roared wildly in celebration of the approaching night. Armed with a flashlight and curiosity, as well as hunger pains, Ben and I made our way back to town to experience Nimbin's evening life. As we crossed the bridge and rounded back into civilisation, the Oasis Café, with signs of life and a title that was similar to our new home, became the first place to catch my attention. I parted the thick veil of smoke that curtained the entry, took note of the freshly-baked goods on display with great delight, and began to make my way inside.

The Oasis Café appeared to be some sort of kin to a speakeasy café, (perhaps its mute cousin,) which, in turn, caused me to immediately feel welcome and at home. The café appeared to be where the entirety of the town's small population came of an evening. Each table was taken up by a group or person that looked to have been sitting there throughout the ages. Their skins were all somehow drenched in Nimbin, their eyebrows arched in the same manner as the mountains, and the shrubbery between their fingertips sparkled in the same green as the forest that surrounded us. Thick joints hung in-between the talking lips of almost everybody there, turning the room into a warm, yellow sauna. The fresh air that I had initially carried into the café with me began to have a midlife crisis, panicking because it could barely recognise itself

Innumerable games of chess were being scrutinised under calculating eyes and hypnotically played between well-versed hands. I watched as the games sprawled themselves out across the tabletops like a checkered octopus with many arms. Following the sound of a guitar, I floated through the foggy air and made my way towards its melody, stopping to take seat at a table that was being occupied by the biggest smile that I had ever seen.

"Don't worry... about a ting." Jonny Ganja sang out into the room from behind a peaceful army of sparkling, white teeth. "Cuz every little ting... it's gonna be alright." Aiming his ivory white light across the table towards me, Jonny Ganja drew me in, as well as everybody else around him, into that bright space inside of his person, just so that we could all feel a part of something larger, part of a collective. Jonny Ganja's dark dreadlocks were loosely gathered in a white turban that perched upon his head, some locks falling down beside the sandy tones in his face and resting beside his mouth as if they couldn't stand to be parted from his smile. His eyes slanted in a combination of heritage and medicinal substance, crowning Jonny Ganja as the first Asian Rastafarian that I had ever met. A group of tourists that had been ejected from their bus for longer than a split second began to gather around him.

"Where are you from?" The tourists asked Jonny Ganja, enraptured by his looks and spellbound by his jovial performance.

"From my mummieeeee." The 'e' curved his mouth into an even wider smile, but as Jonny reached out with phantom hands and touched everybody in the room, he began to look down towards his joint and suddenly creased with seriousness. "Dis medicine for my soul." Jonny held up his joint as though it were a microphone, sharing his answer to a question that, although no one had dared ask, looked to have been teetering at the forefront of the tourists' thoughts. After a moment of reflection, and no further pressing from his spectators, Jonny Ganja enthusiastically rejoined Marley, pressing and encouraging everyone to smoke and sing along with him. As my own mouth began to part in song, I began to understand Jonny Ganja's contribution to existence and defined it in one word, *Joy*; the pursuit of it, the spreading of it and the indulgence of it. Joy, it was apparent, was Jonny Ganja's full-time occupation.

A young girl named Felecia sat in front of me with kind eyes that began to part the curtain of smoke, inviting me to take a dip in their deep pools. It didn't take long before Felecia and I were lost in conversation with one another. I followed her long, mermaid-kissed hair down a lane of memories, where she showed me a version of her that used to be a city girl. Having recently arrived in the countryside, Felecia and I shared similar interests in clean living through a creative life. A guitar sat quietly behind her, waiting patiently until the day that she would play her. Amidst Felicia's silken conversation, I could hear the makings of an enchanting song in her voice and I anticipated the day that she would find courage enough to share it with me. Beneath the sultry light of the Oasis, Felecia's pale, unmade-up skin shone with the first glimmers of freedom, finally unweighted by foundations and all that she had once thought she needed in order to be beautiful. Felecia sat across from me like a ray of hope and we began walking a similar path, one easily falling into the other's reflective company.

Ginger Dave entered the café as if he were a preacher and began to conduct a sermon on the day that he had met Jesus Christ himself. The chess players looked up for a moment, then resumed their game, paying Dave little notice. Through the smoke, I was certain that I could see a demon and an angel playing hide-and-seek upon his tattered shoulder.

Aunty rolled through the waves of smoke, past the tentacled chess games, past the impromptu sermon, and washed up upon our table. With disheveled hair crowning her features, Aunty's thick, black lips fell upon my mouth like a beer-stained comet, momentarily halting my song. Looking back into the room, Aunty began to scream at an unsuspecting by passer that seemed to be related to her. She was water. She was fire.

Back in the forest that night, with the trees guarding over our safety, I swung in my hammock-turned-home and felt that I was close to, or perhaps even exactly, where I needed to be. Ben slept, top-and-tailing beside me, with feet that had been cleansed with the kiss of the river and, for the first time in a month, I did not mind them being so close to me. Nestled into the bosom of Nimbin's forest, serenaded by the trickle of the river below me, I felt safe. And I slowly allowed my thoughts to be carried downstream, where a land of dreams awaited me.

Though, just before I had made it to the promised land of dreams, I was brought back to Nature's Honeymoon Suite… by an overweight raindrop that had decided to take rest upon my cheek.

Divine Intervention

27th December 2014

After a sleepless night, before dawn had even had the chance to try and break through the thick wall of fog that surrounded mine and Ben's encampment, I poured myself out of my hammock-turned-impregnated-pool-of-water and fell onto the sodden ground beneath me. Upon exiting, the tarp that I had loosely placed over my hammock that night brushed my head and, as if to mock me for my futile efforts, burst. A bucket load of rainfall spilled all over me and, for the hundredth time within just a few hours, the tarp drenched me in its watery laughter.

As I humourlessly crouched upon the ground and watched the river in front of me rise through a curtain of flattened hair that draped itself across my eyes, Ben began to remark upon the terrible job that our living quarters had done at keeping us dry. It had rained all night long and, as I looked around at my misty new home that seemed a far cry from the honeymoon suite that Ben and I had once known, it didn't look as though the rains had any intention of letting up. The cold clothes that clung to my back were soaking wet, everything inside of my rucksack was saturated with the poor state of the weather, and my spirits, if it were remotely possible, were even damper. The honeymoon was officially over.

As if to retaliate from the tarp's watery affection, my frustrations began to take a walk upon the pathway of distraction, searching for a victim in which to attach themselves to. Bitterly, I looked across at the disappointed creases that wormed their way across Benjamin's forehead, until...

"Why don't you get your own fucking hammock then, Ben?!" Spewed out of my mouth, tainting everything around me with my foul mood. The sky overhead seemed to grow darker.

Despite how hard I had tried to hold onto it, my harmony with Benjamin was beginning to slip through my wrinkled, wet fingertips and wash away with the rushing river. It seemed as though the sunshine no longer wanted to play accomplice to a girl who had been convincing herself that things were different and it receded into the darkness until I was able to see the light of my own truth. As the clouds wrestled for space in the aggressive, grey sky, I could not avoid the fact that Benjamin and I had inadvertently fallen back into the same old habits. A month prior, Ben had come to me in Murwillumbah full of hopes and dreams and, even though his pockets were in their usual cobwebbed state, I had invited Benjamin's endlessly romantic, hitchhiking heart back into my life.

During the last month that Ben and I had spent together in Byron, I found myself perpetually dipping into savings that I had worked so hard for back in Melbourne in order to take care of us both. I had fed Ben, clothed him, and tended to his many needs without venom. And just like before, Benjamin had allowed me to do so. As well as the free spirit that I embodied, Ben also loved the mother in me, and had taken to resting inside of her womb. In one moment, Ben was a young boy who needed to be taken care of, yet in the next, he would turn into a grown man who wanted to love upon me. My vagina was called to the witness stand for incestuous behaviour and, as I sat upon that damp embankment, listening to Benjamin complain about *my* tarp and *my* hammock, something inside of me snapped.

Once again, I found myself at war with loving Benjamin's beautiful spirit, his gentleness and his unconditional love, but how tired I had grown of his absolute lack of provisions. Ben had no money, no blankets, and no food. He didn't even own his own tent. My ill-patience seemed like a condition of my affection towards him and I could not help but to hate it. I sat in the rain, detesting myself for placing such an emphasis on Ben's lack of financial contribution, but a part of me needed him to step up, to take control of the situation and offer us a remedy that came in the form of a warm, dry place to rest. I looked into the boyish blue eyes of Benjamin, expecting answers.

"It's hard to tell with you, April," he began. "You do so much on your own, without saying so much as a word. It makes it difficult for people to know when you really need help."

Surrendering to Benjamin's gentle, but firm, point, I looked into the rising river and suggested that we abandon our derelict honeymoon suite, leave the impregnated hammock behind, and make our way out of the forest. Amongst our bickering, the indisputable fact that we were completely drowned out could at least be one thing that Ben and I agreed upon.

After wading through thigh-deep water that had once only tickled my ankles, and struggling to stay afloat under the weight of my saturated backpack and heavy heart, Ben and I poured ourselves out into the closest park. The mountains around us arched abruptly into the skyline, softened only by a thick coat of fog that curled around their tips like a misty, white cat. The combination of jagged edges and soft clouds were like two opposing worlds, giving Nimbin a sense of harmonious balance amidst the pressing chaos of the weather. Mother Nature stretched out her claws and, as I huddled beneath a shelter in the park, looking out at the luscious grass, she revealed to me of how she kept her land so green. The rain, undeterred by the pout that extended from my drenched whiskers, marched on and fell upon a shimmering green land that was in love with its dewy affections.

Apologetically pressing cold clothes against one another's limbs, Benjamin and I put our argument behind us, huddled together for warmth, and tried to keep our spirits up. Between chattering teeth, we each read aloud from the pages of a soggy book and attempted to get lost in another, more magical, more inviting, and somewhat drier world. After a few hours of killing time, my saturated fingers decided to quit their day job and resigned from their position of 'page turner.' The report that their tips had filed simply read: *'cannot work under these damp and hostile conditions.'*

Beneath a flimsy tin shelter, the darker side of travel had decided to pay Ben and I a visit, sitting down beside us like an elephant in a room without walls. The elephant's thick, swollen posterior perched upon a park bench beside us that wobbled beneath his weight. And he had skin that was as grey and ashen as the sky. He introduced himself as, Not; Mr. Not-All-It's-Made-Out-To-Be, to be more specific. Focusing on Ben's reading voice

407

above the heavy rainfall, I tried to ignore the elephant's presence. But the dark, well-travelled elephant just stretched his giant ears over his body, in an attempt to also hear the same story as I. I sat with Benjamin amidst our estranged travels with Mr. Not-All-It's-Made-Out-To-Be as our only company, and I began to drift into daydreams. I thought of soft beds and crisp, dry linen. I dreamt of blankets and dry socks, of endless pots of lemon tea and of thick, squidgy macaroni and cheese. The elephant began to lick his lips along with me. There was no denying his presence.

After leaving the elephant of dark travel behind us, Ben and I decided to retreat into the safety of the Oasis Café. As we parted the familiar curtain of smoke, a myriad of bored and damp lips blew welcoming rings of smoke into the room as if they were umbrellas. Jonny Ganja still sat in the corner, singing merrily into his guitar, yet as evening began to approach without consideration for my accommodation, I could not quite believe in his song. Ben took a seat beside Jonny and began to employ the joy that he brought to the table, pulling a joint towards his mouth and tossing his wet hair out of his eyes, as though he had not a care in the world. But inside of me, *every little ting* did not feel as though it could be alright.

Leaving the boys to their smoky song, I perched on the ground outside of the café and, pressing my back against the wall, proceeded to slump over into my diary. My wet fingers (rehired by the same company, but employed under a different job title) began to draw upon the grey that seemed to have infiltrated everything around me. As the dark ink smudged across the yellowed paper of my journal like a suicidal rainbow pressing against a golden sky, a busload of tourists pulled up in front of the café. Armed with a multitude of extended camera lenses that didn't require their owners to subject themselves to the weather, the tourists began to push their boxes out of the bus windows as if they were embrasures. Fogged with momentary perceptions, they aimed their weapons towards a waterlogged and depressed version of me and opened fire. In that small gesture of photographic association, as I crouched outside of the Oasis Café, I knew that I had become a part of Nimbin.

Deserting my damp scribbles, I looked into the back of the bus as it pulled away from the café and silently wished that the tourists had taken me with them; back to bedrooms and hot showers, back to kitchen cupboards and bedroom drawers, back to bookings and reservations, monetary organisations, friends in bunk-beds and simply back to everything that consisted of regular, safe, and plain ordinary travel. Warm pools of water began to slosh around in my eyes; contributing to the wetness, they thought about macaroni and cheese once more and, as if it were too much to bear, they jumped to their death and joined the dampness upon my face, unnoticed. As I wallowed in my own salty tears, the silhouette of a woman slowly appeared at my left-hand-side and stood over me. Just above the incessant pattering of rain upon the single street, I heard a solitary question part from the shadow's lips...

"Are you ok?" The woman's voice was stern and direct. So cool was her tone over the air of my daydreams that, as if to warm themselves against her words, my cheeks morphed into a ruby red fire. The strange woman had caught me off guard.

Looking over my shoulder, my vision fell upon the sight of a mystical being and, as if my eyes required more space to properly see her, they stretched open, becoming wide with astonishment. The woman's long, silver hair fell down to her waist like moonbeams upon a starry night. Galactic messages had been written against her well-aged, pale skin, daring me to try and avoid them. The stern of her jaw held itself in place, anticipating my response and, as I looked upon her beige, flimsy fabrics that looked like the outside, the woman arched her eyebrows towards me in a manner that said she wasn't fucking around. She exuded the same jagged softness as the town of Nimbin and the surrounding mountains.

Recalling the argument that I had had with Benjamin just that morning, I took a moment to seriously consider the woman's question. *Was I ok?* 'Ok' seemed like such a broad manner of mood. Many things could fit inside of its versatile box. One could be ok and still be sad; one could also be ok and still be happy. It was hard to tell what category I fit inside. From a young age, I had

409

been advised that I shouldn't show others my sadness, that I should get on with things and try not to be so emotional because it showed weakness to cry. But, as I sat slouched over my diary with salted cheeks, I knew that it was too late for me. I considered that perhaps it was time to leave those outdated reservations that I had always held inside of me far behind. The moment felt ceremonious and worthy of change.

"I'm soaking wet. I'm pretty cold and hungry. And I just want a roof and a dry bed." Upon admitting my defeat, the saffron buns that sat inside of the woman's deep, glossy eyes began to rise. Despite her cool nature, something in the woman was also nurturing. Yet, after the words had barely made it past the border of my lips, I could only recoil in horror, knowing that I had just shown too much to a stranger. My mouth began to seize up like an old Singer sewing machine.

The woman stood beside me with clothes that looked like the outside, with a multitude of woven baskets gathered at her hips like full and contented children, and looked down at me with hanging limbs that wept from her body like a willow. As if to introduce the two of us on behalf of our own inabilities, a thin aroma of earth and rain ran in between the woman and I; neither of us had offered up our names. She just stood there, indifferent to my remark, and did not seem to be concerned with any pleasantries. Instead, she just stood above me with an icy glimmer of suspicion that flashed across her doughy eyes. Unnecessary pleasantries didn't seem to be with me that day either so, with no further correspondence between the two of us, I simply resumed my writing. But as I put my pen to paper, I could feel the woman standing there, watching me, looking into and penetrating me. In her self-assured quietude, I knew that such a creature did not belong to our self-conscious world.

"Are you the woman that was singing here the other night?" She pressed me, without a hint of melody within her voice. It was a tone that belonged to necessity or to a cold-hearted duty.

I began to chase my memories, until I found a happy and dry version of me; sitting in the Oasis Café amongst chess and billowing smoke, singing with Jonny Ganja and having a grand old time. I nodded in affirmation of her referenced character and allowed the woman to arch her eyebrows further into me. As she felt out my frequencies, I comfortably returned to my journal and allowed her diagnostics of my soul. Until...

"I have a little shack in the woods," the woman began, with a slow and calculated speech. "It's not much. No electricity or plumbing... But, it's dry." The woman paused with an authority that knew I would not interrupt her and I sat there like a child soaking up a bedtime story, hanging onto her every word. "Maybe you could stay there until the rains let up... is it just you?"

Then, as if on cue, Benjamin, with blood-shot eyes and a larger nose than I remembered him having, emerged from the clouded café. Stretching his grin towards the woman as if it were a handshake, Ben broke our quietude with his cute and clumsy tone.

"Hello, I'm Benjamin." Ben smiled a smile that could have stopped the rain in its tracks. Yet, as if to lead by example, the rain continued to pour and the woman looked Ben up and down with eyebrows that also refused to be impressed by his boyish charm. In that one single act of reservation, that strange woman secretly became my hero. She showed me that, unlike other women, she would not be swooned by Ben. She eyed him as if he were an intruder upon her land and something about her assured me that she was a woman who took care of other women. Something else inside of me, something that was made of dreams and magic, something that understood the moment to be definitive and worthy of change... that part of me wanted to follow that witchy woman to the ends of the earth.

"Oh, well." The woman proclaimed, indifferent to Ben's presence, as if she perhaps already understood that there was always another in tow. "Come on, then."

So, gathering my sodden pack upon my goose-bumped back, I began to follow that ethereal creature out onto the street, taking note of how erect her body stood as she walked with the weather. With her baskets swinging against her confident stride, the woman did not hunch against the persistent rainfall. Instead, she faced it head-on and drank it in, allowing the water to nurture her skin. My own posture could not help but to straighten, immediately giving me a new and improved feeling about the day. It was obvious that I had been intercepted with some kind of intervention that could perhaps make every little ting turn out alright.

"I'm April." I called to the woman's silver back, as she began to disappear into the mountains and the fog. Parting the mysterious mist, I tried to catch up with my white witch of divine intervention.

"I'm Granny Breath Weaver." She called back… from the ends of the earth.

Granny Breath Weaver

29th December 2014

Some pathways in life are so well-defined with certainty that they make every other walkway that has come before them seem jagged and unformed. As Benjamin and I emerged from the back of a hitchhiking bubble to find sturdy footing at the base of a small, but prominent, mountain, cloaked in a grey and sunless sunset, I looked up towards a narrow pathway that began to unfold before me.

Granny Breath Weaver slung a few woven baskets over her nimble shoulders and, undeterred by the steep ascent, began marching up the winding road that served as a pebbled backbone to the mountain. Even though I had never before tread upon the path ahead of me, even though it was wildly overgrown and wound off into unknown secrets that the fog would not forsake, I looked upon its definitive curves and somehow felt certain that it was a pathway that I had always been destined to tread upon.

As I began to ascend the mountain, a sea of damp, fallen leaves spread themselves out beneath my feet like a sacrificial offering, comforting and encouraging my steps with their soft, veiny presence. Looking around at the sparkling greenery that lined my pathway, I began to think over the name that the woman had offered me as her own and recited it under my breath. *'Granny Breath Weaver.'* It was such a mysterious name that, upon exhaling its title, it conjured up such mystical connotations that I could not help but to be enthralled by it. When Granny had initially parted with her identity, it had sent a prickly shiver of curiosity up and down my spine, running so many marathons across my back that I had inadvertently begun to run too, following the breath weaver into the fog just so that I could attempt to know who she was. In an effort to solve the riddle of her name, I continued up the pathway and, as if she knew that my thoughts solely orbited around her, Granny turned back to face me.

Through a night sky of sparkling eyes, Granny looked all around her. With her fingertips extended towards the rustling trees, she paused to emphasise the land, ensuring that my attentions were upon them both before she began. "The mountain that I live on… this is a place that I call the Woman's Mountain." Granny had a calm stage that had been crafted into her stern voice, invoking the audience within me to be more attentive than I had ever been. Granny Breath Weaver was pure theatre.

I understood that, through her strong words, her bold pauses and her gentle breath, Granny Breath Weaver was not only a woman who wove baskets, but she also wove powerful stories from the fabrics of her being. Casually spellbound by the woman, I followed the back of her silver hair up the steep mountain and knew that I was being drawn into something larger than myself. Somehow, I had found myself to be walking upon a pebbled pathway that appeared to lead straight towards womanhood.

In an effort not to self-implode, I kept my mouth closed, pressed my reservations close to my heart, put one foot in front of the other, and continued to hike up the Woman's Mountain. Benjamin looked over at me and smiled, his eyes burning with the same sapphire blue that was always a sure sign of his excitement. Pink flower petals peeked out through a magnitude of shimmering green and, from the well-trodden path, they blew salutations into the breeze. As my breath became heavy with the labour of ascension, every leaf and petal began to rustle and turn, as if they were cheering me on in the journey to come. Although my heart was too nervous to admit it, my feet knew that they, undoubtedly, had begun to walk upon a rite of passage that I had long been searching.

Halfway up the slippery slope, as the path wound sharply up to the right and a level of flatness offered a place of refuge, my ears pricked at the sound of a rushing river. The rains had not yet let up and proceeded to deposit each cool drop into the stream below as though it were a safety deposit box, filling the river with an abundance of liquid currency. Stopping to catch my breath in the opening, I looked down into the forest below me. Large boulders brushed shoulders with the sharp blade of a furious river that carved its own pathway out through the foliage and, as the flowers laughed beneath the tickle of raindrops, suddenly the weather didn't seem to be so hostile. It was no longer my enemy, but instead, an accomplice; an element that was perhaps even part of an alliance that had led me to such a place. With woven baskets pressing down on her shoulder blades, Granny floated up the mountain with an ease that is not usually embodied by someone of her age; as I watched her sixty-eight-year-old frame do better than my own, I began to experience a moment of total euphoria.

It was as if I had heard a door, somewhere within the forest, slowly unlock; I began to feel connected to everything that was around me, as if I could be a key part of its tapestry. My shoulders met the rain without fear and, as they collected and deposited nurturing droplets within their bare blades, I saw a vision of me bathing in the stream that hid somewhere amongst the rustling leaves. My heart pounded out of my chest; partly due to being out of breath, but also because I was overcome with happiness. Just a few hours prior, I had been in the depths of despair, yet in the blink of an eye, the world had shifted and saw fit to throw me into the doorway of an ethereal adventure. The world around me felt fresh and clean yet, upon seeing that I had fallen far behind the determined step of Granny Breath Weaver, I tightened the straps on my rucksack and left my euphoria frozen in midair.

After about fifteen minutes of enthusiastic ascension, Benjamin, Granny Breath Weaver and I reached the top of the Woman's Mountain. The only sound that I could hear, save for the persistent rain, was our collectively strained breath. Following our guide through a few snaky paths that slithered through the dense forest, Granny theatrically extended her hands at the end of the pathway and presented me with the accommodation that she had promised.

A small, wooden shack sat nestled in amongst the thick foliage and, without doors or electricity, proceeded to humbly welcome Benjamin and I into its belly. The front porch was overflowing with a collection of bark, sticks and vines, which gave the place an intestinal persona. Inside of the shack, there was just enough space for the bed to have a harmonious existence. There were no drawers, no chairs, no fancy frills, airs or graces... there was just the simplicity of a dry bed that sat below a beautiful tin roof. And never in my life had I been so moved by the protective sight of tin. What I saw in front of my eyes had been everything that I had asked for when Granny Breath Weaver had approached me at the Oasis and asked me if I was ok. There was even a place to make a small fire beneath the patio. The simple things in life began to soften me.

After settling in with our things, which was just a case of placing our backpacks upon the wooden floorboards and offering thanks to our dry accommodation, Benjamin and I made our way over to Granny Breath Weaver's home, where she was said to await our company. Just beside our own temporary shack, a fortress of wood and tin grew like a flattened beanstalk towards the sky, leaving no space for intruders. Stepping in through its doorway, I removed my boots and found my toes wriggling upon a deer skin mat. As I made my way through the dark hallway, I followed the sound of Granny's voice and tiptoed through a sea of beautifully hand-woven baskets that revealed the weaver's second part to her name. The afternoon light did not take long to find my face, showing me that, despite the appearance of entering an inside home, I was still very much outside.

There was not a trace of electricity on the entire premises, no machines sat upon the dusty shelving, no lightbulbs hung from the bamboo ceiling and nothing at all that one would find in a common household appeared to be in Granny's spacious shack. It was a house that did not belong to this time. Transparent tarps were placed precariously upon the few walls that there were and wept thick, plastic tears, perhaps pining over the life of a glassless window. All around the floor were tales of how Granny Breath Weaver had acquired such a name for herself. Her baskets were woven in an assortment of earthy colours, shapes and sizes, exuding the sense that they each had a story of their own that I would come to know. A large pile of wood sat on the border of Granny's outside area, stacked so high that she could have survived a year in the bush with its brittle offerings alone. A collection of bones poked out through various parts of her home and, amongst the fur skin rugs that were scattered all over the floor, the enclosure had a beautifully earthen feel about it. As I looked towards a single bed that stood just a stone's throw away from the outside world, with no wall to close itself off from nature and a simple mosquito net hanging between its sheets, Granny firmly established herself upon the list of my heroes without even knowing it.

As the last of the afternoon sun fell behind Granny Breath Weaver's abundant and wild vegetable patch, a patch that brought the meaning of self-sufficiency up into an entirely new level for me, I pulled a wooden chair out from beneath a stainless steel kitchen table top and took a seat opposite Granny. Removing her large, working hands from a coffee cup's tender embrace, Granny set alight a rusted, blue lantern, placed it upon the silver table, offered Benjamin and I some homemade hemp cake and, whilst we all drank steaming black coffee, Granny Breath Weaver began weaving her stories into our souls.

That night, I lay upon my firm, yet dry bed, with a body that smelled of wood smoke, and I allowed my heart to absorb Granny's mystical stories. I stared at the glorious tin roof, still alive with the dance of raindrops and I knew that it would be hard for me to leave such an interesting place behind. Fortunately for me, I didn't have to leave until the rains let up and the rains... and they continued to fall for two entire days after our arrival. It was the most persistent rainfall that I had ever endured.

During that time, Ben and I spent many of our waking hours with Granny Breath Weaver. By day, she would heat up her gas cooker and water us with offerings of hot, black coffee. Powdered milk was an option, but in truth, wasn't really even a fan of coffee. However, I drank it up anyway, as if the refusal of such a simple gift would prove me to be ungrateful and I began slurping up its steaming blackness until I began to like it. By night, Ben and I would light our little fire that sat in a bed of bricks just outside of our shack, lounge upon the earth-saturated pillows, and silently read our books by the glow of the fire. It was the simplest happiness that I had ever known.

After the two days of rain had finally receded and the sun began to shyly show its rouged face, I found myself asking Granny Breath Weaver how I could repay her for her hospitality. She had not only provided a dry bed and a roof for Ben and I, but had also fed us, caffeinated us, and provided us with the most interesting company that I had ever had the pleasure of keeping.

"There's another shack out here on the property," Granny began casually. "The mountain is not for the weak, you see." Knowing that I could expect another story, I peppered my tobacco across the stainless silver tabletop and began to roll a cigarette, employing my ears as my fingers methodically focused on the task at hand.

"A young girl stayed down there in that shack for a while. And she couldn't handle it. She allowed herself to be carried away with the deterioration of her mind." Granny Breath Weaver stopped momentarily to draw upon the medicinal smoke stream that perpetually curved out from between her working fingers, then exhaled the rest of her story into the air. "The mountain can be a harsh and lonely place. As I said… it is not for the weak."

"There are no walls to hide behind up here. No television to disrupt your true vision and no electricity to distract you from your elemental self. It is just you and nature." Although I was but a guest upon the property, Granny's generalisations seemed to be aimed towards me. "You've gotta be strong up here. That young woman sure wasn't."

Granny's nostrils closed the conversation with an open flare and, through the smoky room, her features took on the calm determination of a bull. Although it was just a story about a young woman that I had never met, some kind of red flag had been waved above Granny's face and she had sent her words towards me at full speed. I did not say it at the time but, in her own way, I knew that the old woman had challenged me. In that same smoky instant, I also caught sight of, not only the bull, but also the cheeky little girl that lived inside of her old soul. Though her jaw line was firm, freshly pressed with a tragic story, I could see a glimmer in the woman's eyes... and that glimmer was full of secret smiles.

"Well... the shack itself... she left it in a bad state." Granny, as always, rounded back to the origin of the story with an ethereal ease. "You could help me with that."

With that last invitation, Granny Breath Weaver's declarations were set. Her eyes glimmered, her nostrils flared once more just for good humour, and I accepted her offer for repayment with the kind of sentiment that knew outside elements to be governing my life. I felt small against the things that were unfolding before me and knew only that I must surrender to them. So that is what I did.

The following day, I arose with the early morning bird, left Benjamin and Granny to their coffee, and snuck off into the forest. As the warm sun shone over my serenity and the flowers stretched their petals towards its golden rays, I walked along a pathway and felt a peace like no other. A baby wallaby hopped and skipped at the sound of broken branches that crunched beneath my bare feet, and I knew that there was something more in the green of the ferns than I could see; it went deeper than wallabies and birds and was beyond just the sun, shining upon and warming the blood red earth. There was something in the air itself. I could feel it every time that I breathed that place in, up through my nose and into my lungs, it would infiltrate me until somehow we were one. Although I wasn't quite sure who the other party was.

As I impulsively made my way through Granny's eleven acres of property with no need for a map, I merged into an overgrown pathway and began to follow it downhill. Through the shrubbery and the trees, through an entire ocean of fallen branches and leaves, I came upon a clearing in the woods. Through the forest, a large, wooden shack that stood defiantly against its abandonment, also stood to attention at my approach. The shack itself had only one wall and as I peered down into its open space, I heard a voice in my head say *'you are here.'*

Trundling towards the entrance, I pushed leaves and branches out of my path and finally came upon a sign that had been scribbled onto a shard of the wall. It read: 'The Last Resort.'

Some pathways in life are so well-defined with certainty that they make every other walkway that has come before them seem jagged and unformed.

The Last Resort

30th December 2014

The first time that I can recall my family and I moving home occurred when I was about seven years old. It was to be the first of many moves that, unfortunately, were not inspired by an endless sense of adventure, like the younger version of me had thought it to be, but were instead encouraged by the ever-rolling wheels of financial destitution; five hungry mouths to feed were never destined to give my parents an easy ride.

As the years went on, my three sisters and I would often find ourselves squashed together in a single bedroom that was void of character and we would either be closer to one another for it, or drift further from the shores of our intimacy due to such close proximity. My brother, being a boy, always had immunity. In 1999, my mother and father, for their own personal reasons, went as far as to drag our whole lives across an entire continent. We each left England with a single suitcase in our hand and travelled all the way to our new home in America. It was to be my first taste of great adventure, yet my family and I found that we arrived at a place where the walls were yellowed and grimy and, save for the simple necessities, there was a clear lack of homeliness. When my siblings and I would wake in the night, trying to remember where the light switch for the bathroom was, an army of cockroaches could often be found marching across our little toes. Yet, amidst the chaos of our accelerated relocations, I recall it bringing out the best in, not only me, but also the most delicate parts of my parents.

Despite the repulsive houses that we initially occupied, my sisters, my brother and I were all fortunate enough to be born beneath the wings of a dreamer. My mother; the artist, the inventor, the fairy seer. A twelve year old version of me would sit upon a restored sofa with restless legs swinging out from beneath her, and she would look upon a paint-splattered version of her mother as she worked her decorative magic. I would feel the difference between the old and the new fabrics between my

421

curious fingertips, breathing in the purple living room that my mother had freshly painted, and I would feel enlivened by her bold choice of colours and arrangements. My father would cast his eyes adoringly upon my mum as if she were the moon and, with a half-smile cast across his dark face like a flash of lightning against a midnight sky and a single golden tooth that shone like the first star amongst his perfect smile, my dad would beam and proceed to tell us that, "That woman could turn a cardboard box into a palace." My father would swell with pride.

I would look up from the sofa at my father's charismatic gestures, his self-assured mannerisms and his features that were the spitting image of my own and, in those moments, my father's loving side would always be a welcome addition to our family. He would pull my mother away from her duties, gathering her into to his large, ever-present body and would bestow his affection upon her in tentative appreciation for creating such a beautiful nest for him and his family. It was a primal kind of love. My restless legs would quicken in their swinging at the fleeting sight of my parents' happiness and, in that moment, I remember consciously deciding to implement all of my parents' *best* qualities into me; my father's unfailing ability at breaking through the seemingly impossible and my mother's creative ingenuity. Even back then, I learned that I could turn the lining from destitute pockets into a pillowcase for me to rest my weary head upon.

As I stood upon the Women's Mountain, before the Last Resort, and peered into its filthy compartments, I understood that I would need to evoke every single ounce of resourcefulness and creative ingenuity that I had learned from my parents all those years prior.

Within the shack, chairs lay scattered across the green carpet as if they had been turned upside-down in a blizzard of abandonment. Spider webs layered the thin, tin roof ceiling in a thick blanket of forgotten isolation and the entire shack looked as though it had not been tended to in many years. As I stepped upon the leaf-drenched carpet, the ashes from the inside fireplace blew around my bare feet in an effort to welcome my attentions, though the fire had been extinguished long ago. I made my way past an assortment of overturned stories that gave clues as to who had been there before me and came upon a disheveled kitchen. There, mouldy china plates sat stacked upon a wooden bench, offering a glimmer of hope that proved of how there had once been a trace of organisation within the shack. Yet, as my eyes fell upon a festering mound of rotting and indistinguishable food that moved with the slow dance of maggots, that organisation felt like a distant memory.

Swallowing down the saliva that, as if to get a better view of the chaos, had escaped my mouth and gathered around my lips, I turned away from the kitchen with a similarly turning stomach and looked towards a small enclosure that stood behind me. Three thick sheets of dirty tarp had been draped around the small room, providing one of the only walls to the Last Resort. At the entrance, a dark green mosquito net had zipped in a mess of foul-smelling objects that had been piled into indistinguishability. The hot air around me congealed with the thick scent of rotting food and, in the still of the morning air, the only sign of life was the dance of the creeping maggots that lived in the kitchen. Everything within The Last Resort had turned itself inside-out. It looked and smelled like the next appropriate step after the salivation of my lips had succeeded in their efforts at escapism. Yet, despite the mess that I found myself in, a determined smile began to chisel its way across my wet lips. With my mother's eyes looking out from inside of me, and the breath of a child who had learned to see the possibility amongst the ugly, I exhaled, 'The Last Resort is amazing.'

Despite the busyness of it, the shack was spacious; it was about the size of a studio apartment. It had a living room; kind of. There was a kitchen; kind of. And the small enclosure that was full of foul-smelling things had the potential to be transformed into a snug and secure bedroom; maybe. I looked once more upon the heavy-duty mosquito net that zipped in the mess inside of it and envisioned it emptied, with the bed that was in the living room pulled inside of it so that *I* could be protected from the creepy crawlies whilst *I* slept... Without being conscious of it, I had

423

automatically began implementing myself into the Last Resort.

I began sifting around in the madness, finding treasures and relics of all those who had lived there before me. Signs of peace and signs of war were scattered in amongst the leaves that layered the floor. Looking upon the pots and pans, I envisioned hanging them from the wooden beams and, before I knew it, my hands, gloved with the thin fabric of OCD, began to search for serenity amongst the madness. As sweat, dust, and spider webs all gathered upon my damp forehead, I was met by the wandering eyes of Granny Breath Weaver and Benjamin.

Granny looked around the Last Resort with a bud of sadness that blossomed within her dark eyes. It was obvious that the breath weaver had not made her way down to that side of the property for some time and the state that the shack was in weighed heavily upon her heart. However, I knew that I wanted to rectify the wrong that had been done to such a beautiful space and, undeterred by the mission that laid before us, Benjamin, Granny Breath Weaver and I began to put our able bodies to work.

Loading wheelbarrow after wheelbarrow with junk, we rolled an endless array of rubbish up to the top of the property and slowly began to empty the shack of its deteriorated belongings. Together, we turned the furniture the right way up, dusted, swept and excavated last year's dinner from the cool box with as minimal retching as possible; the maggots would need to find a new home to dance upon. Beneath the heat of the sun, amongst a wildly overgrown garden, Benjamin and I found an overturned bathtub and proceeded to drag it out from beneath the bushes. Scrubbing it out in hopes of a future starry night bubble bath, each of us cleaned and envisioned a brighter and cleaner future for ourselves. It was hard work, a labour of love that, from day one, is what the mountain would demand of me.

As I attacked the rank enclosure within the shack in an attempt to turn it into a bedroom, Granny went on to tell me that there had once been bat keepers who had lived within the Last Resort. "They were strong women who used to keep bats within this very room." I looked around the enclosure; the earthy, dank smell beginning to make sense to me, and I was enthralled by such a radical concept; a bat-cave-turned-bedroom. Amongst our cleansing dedication, with spider webs wrapped around our hair like silken ribbons, Granny Breath Weaver casually began to mention,

"If you like… you can stay here… for as long as you want." My eyes met hers in disbelief, but Granny's eyes simply twinkled for a moment in that same cheeky mannerism that I was beginning to love, then resumed her cleaning duties without a second thought to her offer. Benjamin worked somewhere in the background, humming and singing to himself and, although Granny had grown to accept the male in him, I knew that her offer had been specifically for me.

My heart, understanding that it had already unconsciously implemented itself into the Last Resort when I had first arrived, began to thud out of my chest. My dream of living in the woods and endeavouring to fulfill a clean and clear life was becoming a reality right before my eyes and, as I stood with a broken broom clasping onto my hand for dear life, I tried to tell myself to remain cool. Granny looked over at me expectantly and I nodded a casual nod of acceptance in recognition of her offer. Granny Breath Weaver's eyes glimmered once more before both of us returned to our cleaning duties.

Just two days prior, I had almost given up on the dream that had already brought me so far; when the will to indulge in magic, spirit, and earth had just about been washed away with the heavy rains. But as I stood within that shack, just as I had witnessed with my parents relocation, the best parts of me promised to surface if given the chance.

With the rains having finally washed away the impossibility to tread upon such a divine pathway, I stood in the shack wearing my father's proud lightning bolt smile as well as my mother's beautiful creative blue eyes…

… And I knew that, during the dark of my own personal storm… I had also stumbled upon my very own last resort.

A New Year

Quietly...

I crawl on all fours

A predator

Wild animal

Across the shack floor sprawls a territorial dispute

Made up of fate and predestined footsteps

Though there is no such thing as war here

I look past walls that were never there

I am outside, yet I am inside

I am inside out

The fire...

Pouting amber lips part like Aladdin's cave of secrets

Burning red, whispering coals, they tell it all...

'You are exactly where you need to be.'

But this isn't the first time that the fire has spoken to me

Benjamin and I prowl around one another, not speaking...
dancing into forever

Teasing, playing, tripping...

Stripping down to our primal bodies

I chose this nose, these eyes, this life long ago

We know these moments to be magical

Separated until equal

We come back together as the clock strikes twelve

*Fireworks explode in the sky like rainbow popcorn without a hint
of salt*

And I release like never before

The floor,

An ocean of my pleasure

A New Year is upon us

*I look around at the work that we have invested into our new
home*

A humble shack in the woods

The floors are scrubbed, cobwebs brushed

A bat cave turned into a bedroom

*Sweat, blood and love have all been inserted into every single
corner of this place*

The forest cradles me and I sit in the palm of its dark hand

Unafraid of its grasp

What magic is this?

I wonder

Standing tall with my hands to the sky

A waterfall of happiness cascading down my rocky limbs

Falling down, down... down

All the way down into Benjamin's laughing belly

He lays on the floor looking up at me

Femininity flows through me

I stand upon a woman's mountain

The breath weaver sleeps

She impregnates me with her stories

Until a teller is born in me

I have been led here by a dream

It now fits together perfectly with reality

Ethereal puzzle pieces

A new year is upon me

And I am exactly where I need to be.

Women's Business

8ᵗʰ January 2015

Benjamin and I sat side-by-side, crouched over the stainless steel of Granny Breath Weaver's kitchen tabletop, amongst offerings of steaming black coffee, homemade hemp cookies and smoking paraphernalia, and together we indulged within Granny's company. It was an image that, over the course of the previous week, had become a familiar scene to us all. Night or day, Ben and I would find each other in such a way; tentatively listening to stories that had been conjured up from the Breath Weaver's history and selflessly offered to us with the same casual care as the powdered milk.

Through a soft layer of smoke that wrapped itself around our heads like a loose-fitting turban, that morning, a story of sovereignty came to take seat with us at the kitchen table. Never hearing of such a word before, I gathered myself like a student beside the bare workmanship of Granny's feet and began to bestow my full attention upon her approaching story.

"Sovereignty is an individual power or authority," Granny began, rearranging her paraphernalia upon the tabletop, until she was sure of mine and Ben's undivided attentions. "Through the simple act of accepting one's name at birth, we each unconsciously enter into a contract with authority." The breath weaver's voice was calm, yet dramatic. Through large, working fingers, she pulled a smoke towards her lips and paused to inhale its medicine. Benjamin and I awaited further instruction without a hint of interruption; only the morning birds chirped in-between our silence. "It is a name that is chosen for you by your parents and asked of you by authority, yet the fact of the matter is... you never agreed to such terminology." Smoke swirled around her arms like grey, lucid wings as Granny attempted to fly away from her distaste of authority. "That is how they trap you... with a false affirmation of your person... but what they don't tell you is that no one can own you or enslave you. What they don't tell you is that we each have the right to choose and create our own identity... for we are all *sovereign* beings."

As Benjamin gulped down another mouthful of black coffee and I swallowed down the term 'sovereignty,' the idea of contracts, personal perspectives and name-giving all swirled around in my empty stomach and began to fill me up. The morning light waltzed in through the doorless door with no need for a key and began to part the air around us, reminding me that it was time to begin my working day. I had previously drawn up a contractual agreement with Granny to work upon her property each day for a few hours, in exchange for accommodation. As I tied my red bandana across my forehead and began preparing myself for another day of hard labour, Granny stubbed out her smoke and looked across the steel table into me, with eyes that mirrored its metallic intensity. She had that same innocent, yet wise, twinkle in her eyes that I had come to love.

"You, dear one, remind me of a deer." I tilted my head to the right in the same way that an animal would do when spoken to. "You have fawn eyes and, although there is great gentility, there is also a deep strength inside of you." I looked down at my body as though it were a specimen that didn't belong to me. "You can choose any name you like," Granny reaffirmed, calling back to me as I departed her shack without answer; upon my back were two black eyes that had been born of a thousand dying stars.

Granny Breath Weaver had been under no false illusions when she had said that life upon the mountain was not for the weak. During the previous week, hard work had found Benjamin and I, whatever the hour may have been, just to prove that mountain life was a tough prospect at the best of times; though I had begun to find tranquility within its daily demands. Tucked away in my bat-cave-turned-bedroom, I would often rise with the blue ache of dawn, unzip the mosquito net, and venture outside towards my favorite place to pee. The birds would sing through the trees, the mist on top of the mountain would gather around my bare body as if to bid me good morning, and the thick walls of the bamboo forest would creak and sway in the warm, summer breeze. Inside the shack, I had devised a new kitchen system; I had a large bucket of water for washing the dishes and a separate bucket for rinsing. A titanic rainwater tank served not only as a partial wall to the kitchen, but also provided a necessary abundance of clean, natural drinking water that made such an outside life sustainable. I would employ its tap, wash the dishes, and then step outside into the back garden and throw its cool water all over my body. Although it was a far cry from the bathrooms that I was used to, as I washed in the rainwater with only a bucket, a bar of soap and the treetops looking down upon me, I had never felt so clean.

In fact, everything around me was clean. The floors had been cleared of leaves, the surfaces had been vigorously scrubbed, and the mammoth spider that had sprawled itself out to the size of my entire hand, whilst attempting to protect its nest of millions of babies, had been safely evicted from my bedroom. Our shack was a cardboard box that had successfully been turned into a tin palace. The bed fit beautifully within the bat cave, a sofa bed sat in the living room patiently awaiting guests, and a rocking chair rocked beside the fireplace invitingly. On the other side of the fireplace, under Granny Breath Weaver's instruction, I had divided multiple piles of wood into small logs, large logs, and kindling, which I placed beside the fire like ammunition.

"You never want to get caught out in the rain without enough wood," Granny had warned Benjamin and I. "Always make sure that you have enough." The breath weaver's eyebrows had raised towards her silver hair line like two pieces of dark driftwood reaching towards a moonlit shore. In her predictable, yet enthralling manner, Granny exhaled a cloud of smoke from her lips in a final and dramatic puff that signified a clouded full stop at the end of her story.

Benjamin and I collected our firewood from the surrounding forest area that was abundant in fallen trees; through their decaying lips, they had promised to keep us warm during the night. In the mornings, I began to practice making a fire that was just the right size to boil a small pot of water upon it for tea, without billowing smoke into the morning air and alarming anyone to a fire.

"A great fragility lies in a small, yet controlled fire," Granny had firmly instructed one morning, after swatting Benjamin out of her way. "It is an art." Benjamin's attempt at making a fire had been enthusiastic and clumsy in comparison to her own; he had piled thick, heavy logs onto Granny's cooking area and smoked us all out of the house. In return, Granny had simply looked at Benjamin as though being a man were an ailment that she could never save him from.

During my daily duties, I became well-versed in the arts of digging ditches. Through sweat and blisters, I surrounded the entire shack with a trench in order to deter the rains, should they fall again in the same manner as they had upon my arrival. The tin roof that perched upon the shack's shoulders had only a few small holes in it and I was learning to work on them, though I settled for buckets beneath their openings until my other duties were done. As I pulled out deeply-rooted weeds and sweated away all of the toxins of my old city life, I began to flower from such exertions. With deer legs, I pushed innumerous wheelbarrow loads full of junk, weeds, and funky, useless things up to the top of the mountain and remembered what it was like to have an athletic body. The sun shone down upon my red bandana, warming my white deer spots whilst songs pressed out from my lips and Granny Breath Weaver encouraged my melody and my power with the soft twinkle of her eyes.

When the heat of the day held us at gunpoint, Ben and I would hitch the 10kms back towards the town of Nimbin and surrender to the familiar faces that resided in the Oasis Café. Chess pieces would be the only thing to move in the afternoon heat and, as sweat gathered beneath my breasts, I came to find myself sitting around the back of the café amongst a group of women. Granny Breath Weaver was amongst them and with privacy and authority chiseled into her dark eyes, she was a singular entity, yet somehow she was also the embodiment of all the women, young and old, that encircled her. Granny sat upon a stone that had been dipped in fragments of coloured glass and carried herself like a queen. I sat beside her throne and listened to the diverse topics that the women spoke about; equality, Aboriginal peace treaties, more on sovereignty, and the necessary safe space that women need in order to come together without being under the scrutiny of men. It was women's business and, although I had grown up in a household full of women, I knew that my connection with them had never been anything to be completely proud of. If I was truthful, I would go on to admit that women, with their weakness and their nagging, had in many ways, always disgusted me. Therefore, I sat as a self-proclaimed tomboy, outside of the Oasis Café, with a group of caring women and surrendered to such unfamiliar business. A whole new world of femininity was beginning to encircle me.

Life upon the mountain had fit upon the sole of my foot like a forgotten glass slipper. Even Cinderella would have looked upon me with pride to witness such momentary glimpses of feminine power; I would lay down my tools with the setting sun, wring the sweat out of my red banana and then disappear into the dark of the approaching night without fear. Without even a hint of electricity, I would stare into the open fireplace and listen to the world around me. My days at the Last Resort were ferocious, yet my nights there were gentle. The mountain encouraged such a balance within me. Even Benjamin had begun to mould to his new environment and seemed to exude a humble quietude. We would each look into the black of the night that surrounded our inside-but-outside shack in the woods and experience a peace so great that neither of us could speak of it for fear of disturbing it with our words.

I could only stare into the embers, blinking my fawn-like eyes into the whip of the flames like a deer that had been caught in the headlights...

...wondering, with all her might, who she would eventually decide to be.

A Perfect Balance

10th January 2015

To feel a sense of stability against the ever-changing backdrop of my life is an imperative emotion to procure. Despite the variety of strange new places that I have consciously and perpetually implemented myself into, the ruffled feathers of disharmony can unsettle even me. Therefore, amidst the wind tunnels of my endless travels, I have learned to find great appreciation in the act of also being still. It is said that a hummingbird can beat its wings at eighty-beats-per-second, yet its body and focus are never affected by the external commotion. Within my current life, I could only aspire to mirror such a perfect balance.

I stood within the safety of the Last Resort, looking into the cozy bat-cave-turned-bedroom and thought over all of the strange places that I had slept in the few months prior to the shack. I had laid upon beautiful beaches and had rolled around in sand that was as soft and white as the clouds above. I had squashed my body within the mouth of a psychedelic bus named Broomhilda and slept with two other little piggies in a zebra print row amidst a tribe of naked hippies. Outside of a tall bank building that had been brimming with riches, Ben and I had tossed and turned upon an unforgiving pavement and, although we had no money in our pockets, we were happy to simply have an overhang above our heads as well as each other. We were rich in our own right. I had found refuge within the woods and had slung my hammock amongst other tree-dwellers, I had slept upon a stage above the toxic flatulence of Nimbin's homeless and had even tied my hammock-turned-home against the barred doors of a public bathroom in Byron, attempting to escape the rains. Hovering over a fusion of cleaning chemicals and faeces proved to be a challenging first night in Byron, yet as I stood in the stillness of the Last Resort, I could not help but to breathe a sigh of relief knowing that I was far from those streets, those flimsy trees, and that filthy, sodden bathroom.

Within the shack, there was ample room for me to store my food without being weighed down with its necessity. I had become the proud owner of a cool box that contained a block of beloved cheese that silently sweated within its enclosure as well as a tub of butter that I could lather upon bread, freshly toasted by the fire. An assortment of books lined the shack shelving without concern for their density, ready and willing to be ravished when the perfect moment found me. Also, mine and Benjamin's rucksacks had finally been laid to rest beneath a bat cave bed that promised to always keep us warm as we slept. The bat cave; yet another strange place in which I had laid my body to rest.

With a broken broom clasped between my blistered fingertips, I swept away the windblown leaves from the grass-green carpet and prepared to receive my first guest at the Last Resort. Back in the realm of Melbourne, in a place that felt like another life altogether, I had partied beneath a bridge and screamed out into the night sky with a boy named Samuel. Sam himself had miracles for legs and a crooked smile that hung like a galactic belt across his face, wrapping itself around my curiosity and parting with the story of how he had, just a year prior to our meeting, very nearly died. Beside the fire barrel, beneath the bridge, Sam had drawn up a tale that depicted a rock climbing accident, where in which he had fallen down from the sky and met the unforgiving, jagged earth; it was a collision that left him with a six percent chance of rejoining life. Sam had broken his ribs and his back, yet somehow his spirits remained intact. The doctors had put a hole in his throat and induced him into a coma in a desperate effort to save his life and, despite his slim chances of survival, Samuel had chosen to keep on living, to keep on walking... with miracles for legs. Sam not only chose to walk, but instead did backflips away from Death's door, singing out in melodies of infinite gratitude for his life. To me, Samuel was a living, breathing miracle.

The morning that I had left Melbourne, Sam had arisen from a sea of red wine bottles and bodies that slept upon my bedroom floor, hugged me farewell and mentioned that he would be in Byron Bay just after Christmas. With Christmas just having passed and Byron Bay just around the corner, I had contacted Sam and invited him as a guest in my new home. Although Granny Breath Weaver had approved of him visiting the Woman's Mountain when I had asked her permission, a pang of guilt had still stabbed into my heart just as the question had torn itself from my lips. I, myself, was torn in-between the maintenance of my old life and the development of my new one. Back in Melbourne, I had been the tomboy, the girl that had not kept many female friends because of her distaste for their susceptibility to weakness; my adoration for rough play and messiness had always conquered my feminine curiosity.

Since childhood, I had seen how women could be broken at the merciless hands of a man and I had never wanted to be like them, be in their position, or in any way resemble their susceptibility to pain. Therefore, I had only ever nurtured the masculine part of me; the girl with the scraped knees who wasn't afraid of a little dirt and who had found great refuge in the climbing of trees and the excavation of worms. Still, there I was on a Woman's Mountain, not quite understanding why, and inviting another guy upon its feminine soil just because I thought he was a miracle and deserved to see such a place. Granny Breath Weaver had only said that she trusted my judgement, so I pushed down the pangs of guilt, concluded that I would understand my placement soon enough, and continued to sweep the shack.

That afternoon, Samuel ascended the mountain with the sands of Byron Bay still stuck to his sun-kissed face; emerging through the trees to greet Benjamin and I with an unfailing affection. The salt from the sea had locked Sam's dreads into further follicle matrimony, his blue eyes emanated the same crystal clarity of the skies overhead, and his crooked smile pulled together in a dimpled bundle upon his right cheek and fell down across his chin like a tipi. As Sam's teeth shone like fairy lights

436

from within the encampment of his mouth, it brought me great comfort to see his familiar and jovial face. I led Sam's body, brimming with stories, down to our shack, and listened as he spoke about, not only a leisurely visit to Byron, but of how he had also tied his professional aspirations into his trip. Sam was in the same line of work as Benjamin and, as I lit the fire to prepare some tea, Ben's ears pricked up as Sam began to impart of how he had just embarked upon a few weeks of massage therapy upon the beach.

"I just had my massage table, my hands, a few crystals and a couple of sarongs... but that was all I needed." Sam held his thick hands, strengthened from years of rock climbing, up in front of his face, as if to acknowledge their duteous efforts, and smiled proudly over their accomplishments. Sam had the captivating kind of smile that was contagious, so, despite a sourness that had unknowingly bruised my lips, I also joined him in his happiness. I sat beside the fire and watched as Benjamin and Samuel swirled around one another with the same brotherly love that they had exuded back in Melbourne and, as the embers roared in anticipation for the tea pot, I thought upon the boys' similarities; their large personalities, their appreciative natures and their common interest in massage therapy. Yet, there was one difference that was as plain as the sun that had begun to set through the trees; Sam was out there making his dreams a reality, whilst Benjamin, with the exact same dream as Sam, was not out there doing massage on the beach as he had dreamt, but was instead living on the Woman's Mountain with me.

After the tea had boiled and Benjamin and Sam had excitedly devised a plan to trip together beneath the light of the moon, in regards to joining them on their psychedelic adventure, I had decided in favour of polite refusal. I was still processing my New Year's journey and had, after all, come to the mountain to seek a clean and sober life. With hallucinogens in the wet of their eyes, the boys respected my dismissal and, as the sun tucked itself into a bed of darkness for the night, I decided to leave Sam and Ben to their fungal adventure. In the deep, aquatic smudge of moonrise, I began following the trails of a forest that had come to be my new home and set my own sails towards the next shack on the mountain. Through the sweltering, damp summer air, Granny

Breath Weaver was silently calling out to me.

With curious deer-like feet that were perpetually attempting to be as quiet as possible, I pranced and tiptoed through the thick, dark rain forest without fear. Yet, the deer in me became startled as the noises that emanated from behind her sounded as though they belonged to a pack of wolves. Benjamin and Samuel's conjoined howling penetrated the silence of the mountain with no regard for the sleeping sun that lay tucked away in a bed of shrubbery. Their journey had begun. And as I pushed my way through a wooden fortress, startled by the sound of wolves, I felt my feet fall upon a deer skin mat and knew that I had also stepped upon the beginnings of an entirely separate journey. I realised that, in the two weeks that I had spent upon the Woman's Mountain, it was the first time that I was to visit the breath weaver without Benjamin.

Usually, it was I who left Granny and Benjamin to their own devices, scurrying off whilst they shared another pot of coffee and a smoke; I, myself, had not long quit and their session was always a welcome excuse for me to indulge in some time alone. But, as I rounded the corner into the kitchen and saw Granny Breath Weaver sitting beside the white light of her lantern, a river of silver hair running down her face, and eyebrows that arched towards my approach like a life raft, I became very aware that our communion immediately felt very different. Pulling up a stool in front of a metallic table that was felt out of context to the rest of the organic house, I, as always, began to state the obvious.

"You know, Granny, this is the first time that I have been alone with you up here."

"I know," was all that Granny Breath Weaver responded, looking out at me through two black eyes that unfolded like the printed pages of a book. Taking my cue for silence, I joined the audience of firewood and dried bones that had been stacked precariously around the shack and listened out for her unfailing guidance. A door to women's business slowly creaked all the way open, revealing a dynamic force that moved from its doorknob and extended out throughout the entire universe. Granny Breath

Weaver and I fell head-first into the breast of a Shakti scented dialogue.

"There is an energetic shift that occurs when a man enters a room that is full of women." The light from the lantern played Snakes and Ladders in Granny Breath Weaver's dark eyes. "Women can forget themselves in the company of men. They become distracted when they are in love and, even in the presence of an unfamiliar man, women can change their interactions with one another just to benefit the ego of the male. We are born nurturers, you see." Granny took another dramatic puff from between her thick fingers and, although we were speaking generally, (of every single woman that pulsed with a warm, red heartbeat,) I understood that we were also specifically speaking about me.

"Women only tend to remember one another when they have had their hearts broken. They crawl back to their girlfriends with their tails in-between their legs and ask to be mended." I meditated upon Granny's cool words, thinking back to every single version of myself that had ever had her heart broken by a boy. And I found truth in her words; I saw a heartbroken version of myself grovelling back to my girlfriends, after months, sometimes even years, of separation and asking them that they be there for me, no matter that I had not been there for them. I realised that the more I allowed myself to be swallowed up by the endless attentions of love, the easier it was to unconsciously allow my sisterhood to fall apart. As I sat talking and connecting with the breath weaver, I took great comfort from our conversation, yet because of that sense of blossoming peace, I also felt a great shame for ever having forsaken my own femininity; sisterhood was never intended to belong upon the backburners of my relationships.

As I looked across the stainless steel table top at Granny, with a dark backdrop of brittle bones and firewood sleeping behind her, with her large working hands, with her skin-tone clothes that looked like the outside and an unwavering respect for women pulsing from her insides, I came to realise that I deeply admired Granny Breath Weaver.

A part of me was startled at such an admittance, like a deer that had heard wolves in the night or been caught in the headlights of reinvention, because the truth was that I had only ever admired small pieces of women, fragments of their persons; a mannerism, or a thought pattern. Never before had I ever been drawn into admiration for a woman's entire being like I was with the breath weaver. Never before had I met a woman strong enough that it would inspire me to mould myself around herself and, upon realizing that, I knew that it was almost a sin not to have had any heroines. Granny sat across from me, surrounded by darkness and ethereal magic and, without knowing it, she climbed to the very top of my heroes list. Granny Breath Weaver showed me that, through my disregard for women, I had also disregarded important parts of myself, long ago. I looked down at my coffee. It was cold.

I could hear Benjamin and Samuel roaring out into the night sky; wild and desperate to exert some kind of bottled-up emotions; they were full of themselves. Full of the man that was within them. I recalled having once employed my tomboy lips to drunkenly roar into the night sky alongside Sam, beneath a bridge back in Melbourne, and it had been a necessary part of my development. Yet, as I sat upon the Woman's Mountain immersed in conversation with Granny Breath Weaver, I could feel myself gradually stepping into the clouded waters of gentility. The deeper that I submerged myself, it was said, the clearer the water would become, though it was hard to concentrate on my depth with all of that howling going on. I began to chew over the masculine energy that was resonating out in my life and searched myself to determine whether or not my lover and I were on the correct pathway to the highest versions of ourselves. But when I looked inside, I saw nothing. I could only feel the cold draught of separation blowing upon my perspiring skin.

Equality, in a financial regard, had become a stranger to Ben and I and, as I sat across from Granny and told her my own tales of disharmony, I understood money to simply be a symbol of Ben's contribution to us. Upon hearing of Samuel's successful massage therapy upon the beach, a sour taste had tainted my lips and I knew that it had been because Ben was not living up to his true potential; a version of who he truly wanted to be. Back in

Byron Benjamin had perpetuated an endless dialogue of the therapy that he aspired to offer beach-dwellers, but he was yet to focus his attentions on anything other than me. Ben's screams cloaked the night air and, through their piercing tone, I knew that I had been the one that was hindering him all along. I was, without a doubt, Benjamin's main concern. He would, and he did, follow me to the ends of the earth with no concern for his own wellbeing, though I would always be concerned for him, for his higher purpose, and for his ability to take care of himself. It felt as though Ben and I were destined to run around in circles after one another... because Ben would only ever care for me. He had even sold himself short of his therapeutic dreams, just so that he could accompany me to Nimbin and help me to follow my own. The jury had spoken. I had become Ben's greatest distraction.

Granny Breath Weaver listened to me wholly, as I poured out an internal dialogue of disharmony upon her stainless steel table top. She gave me room to figure it all out for myself, never suggesting that she knew a better path than my own. Yet, when I reflected upon the fact that I felt safe and at home upon her mountain, that I thought perhaps I would suggest to Ben that it was time for him to go back to Byron with Sam and no longer put his development on hold,

"Yes... I know," was the breath weaver's only response.

Those three words that parted from Granny's lips, pressing themselves into my hungry ears, had felt similar to the stories that she had told me about forsaken sisterhoods; they were words from another person's testimony, but they were also straight from my own soul. As I left Granny's shack later that night, walking alone in the black forest without even a torch, just following the light of the moon, I could see that a time of change was upon Benjamin and I. The murky waters around me had begun to clear.

So, when the blue hands of dawn finally rose up from their

soft bed of shrubbery the next morning, pushing their way through the plastic tarp that lined our bat-cave-turned-bedroom, I began to shake off the slumber from Benjamin's body without a moment to lose.

"Good morning, darling." Ben looked at me, his face cast in blue-grey light, surprised at my early-bird exertions. But I had had all night long to lay awake and think upon that cold draught of separation that I felt blowing in between us. "Come on darling, wake up... you're going back to Byron with Sam today." My statement left Ben with little room for question. "It will be a great opportunity for you to finally make your dreams a reality."

I looked into Benjamin's half-closed eyes with a sparkling reassurance that tried to pry them open like a crowbar, however, he just groaned away my enthusiasms. Disgusted that I would even consider pushing such a statement upon him after such a heavy night of tripping, Ben rolled away from me and attempted to fall back into his tender and considerate dreams. However, once an idea is in my head, there is no running from it. So I shook Ben's body awake once again.

"I've only just got settled in at the shack, April... uhhhh, and last night was just... a wacky night and..."

"It will be fun," I interjected Benjamin's trail of excuses, unmoved by his inability of action due to intoxication, and continued, "I will even come and spend the day on the beach with the two of you. It will be a lovely excursion for us all."

After the morning had slipped into a more appropriate hour, a single backpack emerged from beneath our bat cave bed and reconnected with the familiar curve of Benjamin's back. Waving farewell to Granny Breath Weaver, Benjamin, Samuel and I descended the Woman's Mountain and put our thumbs to the wind in anticipation of another adventure. Knowing that my sisterhood connections, as well as Benjamin's dreams, no longer belonged upon the back burner of our persons, I pressed forward in an attempt to also bring them forward with us. Cars rushed past our faces, mystery thumped within my heartbeat, and the quietude of the Woman's Mountain slowly began to slip away from me.

It is said that a hummingbird can beat its wings at eighty-beats-per-second, yet its body and focus are never affected by the external commotion.

I could only aspire to mirror such a perfect balance.

Dear Benjamin,

January 15th 2015

I sit alone at the Last Resort staring into space, trapped in a place that was once our home, and I know that I am cursed with too much time on my hands. Fondling the slender stick of a returned smoking habit, I'm replaying the events that occurred between us over and over in my mind, but I cannot draw solace from them, nor appreciate their implications as of yet. I find it difficult to keep even one conclusive thought close to my breast. So I write instead... with the black ink of abandoned patience, upon the water-stained paper of desertion, and with the oils of disappointment glistening upon my frantic fingertips; I write to myself... and I only hope that you can hear it.

Never before have I been so disappointed in you, my blue-eyed prince. I try to break the word down, to make it so that I can understand what 'disappointment' truly means to me, but this is the only truth that I can see...

I have been Dis-sed by a love that I had thought to be unconditional. You finally gave up on me, took the easy road that led away from my heart box and disrespected everything that we were to one another. You are a coward.

You made A POINT when you told me that I was too difficult to love, too complicated, with too many layers around my persona. But I wonder, am I so bloated with the love of the world that it makes it impossible for any man to feel contented in their love for me? Is there such a thing as true equality?

MENT... men... the creatures whose carcasses I constantly crave. I cannot escape them, you, him... Benjamin. You see the men that have loved me feverishly and perhaps you would prefer that my limbs were undesirable. If I were an empty shell, a safe kind of love that would never slip from your hands and discourage the word disappointment from ever having to be broken down, would then you feel secure in your position of Man?

444

Darling, I am past the point of being able to be that for you. That emptiness that was once in me has been filled with the light of the world. You see, I am a woman who steps further and further into her power every single day and, although you are challenged by that development, I carry with me the scent of love and poetry upon my rouged skin and only ever aspired to soften your pain. I stand naked before your judgement, unashamed, with painted eyes and a jezebelian smile, imploring that you look into me in the same exact way that you would look into yourself. I never wanted you to be so distracted by me... I only ever wanted you to see the very best version of yourself that was possible. Because I wanted to love him as well.

Yes, I pushed and I pushed, feeling your resistance all the way. You buckled under the pressure of my expectations and maybe I was wrong to have them in the first place, but I knew that you were more than the smitten love that you expected to pour from me. Maybe I would never fuel you with shallow compliments towards your perfect beauty, but the way in which I have loved you went deeper than the unexplored depths of the sea. If only you could have seen... seen past the complications, seen past the layers, but instead... you gave up on me. I knew that it was only a matter of time before you fell into the kind and loving arms of a doe-eyed fawn who would look up at you as if you were a god, but I didn't expect it to happen so soon. Lord knows I never made you feel that way, but this ideology of what you believe to be love... there is greater tragedy in this than you will ever know.

I accompanied you to Byron Bay in order to help you stand on your own two feet. I wanted to witness your impending dreams become a reality, wanted to see you oiling up beach bums and practicing happiness; I wanted to ensure that you actually became who you said you wanted to be. However, we got distracted from that pathway. You hurt your back in the ocean and declared your body to be out of order; once again the therapy would have to wait. You wanted to come back with me to the shack, but I insisted that you stay in Byron and rest your weary bones. You pleaded, but I would not relent. Though, despite the fact that I would not budge, I was not too cold to the touch. I had arrived in Byron with only the clothes on my back, yet I stayed with you for three days and tended to your needs. I helped you to walk, kept you warm at night, and made sure that you had enough provisions. On the second day of your healing, we became even further distracted and decided to take LSD. It was during that night that true sight found me, showing me of the two opposite worlds in which you and I reside.

Upon the shoreline of Byron Bay, surrounded by music and young, swaying bodies, I found myself afloat upon a melodious wave. My body, barely holding me inside of myself, felt light and full of grace. Harmonious tribal song began to pour out from my lips, falling into the deep beat of the drum and echoing out into existence. The heavy-handed sea rolled and crashed over its own body, as if to dance and touch itself at the first sound of music. People sang, swayed and pranced across the shoreline with sand, dreams and pieces of fragmented reality stuck in-between their adventurous toes… and then Benjamin… then, there was you.

Maxed-out in your indulgent ways, you teetered beside me, fueled with a combination of acid, pain pills and stolen whiskey. Your words were few, but as I looked closer, I could see the reason for your quietude boil down to the fact that your mouth had been crammed full with a glass teat. I sang and you drank thirstily from the bottle. Amidst the song and dance, a young woman emerged from the crowd and stood in front of you like a mirror. Her dark, curly hair sprang past her ivory skin and a flash of blue eyes pierced your own with her affection. She looked exactly like you. I wondered if it was jealously that I felt crawling over my shoulder but, as I watched you and the fawn exchange superficial compliments to one another's identical extremities, I only felt indifferent. Separated from something that I could not care to be a part of, I became lost in the music and allowed the drum beat to have the full attentions of my heart.

After slowly encouraging you away from your reflection, we piled into the back of a random van in an attempt to find further fun. In the dark of the night, squashed in against ten other bodies, as sepia street lamps fragmented in through the window like broken film footage and cast you in their half-light, I saw a myriad

*of beautiful jewels glistening proudly upon your bare chest.
Curiously, I crawled over ten tripping bodies and began touching
the glistening treasures that sat upon your skin... only to pull
away, horrified. With wet fingertips suspended in the air, I
discovered that they were not jewels that lay scattered across your
chest, but were instead the result of a purged stomach; LSD,
whiskey and prescription pain pills had all evacuated onto the hill
of your chest with no regard for parachutes.*

*The van swiftly returned us to the beach and, with my bare
hands, I wiped away the mountain of vomit that sat sparkling upon
your bare abdomen and tried not to gag. Whilst you lay
unconscious on the tarmac, I ran to and from the shoreline,
gathering water to cleanse your mouth, your face and your hair.
Sick was everywhere. I held a space of apologetic peacefulness
with the van owners, whose home you had soiled. And I poured
water into your drooping mouth, because you were like a child
who had not yet learned to use basic motor skills.*

*'Do everything to the maximum,' is what you always say,
with your cocky grin and your hungry mannerisms. But this is the
price that you pay. No... this is the price that I also pay; for your
inability to know your own limitations and for your psychedelic
greed.*

*Samuel and I dragged the ghost of your limp body back
down to our encampment and lay you to rest outside of his tent.
Afraid that you would choke on your own vomit, I sat outside with
you all night long, tipping your tripping body on its side and
stroking your damp, soiled hair in an effort of comfort as you
gurgled over your excretions. The night air was full of shivers and
chills; still, I removed my only jumper, placed it over your quaking
body and rubbed my hands up and down your back, in an attempt
to create friction and warmth. Samuel lay in a tarp beside us,
wrapped up like a peaceful cocoon. He slept with dry hair and
clean dreams... and I wanted you to be like him.*

*When I tried to call you back to me, to sooth my artificial
paranoia, you did not respond. It was a version of you that was
not you. A you who lay upon the ground and perpetually evicted*

447

sickness from his insides; an unresponsive lump that quivered, gurgled and made noises of a beast. Each time that the pained beast escaped from your mouth, I would rub your back once more and calmly whisper into your ear that everything was going to be ok. Even if I was unsure. You were so far gone from me that you would never hear my comforts, nor remember a single one of my efforts. I feared that you would never come back to me... and upon recollection, perhaps you never really did.

Still, for six hours I sat in the dark, crouched down beside you, and employed the crashing waves as my only confidant. They stretched their watery hands out towards me over and over again, though, in the same way that I was having trouble getting through to you, they would never reach me. A beam of light escaped the lighthouse and slithered through the foggy beach, parting the very skies before me, demanding that the mist and fog bow down in honour of its light. Byron Bay had a haunting kind of beauty about it, and as I sat in the early hours with only Isolation for company, I witnessed that beauty without you.

After spending many hours alone with my thoughts, the dark skies gradually became lighter and a great sense of relief washed over me. A kookaburra, cast in the soft grey of the early morning light, sat on a branch above me and looked down into my vacant eyes. My empty hammock swung from beneath the same tree that he perched upon and, as you rolled around on the floor, desperately clinging to your back in pain and as I shivered in the cool, isolated air, the kookaburra and I both knew that our circumstance was no longer a laughing matter. Above a blanket of mist that surrounded us like a bad dream, dawn finally penetrated my despair and broke across the hillsides in a ray of hope. Blue and pink hues mixed in with the frothy white dance of the sea. The morning joggers jogged. The dogs stretched their legs, whilst their owners enthusiastically followed their hairy excuses to stay fit and ran towards the breaking sun. The day began as if nothing had ever happened.

You awoke sometime later; your usually vibrant blue eyes had turned a winter's grey. Looking out at me from a storm of confusion, it was even later still before your mind completely returned. Benjamin, I tell you these things, in this unintentional letter that has addressed itself to you, not because I aim to embarrass you, (we have all suffered complications with intoxications,) but darling, I tell you this because the things that you said next will forever define the totality of our relationship with one another...

With sick still crusted in-between the threads of your beard and my clothing still draped over your shoulder blades, you spoke to me (unnecessarily) of your defense. "I felt like I was being led along all night," you began. "I didn't want the acid. I didn't want to get into the van. I didn't even want that other girl in my bubble... I just wanted you. But you didn't want me."

Your first and only explanation in regards to the previous night had escaped your mouth and would never find its way back inside. Pierced with unnecessary deflections, I understood those statements to be a far cry from the responsibility that you should have sought after. You, who parted the crowds in search of LSD. You, who chugged thirstily from the whiskey teat, you, who looked into the similarity of that woman's eyes with surface-layered desperation and you who had done everything that you could to 'do it to the maximum.'

But, being 'led' you said... I could only hang my head in shame.

After spending four days in Byron Bay with you, tending to your needs, feeding you, loving you and supporting a bad back that had kept your from fulfilling your dreams, upon hearing your version of being led, I finally waved a white flag in the air. Enough was enough. It was time for me to surrender and return to my path upon the Woman's Mountain. So, that is what I did. With fingers that were still warm with the friction of dedication and a morning that had barely broken into anything, I split my pouch of tobacco with you, made sure you had enough food for the day and, with sick still clinging onto the embarrassed state of you, I left you there in Byron Bay.

Samuel drove me back to the mountains that day and, as

449

I looked out of the passenger window into the blue, clouded sky, he asked me what I saw. Through eyes that were still smudged with LSD, I explained to him of how I saw a powdery white goddess breathing out fire upon all that she touched. A lion, full of fury and protection, roared out into the horizon whilst a child crouched alone upon a pure white, ever-moving pavement. After six hours of silence, it felt a foreign luxury to be asked about myself. Whilst the wheels rolled back to Nimbin, Samuel and I told one another stories about our lives and, with the clouded goddess as my witness, I finally admitted my own unhappiness.

Still, I returned to the Last Resort with the intention of rejoining my own personal path. Although I was armed with a desire to indulge in writing and music, I was surprised to find that after a few days, a fever had gradually taken ahold of my body. Apparently, despite my best intentions, my health had other ideas for me. It wasn't long before I was snotty, hot, and inflicted with the fevers of a broken heart. I lay alone in my shack feeling sorry for myself and, before long, a week had passed. You were a ghost to me. I tried to reach you, but your phone would just ring and ring and ring. The shack was plagued with silence, the forest became frightful and unhospitable up there on my own and, in the dark of the night, through my coughing and sputtering, I swore that I could hear something coming after me. Yet the only thing that sought me out was an infuriating truth that whispered to me of how you had found somebody new. I knew, in my heart of hearts, that I had finally lost you. So, I coughed and I wept… and I didn't eat for days.

With no word from you, I tried my hand at a beautiful distraction; I visited the outskirts of Nimbin and attended the Echidna Dreaming Festival. Without question, the Aboriginal peoples welcomed me as a sister, and I attempted to dive head-first into their magic. Sitting amongst a group of family, the Aborigines allowed me to assist in painting their bodies in preparation for a tribal dance that was scheduled to occur as a main act. Whilst an Aunty placed ochre upon the brown of my own skin, she invited me to get up on stage and dance with her and her mob in a ceremony of one single family. But I could barely even speak, let alone dance. I was weak, brooding, and confused, so I

450

respectfully refused her offer and accepted her honey and vinegar remedy for my raw throat instead. As Aunty tentatively put feathers in my hair and looked upon me with the concerned eyes of a mother, I fell further into the depths of despair. Knowing that the magic that I had been seeking out all along was finally upon me... only seemed to amplify my sickness. My throat felt all broken up, as if it had been dragged backwards through barbed wire, and I feared that I may never again speak or sing. A sister pulled me up on stage to sing with her and, as my voice shuddered into the microphone, I knew that I was not on top form. It was a strange sensation to find myself, after years of shyness, in front of a microphone with the will to sing. Yet, despite my determination, only croaking frogs seemed to come out of my throat. It was a lesson well-learned, and I promised myself that if my voice were ever to return, then I would sing as often as possible.

After stepping down from the stage and retreating to the safety of Granny Breath Weaver's circle of women, I attempted to take up weaving under her instruction. As each thread wound into the next in an effort of beauty and support, who should arrive at the festival... but Andrew... and his queen of hearts. Andy sat across from me with the men and played music, whilst his queen came right over to Granny's circle and began weaving. Her fingers were beautiful and dainty, her face was blushed with the crimson of an angel's heart and, as I sat with a half-woven basket in my hand, I understood the tapestry of our woven interactions. With Andrew's love sitting right beside me, my broken relationships with women could not have been more apparent. With my blood at a boil, I retreated back to my home upon the Woman's Mountain.

That night, I coughed and I cried so hard into my sheets that, as the blue light of dawn shone through the bedroom tarp, I realised that I had given myself a hernia. An aching lump manifested just above my belly button and caused my eyes to water every single time that I coughed. The Sahara desert had relocated to my throat and I felt weaker than I had ever felt before. My love for you physically hurt. But where were you, Benjamin? When I needed your support... where were you? You were lost in-between the legs of another. The phone rang and rang, but you just

451

wouldn't answer. There was no one to rub my back with friction fingertips, no one to clothe me, feed me, or tell me that it would all be ok. There was no one around to love me in the way that I had loved you. So I began to give up.

Benjamin... my heart won't allow me to eat. I lie in my bat cave bed, bruised with defeat; I have been lying here for so long that, before I could have known, I have become too weak to collect wood. Without wood, there are no fires. Without fires, I cannot cook. My cool box is bare of food, my stomach is swollen and pained with grief, whilst my bones have begun to protrude from my skin, as if even they are trying to escape me.

During a time in my life where I expected to be the strongest, I have never been so weak. I am entertaining the idea that I could die alone on this mountain... and that nobody would even know where to find me.

And you, my blue-eyed prince...

... you are not here for me.

A King's Castle

January 19th 2015

In the midst of my sickness, as I lay in a bat cave bed surrounded by tissues, tears, and my own personal pity party, whilst dreaming of electricity and trying my best not to cough the guts out from inside of my body, above the splutter of my wheezing lungs, I began to hear the sound of leaves frantically turning upon the ground. As my ears pricked towards the commotion, I ascertained their rustling to have been caused by the sound of determined footsteps… feet that were making their way towards me.

Knowing that Granny had left me to my own recovery, and not being in the slightest way ready to receive a guest, I nonetheless draped some light clothing over my fevered body and walked towards the entrance of the shack, in an effort at solving the riddle of the rustling leaves. Standing on unstable and undernourished legs, I wobbled towards the approaching sound, adjusted my reddened eyes to the assaulting white light of the afternoon and, as my vision gradually began to focus, I was surprised to see the jovial face of Samuel making his way towards me.

"I'm just on my way back to the Blue Mountains to see my family," Sam called out from a pathway that promised to lead him straight to me. "I thought I'd drop in and say goodbye to you before I left." Samuel's Cheshire cat smile shone through the trees with the brightness of a thousand hopeful sunrises and, amidst the darkness of my heart, I knew that I had never been happier to see him. Sam; the only person in the world, besides Granny and Ben, that had any clue as to where I was.

I smiled at Sam with all the strength that I could muster, invited him in to my outside home and, as I attempted to find my voice in order to welcome him, I also tried not to splutter and cough all over his face. Sam stood in the doorless doorway,

453

looking me up and down with eyebrows that had suddenly become animated with worry and, without being able to summon any words of comfort, I understood the sorry state that I looked to be in. Raising a concerned and thick rock climber's hand up to my damp forehead, Samuel began to feel the fever that had been climbing across my bony body without a harness and then recoiled in the horror of its carelessness. After touching the shrinking memory of my waistline and looking into me with sherbet-blue eyes that had been dipped in a sticky kind of care, Samuel put his belongings down upon my leaf-saturated floor and, without saying even a word, concluded that the Blue Mountains could wait.

After a few days of rest, the sickness that had once defined my existence and threatened, with or without conviction, to extinguish my flame from the world, finally began to release me from its grasp. Under the tentative care of Samuel, I had been well fed and watered, warmed beside the fire at night, and told a myriad of enchanting stories whilst falling asleep in my bat cave bed until I felt somewhat healed. There was no doubt that Samuel had shown up at exactly the right time and, although I was rarely a damsel in distress, he had proved to be my knight in smiling armour.

Once I had gained strength enough to leave the shack, Samuel and I headed into town to grab a coffee. But, on the way, above the pains of my coughing and inspired by the pitiful tears that clung onto the sides of my eyes for dear life, Samuel had decided it in my best interest to re-route our intentions and instead head towards the hospital, asserting that we needed to investigate the hard lump that had formed just above my belly button, as well as procure some heavy-duty medicine for my chest. The sterile building of the hospital was a far cry from the forest life that I had become accustomed to but, as we patiently sat in the white waiting room, Sam placed his hand in my own and, holding it there, he helped me to at least feel a sense of home.

After diagnosing that there was nothing to be done for a

hernia, but breathing a sigh of relief knowing that it wasn't anything more serious, Samuel and I fell into exploring the local area.

With a rough cough that drummed out across to the Amazon rain forest, fooling indigenous tribes into ritualistic dance, and an ache in my belly that pulsated throughout my watery body in such a high frequency that even salt water dolphins became disoriented, I feebly attempted to enjoy my local tour. As Samuel and I drove through the winding country roads with nowhere in particular to go, Sam proceeded to hold me in a bubble of safety and humour that was altogether healing.

Together, we visited small fishing villages along the coastline and, under the cover of night, Sam and I searched for a boat deck in which we could sleep upon. I had never slept on a boat before and the act of mischief began to cloak me in distraction from my aching heart. Sam and I snuck into peculiar places without tickets or passes and pretended to be king and queen of a crystal castle. We took things that were never ours, passing them on to owners who would better appreciate them and, when Samuel put his bandit arms around me in victory, I looked at him admiringly and felt as though we had always broken the rules together. Despite my sickness, I knew that Sam could see the higher version of me and, whilst he encouraged her to come back out and play, I kissed him for it. Passion sparked and Sam became as familiar to me as the worn pages of my diary.

It was apparent that within the chemistry of Samuel and I lay a great adventure that was just waiting to be discovered. Everything that we did together resonated with such joy and happiness that my sickness began to throw its hands up in surrender. Bouncing off of one another's energy, no idea or plan seemed too great or too far for us to accomplish and we even began to entertain the idea of travelling the desert together. The desert had long been within my dreams and, as I shared them with Sam, he helped me to feel as though they could become a reality. I didn't feel hindered in Samuel's company; instead, I was lifted up by the capable hands of an unconventional love.

Sam and I held hands and ran naked across a public park into a glimmering and inviting lake. Upon an assortment of picnic benches, shocked onlookers attempted to eat their afternoon sandwiches without their dropped jaws getting in the way. Swimming freely in the waters without concern for an audience, Sam had helped me to bring my inner joys into the outside world without fear, because he simply didn't care who was around. As we swam closer to one another through the waters of improbability, cruised around in his car telling stories, and watched the green valleys pass us by in a smudge of beauty, I learned from Sam's relaxed and genuine ways. Although it was a foreign flavour, it felt nice not to have to worry over the provisions of my company. Sam had his own car, his own money, his own journey, and he took very good care of himself. In a time when I needed such affection, he had also taken great care of me and, because of that, a part of me began to love him for it. Sam and I had left the Woman's Mountain to grab a coffee four days prior and, without regard for time or commitments, had simply become lost in one another's fun.

Amongst the carefree escapades that I had shared with Sam, I was not fooled by the definitive danger of jumping from one relationship right into another. Though, at the time, Sam could only ever be an impermanent fixture in my life; the Blue Mountains still beckoned him back to their eucalyptus forests, giving me a free pass to excuse my frivolity. Sam and I, without promising each other anything, just bounced around on the sounds of our rebounded laughter until we bounced all the way back to Byron Bay with goods to sell upon its streets.

Despite Ben's phone not having any place to be other than his pocket or his backpack-turned-home, it still rang and rang without any intention to answer me. Without any verbal confirmation, I knew, through those unanswered rings, that Ben and I had each fallen into the caring arms of other lovers. And, no sooner had Sam and I set up our wares of gypsy trade upon the street, then did I see a coy and wounded Ben emerge from the crowds and begin to approach me.

Taking a deep breath in anticipation of our impending

conversation, I sat upon the streets of Byron Bay, amongst a sea of glimmering things, and cast my eyes up towards a rigid and nervous Ben. Ben hovered above me with a weighted look about him that pushed him down to my eye level and, after a casual ceremony of hello's that could have belonged to any of the strangers that walked past our meeting, Ben looked upon Sam and the strangers around us and asked that I follow him into a private conversation.

Together, Benjamin and I walked through the back alleys of Byron Bay and fondled common conversation upon our tied tongues until we came upon the back of a building and sat down outside of it in order to hold court with one another. Perched upon a few small concrete steps that were not ascending anywhere, I looked over at Benjamin with an empty mouth and ears that were full of the will to listen.

"Well," Benjamin began with caution, clearing and chasing away a bullfrog that seemed to have taken up residency in his throat. "I have gone and done the same exact thing that you did back in Melbourne, April." I looked into Ben's blue-grey eyes that were not only smudged with ironies, but also held the look of one too many intoxications within them. Dark circles hung below his eyes as if to remind me of the hammock that we had once shared and a jagged look of uncertainty resonated out from his crouched body. It was clear that a twisted kind of competition had inadvertently been running marathons in-between Benjamin and I. Without needing further explanation, I knew that because I had fallen for another 'once upon a Melbourne nightmare,' that Ben had seen fit to serve me the same kind of medicine. He searched my face for signs of shock, though I could only mirror the cement that sat below us.

"How predictable you are my prince," was my only answer.

A collection of rubbish bins stood beside Benjamin and I as we sat crouched behind a grocery store and, with their overflowing, foul-smelling mouths, they reminded us of the crap that each of us had created. Boxes of outdated vegetables stacked

457

themselves above our heads and sweltered in the afternoon heat, emphasisng the fact that everything has an expiration date. And, as those that passed us by smiled at a version of Ben and I who sat dangerously close to each other, immersed in intimate conversation, those strangers mistook us for two people who still gave a damn about one another. But how little did they know of our dialogue. *How little will passing strangers ever truly know of us?*

A forest of explanations began to populate inside of Benjamin's mouth. Watered by guilt and fed by the light of his personal journey, Ben's tall tales surrounded me with their thick, suffocating canopy.

"I love her very much, April," Ben promised me. "I love her very much and she loves me in the same kind of way. She's kind and warm and, although I have been denied the right kind of love for so long, she bestows it upon me. She is my joy." The rumble of an overdue earthquake began to echo out across the plains of my heart, fracturing and cracking its dusty land into indistinguishability. Upon hearing the words finally escape his own mouth, Ben began to panic and proceeded to dig himself into a deeper hole.

"I tried to ignore it. I tried to fight it. But it's like two different people are living inside of me." Ben pleaded, the lines in his face creasing, his youthful features morphing into the look of an old man. "A part of me loves you, April, until the end of time and beyond. But a part of me also knows that your love just isn't enough. You can't love me in the way that I need to be loved. April, you know that you can be so very cold to the touch." With Ben's final words, the earthquake in my heart stilled and, as I crouched over the concrete steps like a boy, I became a statue of impenetrability. Knowing that Ben awaited a reaction that would validate my love for him, I instead decided to show him just how cold I could be.

"So, good luck," I announced, without an ounce of emotion upon my sun-kissed face and, disassociating from Ben, I proceeded to address him as if his face were a letter. "Good luck with your future endeavours, Benjamin, I wish you all the joy in the world." Half of me meant it, yet the more prominent half did not. Looking upon Ben's rugged features, I saw that he had not only subjected himself to homelessness upon the beach, but also appeared to have indulged in one too many trips with the hipsters of Byron Bay. I saw my chance to advise, as well as casually strike. "Stop rotting your brains out on psychedelics, Benjamin, you're gonna end up being just another kid that's dazed out and lost on Byron's beach.... I hope you realise that you look like shit." I eyed Ben with distaste and he recoiled with the reminder of the tough and unsympathetic love that would never be good enough for him.

Pointing with two fingers that were cast towards opposite directions of the street, I took the lead and instructed that Ben and I step away from the pivotal point of our meeting. "I am going to walk this way... and you Ben, you will walk that way." The back alley of Byron Bay grew dark and hostile. The discarded vegetables recoiled in rotten horror at the coldness that had been shared between Ben and I. And, as a boy and a girl, who were once star-crossed lovers, walked away from one another in separate directions with their heads hung low, a forgotten cabbage fainted in the thick heat of the afternoon and wilted its way towards expiration.

Once again, my blue-eyed prince and I were parted; we had fallen into the loving arms of others and had reflected one another's journey through the mirrors of a competition that, it seemed, would never surrender. In an attempt to rinse my spirits of heartache, I discarded my gypsy trade upon the streets and began fuelling myself on four bottles of white wine, (one for every year that Ben and I had spent together.)

That night, I sat at the top of a tree and, releasing the coldness that I had cloaked myself with, I cried into its green, bushy leaves. Samuel sat a branch over from me and, with the thrashing ocean as our backdrop, he searched my sadness in an

459

attempt to find a pathway that would lead me back to happiness. Samuel became my confidant as well as my drinking partner but, despite him joining me in my despair, I had become stained with white wine eyes that could barely see the support that was in front of them. I thought so hard upon the image of Benjamin and Joy that fate eventually tired of my dissolute ways and found great comedy in placing the new lovers at a stroll beneath me.

Of all the places in the world to take a romantic stroll, Benjamin and Joy had decided to walk, not only beneath the moonlight, but beneath *my* tear-stained tree. Not realising that I hovered above them, camouflaged by the thick foliage, I looked down upon Ben and Joy, in more ways than one, and watched them like a tree top spy. Joy's small, pale frame almost disappeared beneath Ben's muscular body and, still hindered with a bad back, Ben leant up against her whilst they strolled, arm in arm. Looking up into Ben's spaced-out eyes, pickled with new love and meek adoration, Joy automatically became every single attribute that I despised within a woman. The blood beneath my skin began to boil with the same red fever as a volcano that was on the brink of eruption.

Joy looked up to Ben with eyes that called him a god and, although I could not fathom such a concept, the language of her body placed him above all else. Samuel looked over to me through the leaves and, although he was also an accomplice to our love square, I could barely see him. Besides Benjamin and Joy... the rest of the world faded to black and their silhouettes became the only thing that I could focus upon.

One week apart, and mine and Ben's relationship had been reduced to that scene; me sitting up in a tree with somebody new, and him arm in arm with a lover that was a far cry from me. As the rubbish bins shook their heads in shame, the things that Benjamin had said to me back in that back alley of Byron began to haunt me. *After everything that I had done for him, shared with him, and been with him, how could Benjamin think that I had not loved him properly?* Waves of responsibility crashed in the ocean behind me and, as I became wild and ugly with depravity, I called out to Ben from the tree top in order to ensure that he knew I was there.

"Hey, Ben." His name punched through my teeth like a silver-tipped bullet, shattering the fragile image of his and Joy's romantic moonlit stroll.

"April..." Ben stammered, unarmed and vulnerable. "This... this is Joy." Pushing his prize forward to meet me, I feebly extended my arm from the top of the tree just enough so that Joy needed to stand on her tippy toes in order to greet me. As Joy looked up at me with wild, nervous eyes that could very well have belonged to a deer, I felt the lioness emerge from my fractured heart and roar out into the night sky. Wrapping my venomous fingers around her dainty hand and pulling her slightly off the ground, I shook Joy's hand with an intentional violence.

As Joy retreated back into the folds of Ben's comfort and Ben, as if he could smell the scent of thunder and rain in the air of the pride land, pushed her back towards their encampment, I allowed the storm inside of me to spill out over everyone. Jumping down from the tree, full of ugly rage and fury, I began to tell my side of the story to the jury of Benjamin, Joy, and Samuel.

"You know, Ben," I sarcastically seethed, as my feet touched the tarmac like a villain that had leapt from the sky. "Perhaps I was just too goddamned *busy*... too busy feeding you breakfast, lunch, and dinner from *my* pocket, too busy showering you in tobacco, weed, and anything else that arose from the insatiability of *your* endless greed. Perhaps I was too busy putting clothes on your back, too busy mothering you and encouraging you to utilize your *gifts* so that you may fulfill your forgotten dreams. Perhaps I was just too bloody busy encouraging you to be the highest version of yourself to 'love you properly." My words were a machine gun of malevolence.

Seeing Joy scurry away down to the embankment of the beach, I called out to her turned back. "I hope you have hard nipples girl... because he will suckle until the milk's run dry."

I had become a vision of madness that was and was not me. I thought of everything that I had given to Ben over the years

461

of our relationship and, because of his disregard for it, it brought out the primal beast within me. Feeling mocked and disrespected, I looked towards my leather belt satchel that sat around Ben's waist and knew it to define my efforts. It was a belt that I had paid a hundred dollars for and had never even worn. It was a belt that I had given to Ben so that he could keep his most precious things close to him. And it was a belt that he had worn out in the same way that he had done my heart. As the sea seethed with me, I approached Ben, ripped my belongings from his waist, and screamed out: "Give me back my fucking belt!"

Turning my back upon Benjamin, I continued to scream out into the crashing waves of the sea.

"You think that you're the king of the fucking castle, Benjamin." Wine and heartache swirled around in my body, encouraging an emotional exorcism that no longer gave a damn about the repercussions. Sam sat in the tree looking at us in disbelief, Joy scurried away down the beach, and the waves from the ocean reached hungrily towards our feet. Sarcasm swam around my convictions and, as I threw my hands in the air theatrically, I walked away into the night with mockery upon my tongue.

"King of the castle. He wants it all. King of the castle…well, not *this* castle, Benjamin, not *my fucking castle.*"

As the dark night swallowed me up, a single cabbage rolled out from beneath a forgotten vegetable box and stumbled upon her partner's wilted corpse.

Together, the remaining cabbage and I wept for the certitude in the expiration of love.

Cosmic Advertisement

28th January 2015

After the quaking of my heart had softened to an indistinguishable rumble and the venom in my blood had been diluted down with the currents of time, my life upon the Woman's Mountain became a quiet and simple affair.

Each morning, I stood amongst the thick, pre-dawn fog and watched it crawl, upon veiled palms and murky knee-caps, across the leaf-peppered pathway towards me. Merging with its distorted and disorienting ways, I would allow the mist to crawl all over my body, surrendering to its haunted isolation. My own identity had, once again, become blurred into the life of another, leaving me with an inability to determine who I really was; the bitter lover? The optimist? The spirit seeker? With a heavy heart, I sighed out into the morning air and heard something stir within the rustle of the trees. *'Get a life, girl,'* the forest, my heart, and my subconscious had all quietly, and very sarcastically, said to me. I was taken aback by their unified insensitivity. Some truths are so obvious that, upon hearing them, one can become slightly offended at their frankness.

With a cough still clinging to my chest like a koala to a eucalyptus tree, and signs of mould beginning to materialise upon my pillow case, life felt exactly how it looked; sick, lonely, and mildewed. Nothing felt right to me. Despite being in a position where I should have been at my strongest, my healthiest, and my cleanest, I was, in fact, quite the opposite. Still; clean air, the absence of electricity, and tough tasks of manual labour all begged that I get out of my self-inflicted funk and enjoy them. But as I looked through a bucket of clouded dish water and entertained the universe's invitation of employment, once I had seen the distorted reflection of myself, I knew that I simply couldn't stand the sight of me. But, as the ripples settled, through my coughing, spluttering, and wheezing, I also knew the night to be at its deepest before the light of dawn could ever begin to approach.

I understood myself, as often happens when I am sick, to be going through a process of purging. I was attempting to evict a person that had been living inside of my heart for the last four years of my life and, as the fusion of our soul mates had finally separated and tried to make a break for it, it was not only my heart that was left vacant... my entire being had never felt so empty. Benjamin was more than just a sour taste that had been left upon my tongue; he was my blue-eyed prince, my humble beginnings, my one and only constant in the ever-changing backdrop of my life. Benjamin was, without a doubt, my complete and utter everything. But, there I was, alone in the shack, in the exact way that I had secretly wanted to be. Sam had returned to the Blue Mountains and Benjamin was left in Byron Bay with his new girlfriend. Somehow, it was everything that I had consciously, or unconsciously, encouraged to come into existence. My life was a perfect darkness.

It didn't take long before I convinced myself that I was strong enough to submerge into the demands of manual labour and I began sweating out, as always, my lingering sickness. During my unexpected four day escapade with Samuel, a middle-aged woman named Jen had joined Granny Breath Weaver and I upon the Woman's Mountain. A small circle of women had formed in my absence. Jen had short, thick legs, dirty blonde hair and a plea for developmental assistance that sat upon her soft cherub face. As she looked back into my own eyes, Jen had also registered my brokenness. So, without words or further ado, Jen and I joined forces on the mountain and attempted to make up an entire person.

Jen had decided, with the permission and encouragement of Granny, to build her own shack on top of the mountain. This structure was to be built from the shell of an old shed that was just a stone's throw away from my own shack. I was looking for a sense of purpose in my life, so I had easily adopted Jen's mission as my own and, together, we began to get down and dirty. Two heads would always be better than one.

464

Every afternoon, Jen and I stood on top of a barely-there tin roof, avoided falling in through the deteriorated patches, extracted nails that were deeply imbedded within the rusts of time, saturated our bodies in salty sweat, flexed our muscles into definition, and dutifully ripped off each sharp shard of metal from the structure that no longer served as a working shelter. The longer that I found myself lost in labour, the closer my mind would come to taking some time off. When that tactic didn't work and I was overrun with thoughts of Benjamin, I would then push myself into a difficult task just to demand complete employment of my attentions. My torn hands began to bleed with duty, running red rivers down my wrists and depicting the need for me to stay busy and feel strong. Rusted nails and jagged saws were the only available working tools, but it was that sense of slight danger that kept my demons at bay.

All afternoon, I would dig trenches that were deep enough to house freshwater mermaids, should they choose to join our sisterhood upon the Woman's Mountain. When Jen's shack was deemed safer from the rains and, as I dug deeper trenches around my own home, with soil and sweat mixing around in my eyes, I found a safe way in which to cry. With every trench that I dug, in order to avoid drowning in the murky waters of my abandonment, I also attempted to reroute the rivers of my heart. For hours I would dig, weed, hammer, and rip apart all of the untended parts of the mountain, whilst leeches and mosquitos attached themselves to my skin and ankles, bleeding me without table manners.

I would think of Benjamin, suckling, and then chase him away again. I swatted away the memory of them together holding hands. I dug and dug and attempted to dig myself out of a different kind of hole. As sweat rolled into the corners of my lips, I also attempted to dissolve the bitter taste that had formed in the romance of my mouth. My work became a complete symbol of my own internal garden; overgrown and forgotten. But, despite how bitter I had become, the Woman's Mountain promised to keep me on without judgement, healing me, distracting me, and needing me, even though a half of my flame was missing. The Woman's Mountain seemed to be the only place where in which the sky wasn't falling.

One afternoon, after Jen and I had rolled into Granny Breath Weaver's shack, full of dirt, abandonment, and the hope for empowerment layering our soiled skin, Granny had peered over her coffee cup into our swollen, red eyes and suggested that we sing together. Excavating some forgotten papers from amongst the piles of wood and bones, Granny placed them before the sorry state of Jen and I, then went on to tell us of how she used to congregate with a group of women that sung empowering songs out into the single street of Nimbin each week. Granny looked into Jen and I as if we could use a dose of the same medicine. I took the yellowed pieces of paper from Granny Breath Weaver's hand and watched as she removed a tambourine from the shelving. Granny then began to shake the instrument with absolute purpose upon her slender thigh, singing out into the roomless room with great conviction.

"I am a wild woman," she began, with eyes that glimmered like diamonds and encouraged Jen and I to join them in their richness. "Into the dragon's mouth I go." Granny became animated, dancing around her shack in her skin-coloured clothes. She was a blur of flesh, a lightning bolt of life.

With no reason not to join in on the song, other than the nagging whine of my unenthusiastic heart, I looked upon the lyrics that swirled around upon the aged paper, took a strange wooden frog instrument into my hands, and began clumsily tracing a wooden stick up and down its ridged back in an effort at creating sound.

"I am a bold woman," I began. With all three of our mouths employed in melodic action, Granny, Jen, and I met one another's gaze with a sense of purpose glossing over our eyes. "Seeking love and wisdom, I go on my own." With each spoken word, the atoms in my body began to morph into what they had been sung to be and, as I danced upon a sheepskin rug with bare, earth-stained feet, the affirmation of a bold, strong woman began chasing away my pain. "Seeking love and wisdom, I go on my own... I go on my own."

Granny had dosed me up with the appropriate medicine and suggested that we meet in her kitchen each week in order to go over the list of empowering songs that she kept inside of her. Whilst I laboured beneath the sweltering sun each day, that song began to fall from my lips without thought and became my mantra for development and healing. Because, through seeking love and wisdom, I had found myself on my own.

In the evenings, when the women of the mountain slept and a piercing quietude fell over absolutely everything around me, was the time that I felt most alone. I would sit cross-legged upon my carpet, staring into the fire that I had created, surrounded by complete and utter darkness, and I would ponder upon the source of my empowerment, trying to tap into it like a secret well. There were no walls in which to keep the darkness out and, just as the shack had had to surrender to such a life, so too did my heart. I began attempting to mimic my environment. I would listen to the silence of the night, disturbed only by animals who assured me that I wasn't completely alone, and I began to allow the mystery and quietude of darkness to comfort me. I no longer feared the animals that lived amongst the thick, uncertain forest, because I had decided that fear equated to heartache and I didn't want my heartache anymore.

As I stared into the fire and was hypnotised by its amber glow, I found myself wondering what it was that I *did* actually want. As the flames crawled higher into the air like a blazing tiger scaling an unsuspecting tree, a single, barely audible answer began to stir from the ashes, then spilt itself out from the hot coals and landed at my feet.

'*A friend would be a good start,*' the fire, in a whisper, nudged me.

The sarcastic voice of the embers reminded me of how I had allowed everything to fall away from me with the death of my romantic relationship. I had fallen down from a pedestal of shit and, in the same manner as always, I had arrived on the floor with no friends to catch me. But it was I who had not made an effort to maintain any relationships other than the one that I had with

Benjamin, my twin flame, my best friend. So, it was I who would need to deal with those repercussions.

Through the sarcastic tones of the fire, I also understood that not everything upon the Woman's Mountain needed to carry such a heavy lesson, and that fun was as good a remedy as any. I stared blankly into the fire and felt slightly embarrassed that I had not thought of it before… but some truths are so obvious that upon hearing them, one can become slightly offended at their frankness.

Gathering my thoughts into one large intention, I decided to send out a cosmic advertisement to the universe. It read as follows:

Wanted:

Seeking young female companion between the ages of 20-50.

Applicant must have a zest for life and the ability of endless laughter into the late hours of the night.

Applicant must have a philosophical inquisition ingrained within her third eye.

Those lacking third eye qualifications need not apply.

Applicant must extend her colourful personality into a wacky wardrobe, in order that we may find love in the sharing of our clothes.

It is preferred that applicant be balanced in listening skills, as well as be communicatively inspiring.

Blondes are preferred as they are said to have more fun.

However, due to unconcern for surface layer, physical make up, the former term is negotiable.

Adventure, on the other hand, is non-negotiable.

Applicants may apply from within.

An Angel Answers

30th January 2015

It was a sunny afternoon at the Oasis Café and, as I sat encircled by the women of Nimbin, I curiously looked upon our organic gathering as if it were a scientific experiment that were in need of documentation.

Various shapes pushed themselves out from the assortment of our bodies like a child's shape-finder toy; some were rectangular, some circular, some women were as tall as a straight line, whilst others hunched over into a puddle of scribbles. A collection of varied tones pirouetted out across our voice boxes like ballerinas that had been moved by the sound of music, rising and falling, scraping across the ground, and then soaring off into the clouds without any intention to return. Together, the women and I were a collection of waves that had rolled, in unison, upon the shore of the afternoon and, as we circled one another at the back of the Oasis, each one of us had brought something different to the table.

A pair of older lips parted with discussions of Aboriginal treaties and, as brown ears pricked up and listened attentively, the ownership of certain plots of land were renounced. The topic of treaties was a sensitive subject between the white and the black people of the community and, as I watched hairs stand upon their ends with the rigidness of conflicting emotions, I was also comforted by most of the women's ability to sympathise with one another, no matter the colour of their skin.

A young woman carried a candle of understanding towards the older generation and, as she parted her quivering lips with stories of troubles upon them, the older generation became illuminated with a new-found understanding of the younger generation's disharmony with addictions. The young woman spoke of how methamphetamines had grasped her loved one by the throat and, as she poured her troubles into the safety of our

469

circle, she showed us what kind of payment she had received for attempting to help her partner to step away from the drugs. The fingerprints around her neck had faded into a barely recognisable smudge, though as she rubbed at her phantom bruises with a shaky hand, it was clear that they would always be visible to her. The aged eyes looked upon the young woman, horrified, and a whole new world of narcotics began to open up before them.

An elder, warm and concerned in her nature, immediately joined forces with Granny Breath Weaver and drew the first pencilled outline of a resolution upon our watchful paper faces. "We need to form a support group." The two women looked into one another with respect, their maternal features glimmering beneath the afternoon sun. "We will call it Breaking the Ice."

The young woman shuffled around on the cement seat uncomfortably and, as she locked eyes with me, I felt compelled to tell her of my previous battle with methamphetamines. Although it was a topic that I did not usually speak of, something in me needed to comfort her. The women in the group fell silent, listening as I drew visions of my prior struggles into the afternoon air; a version of me that had been awake for weeks, strung out into unrecognisability and who dabbled in a madness that most people don't come back from. But there I was, back from it… wherever *it* was, and aspiring to provide just a glimmer of hope in the young woman's life. She smiled at me for my efforts and, without meaning to, warmed my heart. Speaking the unspoken, that afternoon, we had all come together as a group of women who aspired to find refuge in one another and for it, each one of our eyes twinkled with the light of community within them.

In many ways, Nimbin is a carefree, coffee-drinking, pot-smoking community. The town is comprised of old-school hippies that you can find walking the single street back and forth with feathers in their hair and nowhere to really go… but with everywhere to be. The tourists pull up in their busses with their flashy cameras, stop at the café's, smoke a few joints, and take a few pictures, just to prove that they were there. Then they disappear back to wherever they came from with a feeling of accomplishment stored in their memory cards. But the truth of the matter is that they rarely ever skim the surface; a tourist rarely does.

Beneath the top layer of the towns carefree façade, there is a powerful underbelly that consists of the real Nimbin. The town is full of politics and women's business, Aboriginal communications and chakra related poetry, rich, yet poor, characters, peace treaties, drug addictions, and unsettled disputes towards the land. All of these things gather themselves into the small cafés of Nimbin's single street, hide beneath a superficial layer of greenery and try not to be seen by those who are not equipped to handle them. But I had been in Nimbin long enough to understand the depths of its true character and, although I had initially been uplifted by the town's unique and lighthearted charisma, I also knew Nimbin to be a weighted place.

Parts of the town were heavy and unforgiving, pressing down upon me with a serious disposition, even when I tried to look at them from a distance. Back on the Woman's Mountain, I had also begun to find myself gasping for air, unable to breathe in the pressure of such a mysterious place. So, as I sat in the thick air of the women's circle, I understood the ability to have fun to be an imperative practice that I needed to employ immediately, should I wish to survive.

Whilst the women continued their dialogue, my thoughts began to drift back a few weeks prior to that moment, settling upon the day that I had left for Byron in order to assist Benjamin with his dreams. It was before the hitch, before the tears, and before I had jumped down from the tree like a madwoman that had been inflicted with the temper of a villain. Before any of those events had transpired, as Ben, Sam, and I had scurried around gathering provisions for our trip to Byron, we had also met a pretty little pixie who had sat cross-legged upon Nimbin's single street.

The young woman had looked up at me and, with a smile that promised to keep me safe, she had beamed a thousand moonbeams into my being, stopping me dead in my tracks. The round of her ivory face had been curtained by a string of beached curls that wound themselves into one another like golden chains on a precious locket. Curling and bouncing across her nimble shoulder blades, her locks moved like dancing snakes that had been dipped in a raging sandstorm. As I fell into the mud bath of the girl's eyes and began bathing myself in their rich, earthy pools, I knew that something about her was just as powerful as the sandstorm. Sitting amongst a bed of necklaces that she had made out of pinecones, the girl extended her soft, generous arms out towards me and, with her tone wrapped up in the blanket of a Bristol accent, she introduced herself to me as Florence. Pulling away from her embrace and looking into the twinkling mischief of Florence's features, I saw that she had the kind of eyes that a person often finds themselves wishing upon.

Although I had undoubtedly been drawn to Florence from the very beginning, after Ben and Samuel had begun hovering around her and her friend, Luke, indulging in connected conversations that pertained to the meaning of life, I saw a version of myself sliding into the background. I had been quiet and introverted, with only the ability to watch as a sideline participator whilst Ben and Florence's friend, Luke, hugged one another; man to man, beard to beard, and teared up over their connection. I just leaned against a lamppost, listening to Sam and Florence talk wildly about poetry. With animated features, they exchanged quotes from Rumi and, although my love for poetry was on the tip of my tongue, something had cloaked me in reservations and stopped my interjections from escaping.

I found that I was distracted. The meeting with Florence had felt like a sidetrack, an off course, or even a backtrack, when I was just trying to go forward. I had only wanted to find the track that could lead me into the grassy verge of relationship equality and I couldn't possibly stop here; I was the one that had built my bedroom in a cave, therefore I knew it to be bat country. However, before I hit the road with my restless feet, I had exchanged phone numbers with Florence, the street pixie.

472

As I returned to the present moment, brushed away my daydreams, and looked around at the women that encircled me, I tried to focus upon their stories but my thoughts had a mind of their own and continued to pluck that pinecone pixie from my memories, pushing her forward into my reality. No matter how hard I tried to pay attention to the group of women that spoke around me, the light of Florence's smile and the brown pools of her mischievous eyes continued to find me and refused to leave without proper acknowledgement of their beauty. So, surrendering to the imagery of Florence as she floated in-between my thoughts like a love note that had been lost in the wind, I involuntarily began to envision a friend in which I could have a little fun with. Something strong seemed to be calling out from behind the curtain of daily life, whipped up by a wind that belonged to a sandstorm and, as I felt the warm breeze blow across my sticky skin, the curtains parted and I remembered my cosmic advertisement.

Knowing that I had unfinished duties to tend to upon the Woman's Mountain, I quietly excused myself from the weight of the circle and thanked the women for their company. However, I had barely made it to the back door of the café before Florence's name called out to me once again. Surrendering, I decided to take a seat in a quiet corner and honour my random obsession with Florence. Removing my dusty, unused phone from my rucksack, I scrolled down my contacts and dialled Florence.

"Hello!" A young woman's voice answered the phone, full of frantic desperation. Her tone, wobbling through the sound of whipping wind and cracking like a china plate under the pressure of a Greek wedding.

"Hey, Florence," I began, with a calm nervousness that was akin to asking a stranger out on a first date. "Would you like to meet...?"

"I'm not in Nimbin anymore," Florence abruptly

interjected; the wind distorted her softness and suggested that she could have been driving. Florence sounded all cut up, rushing. "I just had to get outta there. That place, Nimbin, it was getting to me!" Her breathing was laborious. "I'm on my way to Byron now… I just needed to get out of there… I'm just… I think that I need to go back home to England. The energy there… it's just too intense!"

The sound of silence sniffed me out and, like a hound dog, it sat at my feet and awaited my response. I digested Florence's testimony and, knowing that it was perfectly aligned with my own, I sent a silent *amen* up into the cloudless sky. With just those few words that she had spoken, I could feel the truth in Florence's tension. The draught of her isolation rushed up through the phone and pushed its way through the speakers into me and I recognised it to be the same isolation as my own. So, as Florence fled Nimbin, looking for a sense of peace and home, I casually assured her that she needn't feel rushed to leave.

"I'm here at the Oasis if you want to talk to me," I suggested. Florence and I made no promises to one another and, before I knew it, the line was dead.

For ten minutes I sat outside of the Oasis café, thinking over mine and Florence's odds; two strangers who felt the exact same way, in the exact same moment, and had been pressed, by unknown forces, into contacting one another. As mine and Florence's brainwaves consciously and subconsciously tried to align with one another, fighting for space to exist over the heaviness of Nimbin, I received a text message on my phone. It read:

'If I drive back to Nimbin, will you still be there?'

Whilst I sat in a deserted corner of the café, allowing the shade of a palm tree to cast riddles upon my face, I thought over the responsibilities that were calling me towards the mountain, (the trenches, the weeding, and the building of a bamboo shack,) and I decided to put them all aside for the day. Sisterhood was also calling out to me and, somehow, I knew that Florence needed me.

And even though I needed her too, it was a longing that was without desperation, a longing that was not even fully formed and, as I pondered over our meeting, I knew it to be a longing that had barely been recognised as a reality.

'I will be here.' I replied, perhaps answering Florence's very own cosmic advertisement.

Ordering another chai tea, I sat upon a crooked chair and tried to avoid getting too high from the second-hand smoke that perfumed the air around me. The women still sat behind me, talking amongst themselves in serious tones, their shapely bodies moving and changing forms with the light and shadows of day. Florence had postponed Byron Bay whilst I had pressed my mountain duties back into the list of things that could wait. I thought upon her starlight eyes, but had no need to make a wish upon them.

Because whether it was subconsciously, accidentally, or on purpose, I knew that an angel had already answered me.

Heartbreak's Hold-up

2nd February 2015

After meeting Florence at the Oasis café and having had sufficiently introduced, reflected, and submerged ourselves in the language of our hearts, it didn't take long to see that the pixie sailed a similar ship as my own. The waters of our affections were at different depths, yet it was apparent that Florence was nonetheless as romantically troubled as I.

As a result of our reflections, I knew that Florence and I had been aligned for a reason that was yet to be determined to either of us so, after a brief word with Granny and her trusting my judgement without question, I returned to the shaded corner of the café where I had been sitting, and asked Florence if she would like to seek refuge with me at the top of the Woman's Mountain. Florence accepted my proposition with curious intrigue, a shower of meteorites flashing across her dark, mysterious eyes.

Rounding the corner of the café and spilling out into a car park, Granny, Jen, and I came to a halt in front a boxy, old campervan and, as Florence proudly extended her arms towards it, she theatrically introduced us to her home on wheels, Millie; the red box wanderer from '85. After we had each admired Millie, crammed our curvaceous bodies into her angular one, drove up the winding country roads with the rattling windows down, laughed at Millie's lack of registration, and finally come to a halt at the foot of the Woman's Mountain, we exited the red box wanderer, stained with adventure, and began charging the steep hill towards home.

As the women and I walked across an endless blanket of damp leaves that paved the way towards our separate shacks, my eyes gravitated towards Florence. Her own dark eyes were as large as two vinyl records and, as she pulled everything around her into them, they spun around and around, dizzy with the force of beautiful funk. Florence's slender jaw dropped to the floor, politely upsetting the leaves as she walked and, as she entered the Last Resort, my new friend took a look around her new home for the night, inhaled a deep breath, and expanded with all of the beauty that surrounded her. Florence stood in my doorless doorway looking ten feet tall, as if the magic upon the mountain was so potent that it had physically filled her being. Looking upon her wanderlust, I felt as though I were also seeing a version of me that had just arrived at the Woman's Mountain. Our wanderlust-struck reactions had been one and the same.

That night, Florence and I cooked dinner together beside the soft light of the fire and, as our pot of pasta gradually came to a boil, we found that we had already poured over an endless array of comedic and tragic stories without even burning our tongues. The familiarity of England had served as our common ground but, as I watched the fire wrap itself around the soft curl of Florence's hair, I understood that the Last Resort would substitute for our new foundation. Our laughter echoed out around the still of the night, startling creatures that had become accustomed to my silence and my tears. Through the silliness that protruded out of Florence and I, I knew that companionship had found me, and for it, my bitterness began to retreat. The power of laughter proved to be the most healing of things.

That night, after the mosquito net had tucked us in like a nurturing mother who aspired to protect our new-found friendship, Florence and I lay peacefully beside one another in my bat cave bedroom and allowed the world to quieten around us. I could feel a regenerative force brewing inside of me as if, with Florence by my side, parts of me had already been pieced back together. Through the cloak of darkness, I looked upon Florence's pale skin, shining like a woman-shaped moon amidst an ebony sky. I followed her lungs as they instinctively moved up and down, inflated with languid, shallow breath, rocking like a tin boat upon a calm, yet powerful, sea. I traced the glow of electricity that seemed to emanate from and encircle Florence's entire being, glowing like a beacon through the opaque night. And I knew right then and there that I wanted to know everything about Florence. With our bodies lightly touching, a slither of human contact inserted itself in-between us and, as I closed my eyes, (eyes that still saw bolts of electricity flashing across their lids,) that human contact began rocking both Florence and I into deep and humble dreams.

The next morning, I awoke to an empty space in the bed. Upon hearing the teapot singing out in an almost-ready melody, and smelling the thick smoke of an early morning fire penetrating the fresh air of a new day, I slumped out of bed and made my way towards the commotion. As I rounded the corner into the living room, (kind of,) I found Florence huddled over a roaring fire. With elongated fingers that cupped her face like a cake liner, and firm features that looked to have been transfixed for some time upon the pulsing flames, I was surprised to look into the eternity of Florence's eyes and discover that she had been crying.

"Are you ok, Florence?" I inquired, with a sluggish, early morning concern.

"I've never lit a fire before," Florence replied, looking up to me, her damp, beige face catching the light of the fire like a mirage upon desert sands. "I wanted to do something nice for you. I wanted to make you a cup of tea." Her eyes wept with contentment and, as she cast them back towards the fire, a half-smile formed upon her perfectly curved lips. "And this... this is the first fire that I've ever lit. I was always too scared before..." Florence trailed off into silence, becoming lost in her own memories.

After touching her brittle shoulder blade affectionately, and feeling touched by her testimony, I left Florence to her early morning conquest and stepped outside into the blue break of dawn in order to prepare for a wash. I filled a few small buckets with cold rainwater and, in my usual fashion, armed myself with a bar of soap and a sarong. It wasn't long before Florence stepped outside onto the deck and into the bathroom, (kind of,) to join me.

The rising sun reached its way out through the trees and fell upon our fabrics, unbuttoning our trousers and pulling away our tops with golden fingertips. As Florence and I poured buckets of cool rain water all over our skin and began washing, the sun, as if unable to control himself, fell head-first onto our bodies and, along with the soap, began to lather us in his glimmering affection. The cool morning air pushed my nipples to attention and, as I looked over at Florence, I could see that the temperature had the same effect upon her. It was unusual to know someone for such a short amount of time and already see them naked, but the mountain demanded such an openness from all of its guests. So I went along with it, gladly, casting my nervous eyes across the perfectly-formed body of Florence. Her slender frame was about the same height and weight as my own, but as my eyes slid down her hip bones and picked up momentum in the deep curvature of her waist, as if on a waterslide, my eyes shot out into the surrounding day. Blushing and intrigued, I continued my wash with a growing affection towards my new guest.

That afternoon, I took Florence up to Granny Breath Weaver's shack. After sitting upon sheepskin rugs together, drinking coffee with piles of woven baskets and bones as our backdrop, and connecting as supersonic women, it was soon decided that Florence had been called to the Woman's Mountain. With her gentle theatrics, Granny had not only accepted such a truth, but had also strongly encouraged that we all begin to build our own legacies from the materials within her forest.

"You can stay here as long as you please," Granny had assured Florence, parting with that secretive twinkling smile in her eyes that I had come to adore.

So, without needing to have her arm twisted any further, Florence put behind her the idea of returning to England, and had decided to stay on the Woman's Mountain with me. After a week with her upon the mountain, what was once *my* labour of gardening, wood collecting, and digging, soon became *our* gardening, *our* wood collecting, and *our* digging. Wearing headscarves tied around our heads, and clothes that were joyfully soiled in mud and dirt, Florence and I began to dedicatedly repay the land for having us upon it. We worked together, laughed

479

together, and healed together, offering sweat and blood treaties for the mountain's service; we selflessly offered the service of ourselves in appreciation of being brought together. Each day, Florence and I cooked together and slept together and, when we bathed together, neither one of us no longer blushed. Together, we had imprinted the kind of connections and mountain rituals upon our skins that would never wash off.

So it was written that the loneliness of my heart just rolled away with the morning fog, dematerialised at the first sign of true friendship, and was never to be heard from again. The Woman's Mountain had played its part. After a week of hard labour, Florence and I decided to take some time out and rinse away the dirt from our skin with the pure, cleansing salt water of the ocean. Byron Bay was calling.

With the windows all the way down, and the breeze teasing out an impromptu dance from our wild hair styles, Florence and I cruised around in Millie, the red box character from the 80's. Each time that Millie stalled, (which was often,) we had to stop the van in order to jumpstart her and, as we drove away undeterred after each breakdown, I began to understand Millie's damaged battery heart. Florence, Millie, and I drove through the snaking roads that lead away from Nimbin, talking, singing, and laughing harder than we have ever laughed before, neither of us desiring to be held hostage by our hearts, and each of us honouring and blossoming from the beginning of a fresh jumpstart.

As I listened to the hilarious stories that spilled out from Florence's animated mouth, and allowed the funky music that pulsed from her portable speakers to get drowned out in the whipping wind and my daydreamer thoughts, I knew Florence to be a cosmic comedy that was bringing out the very best in me. We drove into the afternoon's decline like Thelma and Louise, in search of sunsets and crystal-white beaches. With callused and cut fingers, I reached over to the speaker and turned up the music until it spilt out all over the little red van and crept through the open window, saturating the green, fertile land with a flex of pumping good times.

Florence and I looked over at one another through the lyrical haze of frantic music and, without speaking it, laughed once more at all of the serious situations that had recently befallen our delicate emotions; scenarios that had curled us up, like little heartfelt creatures, into pitiful balls of sadness. Knowing that I could finally fully laugh about my previous heartache was a sure sign that I was resurfacing from my self-imposed depths of immobility. So, mocking my old susceptibilities, I felt strong enough to begin chasing after the grinches that had stolen my fun, who had stolen *our* fun. Florence and I were Thelma and Louise and, with our plastic guns waving carelessly in the air above a fury of wild, curly hair, we knew that we had been pushed to the edge when we had been robbed of our love. The only way to reclaim our things, it was decided, was to hold Heartbreak up at gunpoint, (though we would never tell him that our guns were plastic.)

'Give us back the goods!' I imagine myself screaming fiercely into the confused face of Heartbreak, my fear dissolving into a motivation of strength. Heartbreak isn't used to such direct confrontation and, unsettled, he looks out towards Florence in a hope of distraction.

'Don't look me in the eye again, Heartbreak, or I'll blow your fucking face off!' Florence aims her fury towards him, releases in verbal abandon and, although a sweetness still hangs about her assertions, Florence has dark sunglasses on that swallow up and mask her soft, poetic features. Her disguise is perfect.

Florence and I are empowered within our sisterhood. We surround Heartbreak like a pack of wolves and press our weapons to his genitalia, looking him in the eye with a promise to pull the trigger. With this act of treason, Heartbreak knows that there's no more fucking around and shakily begins to hand us over the goods that he had stolen from us; offering his riches to Thelma and Louise... to Little John and Robin Hood.

With callused, bleeding fingers, I snatch the bounty from

481

Heartache's trembling hands and count our returned riches aloud, just to ensure that they are all there.

'Strength... forgiveness... happiness... and love.' I look towards Florence, ready to make a run for it. "It's all here, Thelma," I promise.

'   What about our gratitude?' Florence calls out to me, with wide eyes that could no longer stand to be draped with wool.

Pushing Heartbreak back up against the prison wall, I frisk his soggy, selfish pockets in search of our forgotten gratitude. Heartbreak perspires, cowers, and shrinks, until he is half the size that I ever imagined him to be. And, as he deflates, the final treasure needed for our healing expands and finds me. I fondle the translucent shard of *gratitude* in-between my overworked fingertips and sigh out with relief. 'Got it.'

Together, Florence and I, Thelma and Louise, Robin Hood and Little John run out of Heartbreak's prison, filled to the brim with all of the goodness that we seemed to have lost along the way and we scream out triumphantly from the lips of our new identities. We throw our plastic weapons down upon the ground and, instead of violence, we opt to take one another's hands, choosing love instead. Falling into our getaway vehicle, (Millie the red box wonderluster from the 80's,) Florence and I pull *gratitude* out from my pocket and place it upon the dashboard amongst our other spoils of war; *strength, forgiveness, happiness, and love*. We smile into one another's success. Millie roars into life. The wheels begin to roll forward and, with our increasing motion, we are finally able to see the beauty in all of our troubles... because we have the secret weapon... *Gratitude*. And I vowed to never again allow gratitude to be taken from me.

Driving towards Byron, laughing, healing, and holding tightly onto one another, Florence and I disappear into an animated and slightly mad sunset, screaming, 'THEY'LL NEVER CATCH US ALLIIIIIIIVVVVEEEEE!!!'

A heartbreak's hold-up; such was the journey of Florence and I.

Sleeping Lovers

4th February 2015

My curious eyes fell upon the body of an acoustic guitar as its deep, wooden curves transformed themselves into the face of a shimmering drum. The guitarist's thick hands came slapping down upon the instrument's glossy body, awash in the momentum of transformation. And, as I listened to the sound of heaven being pulled down from the sky and felt it pound upon the tarmac so hard that it caused my entire body to move with the beat, I saw that it could be excusable to forsake one's intended purpose when need be.

I had arrived in Byron Bay that day with my own simple intentions of soaking up some sun with Florence and retrieving Samuel's pocketknife from the police station, (a possession that had been confiscated from me when last I was in Byron.) But, after both of those things had been done in a day, fate had pushed me in another direction. After I had retrieved Sam's pocketknife from the police station, and began walking down the street, clutching the blade to my chest like a cat who got the cream, fate had seen it fit to place my past directly upon my pathway. Looking up from my chest, I had been taken aback to see Benjamin walking straight towards me.

Remembering our last encounter, and internally cringing at the terrible behaviour that had emanated from my animated temper, my creamy victory soon faded into a hot, fiery blush. As Ben and I walked closer, looking bashfully into one another's features, it was apparent that neither Ben nor I could hide our embarrassment in what had become of us. Sorry's crossed over our eyes and, with the badge of an ex placed over our vision, we fell into an awkward and boxy embrace. However, as Benjamin wrapped his arms around me, I smelled the warm coconut of his

483

skin, breathed him in, and felt that familiar feeling of home that I had always known whenever I was with him. In a world where everything was constantly changing around me, it felt good to be in Ben's company once again.

So, Ben and I, without intending to, had just kept walking together through the streets. Before I knew it, amidst a tornado of conversation, we had unconsciously been blown back to our old encampment upon the beach. As Ben and I approached, the same two palm trees that had once held our hammock up and watched over us as we had slept, now looked upon us shyly like two children who had seen their divorced parents in bed, wondering what the hell they were doing there together. And I found myself wondering the same thing, but although the palm tree children may never understand, Ben and I had merely trodden the only path that we knew how to walk together; the pathway that led towards home.

Benjamin and I sat in-between our confused palm tree children, with the ghost of my hammock swinging behind us on a phantom breeze, and with the faint outline of our top-and-tailing bodies still imprinted into it. Looking into Benjamin's radiant eyes, I thought over all of the deep imprints that we had made in one another's lives. Then, casting my eyes towards a myriad of rolling emeralds that turned and danced upon the transparent skin of the sea, shimmering towards the end of another day, I felt hopeful that Benjamin and I could, despite the finality of the setting sun, also aspire to find some kind of clarity.

I knew that I was sitting beside the man who had regularly, and enthusiastically, laughed with me until neither of us could find the energy to breathe. Whether it be night or day, amongst public or private places, the wild children within us had shared endless amusement in poking and prodding at one another's fun. In addition, I knew myself to be sitting beside the man who had also watched me melt into a puddle of despair on more than one occasion and, as I had leaked into every corner of existence, I had watched that same man, despite the liquid mess that I was, just try to pick me up and piece me back together with his saturated hands. Benjamin had been the man, the boy, and the lover; he had cradled me in the deep of the night, listened to my joys and my fears, adopted them as his own, had brushed my hair out of my eyes and, for four beautiful years, had always ensured me that we would get through anything that life threw at us, together.

I was sitting beside a man whose skin I had washed and bathed in bathtubs all over the world, whose hair I had brushed and encouraged to grow wild, and a man who used to lay beside me in the dark of the night and speak only to me of his deepest, darkest fears. For that intimacy, I had guarded Ben fearlessly and, in turn, he had done the same for me. I had stolen for him, fought for him, and I had even waged wars for him. But, as my warrior heart sat so close, yet still a world apart from him, I understood there to be a time for peace and a time for war. A grain of understanding rolled across my feet with the sandy wind and tickled me, pressing me to laugh, somewhat sadly, at the circus of what Ben and I had become. So I acknowledged Ben as my ultimate heart healer, placed my weapons down in the disappearing sands of time, and apologised for all of the wrong that I had done to him. Ben also said sorry for that which he had done to me, both of us knowing the time for peace to finally be upon us.

Later that evening, after the sun had set, Benjamin and I continued to walk with one another across the beach and back into the streets of Byron Bay. Although Florence and I had not intended to stay the night, I found that I couldn't quite leave Benjamin's side. So we walked, side-by-side, and our bodies clumsily bumped into one another because, to me, the space in between our bodies felt unusually vast and it had begun to throw me off balance. Stopping to find my footing in a gathered crowd, Ben and I had paused beside a boy busker who proceeded to turn his guitar into a drum, forsaking the original intentions of the instrument.

As I listened to the brown-skinned boy pour passion from

his plump lips, giving romance and heroism an angelic, yet ferocious, voice, I placed my hand within my pocket and remembered that I carried a secret weapon inside of it. Twirling a small, secret package in-between my index finger and my thumb, I wondered if it was the right time to use such a tool, considering the fact that I had not long ago resolved to place my weapons down in the sand. Closing my eyes, I tried to feel it out; the guitar-turned-drum travelled up and down my body, asking me to mirror its passionate movement. Benjamin stood beside me with eyes that looked like unclosed doors, swinging on the hinges of hope and, despite the fact that I had previously warned him away from psychedelics, I also knew that there was still much to be said between the two of us.

Ben and I were rigid, clumsy, and distant; in need of so much more understanding than we were both armed with. So, placing my hand in a pocket that would never speak of the company that it kept, I excavated a single tab of LSD and slyly looked at it beneath the glow of orange streetlights. The tab had, intentionally or unintentionally, split itself in two. So, seeing the division as a sign from the psychedelic gods, I placed one half of the tab beneath my tongue and said my prayers. Then, I placed the other half in Benjamin's palm and watched as a cheeky smile broke over his face. Disappearing into the night together, full of secrets and weapons, I could not help but to laugh. And, as the tab dissolved on my tongue, so too did the division that had once existed between Ben and I.

Down at the water's edge, where the land meets the sea, the usual scene of 'Friday night silent disco, dance upon the powdered sand beneath the waning moon to your own private, funky tunes, until you turn into a super space cowboy,' was in full effect. Benjamin and I fell into the scene with ease, dancing out the rigidness from our unified bodies, as droplets of bassy nectar pushed out from individual headphones and seeped into our separate ears. As I danced to my own melody and pirouetted across a field that overlooked the ocean, I was ecstatic to discover

486

Florence sitting on the grass in front of me. Byron Bay appeared to be a land where fate placed those that I needed or desired to see right in front of me, without us having to technologically arrange anything.

Linking eyes with Florence, I was pulled into her muddy whirlpool of vision and watched her like a painting. She sat cross-legged upon the grass like the pixie that I had first known her to be, the moonlight bathing her pale skin in a rich, milky light. And, as Florence had smiled a smile that sparkled in time with the stars, I proceeded to dance my way across Venus and Mars just to get to her.

Swimming in the same kind of eyes that strangers find themselves wishing upon, I yelled out to Florence, forgetting that my headphone's sounds were a private affair. "I feel like I'm on a SPACESHIP!" I informed Florence, whilst listening to glitchy, out-of-this-world music, shattering the silence around us in the process. Florence smiled up at me with features that were as warm and as sweet as cake and custard. And, as I proceeded to look further, I saw that Florence's old heartache, Luke, sat on the ground beside her. Cast with the winds of unification, both Florence and I had been simultaneously blowing around in Byron's breeze, whilst attempting to work out the kinks in our heart string symphonies. My heart warmed with our perpetual similarities.

Walking upon the soft, wet sand with a body so light that it could have blown away with the army of forgotten seagull feathers that lay guarding the empty beach, I began tracing the spine of where the land met the sea and, as I looked over towards Benjamin, I felt certain that I could also realign and meet somewhere in the middle with my blue-eyed prince. The water paid homage to the sky and reflected it, the black tar sky did the same thing for the sea and, as I looked around at the sticky symmetry of the world, I found that I was happy to have Benjamin reflected back inside of me.

The moon shone above our heads like a ball of vanilla ice cream; from full, it melted towards half, and then disappeared altogether, into the clouded appetite of the sky. Benjamin and I were on a mission that led us towards his tent, in order to acquire some provisions for the night. But, as I became tangled up in the silver shoreline of the sea, its damp ribbons wrapping themselves around my practicality and pulling me towards its eternal fantasy, I couldn't quite remember what those provisions even were. However, as my ears adjusted to the silence and the silent disco fell behind us, I was sure that they couldn't have been very important to begin with; certainly I had everything that I would ever need right there with me.

As I opened my mouth in an attempt at discovering words, I found that the orifice itself was completely vacant. No 'point to make' had been hiding in-between my teeth, and an assortment of guarded doors had not been slotted beneath my tongue. I was as empty and open as my mouth itself. Breathing in the world around me, I could not determine there to be any scent of conflict or expectation in the air, instead everything just smelled of salt and cold and new. As Benjamin strolled alongside of me, speaking in soft, gentle tones, there was no evidence of our prior anger towards one another. Bitterness and resentment, it appeared, had left us and, as the world shifted a few more perspectives to the left, (hoping to one day have shifted enough to complete a full circle of perspective,) I knew that those qualities were a sacrifice that had to happen, just so that the present moment could emerge.

As I scurried up the sandy embankment towards Benjamin's tent, hot on the trail of his freshly-pressed footsteps, I wondered how many times I had followed those imprints across the world. I wondered how many times he had also followed mine and, as the sand fell over on itself and became an accomplice, covering up our tracks, I found myself wondering if it would be the last time that Benjamin and I left footprints together in the sand. Benjamin's pace quickened and, as we rolled over the embankment like a breaking wave, Ben eagerly pushed through a thicket of bushes and trees and led me to his plastic dwelling.

At the far right-hand-corner of the beach, below the shimmering tower of the lighthouse, deep in the thicket of anonymity, Benjamin had constructed a camp for the lone wolf that had emerged within him. As he gestured for me to go inside of his tent, I cast my eyes to the outside world as if to say goodbye and thought that I saw a glimmer of pride shoot across the sky, drip down from the curve of the vanilla moon and fall upon Benjamin's smiling face.

Inside of the tent, every single item of practicality had been perfectly placed and arranged in harmony. It was as if Ben had known that I would come to him, as if I were a bird and he were my mate; such was the nest that he had proudly made for us... I could see it written across his entire face. The blanket that lay perfectly-made across the floor spoke to the familiarity within me and, because I remembered it from Melbourne, it made me feel as if I were home. As the moonlight poured into the open tent and illuminated a world of safety and comfort, I knew that Ben and I would not return to the silent disco, for amongst the rubble of our old lives, we had much to discuss. The world around us began to fade to black until all that I could see was *a version of you* and *a version of me*. The night belonged to us.

Literally, the world around us had faded into darkness. Benjamin and I were without torches or candles and, after entering Ben's tent, the vanilla cone moon had been completely consumed by the ravenous blackness of the night. As Ben sat across from me and LSD swirled inside of my brain, fragmenting and rearranging my patterns, I became consumed with the need to understand what had happened between us. Rummaging through my backpack, with a mouth that was still struggling to find words, I pulled out the letter that I had written to Benjamin and knew that I needed to share it with him. I needed Ben to walk a mile in my shoes... I needed him to understand.

By the orange glow of a cigarette lighter, I squinted my eyes into the crumpled paper and began to read my *'Dear Benjamin'* his letter. Through the dark of the night, words of disappointment began to fall from my lips and, without needing night vision goggles to see, they began making their way towards Benjamin. His silence was all that I could have asked of him. As I began to bring my testimony to a close, the lighter burned blisters upon my fingertips, flickered in the deep of the night, and attempted to give up on life, but I was relentless in my need to express. So I kept the fire light going and, amidst my struggle for vision, I pushed through to the very end, for I knew that I was struggling to see in more ways than just physically.

Proceeding that heavy reading, the thick ice between Benjamin and I had finally broke. Sometimes a person has to go in there deep in order for everything that follows the situation to appear lighter and easier. Armed with our new-found understanding, Benjamin and I began floating out of the darkness together. Twirling around my recounted version of the events that had occurred when we were last in Byron, (unanswered phones, acid eyes, sick-crusted beards, disjointed paths, and both of us falling in love with everybody else except each other,) Benjamin appeared bewildered.

"I don't remember anything about it," Ben admitted, after much thought. "All I can remember is waking up feeling worse than I've ever felt in my life and, with nothing to call my own, I awoke just in time to see you hightailing it out of Byron Bay... leaving me behind."

As our stories merged together, itt was apparent that both Ben and I had been blinded. He had awoken to a feeling of empty support and had watched me turn my back and disappear without a second thought for him, his back riddled with pain and the jagged remainders of a drunken night still clinging to the hurt upon his body. Meanwhile, I had finally thrown in the towel and screamed that I had had enough of Benjamin, (never thinking that he wouldn't recollect the reason as to why,) and cursing him for his lack of responsibility. Despite the secret language that we had spent four years perfecting, it appeared that Ben and I had had a major breakdown in communication.

In that tent, I had tried on a pair of glasses that allowed me to see through Ben's eyes and even I didn't like the sight of me. Remembering what he had said back in the back alleys of Byron Bay, (with overflowing rubbish bins that had looked at us disdainfully and a wilted cabbage that had been so affected by my coldness that it had been pushed into fainting,) I finally understood what Ben had meant when he said that I hadn't loved him in the way that he needed to be loved. As the words clanked around in my head, I accepted them and, for the first time, I actually felt them. I met that responsibility head-on and faced it, embraced it, and even went on to become it. Benjamin mirrored my change of heart and we looked at one another through, not only each other's eyes, but also the pupils of two birds that soared up so high that they could see everything without having to be too close to it. I was able to see Benjamin and I; how we had tried to make it, to save ourselves, to save one another. We had done all that we knew how to do but, as I sat in the dark of the tent, knowing that we had not made it through to the other side, I understood that there had always been a limit to our love.

"What was it like to be with her... Joy?" I asked Benjamin, in a breath that held no shadow of reservation, her name not lost upon me. Even though Joy had since returned to her home country, I wanted to know what it had been like for Ben to have known her emotionally. I wondered what it had felt like for him to have experienced her body, her mind, and her soul. More so, I wanted to know whether or not Ben had found the right kind of love that he had been searching for... within her. Without jealousy, I needed to measure Joy's love up against my own and try to grow from it.

"Now I understand why you were reserved with me for so long, April." Benjamin's tender voice was just a whisper above the whoosh of the ocean. "I was Joy to you from the very beginning." Ben's personal understanding flashed across his eyes in a secret language and, without further explanation, I knew exactly what he had meant. With his shadowy features softening and a sense of adoration slipping in-between his tone like a burglar on the prowl for the best of the situation, Ben continued, "But, it was nice. She was good to me." From that contented tone, I knew that Ben had, in his own way, loved her.

I went on to tell Ben of my affection towards Sam, speaking fondly of how Sam had picked me up when I had been buried ten feet underground. I spoke of the adventures that we had embarked upon, of our potential idea to go to the desert together and, for a moment, both Ben and I found ourselves appreciating Sam's warm heart and crooked smile. Although it was a strange topic to verse, mine and Ben's open correspondence, in that moment, was not weird, nor even difficult.

"I'm thankful to Joy." I spoke into the dark of the night; the absolute blackness allowing both Ben and I to say what we really meant without being distorted by too much light. "I'm glad that she was able to love you when I no longer could."

"And I'm thankful to Sam," Ben promised. "He's a solid guy and I'm relieved to know that he took care of you when I could not."

In that moment, both Ben and I understood that everyone, no matter what, and without any exceptions, simply needed to be loved. And that we each, every single one of us, would go through great lengths to feel the warmth and care of another.

Somehow, eight hours had passed us by and, as Ben and I had awoken the new people that we were to one another, that single truth seemed to be the crux of the night.

As the sun began to rise through the darkness, casting its beams through the air in the same way that the lighthouse had done all night long, mine and Ben's spirits too rose with the sun. Laying upon the familiarity of Ben's blanket, I watched the world slowly come into focus. Ben's eyes hovered over me like two vanilla moons that had been dipped in blue icing. Effervescent fairy lights seemed to glow out from his skin and, as he leaned in closer towards me, as always happens when I really look into him... I saw forever in Benjamin.

Ben's soft hands began searching my skin and, as if he had never before touched me, he drew me closer into him with a hunger that was new to me. The X's uncrossed from our eyelids and returned to the stars where the lovers in us had met, crossing. Not knowing what would arise from our unity, Ben and I made no promises to one another outside of the tent and simply surrendered to the love that would always flow between us. Upon hearing the soft exhalation of appreciation escape from Ben's mouth into mine, my mind floated over the vision of him and Joy kissing for the first time. As I felt Ben's hands search out the mounds of my breasts as if they were treasure maps, I thought of Samuel and how he had also loved my body. As Ben and I kissed, Sam and Joy also swirled around in the saliva of our mouths, though there was no bitterness in their memories. In fact, it was a sweet taste, born of crushed green jealousy.

"Each of our bodies have both been loved by another, Ben…" I whispered into the morning's fresh yearning, "and it's ok…."

As the sun fiercely sent his soldiers of light out upon the rays of a new day and, whilst Benjamin and I made a love so sweet that it would have given anyone else a toothache, I understood that there would always be a battle of peace and of war waging between Ben and I. We were eternal, fractured, a fresh beginning, but somehow also a cycle that had been completed. And although we had the potential to be everything to one another, Ben and I rolled around in his tent and loved one another with such a desperate fever that it also felt like the end to a story.

After our love making had had its way with our bodies and we lay breathless in the tent together with lighter hearts, but weighted eyes, both Ben and I knew, as he kissed my eyes into a close, that it was also time for us to lay our love down to sleep.

And the flame in my soul whispered to her twin: *'As the sun does rise, and our bodies fall into peaceful slumber… goodnight my blue-eyed prince. I know that we will see one another on the other side, either somewhere over the rainbow… or where the land meets the sea. Because, through depth over distance, I will never truly be separated from you… and you will never truly be separated from me. Upon the spine of two separate worlds, below a melting vanilla moon, one day I will follow a path that will take me back to you. But for now, we lay our love to rest. Our depth shall soften our distance. Close your eyes and sleep now… my forever blue-eyed prince.'*

And with that, a single flame found itself extinguished.

Earth Frequency

18th February 2015

As it often comes to pass, when one door closes in your face, another portal of opportunity finds the room to open up before you. So, as I sang a lullaby to the love within Benjamin and I, somewhere on the other side of what we were, a door to another world began to slowly creak open.

Sitting upon the shack floor one evening, and staring into the animated flames of the fire, I found my thoughts drifting back to the time when Samuel and I had been out adventuring with one another, being crystal gypsies and fun-havers: We had blown into a dusty old town on the outskirts of Nimbin in order to fill his petrol tank up and, whilst Samuel had wrestled with a rusted pump, I had stumbled upon an advertisement to a festival called Earth Frequency. Looking upon that single sign through the dusty window of the petrol station, something in me had felt compelled to make an appearance there. And, after speaking with Sam and discovering that he had enjoyed innumerous festivals, I went on to admit that I had never been to a real festival gathering and that I would like to attend one. Although Sam was being called back to Melbourne in order to pack up his city life and start again in the country, he had envisioned himself making it back to the mountain in time for us to go to the festival together.

However, as I sat on the floor of Last Resort, feeling the warmth of the fire blush my face, I realised that the weeks had passed Samuel and I by without regard for our good intentions. The time of the festival was almost upon us, but Sam was still back in Melbourne sorting out the necessary transition within his life. Reflecting over that truth with an air of sadness, I began to tell Florence of my plight.

"You've never been to a festival before?!" Florence asked, her eyes shining with the same fever as the fire.

"Nah, just small day ones, but not a proper one." No sooner had the confession fallen from my lips, did Florence then pull herself towards me as if my body were a magnet and her skin were made of iron. A jar of grins pickled her face and, as her body stretched and moved, threatening to burst out of its skin, Florence whispered, "Oh April… festivals were made for you."

So, despite us being broker than the most distasteful of jokes, Florence and I gathered our pennies for petrol, poured ourselves into Millie, (the red box campervan from outer space,) and decided to take a break from our Mountain duties for the weekend. Not being able to fathom the fact that I had never before attended a festival, Florence had decided to make it her personal responsibility to ensure that I did so. During the four hour drive through the winding mountain roads, fuelled, as always, on our hopes and dreams, I made it my duty to assure Florence that, no matter the destitution of our pockets, we would arrive at the festival and somehow find a way in… even if we were pushed into becoming ninjas of the night.

Florence and I arrived at the festival site, drove past the entrance and then, after following a dirt track that lined the festival for some time, we abandoned Millie on the side of the road. Florence left an unconvincing, yet very endearing, note upon her windshield, stating that Millie was on old girl and that she had broken down. After signing the note with kisses and cosmic blessings, Florence and I began to creep our way towards the festival.

As Florence and I walked through the dark of the night, attempting to follow the tree lines and tall barriers that lined the festival towards any point of safe entry, I began to hear the sound of music pulsing out through the thick forest. Following those glitchy, bassy sounds like a melodic map, it didn't take long before we were able to see green lasers shooting out through the trees, lighting up the forest like a spaceship. Stealthily, I tiptoed closer towards the commotion and, with branches at a break beneath my feet, I adopted the best ninja persona that I could muster.

Through the black of the night, I could see the white of Florence's eyes following behind me, wide with anticipation, danger, and excitement. After crawling beneath a barbed wire fence, (whereupon my favourite leopard-print dress gotten snagged in its razor-sharp teeth,) and then trudging through more thick forestry, as the trees came to a clear, I was surprised to discover the place in which I had intended for us to enter... to also be clear. The tall, wooden fence that had loomed over us as we had followed the tree line, now just disappeared at my feet, leaving nothing in between the festival and me.

Not quite able to believe my eyes, I looked back towards Florence and saw that her disbelief mirrored my own. Suspiciously, I poked my head out from the end of the fencing, expecting to see an army of security, though I was further surprised to see that there were none. Instead of trolls or guards, there was just an empty field and then, off in the distance, a crowd of dancers and fun-makers twirled around one another beneath the waning moon, inviting us to join them. *'Go on girls...'* I heard something whisper out from the cool evening air. *'Go forth my children... and play.'* So, before reaching back and taking Florence's hand in my own, we spoke to one another in army signal waves and, with our ninja eyes blazing with the mission at hand, we began to briskly walk across the field to the sound of music... until our stealthy steps turned into dance.

Florence and I boogied our sneaky little bodies all the way down to the main stage, shaking and grooving in the same ways that everybody else did, until we were sure that the coast was clear and we would never be discovered as imposters. As we fell into a bountiful pool of gyration and joy, I looked into Florence's sparkling brown eyes to discover glossy secrets twinkling and reflecting back at me, and was contented to know that we had been successful in our mission at hand. Dancing in celebration, Florence and I allowed the festival to swallow us up.

We danced until there was no question of our belonging to the festivities. However, after our breath had been worn out with exertion and our bodies had sweated all of their juices out from inside of them, a new mission surfaced and demanded our attentions; we needed a place in which to lay our heads for the night. Florence and I had been so tied up in our previous mission, ('become one with the night,') that we had not furthered any other thought beyond that. Having only the thin clothes upon our backs and realising that we also had no provisions to sustain us over the three day festival period, Florence and I looked at one another through the sway of careless bodies and were each shadowed with the darkness of a tardy caution.

The cool of the night came out to greet the stillness of our bodies wearing black, spiky gloves and, as we shook hands in introduction, geese began to bump all over our skin, shaking to their own frantic melody. With no food, no water and, more importantly, no tent in our company, Florence and I decided to send a faithful message to the universe. It read:

Dear Universe, (because, to me, every piece of correspondence is destined be a letter,)

The night has brought a cold war upon Florence and I that we are not equipped against. We shall do our part in chasing such chills away through the act of fevered dance until you have found the time to align something better for us. Please note that the reins have been enclosed within this letter; I pray that you take them in good faith and do with them as you please. We surrender to your embrace and trust you, without question.

Yours faithfully,

April and Florence

XxxoooxxX

As my heart beat in unison with the filth of the trance beat, the unpredictability of our response from the universe felt like a dance with the devil, but the music was surely being played by God's own dirty, harp-fingered angels. So, Florence and I moved the blood around our bodies without concern for our outcome and, because it was a far cry from the silence of the Woman's

Mountain, continued to enjoy the cool chaos that we had found ourselves in. Until, from the depths of a sweaty crowd, I saw a familiar pair of eyes part the salted bodily seas and begin making their way towards the sight of me.

Although the night was dark and the neon lights were blinding, I thought that I recognised the brown skin that sat upon the approaching figure's face; a face that bore that same soft, wide smile that was actually in need of being quarantined because of its contagious qualities. As the figure and I danced towards one another, I realised that I had looked upon that same face back when my solo journey through Brisbane had begun; the house party on the hills, the lone microphone calling out to me, and him... encouraging me to tend to it. I had also met him on the streets of Byron Bay, whilst Sam and I had been selling our gypsy wares; he had embraced Sam as a friend and then, after placing his fingers upon Sam's bare chest and tracing two tribal whales that he had tattooed upon him, I had been introduced to Lolito's real and higher person. Lolito; the ink artist, the spirit seer.

It was as if the universe had been working on overtime for me; during the scarce occasions that I had left the Woman's Mountain, the universe had proceeded to pluck the most appropriate and angelic people to assist me in my personal development out from the heavens and then place them down beside my own two feet. Lolito would become mine and Florence's festival saviour.

Looking upon two beautiful women who had nowhere to go for the night, Lolito had furrowed his eyebrows with concern and then draped his brightly-coloured clothing around our chilled bodies in an effort to chase away our pesky goosebumps. After conversing with one another a little more beneath the chai tent, and feeling one another's friendship out beneath the late hour of the night, Lolito invited Florence and I back to his camp, where we were offered a warm place to sleep. Like three little piggies, we all squashed into the back of Lolito's van and, from between two other entwined bodies, I thanked the universe for its prompt and sufficient response.

The following morning, the sun rose with such a firesome fury upon its face that, as I stared into its yellow rays with the shadow of immobility cast upon my movements, I thought the sun to be a cousin to Medusa; except instead of turning us to stone, it melted everything that it glanced upon with its golden tendrils. Ignoring the sun's unforgiving glare, Florence and I proceeded to strip down to our underwear and, braless as ever, began cooking breakfast for our new hosts. As Lolito and his best friend, Jake looked upon mine and Florence's nudity in amusement, I knew that the wild ways of the Woman's Mountain would forever be within us.

Later that afternoon, I found myself deep in the wardrobe of a tipi tent that, through the foliage of coat hangers and psychedelic fabrics, allowed strangers to exchange their clothes with one another, without the audacity of money's greedy presence. After being offered some fungal magic from a male wardrobe character that was casually wearing a pink tutu, Florence, Jake, Lolito, and I sat outside the tipi in a circle of acceptance and began a ceremony of personal intentions for our trip. With a strange, new, and very theatrical world beginning to open up before me, I, myself, amongst a wardrobe of purple suede shoes and radical new identities, set the intention of trying on the outfit of a wild and free festival attendee.

With a dusty body of movement swirling upon the horizon, and sounds so thick and sticky that their waves imprinted our waxy eardrums, the gang and I allowed the commotion of the main stage to swallow us whole. Beneath the watchful eyes of the burning sun, hundreds of bodies gyrated their parts, stomped their feet down upon the dry, cracked earth and, as dust swirled around our limbs like a smoke machine, we all danced as if no one were watching.

Mounds of thick, twisted dreadlocks swung out, like charmed snakes, from beneath many of the dancers' waists, then slithered their way up towards their heads, gathering and unfolding their follicles like budding lotus flowers. Beneath intentionally-tattered skirts and transparent leaves that had been pressed against their breasts immodestly, a kaleidoscope of beautiful women swayed their hips to the sound of a birthing drum. Tribal, yet gentle, they extended their limbs towards the savage sun in a ritual that was dust-covered and ancient. Large feathers peeked out from nests of knotted hair and offered their owners flight, seeing them for the true bird children that they were. Corsets crossed themselves over my eyelids, and dusty skin that had been painted with the oranges of a Bengal tiger swayed and danced to the rhythm of Africa, whilst topless fairies fluttered their dainty wings out across existence, demanding that we finally believe.

All around me, complete strangers began abandoning their steely reservations and hugged each other with such fever that I was also drawn into a crowd of them. Despite not knowing a single person's name, in that moment, the huggers and I each became long-lost friends. Looking upon colourful and loud attire that screamed out, *'hey, this is my contribution to existence,'* I accepted everyone for who they were and allowed my heart to soar at such magic. Even the brutal sun softened at the sight of our affection.

Looking over to my left, contrasted against a psychedelic sea of rainbows, a tall and slender figure stood out amongst the crowd. All dressed in black, like a pillar of strength amidst the translucent intangibility of magic, the woman parted the crowd with searching eyes. Her silken black dress, clinging to a body that was cloaked in authority, reached down towards the cracked floor as if it could moisturise even the ground with its shimmering richness. The blonde ash of the woman's hair feathered her angelic features with its own kind of wings and, as I looked closer into the forestry of her searching, luminous eyes, I was surprised to see that I could recognise those orbs of perspective and even name who they belonged to. It was none other than Ola.

Immediately, I fell into memories of my previous connection with Ola, depicting a cracked and fragmented sisterhood that had been disrupted by the presence of man. For but a moment, I allowed the same bitterness that had passed through me when I had heard of Ola and Ben's romantic involvement, to surface. However it soon became apparent that my fractured relationships intended to follow me around incessantly until I had learned to finally release them. Through the dust and the dance and the drugs that were beginning to take effect upon my caution, I grabbed that bitter feeling around its neck and pulled it closer towards me. Looking into its unnecessary face, I threw my bitterness to the ground and decided to honour the lessons that the Woman's Mountain had taught me. Because my heart no longer had room to fester beneath trivial and unfair expectations, my spirit could no longer be weighed down with grudges or venom and, as I began making my way towards Ola in a stride of reestablished friendship, I wanted only to honour my connection with women.

As I danced my way through the crowd and pushed my body in front of Ola's searching, emerald eyes, a look of pale surprise washed over her being. Halfway across the Australian soil from whence we had first met, from Melbourne's mythologies straight up to the frequency of the earth, Ola and I had been placed, once again, upon one another's path. In an attempt to calm the uncertainty in our bodies, I pulled Ola into me and embraced her wholeheartedly, breathing one another in as sisters once again. With that sincere hug, all of the sourness and misunderstanding that either one of us had been keeping began to seep out of our squeezed bodies and then disappeared into the dust of a dancing storm.

Pulling away from our embrace, Ola and I locked eyes with one another. The glitchy music pumped with such vigour and enthusiasm that it made conversation an impossible mission, so instead, Ola and I spoke to one another through our eyes. I told her that I loved her as a sister and that nothing else mattered, whilst she wordlessly exchanged the same truth. As I pranced back into the crowd in search of Florence, despite the thick dust that had attached itself to my lips and my lungs, I felt as though I could breathe a little better. Suddenly, the world around me began to look epic.

Surfing through the tireless crowd, it was as if I were riding on my own magical carpet of good time sunshine vibes and, although the eccentric music drowned me out, "Jasmine and Aladdin don't got shit on this," fell out of my private mouth. Bodies wound around me, turning themselves inside-out just to show the world what they were working with and, as I looked upon their varied curvatures, I knew that I had finally found my tribe. Attempting to capture some of those majestic beings in action through photograph, I clumsily fumbled with my camera phone, before ultimately deciding it to be a toy that was in need of immediately being destroyed.

Amidst my wrestle with technological difficulties, a frantic crowd began to gather behind me, puffing up clouds of dusty disbelief into the fiery afternoon sun. Through the scuffle of accelerating commotion, I thought that I could see a body laying upon the ground and, under the scrutiny of my tripping eyes, I soon determined it to be true. As I walked towards a pair of pale legs that stuck out of the crowd, parting it like an ice cream cone, I began to take note of the shoes that were attached to the extended legs… they were the trendy trainers of Lolito's best friend, Jake.

Pushing my way through the crowd, I discovered Lolito to be bent down beside Jake's flat-lined body, where he proceeded to gently slap him across his dusty and lifeless face. Jake's skin had turned the colour of a wilted white rose; pasty, yellowed at the edges, and dripping with a dew drop sweat. As Lolito tried to encourage his body to return to us, Jake's mouth parted itself in absent slumber and ensured us all that nobody was home. Looking down towards my own feet, I saw Jake's discarded sunglasses strewn across the dusty floor and, not knowing what else to do, I picked them up and held them close to me. Everybody was so involved with the scene that was unfolding before me that it made it difficult to contribute in a productive manner. People with large, flying saucer eyes loomed over Jake's body and tried to take control of the situation, but through their jagged attentions, they only seemed to make matters worse.

Lolito, above the rise of fearful frequencies, kept a strong and impenetrable calm whilst guarding over Jake's empty body, holding down a space of safety that emanated around the two of them like a force field. Jake's eyes were wide open but, as they stared out blankly into the blue bustle of the sky, we all knew them to be far from truly seeing anything. His blue eyes swam around in an ocean of oblivion and, having never noticed their colouring before, I looked upon them in regretful appreciation. Florence, her own eyes wide with horror, parted the thick and rowdy crowd in order to find her way to my side. As she tenderly touched my arm in order to show me that she was there, I twirled Jake's sunglasses around manically in my hand and allowed the moment to stretch out into forever. In a language that was worn across everybody's distressed faces, each of us silently began to entertain the idea that, without having any need for a ticket, Death could join us at the festival whenever he wished.

Just as my heart tried to escape the moment by climbing up and out through the passageway in my throat, causing lumps to form and tears to press out and blur my vision, Jake's blue-stained eyes flickered beneath the sun like a butterfly that had just taken first flight. After having finally returned to the cocoon of his body, Jake appeared to have been just as shocked at his temporary departure as his audience was.

An assortment of concerned faces loomed over Jake's horizontal body like chaotic city buildings that towered above a murky river. Clouded by the unexpected turn of events, Jake's nervous eyes began to frantically search out his new environment until the waters calmed and he recognised the nurturing eyes of Lolito staring back into him. Despite the frantic crowd that had gathered around their bodies, for but a moment, as sparks of recognition shot out of their eyes, the world only seemed to exist for the two of them. Lolito firmly held Jake's hand in his own, softly bringing him back into existence and, as I looked upon their friendship, I began to understand a universal truth; amidst the chaos of our self-imposed struggles, if we are at least able to look into the familiar eyes of a loved one and know them to have our backs 'til the bitter end, then life doesn't seem so bad.

Looking back towards Florence, I felt as though she had just experienced a similar truth as my own. With a nervous smile drawn across our faces and, after placing Jake's sunglasses back over his eyes so that he could receive a little privacy from the crowd, Florence and I watched Jake and Lolito leave the dancefloor behind and disappear into the capable hands of the medics. The burning sun looked down upon us triumphantly, knowing that his hot temper had played a great part in Jake's temporary departure.

With life and death still staring at me through the Jake-sized hole that had been left on the dancefloor, Florence and I decided to leave and seek out some much-needed serenity. It wasn't long before we found the perfect place for our peace and placed our tripping bodies down upon a soft, grassy verge, right in the middle of the festival. Together, we lay upon our dustless patch of grass for hours and, lost in the depths of stories and connections, Florence and I allowed the majority of the day to pass us by. We were full of deep dialogue and wove the kind of stories into one another that would have made even the Breath Weaver proud.

With the afternoon having fell upon Valentine's Day, and with Florence and I having placed our bodies in the way of many who would pass us by, we involuntarily became subjects of great affection. Freshly-picked daisies, handcrafted jewellery, and even a few A capella songs were all bestowed upon us, affirming that the best things in life truly are free. A cowboy wearing a wild western hat even stopped for a spell to chat and then, before riding off into the sunset, left a few mushrooms in the palm of my hand. I watched lovers walk, arm-in-arm, all tangled up in one another's lives and linked by things that I would never be able to understand from such a distance. However, I was familiar with the look of love that seemed to resonate out from every single person.

Florence was sprawled out on the ground beside me, the green grass contrasting the creamy wash of her skin. As I traced the placement of her arm up to the cradle of her golden head and looked upon a forestry of hairy armpits that displayed themselves without embarrassment, I knew Florence to be a creature that held no fear. A handmade necklace of animal teeth and bones lay across her breast in a primal display of beauty and ferocity. Her caring, fawn eyes stared out from beneath their brown puddles and, daydreaming, appeared to be lost in the dance of the sky. As her body moved up and down in a gentle ceremony of breath, Florence became the most radiant and alive thing that I had ever seen. She looked into me sweetly and, as if reading my thoughts, simply smiled at me in return. With warm gestures that felt so familiar to me, I knew Florence to not only be my valentine for the day, but I also understood that she had become a lifelong companion from there on out. Florence was my star child, my heart reflection and in a way... my very own happy ending.

A splash of animated gangster girls came rolling down the hill and danced past mine and Florence's Valentine moment. With pink, puffy afros that crowned their heads like marshmallows, and blasting boom boxes that perched upon their shoulders, shouting out like caged, black-box parrots, those women were a comedic sight to look upon. As they passed us by, possessed by their festival characters, their ghetto booties wobbled and wavered to the sound of music and almost broke out of their neon pants. A trail of rap melodies followed their theatrical dance.

As the world around me began to open up once more, I saw a bald-headed man sitting in a corner of the chai tent, wearing an outfit that was the spitting image of Johnny Depp in *Fear and Loathing in Las Vegas.* The bald man, from behind dark sunglasses and a putrid Hawaiian shirt, talked theatrically with a flow of strangers that continually approached him. A never-ending cigarette hung in-between his fingertips with a railway line of ash that looked over to me and begged to be flicked off its tracks. The man even carried a brown leather briefcase in order to assure that he would get the part and, as I rolled around on the grass and prepared to rejoin the interactive world, I began to look upon the loathing character in a different light. His stream of endless friends soon showed themselves for what they were... customers. From the leather of his briefcase, the man would extract a compilation of good times, exchanging them for a wad of damp cash that was passed between cautious, yet impressed hands. Wanting to run over and give the man an award for Best

Dressed Costume, but not wanting to upset his cool, I settled for, as his new attorney, silently crowning him the most inventive drug dealer that I had ever seen.

To my right, four exotic women danced towards me, embracing the four elements in their distinct personas. Flowing through the crowds of grass-dwellers, cowboys, love-linkers, bone necklaces, fear, loathing, and hairy armpits, the women brought their own theatre to the grassy table. One of the women, embodying the essence of wind, allowed her white clothing to flow from her limbs like a beautiful haunting. The woman of water pulsed out blue hues that mirrored the fluidity of the skies and I found myself submerged in her depths. A firesome creature created a stampede around her and, with her body glowing in orange embers, she looked me straight in the eyes and sent a fever up my spine. The woman of earth wore tree limbs for fingertips and, as her long, majestic body groaned through the crowd, I began to grow alongside of her. Roaming with great conviction, those four elemental women danced away into the distance, sprinkling their magic upon everyone who looked upon them.

To my left, a pudgy man began to hula hoop as if his life depended on it. Following the guidelines of a musical melody, the man circled his generous hips around in an effort to keep the hoop afloat. With his armpits hovering over his head in concentration and distinguishable patches of sweat forming below his overworked pits, I began to read a sign that had been imprinted upon his white, sweat-saturated shirt. It read: *'drugs saved my life.'* As I looked upon the immeasurable happiness in that man's swing and, assuming that he was having the time of his life, I thought that perhaps his shirt could be truthful in its testimony.

Enlivened with the sight of action, my own limbs began to rouse from their haze of spectatorship. I too wanted to swing my hips with complete abandon and find a joy so pure and so true that it couldn't be challenged. My psychedelic bikini wrapped itself around my body and began to hold me closer in anticipation of our movement. Take off was inevitable. I could feel it tingling in my bones and, as I began skipping towards the dance floor, I felt the music rise and fall in my buttocks.

Once I was submerged in the groove of the world, I began to shake my body without control. Something fantastic was coming over me and the only way to express it was to have no reservations and simply let it out of me. It had never felt so good to be in my body, in my booty, dancing and swaying my hips. And just like the hula-hooping man, I began enchanting people into doing the same thing. Boys began to hoot behind me, but my moves were not for them. They were mine alone and for them, I was beginning to find my own personal groove. It was coming straight for me and it pushed me into a swirling gyration that was overflowing with the kind of galactic rhythms that had always been governed by something that was not of this world. Reaching a dancing climax, I was consumed by the joy of being a vibrant, free, and wild young thing; a woman and a girl.

"April!" Florence yelled out to me from across the dancefloor with a voice that dove through the high pitch frequencies and tried to surface into distinguishability; a couple of carefree hands raising themselves up towards a roofless roof.

"You... are... BOOOOMBASTIC!" She continued, with great enthusiasm. Smiling wider than a load of moving cargo, I privately documented the term *'boombastic'* in my head as the coolest thing that anyone had ever called me.

After our lungs had sufficiently lunged out with exertions and our bodies had adequately swum through the commotion of impromptu dance, Florence and I decided to head back to Lolito's van so that we could check on the boys and gather ourselves. Through the orange decay of sunset, we were surprised to find our encampment empty, but instead of despairing, Florence and I took it as an opportunity to roll around beneath the blankets. With pins and needles in our chests and aches in our bellies, we began to laugh ourselves towards the gates of insanity, demanding that they let us in. Comical stories filled the van with a hot, humid air and, as Florence held her bare butt outside of the van to relieve herself, I decided her to be the funniest creature that I had ever met. I couldn't even look into her cheeky face without being pressed into fits of laughter.

Besides the sharing of our endless humour, Florence also held an interest in my life like no other. She would constantly press me into telling stories that, whether it was due to shyness or the inability to think anyone would find my life interesting, I had never told anyone else before. Florence was my great explorer, digging deep into the chambers of my memory bank and finding treasures that were worthy of sharing. Her genuine curiosity and ability in allowing me to be a complete and whole person began causing me to be bolder and more theatrical than I had ever been. Before long, I jumped out of Lolito's van, ran around our encampment, and pretended to be a version of my grandmother just after she had experienced the Holy Ghost within her. I could not have known it then, but that theatre would be a pivotal and holy moment in my development.

That night, after Florence and I had finally pulled ourselves out from beneath the blankets, we made our way back to the festival with the intention to have a wild and wonderful night beneath the stars. Stopping off at the bathrooms first, I found myself looking upon a single mother and her young baby with great affection. And, swollen with pride for her strength and particular mindset that allowed festivals to also be a family affair, I decided to throw my verbal contribution into the acoustics of the room. "You really inspire me as a woman, ya know." The woman looked into my eyes with a new sense of pride and, as if allowing her guard to fall in our new-found friendship, let me in on her little secret.

"Thanks, umm, my girlfriend who I came here with… well, she got a little bit too out of it," the woman began, with a casual, yet somewhat sombre, tone. "And now here I am, left on my own… with this little one." Looking into the bright blue wide eyes of her little one adoringly, the mother tickled his toes and looked back into me with a weight of sadness pressing down upon her features.

So, without further ado, Florence and I, women of the Woman's Mountain, left our plans for a wild and wonderful night behind us and swooped in to assist the quiet call of our fellow sister. I took the handles of the woman's pram and, as I watched

Florence relieve the weight of the baby bag from upon the woman's shoulders, I began pushing the buggy forward with the force of girl power. After escorting the appreciative woman back to her camp and determining her to be in need of a heavy dose of adult time, Florence and I sat with her and talked for most of the night. The party went on without us but, through our act of devotion, neither one of us minded. Because, although we were both far from our home and cast into a world of strangeness, through that unconscious act of sisterly support, I knew that Florence and I would always be women of the mountain.

During the next three days of the festival, a myriad of beautiful and healing scenarios fell at my feet and, although Earth Frequency was the first festival that I had ever attended, as it came to a close, I promised that it would not be my last. It had awoken something inside of me, something that I knew was only just beginning. Within the festival, there had been great healing. I had found my tribal family, whose only interest was to see the inner child within me come out and play, and because of that, they had really transformed me. We had created art together, and music, had danced beneath the stars together, and had connected in the kind of way that is imperative to the development of aspiring human beings.

Earth Frequency had been a place to play, like a giant playground for kids and adults alike, but more than that, it had been a safe body of land upon which everyone could reinvent themselves. Quietly blushing, I thought upon my illegal entry into the world of fun but, because the festival had blessed me in such a life-defining way, encouraging that the story-teller awaken within me, I knew that I would pay for it in my own way.

The last day of the festival found me encircled by thousands of other bodies. With our arms linked and our tail bones connecting to the earth beneath us, we each thought of good intentions and pushed healing out into the entire world around us with the calming sound of Om. Our surroundings buzzed and vibrated with so much potent love that, being the most powerful feeling I had ever experienced, I could not dispute of how we really were changing the frequency of the earth.

Florence and I walked back to Millie, (the little red box camper from the eighties) and, as she stood there glossing with rouge loyalties beneath the golden sun, Millie looked like a different van altogether. Gazing over at Florence, I remembered how she had stood amidst the dancefloor with her journal in her hand and, over the sound of the heavy bass, had poured out ideas of invention from her enthusiastic mouth into my hungry ears. The festival had changed her too, inspiring Florence to walk down her own pathway towards making a better world. I thought of my time upon the mountain, the women, the shacks, the fires... and I knew that they had each served me well. A big part of myself also felt changed and, as we walked closer towards Millie, (the same camper that she had been since the eighties,) I could not shake the feeling that something was coming to an end.

Amidst my tender reflections, I was brought back to reality by the sound of something flying through the air and jingling as if it belonged to the bells of Christmas morning. Instinctively, I threw my hands up in the air, reached up, and caught it.

"You're heading out to the desert soon and I'm gonna to go to New Zealand, so... April... meet Millie. I would like for you to keep her."

Opening up a closed palm that was full of disbelief, I found a single silver key glistening beneath the sun. Attached to the key chain was a bronze banana dick.

Christmas day had come early that year, and with it also came a magical, though perverted, kind of humour.

A Forest of Farewells

20th February 2015

Back on the Woman's Mountain, the mid-day sun hovered above my head like a ferocious beast, surrounding me, taunting me, and flaring a sun-kissed nose that had been stained with the salted scent of my labour. After sniffing me out, the golden beast pushed its way through the thick tree tops and, hot on my trail, relentlessly hunted me without sympathy. Every inch of skin upon my body felt prickly and itchy, furiously burning with the fever of an Australian summer's day. Dirt and soil had pushed their dark crumbs deep into the caverns beneath my fingernails and, as the pinks of my nails had long turned to black, the dirt dreamt of a day where it could be acknowledged as organic nail polish.

With salt stinging my eyes and skin peeling down from my bleeding hands, I finally discontinued my morning tasks with triumph and looked affectionately upon the rusted tool that I had become so familiar with over the last few months. Knowing that it would be the last time that I would employ such an action, without further ado, and with great private ceremony, I threw my spade to the ground and laid it to rest upon the Woman's Mountain.

After sharing a quiet moment of appreciation with my spade, honouring the depths that we had pushed through with one another, I wiped the sweat from my eyes and looked out across the property that I had come to know of as home. Upon various patches of land were tales of my devotion to it, and even though I knew that nature would take it all back before long, I was contented to see the majority of weeds gone and the fresh smell of turned earth permeating the humid air. Through the foliage were also signs of recent organic construction and, as my eyes fell upon the beginning stages of a bamboo shack, I smiled proudly at the memory of its development:

511

A few weeks prior, Jen had decided that she wanted to build her very own shack on top of the Woman's Mountain and, from the shell of an old tool shed, Jen had found the perfect host for her 'no men allowed' new home. Florence and I had joined forces with Jen and, with the encouragement of Granny Breath Weaver assuring us that we didn't need the assistance of male counterparts, we had begun building the shack from the ground up. After digging trenches, re-routing the draining systems, and vigorously pulling off an old, rusted tin roof, the women and I had decided bamboo to be the best tool in which to build the shack's walls from, due to its abundance within the forest. For weeks, Florence, Jen, and I took rusted saws to the base of those bamboo stalks and began cutting them free. Though, after much labour, we soon discovered that once the green cylinders had been sawed all the way through, because of the leafy bunches that gathered at the crown of the circular forest, it made it so that the trees would not fall with gravity. Instead, due to their entwinement, the bamboo stalks would just hang there, suspended in midair with no intention of screaming 'timber!'

Undeterred by our problem, Florence, Jen, and I had feverishly pulled at the bamboo, yanking it down towards us with an unbridled aggression. We sweated and swung in unison and, in an attempt to bring the stalks down with our weight, (along with a little assistance from gravity,) we clung to the stalks like monkeys swinging from the trees. With a hammer in her left back pocket and a measuring tape in her right, Florence had run towards a single suspended stalk with such unparalleled force that her body had instinctively scaled the green cylinder and almost reached the very top of it. I jumped on the bottom, pulling the bamboo stalk down towards me and, as I looked up to Florence's determined derriere swinging in the air with the force of girl power, I knew that I had never loved her more.

Although we had only made it halfway through the construction of Jen's new home, as I stood beside my sleeping spade, looking fondly upon the work that we had done together, I also knew that I could not soften my need to continually roam. Amidst all of the alternate versions of people that live inside of me, the traveller is predominantly who, since the tender age of fifteen, I have always been. Therefore, once a place has nurtured me, changed me, and filled the empty parts of me with its transformative beauty, despite how enchanting or perfect it may be, I start to feel the pull to leave it. And that pull, the one that I felt sticking out of my wiry hair like knives of electricity that could challenge even the beast of the sun with its intentions, could not be softened.

Making my way through a myriad of dirt tracks, I admired the pathways that I had walked, day and night, back and forth, between mine and Granny's shacks. So familiar was I with the pathways beneath my feet that I could, and often did, walk them in the dark of night, with only the moon or my memory to guide me. Those tracks were as familiar and endearing to me as the first scent of an approaching spring. Brushing past the flowers and the fairies and, registering the lean of abandoned shelters with warm appreciation, I began making my way towards Granny's shack in order to attend the first and last meeting that I would call upon the Woman's Mountain.

Sitting beside a misplaced stainless steel tabletop, Granny Breath Weaver looked upon me as I entered her home and greeted me with a warm smile. With leaves sticking out of her hair, dirt pressed against her soft, aged skin, and a kind of satisfaction cast across her face that could only come from a hard day's labour, Granny placed the kettle upon the fire and offered me a hot drink. With the same dirt beneath our nails, Granny and I each cradled a steaming cup of coffee in our hands and, with salt-stained eyes and similarly sun-kissed kin, we each silently acknowledged one another as women who enjoyed working the land. As a large carpet snake sleepily rose from its slumber, leaving its woven basket bed behind and fearlessly slithering up a shack beam that stood in front of us, I settled my own fear, sipped my black coffee, and knew that I had fallen into complete communion with body and land.

I had left the festival the previous week with fresh ideas

pulsing out from under my skin and, after being gifted Millie, (the coolest retro van in history,) those ideas were about to burst out of me. I knew that a time of change was almost upon me; it had only been accentuated by such a radical and fantastic gift as Millie. I had always dreamt of a campervan to call my own; a vehicle in which I could endlessly roam the wilderness of the world, yet always have a place to feel safe within and call home. Though, I had never been able to afford such a luxury. However, because of Florence's selfless vehicular offering, that dream had become a reality and, as I sat in Granny's kitchen, watching the snake slither above our heads, whilst still framing every single moment in appreciation, I knew that my time upon the Woman's Mountain was about to become but a memory.

Calling a meeting upon the mountain felt a very official and heavy affair, however, it was the only way in which Nimbin seemed to roll, so I decided to roll along with it and follow its serious example. I wanted to discuss my will to leave with all of the women that I had come to greatly respect upon the mountain as a collective audience, therefore a meeting of women had been called. As Granny, Florence, Jen, and I sat on the floor together upon an assortment of sheepskin rugs, with piles of bone and wood as our backdrop, whilst a slumberous snake returned to a basket that had been woven by Granny's capable hands, knowing that it would not be taken lightly, I began to plead my case.

"Women of the Woman's Mountain, it saddens me to inform you that I've decided to leave our home behind. I've lived amongst you all for what feels like a lifetime, a lifetime in which I have learned many a great and powerful lesson from each one of you. Despite my imminent departure, I will always hold a tender place in my heart for our wild, warrior woman ways and will aspire to transmute them into inspiring memories. Granny... you have provided me with not only an opportunity to rid myself of overwhelming masculine energy, but have also given me the time to look into and recognise the feminine part of myself, in order that I may become well-acquainted with her. For that, I will be eternally grateful and softened in a way that has been necessary to my personal development. You have also woven your stories into me, impregnating me with your spellbinding theatrics, and I must admit to you that, even though most women have learnt basket weaving from you, I have found a sense of my true life purpose within the breath that you have woven. You have done more for me than you could ever know and I thank you. I thank you for looking upon a drowned-out version of me that had, many months ago, once sat crouched outside the Oasis Café with a damp notebook in her hand and, after looking upon her tear-stained face, decided to rescue her. I thank you for everything that you have been for me."

Florence watched me as I spoke, already knowing my intentions and the confusion that I expected to be met with once I had vocalised them. Jen, as often was her manner, watched Granny and awaited her response so that she may mirror it, whilst Granny looked into me and eyed my assertive declaration with a casual suspicion. As we each stared into one another, despite how eloquently I had put my words, I also anticipated the women to feel a sense of abandonment from them. From Granny, I expected nothing less than dissuasion, because I knew that she felt a sense of responsibility over me, the young woman that she had rescued from the Oasis Café. But, knowing that I had always been a big girl in an even bigger world, I sat upon the sheepskin rug with an air of certainty upon my face and attempted to hold my ground.

I needed the women to understand me. I wanted them to know that there had been an impermanence under my skin for as long as I could remember. And that restlessness, despite all of the beauty in the world, (or, perhaps, because of its beauty,) would perhaps never settle. My departure was not a reflection of an inadequate love. There was a calling that had been haunting me for some time and whether it was or was not grand, whether I did or did not understand it, I had always followed that calling to the ends of the earth without question.

As I sat upon a sheepskin rug, with bones, snakes, and powerful women surrounding me, I knew that I had learned what I needed to learn from the mountain and its powerhouse occupants. No longer could the call of the desert be stilled. In the evenings, in the privacy of my bat cave bedroom, I had begun dreaming of a world far away from the thick and luscious rainforest that surrounded me; a world of wide open spaces, dusty red-earth deserts, echidnas, Dreamtime, and skin that was as black as the moonless night. Through a parched and cracked mouth, the desert had been whispering to me and I could not pretend to ignore it, especially after being given such an incredible gift that could get me there; Millie, the red-earth wanderer from the 80s.

Yet, amidst the calling of a women's meeting, I could see that my desires were met with reservation. So, as the meeting drew to a close, "we'll see," became the final verdict, and I quietly respected its compulsive and well-intended, yet somewhat unnecessary, protection, because we had all inadvertently become family upon the Woman's Mountain; we were mothers and daughters, sisters, grandmothers, aunties, and forever friends. We had sweated together, laughed together, cried together and, with rusty saws and overused spades, we had each run full-force into girl power, together. Even if they were yet to understand, I knew that those women would always be a part of me. Granny sat directly in front of me, Jen continued to look over at her, Florence looked upon me in encouragement and, as I looked into Granny's proud figure leaning against a wooden chair, I knew her to be the first woman that I had ever really looked up to.

Undisturbed by my sentimentality, Granny, first drawing from her cigarette, and then ensuring that she had a full audience, began to weave words of warning into the thick, humid air around us. "There's a cyclone coming tonight, you know." The cool fantasy of her warning chilled the air around my body, sending goosebumps running up and down my spine. "It may not be a good time to leave… the cyclone will come… tonight." As she drew one more puff from her cigarette in order to emphasise the importance of her words, the brown pools of Granny's eyes rippled out with animation. But, standing up in departure and kissing her on her soft, earthy cheek, I promised to heed her warning about the weather and be safe during my departure.

"I'll make sure to stop in tomorrow morning before I leave and say goodbye, Granny." Then, with the same childish twinkle in my eye that I had seen her adopt many times, I began making my way towards the small town of Nimbin.

Walking down that town's single street, I was awash in a complete wave of nostalgia. I sat in the Oasis Café, watching chess pieces slowly move in the heat of the day and, as I listened to Jonny Ganja's musical contribution to life, I watched the smoke curl around my eyes and clearly felt an unparalleled appreciation for the time that I had spent in Nimbin. Walking down towards the stream that Benjamin and I had once briefly known as 'the Honeymoon Suite,' my heart warmed with tender memories. As my eyes dampened with the same wetness as the stream, the flowing river, as if to comfort me, promised that everything would always stay in motion... even me and Benjamin. The rustling leaves, as if to follow suit, encouraged me to understand that everything would always be subject to development and growth. I honoured Nature's advices and, putting my thumb back out towards the wind in an attempt to let sleeping lovers lie, left the past behind me.

ॐ

As the sun came to a set, Florence and I returned to the Last Resort, made a roaring fire, and cooked our final supper upon it. In preparation for the cyclone, we had gathered piles of wood and had stacked them, at a safe distance, beside the open fire, allowing me an opportunity to pass the ways of the Woman's Mountain on to Florence, the next keeper. Pulling out a tub of fragrant honey that I had harvested myself, just a few days prior, I sweetened our tea and, resuming my position by the fire, looked out into the transition of the world. Evening was approaching and the golden hands of the setting sun smudged and swirled the sky up with such perfection that it replicated the same motion and colouring of our steamy tea. As the rains began to fall from a swirling honey-tea sunset and the tin roof began to serenade us with gentle music, I sipped from my hot tea with a mouth that had never known life to be as sweet.

Extracting myself from my daydreams, I looked over

towards Florence and saw that she was crouched down beside the fire, journaling. Besides the gentle patter of rain, the shack emanated a silence that called out to be broken and, remembering a treasure that Benjamin and I had excavated when we had first arrived at the Last Resort, I gasped aloud, "Florence, let's have a bath!"

The first day that I stumbled upon the Last Resort, amidst my fevered cleaning and gardening, I had discovered a porcelain bathtub that was buried outside in the back garden. Benjamin and I had turned it the right way up, scrubbed the dirt out of it, propped it up so that we could light fires beneath it to warm the water... and promised to one day bathe in it. Three months had passed since then and, with it being my last night on the Woman's Mountain, I knew that I could not miss the opportunity to have an open air rainforest bath. It was too damp outside to build a fire beneath the tub but, as I looked around the shack, I saw that we had a titanic water tank, a roaring indoor fire, and two massive cauldrons that were usually nominated as places in which to wash and rinse the dishes. With all of the necessary ingredients at hand, I frantically began working against the setting sun, filling the silver cauldrons with water and tediously placing them upon a flimsy grate that stood over the fire.

Full of humour, Florence looked up from her notebook devotionals and, accepting my bathtub offer, laughed aloud at the possession that had come over me. Frantically, I began carrying each pot of boiling water across the sodden garden, allowing the mud to squelch in-between my toes and then emptied their steamy contents into the willing bathtub. Against a setting sun that had been enjoying its own honey-tarnished tea party, the steam from a rainforest bath began to rise up into its golden light, becoming lost in blissful delight.

In the same fashion that we had done so many times before, Florence and I stripped down to our birthday suits. Full of goosebumps and giggles, we held two broken umbrellas and, squelching mud between our toes, ran through the cool rain towards our own version of heaven. After rinsing our feet in a bucket that I had placed beside the tub specifically for that purpose, Florence and I entered opposite corners of the bathtub and submerged in its angelic waters. Neck-deep in the most ·wonderful kind of warmth, the steam reached its long fingers out of thc bathtub and brushed away the residue of the setting sun, until a blue darkness finally fell upon us.

The crickets began their dirty bass symphonies and, playing to two pairs of feet that wiggled around and stuck out of the tub, their sounds pulsated throughout the entire forest. Cool droplets of rain fell down upon the parts of my skin that weren't submerged in the hot water and brought my temperature down to a calm. It was a perfect harmony of hot and cold. Then, when the rains became heavier, Florence and I opened our umbrellas up over our damp heads and slipped into a comfortable silence. Through the darkness and the steam, the thick song of wild animals, and the increasingly heavy, heavenly rainfall, I looked upon Florence's contented, closed eyes and chiseled her image eternally into my mind. With a purple umbrella hovering over her head, Florence wore the rouged face of relaxation. Somewhere, deep inside the shell of luscious rainforest, Florence and I, through our hard labour, dedication, and strength, had finally put our weapons down and had transformed into two beautiful, steaming pearls.

There are unique moments in a person's life where the infinity of imagination meets with the diversity of reality and each point of position is caught in a standoff of who came first. That moment, submerged in a steaming rainwater bath, amidst a musical, dark, and damp rainforest, was one of those moments in which it became hard to determine whether I had imagined it into existence, or if reality had manifested it to be true. Either way, with a black umbrella sheltering my head, hot water spilling out either side of the bath, and four knee caps that rose up from the water like the Loch Ness Monster, I could not quite believe the overflowing state of my happiness. As the night fell into complete blackness around us, Florence pointed out an assortment of luminous glowing mushrooms that had sprouted up around the forest and, as two Amazonian priestesses reflected over their journey together, of the present, the past, and the future, our ambient backdrop couldn't have been more magical.

That night, when Florence and I returned to our bat cave bedroom, we took with us a piece of wood from the forest upon which blue, ambient mushrooms grew. Placing the wild mushroom stick in the corner of the room, Florence and I extinguished our single bedroom candle and, knowing that we may never again need electricity, gave ourselves a new and improved nightlight for which to sleep beside.

I watched Florence's alien-coloured skin fall into a peaceful slumber and, as the rain gently tapped upon our tin roof and my skin radiated with an internal warmth that seemed to be sourced from more than just the rainforest bath, I began to follow her into the land of slumber...

...all the while, amidst a forest of farewells, I knew that my dreams could not even come close in comparison to the life that I found myself living.

Cyclonic Sisters

22nd February 2015

Deep in the nucleus of the night, my bat cave blanket began to sprawl its damp, mouldy hands upon two restless bodies in a spiteful effort to keep them from their dreams. The earthen scent of wetness and mildew arose from within the soiled fabrics of my pillow case, floated lightly around my face, and then climbed up into my nostrils, only to splash down into the green pool of my saturated lungs.

Spluttering out into the darkness with an echo in my chest that could have put the Grand Canyon to shame, I feebly tried to fight a cough that had been settled in my lungs for months but, as the rains moistened my entire world, I could only lie in bed and surrender to their persistence. Wheezing, I tried to chase sleep, but the thin tin upon my shack roof aggressively shook as if meteorites were falling down upon it and constantly rattled me awake. All night long, I listened to the chaos of metallic smashing and crashing until it began to feel as though the rains were permeating through the tin roof, pressing down upon my very bones and clawing their watery way deep into my marrow.

The memory of the warm rainforest bath that I had enjoyed not hours before became a world that was a far cry from the slow torture of the night that I had found myself experiencing; that memory pulsed from my sweaty skin like a lucid dream that I could not wake from. In the thin layer between sleeping and awake, nothing felt real to me, not even the storm. I turned wildly in the night, lost in an entranced state of being, hypnotised by the sound of soldiers banging their wet hands against rusted tin drums whilst suffocating in the scent of mould rising up through my sheets like the ascension of a green sun. I could only be brought back to a slither of reality by the aid of an arm unconsciously smacking me across the back, or a leg twitching and kicking my calf. Florence, I was certain, had also become afflicted with the same spell of the weather as I. Our naked bodies lay tangled in the sheets, as well as one another's; restless, twitching, and wondering what had happened to our tea-stained dreams.

Unable to find peace amongst the rain, all I could do was wait for the sun to rise in the hopes that the fury of the night would soften by the new light of dawn. Just as my hernia tightened around my guts like a lock to a safety deposit box and the rumble of my cough began registering on seismographs all the way across the Tasman Sea in New Zealand, I finally began to see the drowned face of dawn pulse in blue waves through my plastic bat cave tarp. Amidst my delirium, I had never been happier to see the sight of morning.

As the alien-stained glow of mine and Florence's mushroom nightlight faded away with the approach of dawn, its gentle ambience was soon replaced by a dark shadow that materialised and lingered outside of my bat cave bed mosquito net. Although my blurry morning eyes registered the slow theatrics of the shadow's movement, as it paced back and forth across the floor, my logic had not yet adjusted to any sense of reality. When the shadow began to speak, I could not, at first, even distinguish a single word that it was saying above the loud clatter of rain upon tin that was filling up every empty space in my head. But, as my mind slowly adjusted to practicality, it wasn't long before the dark shadow dissolved into the concerned body of Granny.

Slowly bringing a working hand up to a pressed mouth, Granny pulled upon the nurturings of her homegrown and inhaled with the force of a tornado. As the Breath Weaver stood outside of the net, waiting for Florence and I to wake from out catatonic state, I saw a bolt of lightning flash across her eyes, extinguishing the playful child that usually lived in hiding inside of them. Granny peered at me through the deep green of the net with a serious disposition that moulded itself across her features. Creases of displeasure had gathered and furrowed her brows into matrimony and, although their hairy union was noteworthy, as I bolted up from my bed and unzipped the net, I knew that there would be no need for ceremony. Granny exhaled a deep breath from her medicinal stick and, as the grey smoke swiftly merged with the grey fog of the mountain, I could not quite determine which realm of reality I was in.

"The cyclone... is here," Granny began, in slow, calculated tones. A combination of adventure and disaster swirled around like a whirlpool upon her features, contorting and changing her face into different people. As the Breath Weaver took yet another drag, the smoke seemed to pass through her mouth and then impregnate her eyes, swelling them like two brown balloons.

Looking upon Granny Breath Weaver, I realised that she looked more like the outside than ever before. Her long, white hair rolled all the way down to her waist like a white-crested wave that was just about to break. Her skin-coloured clothes clung to her body, damp from being consensually kissed by heavy dew-drop lips. Granny, with bare feet that had been moulded and shaped by the flatness of the ground, paced the floor outside of my bat cave like a hurricane with legs. And as she looked upon me with lightning bolt eyes and whirlpool features, I realised that Granny Breath Weaver, as if possessed by the spirit of Mother Nature, had become the storm itself.

"Need to wake up," Granny encouraged towards Florence and I. "Need to dig your trenches out before they flood. Need to fix the leaks in the roof and make sure you have enough wood for the fire." Granny's footsteps rang like alarm bells in my head, her words the reminder. "The cyclone... is here."

Instructions reverberated against my sodden bones, ringing in the same high pitched frequency as the tin roof. Knowing that I had never before experienced such persistent rains, I shook the slumber from my damp body, looked across to Florence, who wore the same surprised expression as I, and knew that we were both in for a wild ride.

"Need to build a fire!" Granny reiterated. "Need to dig deeper trenches...The mountains... are no place for the weak!" She promised.

With that, I felt the weight of the sky begin to fall upon

our heads. Jumping out of a bat cave bed, Florence and I ripped our way through the mosquito net without concern for it and ran through the shack like two electrified kittens without fur. Crouching down beside the fireplace, I began fumbling through our piles of wood, counting and calculating how much there was in proportion to the heavy rainfall. Unfortunately, due to the previous night's steaming hot bath, (wherein which I had constructed a roaring fire to boil a tub's worth of hot water,) Florence and I had been left without any particularly good odds of future warmth. And although that little piece of heaven had been worth it, it did not detract from the cold fact that our stock had been officially depleted. Knowing that I would need to source more, I looked out towards the saturated forest with a dismal feeling upon my damp heart.

Taking from the remaining store of firewood, I began constructing a small fire in an attempt to keep us all a little drier, but the air in the shack had become so thick with moisture that it spread and seeped into my 'dry' storage of wood, dampening it. Whilst I crouched down beside the whisper of a flame and attempted to blow it into life, clouds of thick smoke billowed into my eyes and lungs, tickling the cough that lived inside of them. Seized by a coughing fit, it was as if the mould particles were partying in my chest, clanking their beers bottles together until they carelessly spilt their liquids all over my lungs, adding to the wetness that clung to everything.

As the smoky dampness of my eyes bled themselves onto my cheeks, offering me my vision back, I caught sight of Florence cloaking her naked body with a waterproof trench coat. As the plastic jacket hung down her torso, unbuttoned and unashamed, Florence ran outside of the shack as if she too had been possessed by the storm, subjecting her milky skin to the ferocious rain and wind. A look of duty and obligation began to harden Florence's usually soft features as she clenched against the rainfall, grabbed the spade from a bed of dirt, and took to it like a sword swinger. Looking down upon the almost-overflowing trench that surrounded our shack like a moat, Florence plunged the face of the spade into the dirt without even offering it goggles first.

Whilst Florence worked towards deepening our trenches before the rains spilled over onto the carpet, I began frantically searching the shack for pots and pans to place beneath the leaking parts of the rusted ceiling. Half of our sofa bed had already been saturated by a sneaky hole that arose somewhere beside the water tank and, as its fabrics added to the mould and mildew of the Last Resort, I resorted to placing a plastic bucket beneath it. Then, running outside to gather more wood in the hopes that I could dry its bark by the light of the fire, my feet swallowed up a mudslide that proceeded to propel my barely-clothed body straight into a mound of dirt.

Undeterred by my collision with the earth, I clambered up onto my feet again and ran into the forest so that I could collect more wood. Florence continued to furiously dig away our trench-turned-moat whilst Jen came running over the hill, yelling that her shack had been completely flooded out. In an effort at a last resort, Jen began attempting to glue the rusted holes that were causing the roof to leak, though water and glue quickly became two materials that would never work together. Jen's screwed-up face became the new bucket in which to catch the unruly water. I scurried around with rock-hard nipples that pushed their way through the wet piles of wood that were gathered at my chest. Florence dug a trench wearing only a trench coat whilst Granny, after enchanting us all with the theatrics of the storm, had disappeared back into the fog from whence she came.

Although wet hair pressed flatly down across my eyes and disturbed my vision, for but a moment, it was as if I had stepped outside of myself and could see us all in perfect clarity; we were a damp, semi-nude, very muddy, and absolutely hilarious sight to look upon.

I could not keep myself from dropping my sodden sticks to the ground and doubling over in manic laughter. I felt as though I had just awoken from a trance and laughter seemed to be the only thing that could break the spell. Through her dutiful dedication to dry land, Florence looked across at me with caution in her warrior woman eyes, uncertain of what I had suddenly found so funny. But as I continued to laugh at the sight of us, it wasn't long before Florence threw her un-goggled spade down towards the floor and joined me in my madness. Amidst her sticky task at hand, a slender smile had even glued itself to Jen's determined face.

"Anyone want a cuppa?" I called out through the glistening rainforest. "I think that we should start the day over."

With a steaming cup of tea finally folded in between my shivering hands, and honey swirling around the saucer in the same way that the storm twisted and tangoed in the sky, I warmed myself beside the fire and, as suggested, began to start my day over. Smoke and fog danced around my body and, as if making their way into my mind, made it hard for me to determine what to do with the day. Originally, I had planned to leave the mountain behind, but just as Granny Breath Weaver, (my White Witch of the Woman's Mountain,) had predicted, a cyclone had sought us out. With Jen having disappeared in search of Granny, and Florence sitting quietly beside me, I simply sipped from my tea, allowed its warmth to remedy my indecision, and began feeling the scenario out without the grandeur of theatrics.

Before Granny had disappeared into the fog, before the trenches had been dug deeper, before the glue had fused Jen's fingers, and prior to my fit of mad laughter, whilst Granny had attempted to wake Florence and I from our slumber, her final words had implied that the mountain was not for the weak. Remembering those words, it was as if a serpent swam up and down my spine, sending my body into shivers. I recalled the day in which I had decided to call the Woman's Mountain home; it had been a day when Granny had first said those words to me: 'the mountain is not for the weak.' Almost three months had passed since then, yet the day that I planned to leave the mountain behind me, Granny had seen fit to make that same statement once more.

I twirled the word 'weak' in the fingers of my thoughts over and over again, wondering if Granny had been implying me to be weak because of my will for desertion. Though, after checking in-between my legs for signs of tucked tails, I only saw two damp, muddy thighs that clanked themselves together in an attempt to stay warm. Above the sound of tin and rain, I tried to entertain the idea that perhaps I was weak, though as I remembered all that I had done upon the mountain, I could not settle upon such a verdict.

Surely I had not lived atop of the Woman's Mountain for almost three months in exile of every creature comfort that I had ever known, only to think of myself as weak. I had handed over my privacy to the forest, had knelt down beside it, giving my power over to something greater than myself. I had lived without walls and without noise, save for that which originated organically from within the woods. I had known only cold bucket baths and couldn't even remember what a hot shower felt like upon my skin. I had sweat and bled into the red of the earth until I had become one with its soil. I had even forsaken *electricity* and had often sat in the darkness with only myself for company. Toilets with flushing systems had become an ancient relic that my ancestors once used. Upon the Woman's Mountain, in more ways than one, I had learned to deal with my shit. I had endured and, for it, surely I was not weak at all.

It was during that moment of reaffirmation, as I sat beside the smoky fire, sipping my honey tea and shivering the cold weather out of me, that I came to understand my final lesson from the mountain; knowing when I should and should not leave. For, although I was happy and contented upon the mountain, I also knew that there could be too much of a good thing. So, despite the force of the cyclone, despite the flooded trenches and the whispers of weakness that had dampened me, I decided to follow through with my plan, stand my ground and keep my word, if only to myself.

"Today's the day that I'm gonna leave, Florence. No

matter what." Interrupting Florence's fire-kissed gaze, she pulled her eyes out from the flames and looked over to me with caution. "Why don't you just come with me?" I asked, attempting to prolong our friendship for as long as possible.

However, I could see similar thoughts of desertion and weakness swimming around in Florence's deep brown eyes. Her promise to further assist Jen in building her shack began to furrow her brow and, as the rain whipped the tin roof and tore holes upon its body, duty and desire settled upon Florence's shivering limbs.

"There's nothing that you can do in this weather," I promised.

Without being able to dispute the obvious, Florence and I sat cross-legged upon a rained-out, leaf-sodden living room (kind of) floor and began drawing out a rough plan for our escape. I found that my thoughts kept drifting towards Byron Bay. I thought of Benjamin's little blue tent subject to the fury of the weather and, even though we had parted ways with one another, I knew that I couldn't just leave him at the mercy of the cyclone. Surely I could help him somehow.

When Florence and I had left Earth Frequency, Lolito had also offered for us to visit him at his home in Byron and, the more I thought upon it, the more I found myself wanting to take him up on that offer. I had formed a deep connection with Lolito over the course of the festival period and my affection towards him, as well as a desire for dry shelter, began carrying me away from the Last Resort.

It wasn't long before Florence and I had scurried around the shack, packed our mouldy belongings into cardboard boxes and prepared ourselves for takeoff. Running through the squelching mud, I poured myself into Granny's shack, beaming with my journey at hand and, as expected, was met with cautious eyes; eyes that belonged to the storm, warning me of wet and treacherous roads. Though, without being deterred, I began my farewell to my White Witch of the Woman's Mountain. My eyelashes dripped with cyclonic gratitude as I kissed the lunar magic of Granny's soft cheeks and thanked her, once more, for all that she had been to me.

"I came here with the rains, Granny… So, it's only fit that I leave with them too." And with that, Granny could do nothing but twinkle that secret twinkle in her eye and smile as I clumsily ran back into the rain, waving her a final goodbye.

With cardboard boxes atop of our heads like two drowned African queens, Florence and I began the first of two trips down the backbone of the mountain. But, as the morning had slipped into afternoon, the cyclone had also gathered speed and ferocity, shooting fat raindrops from its grey-clouded gun without fear of casualty. Therefore, everything that Florence and I carried over our heads quickly became saturated. Boxes sagged into nothingness and then spilled their contents out all over the forest floor, rolling down the hill without regard for their owners. Beneath my bare feet, wet leaves became like roller blades, pushing me down the hill at an alarming speed without any concern for brakes. As I picked my muddy body up from the ground, I felt leeches nestle their razor-sharp teeth deep into my toes and ankles, desiring one final taste of me. Everything felt as though it were flowing against Florence and I and because of it, I knew that the mountain wanted to keep me.

The second trip was even harder still, because the chill of the air felt as though it had settled deep in my bones, making mobility difficult. However, as my feet bled out in rivers beneath me and I pranced down the hill on scrawny legs, I thought about the deer within me. I recalled the pending decision that Granny had advised me of when stating that I could choose anyone or anything as my new and improved identity. It had been an exhilarating concept. Though, three months later, it was still my name that pushed itself out of my lips whenever I introduced myself to a new friend. As rainwater pressed its way into my mouth, droplets of blood stained the leaves beneath my feet, and hair crossed over my eyes, I realised that I liked my story, my identity, and my name… *April Lee Fields*. As I slid down the hill towards freedom, I decided then and there that I would never change my name from its origins.

After Florence and I, cyclonic sisters of the Woman's Mountain, had finally loaded our belongings into Millie, (the little red box that's been dry since the 80's,) we then threw our goose-bumped bodies into her red, loving arms. With soggy clothes thrown into the back seat-less seat and windows fogging up as if to mirror the mood of the sky, I knew that I also mirrored the wet version of myself that had arrived at the foot of that mountain three months prior. I had become a complete circuit. And as I prepared to leave the Woman's Mountain behind, I thought of everything that it had selflessly taught me and could not help but to feel as though a new woman had been born inside of me; a new and improved version of me.

Putting a bloodied foot to the pedal, I sparked Millie into life and, without fear, began driving head-on into the approaching cyclone…

… because, as they say, the mountain knows no gentility for the weak weak.

Flight of the Hummingbird

25th February 2015

With bodies that looked like the outside and eyes that flickered with wildfire lightning, Florence and I blew our way through the tempestuous storm towards Lolito's house with the force of the cyclone upon our wet backs. As we pulled into his driveway, Lolito looked up from the comfort of an outside sofa, settled upon the sight of mine and Florence's filthy bodies as they shivered their way towards him and, foregoing the pleasantry of introductions towards his sofa-side companions, Lolito kindly put his arms around our shaking shoulders and ushered Florence and I straight into the shower.

Hot water. Hot water. Hot water. As boiling beads of moisture rippled down my brown skin, then and there I knew it to be a luxury that I would never again take for granted. Whilst Florence and I huddled in the boxy shower together, washing away the mud from one another's bare skin and pulling the leaves out of our locked hair, we each wordlessly surrendered to our survival and allowed the steaming liquid to rinse away our transitory troubles. Through the steam, I could see that Florence's eyes were as wide as my own with disbelief towards the supernatural force that we had just experienced. Through storms and magic, leeches and downpours; through the deep thicket of white witches, soul-sorcery and the cyclonic sisters that had been ignited within Florence and I, the Woman's Mountain had finally released us.

After turning the shower up to the hottest temperature that our bodies could take, I watched the steam replicate the weather that we had just endured. I invited the hot air into my damp lungs with warm appreciation and, not knowing or caring whether we had or had not just awoken from some ancient dream, I fell back into the present and proceeded to join Florence in a fit of steaming giggles. As our witchy laughter bounced off of the tiled walls and echoed around the bathroom without regard for who was subjected to its hysteria, Florence and I gradually giggled ourselves clean.

Though, it was discovered that some things, such as magic and the business of women's deep dreaming, would never wash away from our skin.

It would take four days for the storm to completely pass, for the sky to smudge itself with the wispy blue paintbrush of a brand new day, and for the sunshine to stealthily escape its grey imprisonment so that it may finally rest its golden tendrils upon the world once more. During those four grey days, Florence and I were taken great care of by our host, Lolito. We were well fed, well loved, and were provided with warm beds and dry sheets that had never known the touch of green-fingered mould, nor felt the cold, damp breath of mildew upon their fabrics. I would often come to find myself in Lolito's company, lost in tender reflection with him, wherein which we would speak for hours of our hopes and dreams and linger over one another with a pure kind of curiosity. Whilst the rains kept us indoors, I proceeded to draw stories of red earth dreaming with a dusty pen that was full to the brim with the inks of my wild imagination. Yet, when I flew too far across the lands of time, Lolito would only need touch me with a caring brown hand to bring me back to the present moment with him.

Lolito had a quiet strength about him that I had never before known; it was the kind of strength that is born from the essence of a man that has matured and, knowing what he wants out of life, has been defined by those accomplishments. That comfortable courage drew me all the closer to Lolito and I began to envision what it would be like if I were to stay in Byron Bay in his company. Although our time together had been brief, I had learned many a great lesson from Lolo...

...One night, after putting clean living temporarily aside and drowning myself in one too many glasses of Dutch courage wine, I had aggressively seized the microphone at a bar and had sung into it without regard for anyone else around me. During that moment in time, I had only known how to express my creativity as if it were a poltergeist that had taken hold of and possessed my spirit, instead of a fluid wave that ebbed and harmoniously flowed through me. Lolito, with my best intentions at heart, had spoken up and simply encouraged that I soften my wild side, be gentle, and understand how to allow other musicians the space to grow and unfold alongside of me so that we may make something not only magical, but also well balanced. Although Lolito's guidance, though said out of kindness, was slightly embarrassing for me at the time, the musical mathematics that he spoke of would go on to become a piece of advice that would lend me great service for many years thereafter.

I also came to drink from the company of Lolito's friends as if my admiration for them were a hummingbird's slender beak and their golden hearts were a sweet nectar. Those companions formed a close circle that was comprised of musicians and artists who were a beautiful reflection of Lolito's creativity, as a tattooist and an artist in his own right. From amongst their company, I connected with a young Mexican woman named Janaki who, with tribal rhythms pulsing through her blood and a bird claw earring hanging from her lobe, had blown in with the wind and fallen like a wild autumn leaf beside my feet. Not having a plan of where she would go forth from Byron, I had advised Janaki of the Woman's Mountain and offered to take her there if she felt called to it.

Once the rains had finally let up, I began organising and preparing Millie, (the cyclonic survivor of the twenty-first century,) for my complete ownership and our impending journey together. Adopting my personal cares as his own, upon the afternoon that I planned to leave, Lolito thoroughly checked over Millie's engine in order to determine whether she could make such a demanding journey. After coming to the conclusion that her engine was solid and akin to that of a lawnmower, I felt satisfied that Millie and I could make it to wherever our hearts desired.

Sitting upon the same outside sofa that Lolito had perched upon when Florence and I had first arrived, I found myself looking into the soft care of Lolito's brown eyes and prepared to bid them farewell. Then, through soft, full lips that were stained with an exotic French-Italian accent, Lolito asked me a single question that, upon reflection, would, in its own way, change my life.

"What is your spirit animal?"

"A hummingbird," I replied, without hesitation.

"And… what does the hummingbird mean to you?" Lolo gently pressed.

"Well, hummingbirds, to me, are the perfect balance of strength and gentility," I began. "They push their tiny wings up and down with such effortless force and speed that, well, even the flowers seem to bow down to them." With that, Lolito took a pen from his back pocket and began drawing upon my right arm. Unconcerned with the tickle of his doodling, I looked towards the cloudless sky and resumed my feathered musings.

"Hummingbirds hum and they hum and they hum… and, for whatever reason, I can relate to their frequency. I can feel that vibration inside of me when I speak… and I'm even beginning to hear it in my voice when I sing. Unlike other birds, hummingbirds can fly both forwards and backwards with great ease and, with every casual step that I take backwards and forwards across the globe, I can relate to their unique flight. Even though I have only ever seen one in real life, since I was a child, hummingbirds have turned up in the most auspicious of places, always gently reminding me that I am on the right pathway. They have shown face upon the doormat of a house that I was destined to visit and have been discovered hanging from a necklace that was found in my grandmother's belongings after she passed from this world. The hummingbird has even gone so far as to place its imagery upon the bottle of a perfume… called 'April Fields.' And that's only naming but a few scenarios… it's uncanny how often I see the hummingbirds symbology perpetually fluttering around me."

After I had finished imparting the story of my personal connection with the winged creature unto him, Lolito looked me deep in the eyes and began his own testimony.

534

"I am gonna tattoo you the hummingbird. I can feel its magic from the story that you tell and, if you trust and allow, I will put that magic into you... to keep."

My ears almost tripped over themselves as they tried to catch the words that had fallen with a resounding clang into their hollow drums. Swollen with gratitude towards Lolito's spontaneous and selfless offer, I readily postponed my plan for departure and offered the only thing that I could in response... my complete and ultimate trust. Taking Lolito's hand, I followed him into the warm ambience of his home studio where African fabrics and red-brick walls mixed together in a harmonious tranquility. Then, sitting upon a black leather chair, I followed Lolito's gentle guidance and gradually submerged into the deep seas of a sacred tattoo ceremony.

With a thick stick of sage pressed in-between his attentive fingertips like a builders pencil, Lolito began to trace the outlines of my body with it as if I were the drawing itself, allowing the cleansing smoke to rise and fall around us both in a ceremony of purification. As the smog curved its way around me, filling my every outline in, I felt its sweet perfume pour into me until I became one with its healing. With Lolito having studied beneath the sacred wings of a Mori tribe some years prior, he parted his plump, brown lips and, through the fragrant sage, proceeded to bless me with their prayer. Although it was a language that I did not understand, I felt its meaning without need for translation. Then, drawing upon me in the same way that I had drawn upon him with my feathered words, Lolito, the spirit conjurer, began to work his magic.

With no design to hide behind and a free hand placed upon my skin, Lolito and I fell into a complete state of trust with one another. I gave Lolito permission to tattoo upon me that which the spirit allowed him to see, whilst he in turn entrusted that I would allow my body to exist as a medium between two very separate worlds. As Lolito became lost in his ability to conjure spirit through the fine point of a needle, I found myself falling into a state of deep meditation. The previous four days at Lolito's house had offered me the perfect opportunity to reflect upon everything that had happened over the last few months of my life without any interruption from the outside world. As I leaned over a tattoo chair, attempting to discover ways in which to chase away the gentle sting of the needle, I began to further those reflections and, through meditative breathing, allowed the world to completely stop spinning.

I saw visions of the Woman's Mountain from which I had recently been released and, although it was already beginning to become a distant memory, I smiled, knowing that my time upon that mountain would be a story that I would one day tell my grandchildren... as we huddled together beside an open fire without walls nor electricity.

As the needle hit a bone and pressed me into further vivid daydreams, I thought upon every single version of me that had emerged over the past year: the wild party girl that was lost on an island somewhere in Cambodia dancing beneath a silver-kissed moon; the devoted sister and the remembered daughter that had remained back in Florida with her family in order to piece together the missing links of her life into a long-awaited harmony; the wild woman who, with a rusted saw in her hand and fire blazing in her hazel eyes, had continued her life upon the woman's mountain and had become a natural force to be reckoned with. As Lolito enveloped me in sage-scented magic, I could not help but to think upon the version of me that stayed with him in Byron and, because of it, blossomed in her creativity. I romanticised over the version of myself that had rescued Benjamin from the clutches of the storm just in time to drive off into the sunset within an alternate version of Millie, (the heart-shaped camper who was always destined to be our saviour.) Then, at last, I entertained the unformed future version of me that decided to go forth with Sam and begin traversing the unknown desert lands together and wondered how much reality there really was in such an idea.

Existing beyond the limitations of time and space, there are a thousand alternate versions of myself out there in the world, each having taken a path that my present person chose not to and each version living out a life that I have but momentarily stepped into… if only for a blink of the eye. However, as I leant against the back of a black leather chair with a body that felt like a still life masterpiece, I returned from my dreamtime, slowly focused on the magic of the moment, and found that I was contented with the version of me that had been led to the present. As always, the hummingbird, through its infinite guidance, showed me that I walked the right path.

After many hours had passed us by, caught under a spell of two separate states of ethereal and personal meditation, Lolito put down his tool of dedication, gathered our energy into the unified moment and brought the sacred session to an end. Then, smiling into my body like a proud parent at the sight of their child's first missing tooth, he placed a mirror in front of me and allowed my gaze to rest upon his creation. As my eyes fell into harmony with my reflection, droplets of salted water gathered at the creases of my eyes and stood to attention, threatening to jump… because they were happy enough to die.

Sprawled out across the length of my right arm was the most beautiful tattoo that I have ever laid my eyes upon. In a perfectly balanced combination of gentility and strength, Lolito had seamlessly blended a tribal warrior design that was ripe in dark, protective symbols and fierce imagery, with the soft femininity of a feathered wingspan that blossomed its way across my shoulder blade with incomparable elegance and grace. As I traced a long, fluid tail that followed the curvature of my arm to perfection, it was apparent that, as Lolito was master of his craft, he had also effortlessly mastered the language of my body. The hummingbird wrapped itself around me like my favourite leather jacket and promised to never let me go. Through his love and dedication to his chosen profession, Lolito had done what no other person had ever been able to do for me and I knew it to be a blessing that I would never forget; full of magic and spirit, Lolito had given a hummingbird her wings.

After thanking Lolito for everything that he had done for us, Florence, Janaki and I all piled into Millie and began making our way back towards the town of Nimbin, with only one stop to make along the way. As we pulled up alongside a curb that lined a random back street of Byron Bay, I watched as the girls disappeared into the horizon in search for our dinner, whilst I crouched upon the curb... and waited for Benjamin.

Despite our best efforts at reaching one another, during the four days of the storm, the cyclone had seen to it that Benjamin and I were kept at an undisputed distance. After leaving the mountain with the intention of coming to assist him, when I reached Ben on the phone, he advised me that he had already made his way to higher ground... but found himself flooded in atop a mountain. When the rains had finally ceased and allowed him to descend, it was I who was then unavailable... submerged in another version of myself.

As Benjamin rounded the corner to meet me, a large smile wrapped itself around his mouth like a car colliding with a street lamp and, despite his projected happiness, a tired look of defeat began to flicker across his pupils like two worn-out blue bulbs. After embracing one another in a love that would never truly expire, Benjamin and I began exchanging stories regarding our plight with the storm and, before long, each of us knew that Mother Nature had kept us apart for her own reasons. As I resumed my crouch upon the pavement and Benjamin sat down to join me, his features, as if affected by the concrete below him, began to harden.

"April," he started, "I'm gonna go back to England. My ticket's already booked... I've... I've just had enough." Benjamin's words washed over me in shaky waves of uncertainty, searching out my reaction with a measured caution. Looking across at him in disbelief, I was taken aback at such a statement because, although we had been in Australia for almost a year, his premature departure was something that I had not expected. Even

Millie blinked her headlight eyes in shock of Ben's final decision because, although she would never say as much, she had heard me silently entertaining the idea of asking Benjamin to accompany me into the desert. But, as the finality of Benjamin and I came riding in on a gallant white horse, dismounted, and then sat down on the ground beside us with his head pressed into his hands in sadness, I knew that that version of ourselves could never be a reality. As I looked into Ben's jaded blue eyes and saw the makings of their own storm swirling around inside, I understood his exhaustion towards life on the road and could only learn to accept his final decision to return home.

"Where will go you, April... what will you do now?" Ben, concerned as ever, asked.

"I don't really know, Ben. The desert is calling to me and... I may still go with Sam, but that's as far as I've got in regards to any kind of plan." As I looked off into the distance, trying to imagine what my future looked like, I felt Ben touch my arm and draw me back into the present with him.

"I would rather that you go with Sam than ride out into the desert on your own... I know you, April. And I would rather you not go such a distance alone." Despite the difficulty that those words would have had making their way out of Ben's caring mouth, my blue-eyed prince never ceased to amaze me with his unconditional and unfailing love.

As we sat upon the warm pavement, sharing cigarettes and tenderly reflecting over everything that had happened to us over the past year, Ben and I took one another's hands and held them together as if our fingers were links to an eternal chain that would never break. Not knowing when we would have the opportunity again, we sat as close as we could to one another, allowing our skin to press into one common body that no longer minded where one of us began and the other ended. And, as the moment swayed and changed with the salty sea breeze, an alternate version of myself decided to stay there with Benjamin for all of eternity.

It wasn't long before Florence and Janaki returned with boxes of pizza cradled in their arms and, as if the steaming slices were an egg timer, they silently encouraged that the moment move on. Three womanly, yet girly, bodies climbed aboard Millie, stuck their slender arms out of the open windows and, as the wind whipped their hands around like fleshy kites, they waved goodbye to a boyish man who stood beside the van alone; a boyish man who was destined to return home inside of a different body than he had originally left in, gently waved back. And, as a bird claw earring swung in the salted breeze, I called out to Benjamin through the gaps in between my fingers, "See you back home in a month." But as those words of assurance left my mouth, they rolled around in a mud bath of uncertainty before going out into the world; once they were subjected to the light of day, they quivered and realised that they were unclothed. The truth of the matter was that neither Ben nor I could be certain as to when we would see one another again. But Benjamin, amongst a secret sadness that lined his features, simply offered me a generous smile that clothed my indecision with its warmth. Glimpsed in the rearview mirror, a retreating version of Benjamin, without warning, turned into a single black line upon a beach-stained pavement and faded into the past.

I arrived in Nimbin just in time to catch Granny Breath Weaver at the Oasis café before she made her way back towards her home upon the mountain. As I made my way through the usual thick layer of smoke towards the silver glow of Granny's hair, her eyes were set aflame at the sight of my return, lighting like a beacon in a stormy night and warming in the same way that a mother's would upon the sight of a returned daughter. As I recognised that burning ember of affection within the brown pools of her theatrical eyes, I knew that, although I was destined to leave the Breath Weaver behind, I had never been closer to her. After offering Granny a new warrior woman for the mountain and watching her engage with a bird claw earring that swung in the breeze like a pendulum, I knew that my work upon the Woman's Mountain was finally done and allowed the scene to be swallowed up by the thick, ever-present smoky breath of Nimbin.

Florence followed me back out to Millie, (the new red box shape of my own heart,) and, as I prepared myself for departure, she began applying red lipstick to her soft, kissable lips. Then, in her own ceremonious act of love and devotion, Florence pressed her mouth against the sun visor and left her rouge imprint upon its protection. Through the dampness of the day, Florence and I pressed our sticky bodies against one another for the last time and, stained with the sweetness of tears, finally said our goodbyes. As I drove off into the horizon, leaving the single street of Nimbin behind me, I looked into the rearview to see a star-kissed hand that would never stop waving. And I knew in my heart of hearts that from there on out, Florence would be with me wherever my heart-shaped box decided to take me. She was, after all, my very own happy ending.

It felt good to finally be alone behind the steering wheel with only my own desires to consider and, as I drove further into the distance with no plans upon paper, I slowly allowed those desires to become clearer. I kept on driving. For hours, I drove and I drove and I drove into nowhere in particular, because I simply needed to know what it felt like to be a woman with her own van and with her own sense of purpose that was unaffected by the responsibility of others. I allowed my new way of life to settle into me and, with a single bed in the back of the van, a few cans of food, and a full tank of petrol, I felt that those simple things were a good enough plan and would suffice, if only for the moment. I continued to drive until every connective cord of entanglement had fallen away from me, but as the horizon stretched out into eternity, one single cord still clung on for dear life and wrapped itself so tightly around my heart that it became difficult to breath. So, surrendering, I pulled over on the side of the road and dialled Benjamin.

"Hey, Ben... I can literally feel the distance growing between us with every single mile that I drive further away from you. There will be no going back soon," I admitted vulnerably, through a slow wave of hysteria that had begun to outline the Ben-shaped hole that had appeared in my universe. The fact that Ben would be halfway across the world from me in just a few days had finally sunk in and paralysed me because, despite the troubles that we had endured, he was my Benjamin, my blue-eyed prince, and for the last four years of my estranged life, Ben had been my one and only constant.

"I know, April... I can feel it too. But I think it's gonna be ok... It will be ok."

As Benjamin and I ended our phone call, so too did we end our walk. We ended a walk that, through golden fields and half-formed rainbows, bustling markets and ruined temples, moonlit beaches, ravenous cities, and countless other incredible and mundane places that I may or may not ever remember, had been the most intimate walk of my life. I had never been closer to another as I was with Benjamin and, for it, I had become closer to myself. As I listened to the line ring with dead tones that pressed themselves into my ear, symbolising the birth of something new, I looked around at the beautiful world that surrounded me; the green rolling hills, the sun-drenched blades of grass, the open road... and I realised that Benjamin had been right. It was going to be ok.

All that was left for me to do was to take a seat upon my red box throne and, as I had desired all along, to take the wheel of my own destiny. As my heart began to pulse with a new sense of adventure resonating out from it, I started the engine and passed the rolling hills by without sentiment, knowing that everything was destined to change. A road paved to Nowhere sprawled out in front of me. A map of Australia sat on the passenger seat beside me and a piece of paper with Samuel's address scribbled upon it sat crumpled up against the dashboard, full of half-made promises.

As the setting sun stung a tattoo that rested upon an arm that extended itself out of the open window, I felt as though I were just about to take off. And it was a flight that belonged to the hummingbird alone.

After fumbling with the radio in an attempt to determine whether it still functioned, "You can go your own way," began pushing its way through the crackling speakers and waltzed out to greet my wind-whipped ears, courteously asking them if their loopy lobes would care to dance. As a circular smile curved itself around my teeth like a goldfish tank, the moment could not have been more surreal. And, although nobody was around to hear it, I turned the radio up full blast and sang out with as much force as my little-big heart could muster.

"You can call it another lonely day. You can go your own way. Go your own way."

In the privacy of Millie, as Fleetwood Mac sung out only to me, I did not feel lonely; instead, I thought over every single person that had crossed my path and changed it into something that it would have never have been without them. I pondered upon my lessons and, as I went my own way with fresh wings pressed into my warm skin, I thought of every single event that had transpired in order to get me there; the heartbreak's hold ups, the rebirth, the toe infections, the trenches, the terrible job interviews... the untimely death of a friend. I recalled the falling in and out of love that had become one of my greatest catalysts for change, the black-eyed bar fights, the sorcery of women's magic, the tough love that would always be a part of me, festival frequencies, cyclonic sisters, robberies, and the melodic dances that I had employed beneath many a waning moon. More than ever, I thought upon the loss of my one true love.

But as the music sung me a private symphony and my heart ripened in gratitude, I understood that nothing was ever truly lost. With a fresh journey upon the horizon, I wrapped my hand around the steering wheel tightly and felt as though a great chapter of my life was coming to an end, in order for a new one to begin. As anticipated, it had been my greatest adventure thus far, my story, and, whether or not anyone else could ever understand it as such, it was my very own personal truth.

Yet, as I looked at my reflection in the rearview mirror, beside the eternal imprint of Florence's love, I saw that I no longer looked like the same girl that had left home a year prior. My eyes were wider and my reflection looked softer and not quite like my own. It was as though my features had changed with every single person that I had touched souls with upon my journey, as though I had inadvertently taken a part of their beauty with me. Over the course of a year, I had smudged alongside of the liberated and the broken. I had gotten down and dirty with the spiritual as well as the empty-hearted and through all of the ups and the downs, I had found great guidance in every single version of their diverse and unique persons. For, my story, as I have tried to capture but a glimpse of the prints that people have left upon me, is ultimately a story about such connections.

As the golden sun finally fell into a bed of iridescent grass and the open road laid itself out before my desires like beckoning a lover, I glanced into the rearview mirror once more at my hazel eyes. And, as the sun caught them like a prism and allowed my iris's to glisten with beams of greens and blues... within their colourful kaleidoscope, I saw that it was not only myself looking back at me...

... But it was also a version of you.

Acknowledgements

First and foremost, I would like to thank Benjamin, my very own blue eyed prince, for offering me the complete freedom to write about the journey that he and I embarked upon in this world together. I understand that it takes a rare kind of person to allow such an intimate connection to be shared with the entire world and through better or worse, Ben has proved himself to be that person. Even back when the book began as a humble blog, Ben constantly supported my endless desire to document every single chapter of my life and went through great lengths to ensure that my creativity was nurtured, despite what kind of light it cast him in. Ben, this book is but a glimpse into the connection that you and I have shared, my very own version of you and I, and I cannot thank you enough for being such a humble and selfless muse, despite the pains that it may have caused you. Your unconditional love has offered me the greatest kind of healing.

I would also like to thank Heather for providing me with such a tranquil environment for me to write my book within. Behind the walls of Heather's ivy fortress, upon the most comfortable window seat that I have ever had the pleasure of morphing into, I spent eight consecutive months in a completely possessed state of mind where in which nothing could exist for me except the finality of the book. Heather, after sharing my stories with you and looking into your warrior woman eyes, your maternal support and incredible encouragement gave me the strength to dream bigger than I have ever before dared to dream. And from those dreams, I feel that I was able to find my true purpose in life. Without you feeding me, washing my clothes and ensuring that I showered at least once every few days, there is no disputing the fact that, without you, I would have surely perished. Therefore, I will forever be indebted to the kindness in your heart.

In the midst of my book journey, the universe saw fit to place me in the company of a fellow word lover named Rosana, aka my koala girl. Rosana, your unparalleled interest in my book and absolute dedication to the editorial process of it, undoubtedly turned its pages from the scattered thoughts of an introverted poet and transformed them into something that others could understand. Your second pair of eyes and attention to every minute detail is something that I will never be able to master, but merged together, you and I were truly a novice force to be reckoned with. After joining me behind the ivy fortress, Rosana spent countless hours, weeks and months endlessly editing with me where in which she persisted with her work based purely upon the fact that she truly believed in my story. And that in itself was the greatest motivation for me to bring such personal pages out into the world. My sleepy Koala girl, I will be eternally grateful for your dedication, your thoughtful nurturing and your beautiful friendship.

During the final part of my book journey, I found myself back in Australia and although I was fuelled upon hopes and dreams, in reality, I had only a few carrots tucked away in my rucksack and barely two pennies to rub together. I would also like to thank Andrew for housing me, nurturing me and for spending so much time on getting my van, Millie, back on the road so that I may bring my story out into the world. Andy, thank you for your love, your support, your musical contributions and for each transformative lesson that you have taught me. You will forever be a prominent figure within my life.

Finally, I would like to thank each person that has allowed me to write about them and our connection together. I appreciate the fact that it is an unnerving thing to be written about from the perspective of another and can only hope that I have been able to capture you in a light that honours your person and your incredible contribution to this existence. Your presence in this book is evidence of the absolute love and dedication that I have for each and every one of you.

Our connections have been the source of my life force.

Made in the USA
Charleston, SC
15 March 2017